Ayu
Watanabe

L♥DK

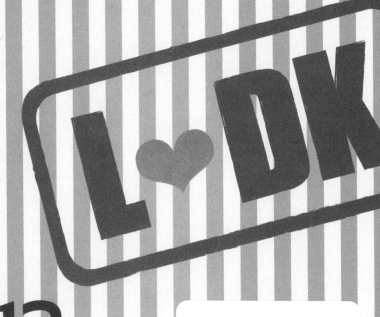

12

L♥DK

Ayu Watanabe

12

contents

L♥DK

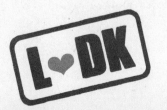

#45 Night of Punishment

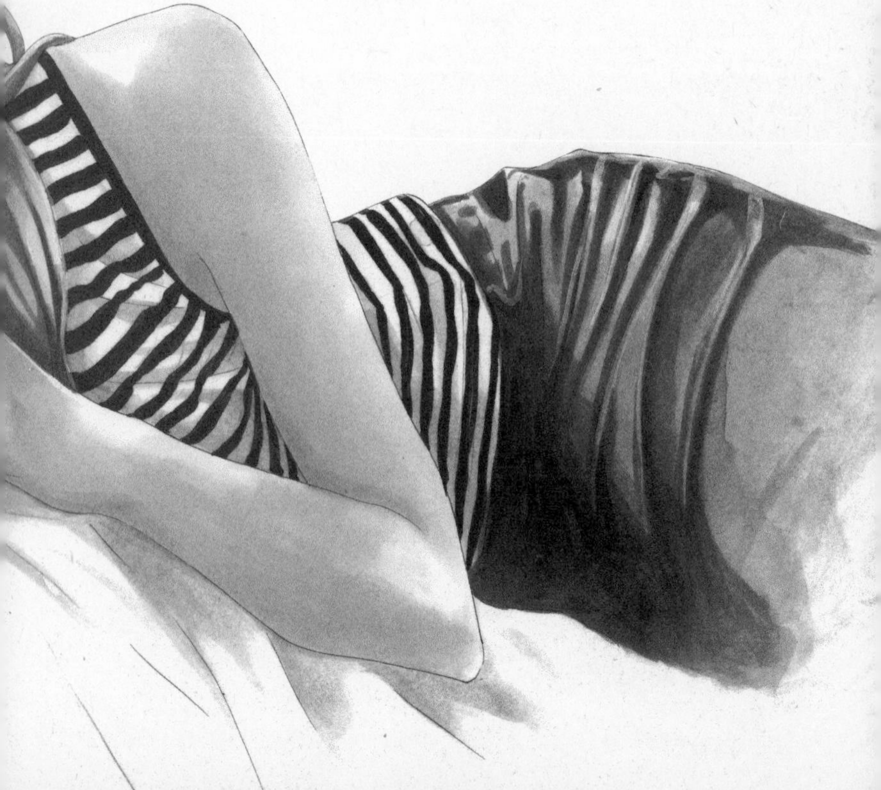

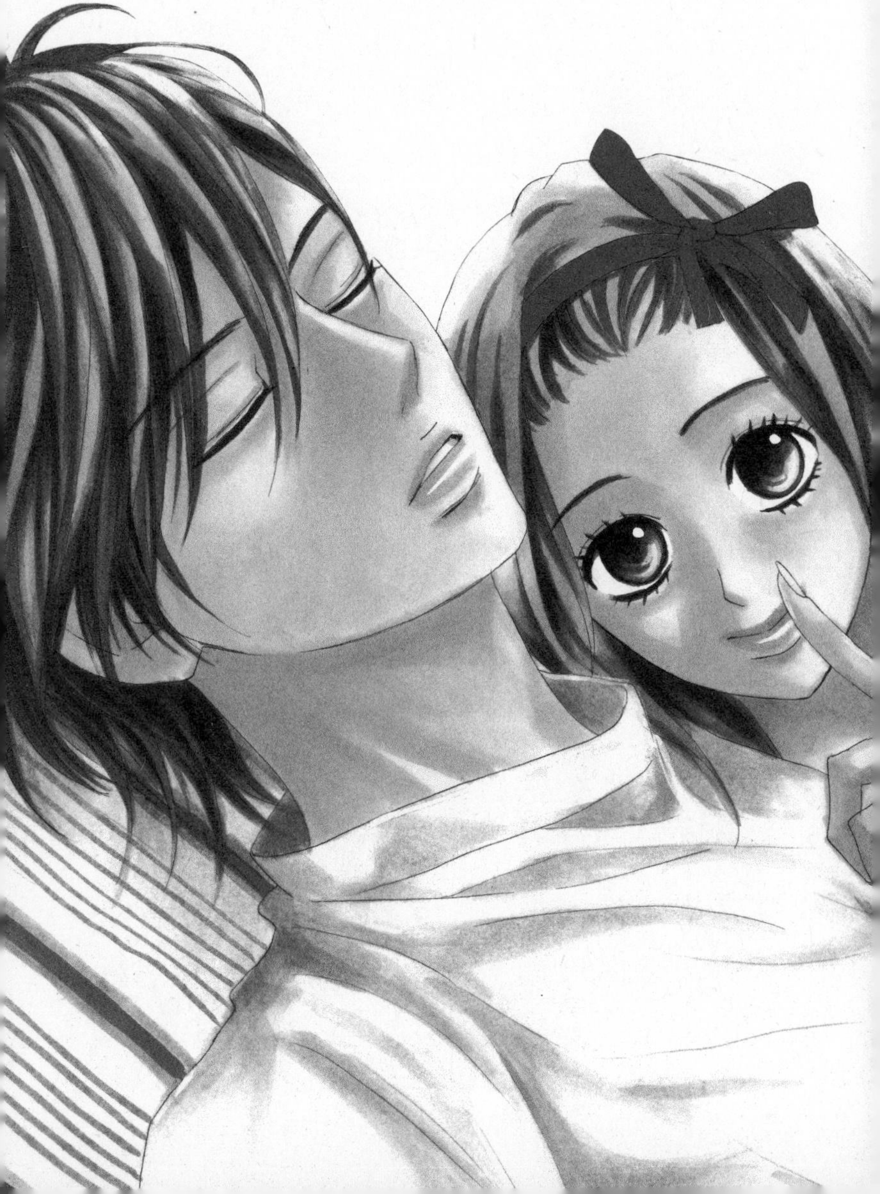

Story So Far

L♥DK

Story

Aoi learns that her classmate Haru is in love with Shusei. Then, Haru's best friend Kaede discovers Aoi's and Shusei's secret living arrangement and threatens Aoi, saying, "If you get in the way of Haru's love, I'll tell everyone about you and Shusei." Unable to turn to her boyfriend for help, Aoi suffers alone in quiet agony, but when she overhears Haru about to confess her feelings to Shusei, Aoi desperately puts a stop to it! That's when Shusei tells Haru he can't go out with her because he's in love with Aoi. But what about Kaede...?!

Cast

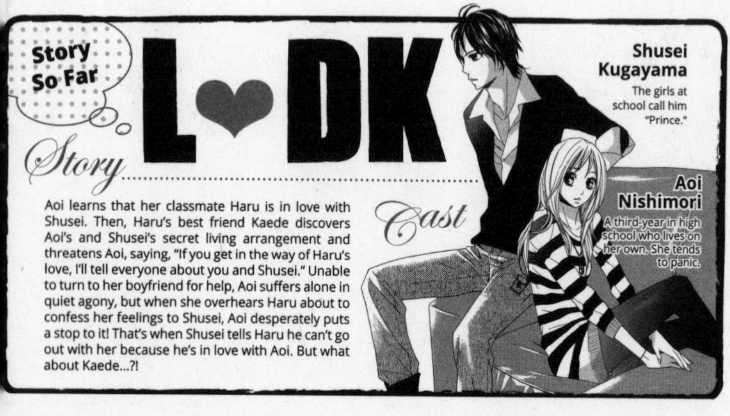

Shusei Kugayama
The girls at school call him "Prince."

Aoi Nishimori
A third-year in high school who lives on her own. She tends to panic.

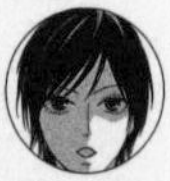

Haru Ono
Aoi's classmate. She was in the same basketball club with Shusei.

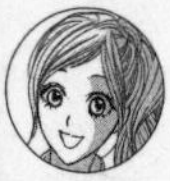

Kaede Igarashi
Also a classmate of Aoi's. She's good friends with Haru.

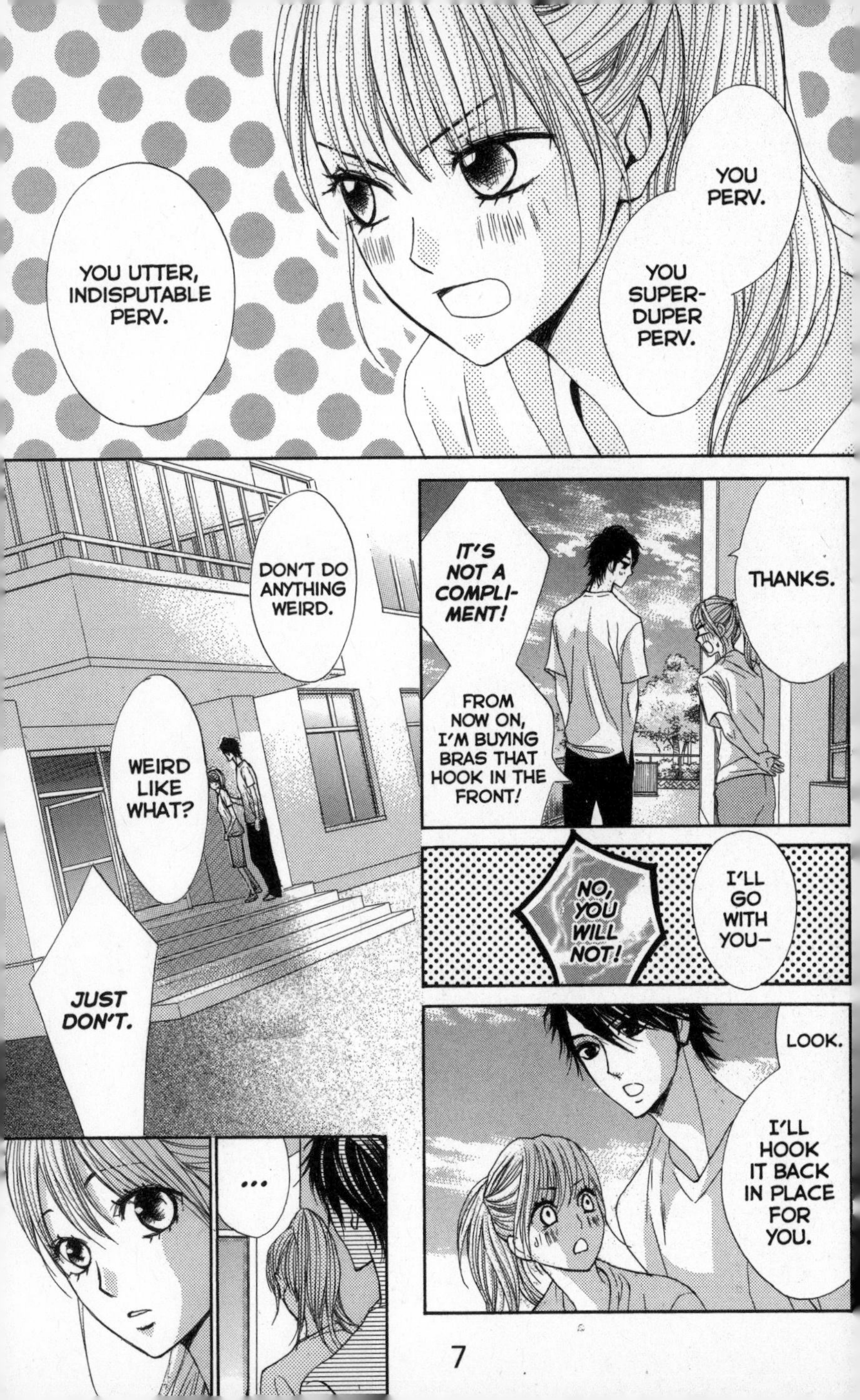
YOU PERV.
YOU SUPER-DUPER PERV.
YOU UTTER, INDISPUTABLE PERV.
THANKS.
IT'S NOT A COMPLIMENT!
FROM NOW ON, I'M BUYING BRAS THAT HOOK IN THE FRONT!
I'LL GO WITH YOU—
NO, YOU WILL NOT!
LOOK.
I'LL HOOK IT BACK IN PLACE FOR YOU.
DON'T DO ANYTHING WEIRD.
WEIRD LIKE WHAT?
JUST DON'T.
...

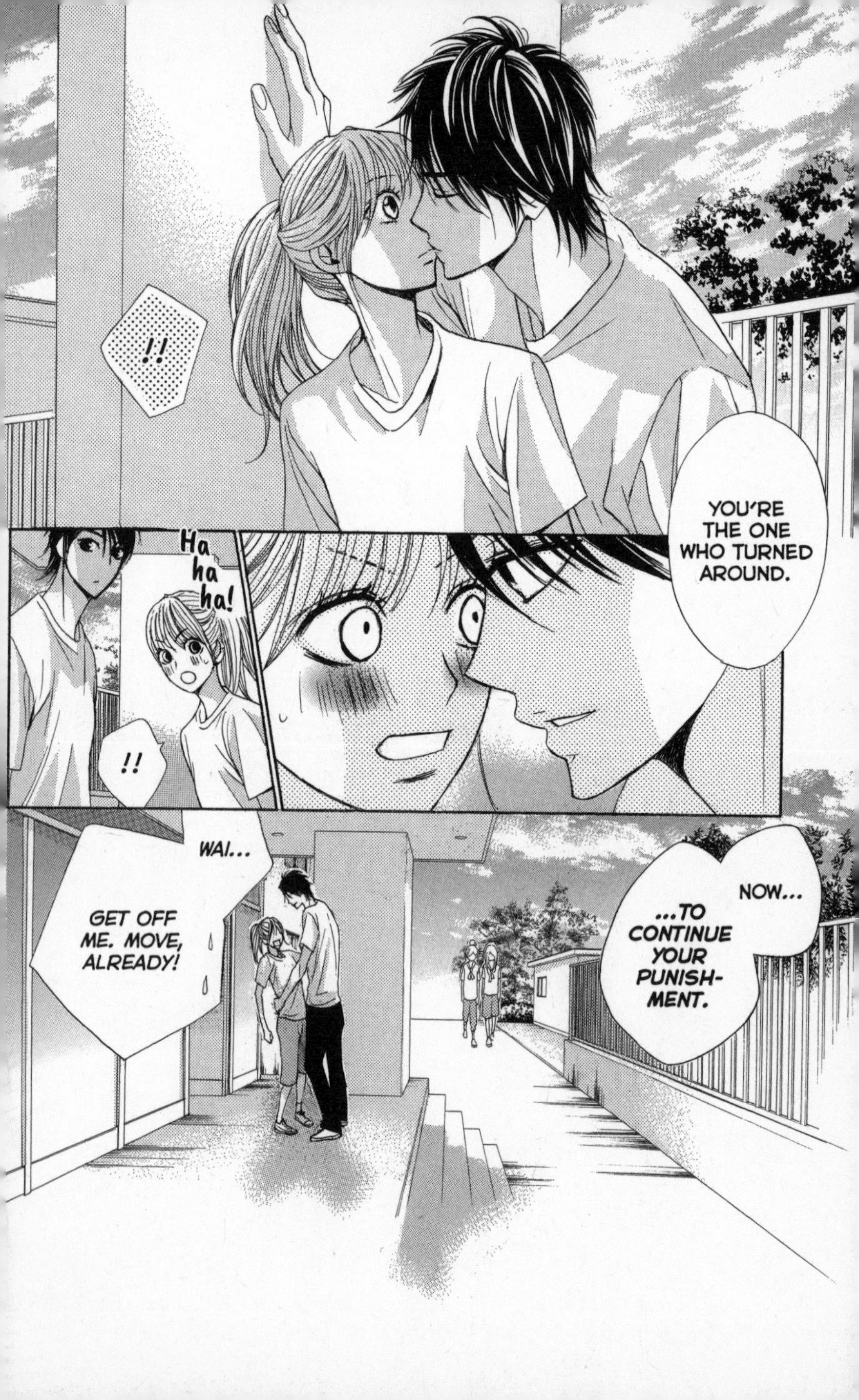
!!
YOU'RE THE ONE WHO TURNED AROUND.
Ha ha ha!
!!
NOW... ...TO CONTINUE YOUR PUNISHMENT.
WAI...
GET OFF ME. MOVE, ALREADY!

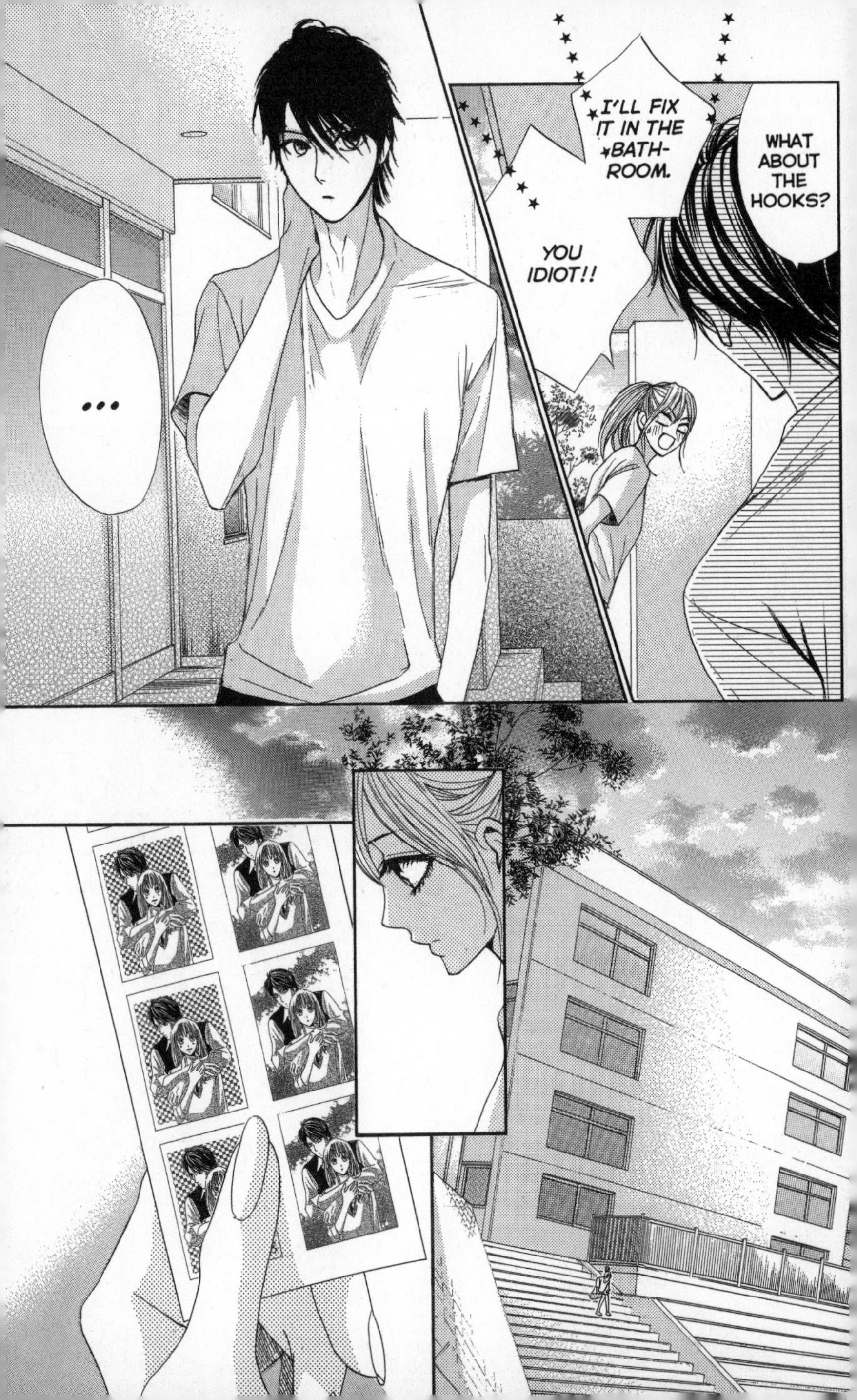
WHAT ABOUT THE HOOKS?
I'LL FIX IT IN THE BATH-ROOM.
YOU IDIOT!!
...

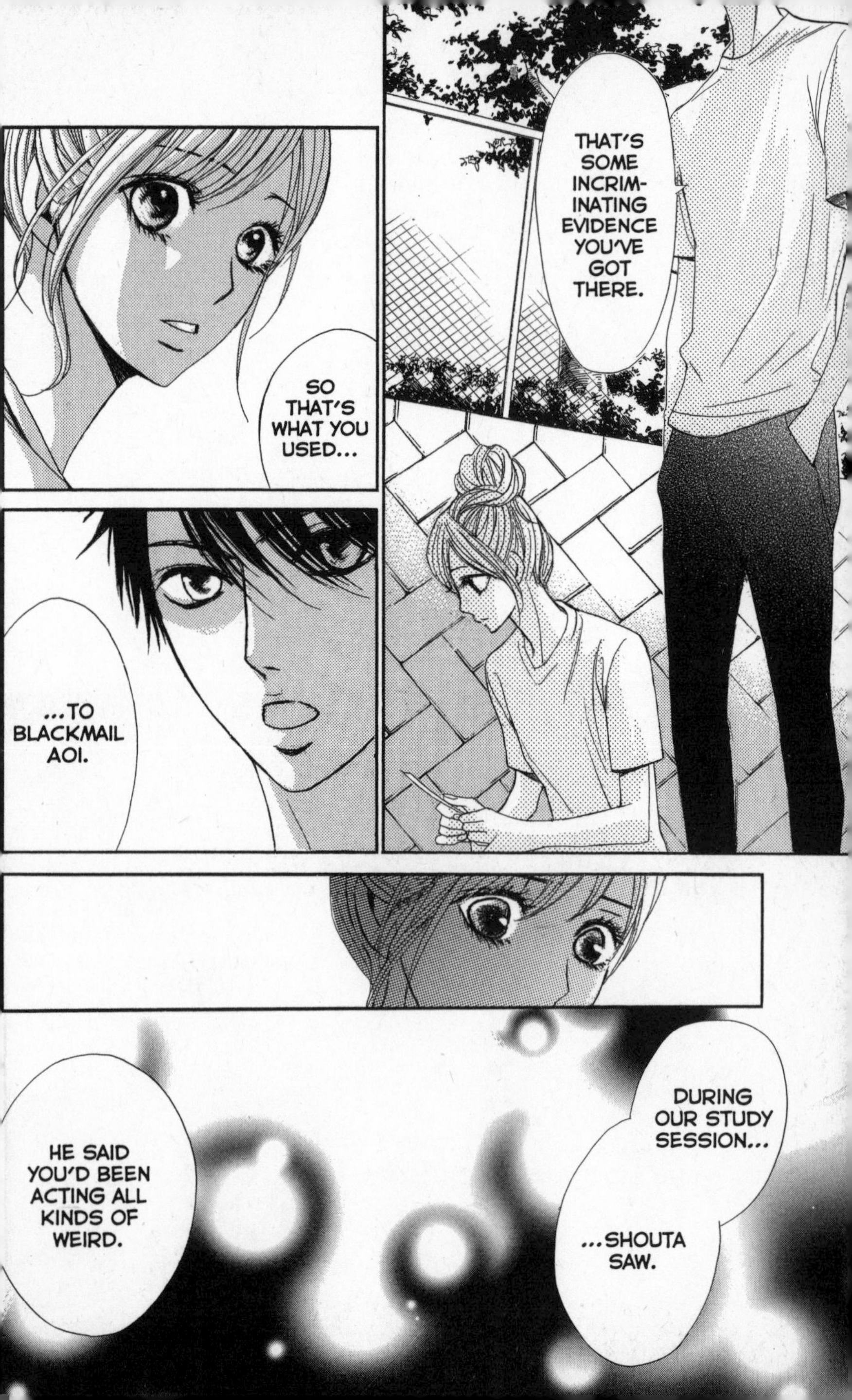
THAT'S SOME INCRIMINATING EVIDENCE YOU'VE GOT THERE.
SO THAT'S WHAT YOU USED...
...TO BLACKMAIL AOI.
DURING OUR STUDY SESSION...
...SHOUTA SAW.
HE SAID YOU'D BEEN ACTING ALL KINDS OF WEIRD.

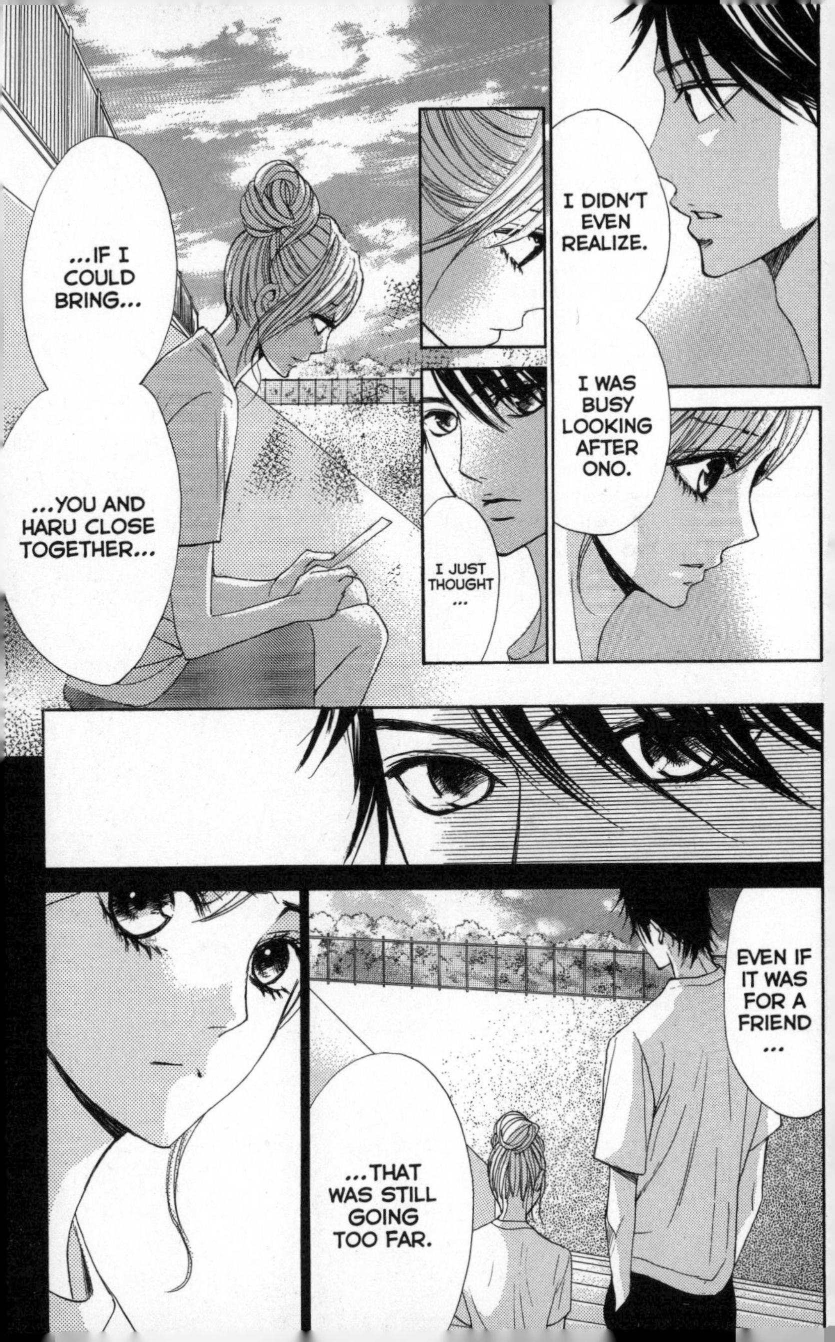
I DIDN'T EVEN REALIZE.
I WAS BUSY LOOKING AFTER ONO.
I JUST THOUGHT...
...IF I COULD BRING...
...YOU AND HARU CLOSE TOGETHER...
EVEN IF IT WAS FOR A FRIEND...
...THAT WAS STILL GOING TOO FAR.

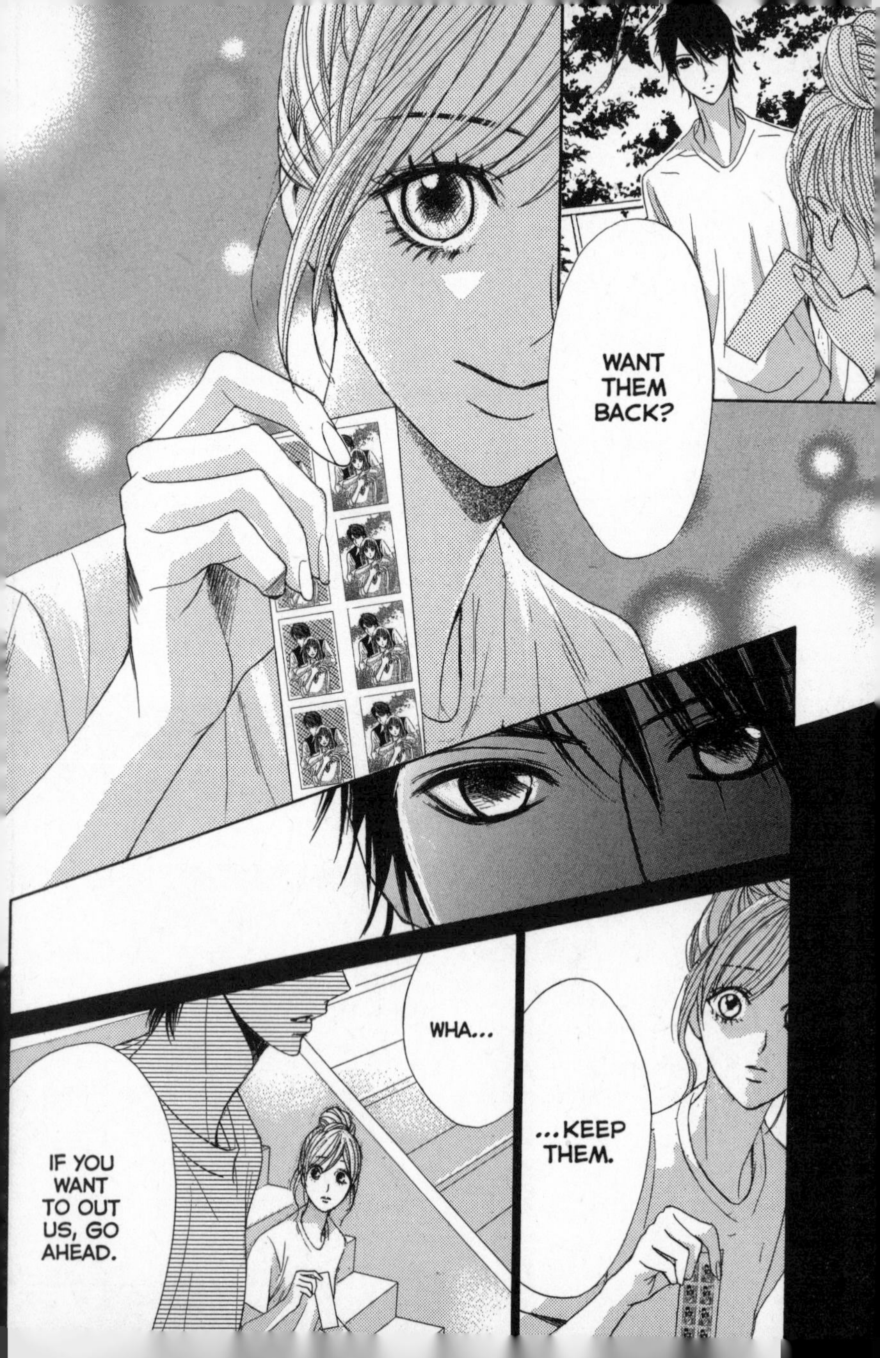

WANT THEM BACK?
...KEEP THEM.
WHA...
IF YOU WANT TO OUT US, GO AHEAD.

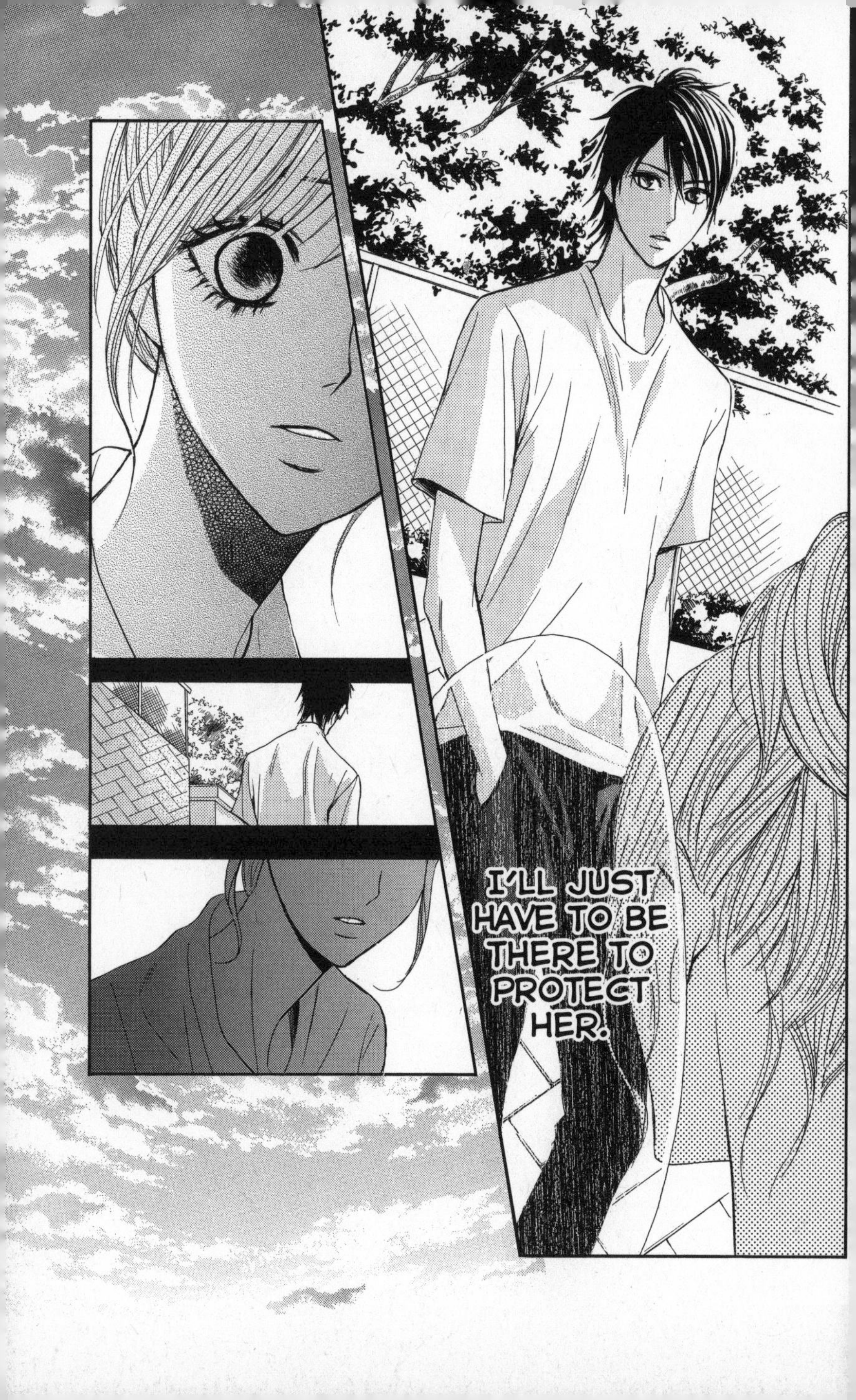
I'LL JUST HAVE TO BE THERE TO PROTECT HER.

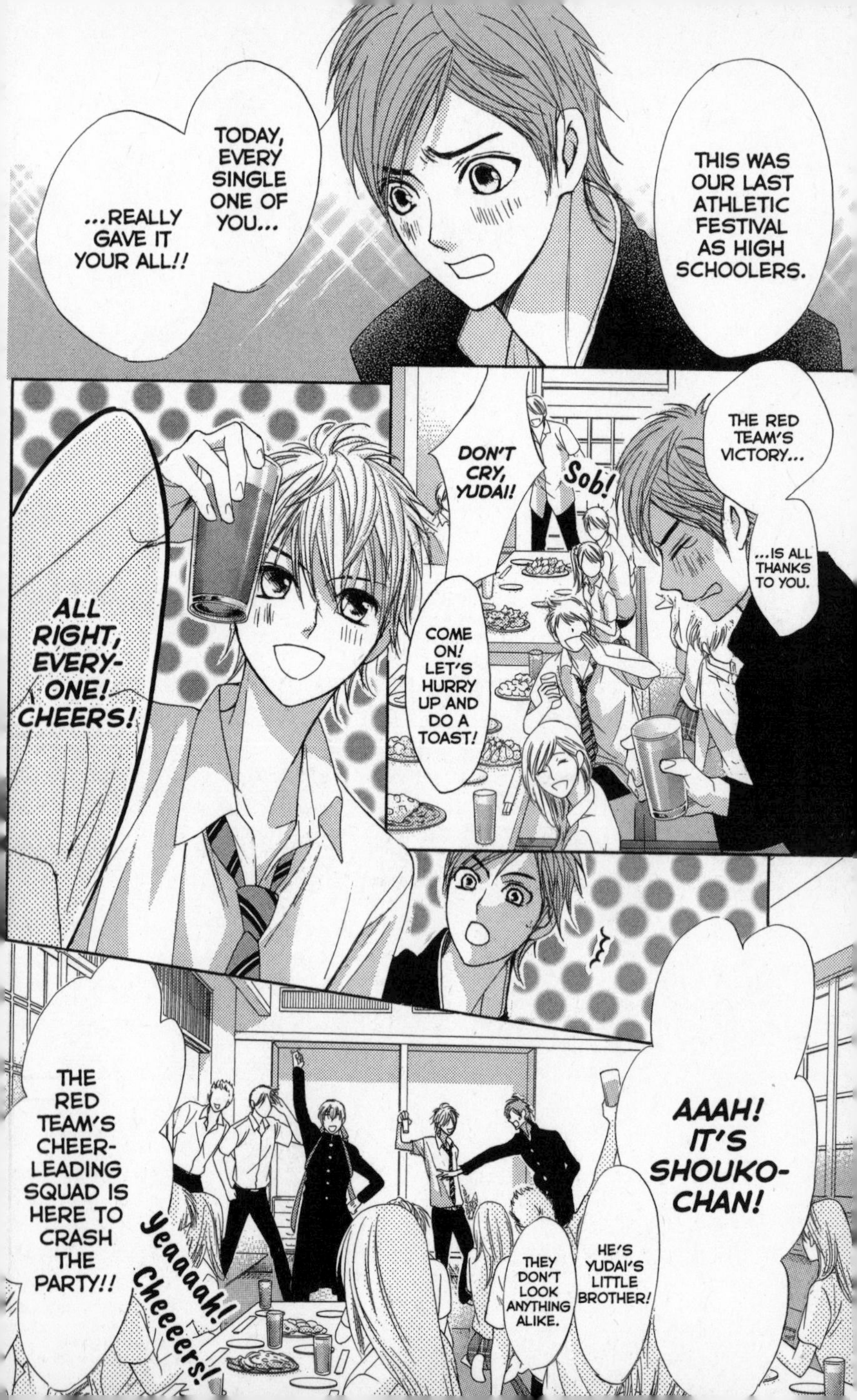
THIS WAS OUR LAST ATHLETIC FESTIVAL AS HIGH SCHOOLERS.
TODAY, EVERY SINGLE ONE OF YOU...
...REALLY GAVE IT YOUR ALL!!
THE RED TEAM'S VICTORY...
...IS ALL THANKS TO YOU.
Sob!
DON'T CRY, YUDAI!
COME ON! LET'S HURRY UP AND DO A TOAST!
ALL RIGHT, EVERY-ONE! CHEERS!
AAAH! IT'S SHOUKO-CHAN!
HE'S YUDAI'S LITTLE BROTHER!
THEY DON'T LOOK ANYTHING ALIKE.
THE RED TEAM'S CHEER-LEADING SQUAD IS HERE TO CRASH THE PARTY!!
Yeaaaaah!
Cheeeers!

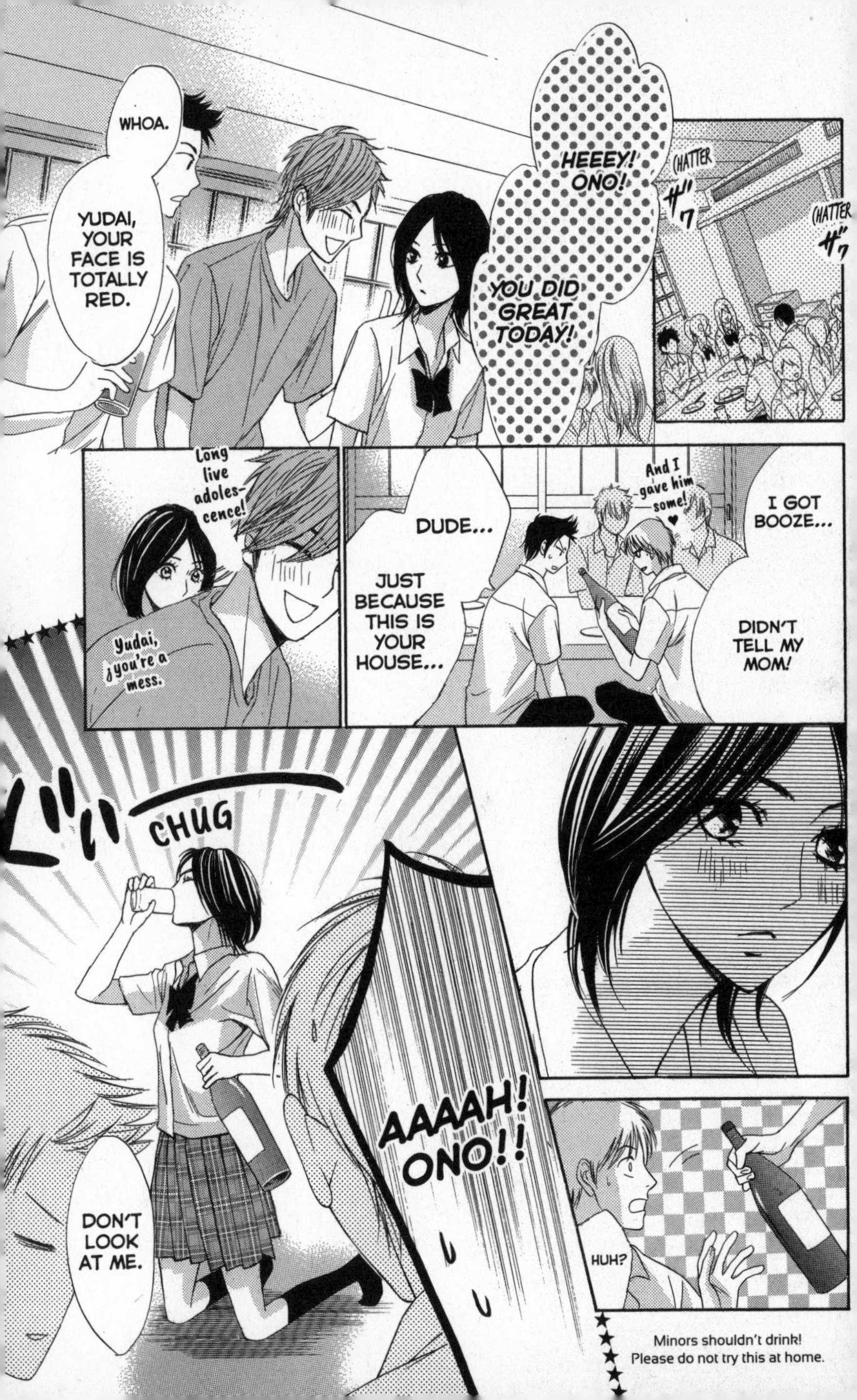

CHATTER
CHATTER
HEEEY! ONO!
YOU DID GREAT TODAY!
WHOA.
YUDAI, YOUR FACE IS TOTALLY RED.
I GOT BOOZE...
DIDN'T TELL MY MOM!
And I gave him some! ♥
DUDE...
JUST BECAUSE THIS IS YOUR HOUSE...
Long live adolescence!
Yudai, you're a mess.
HUH?
CHUG
AAAAH! ONO!!
DON'T LOOK AT ME.
Minors shouldn't drink!
Please do not try this at home.

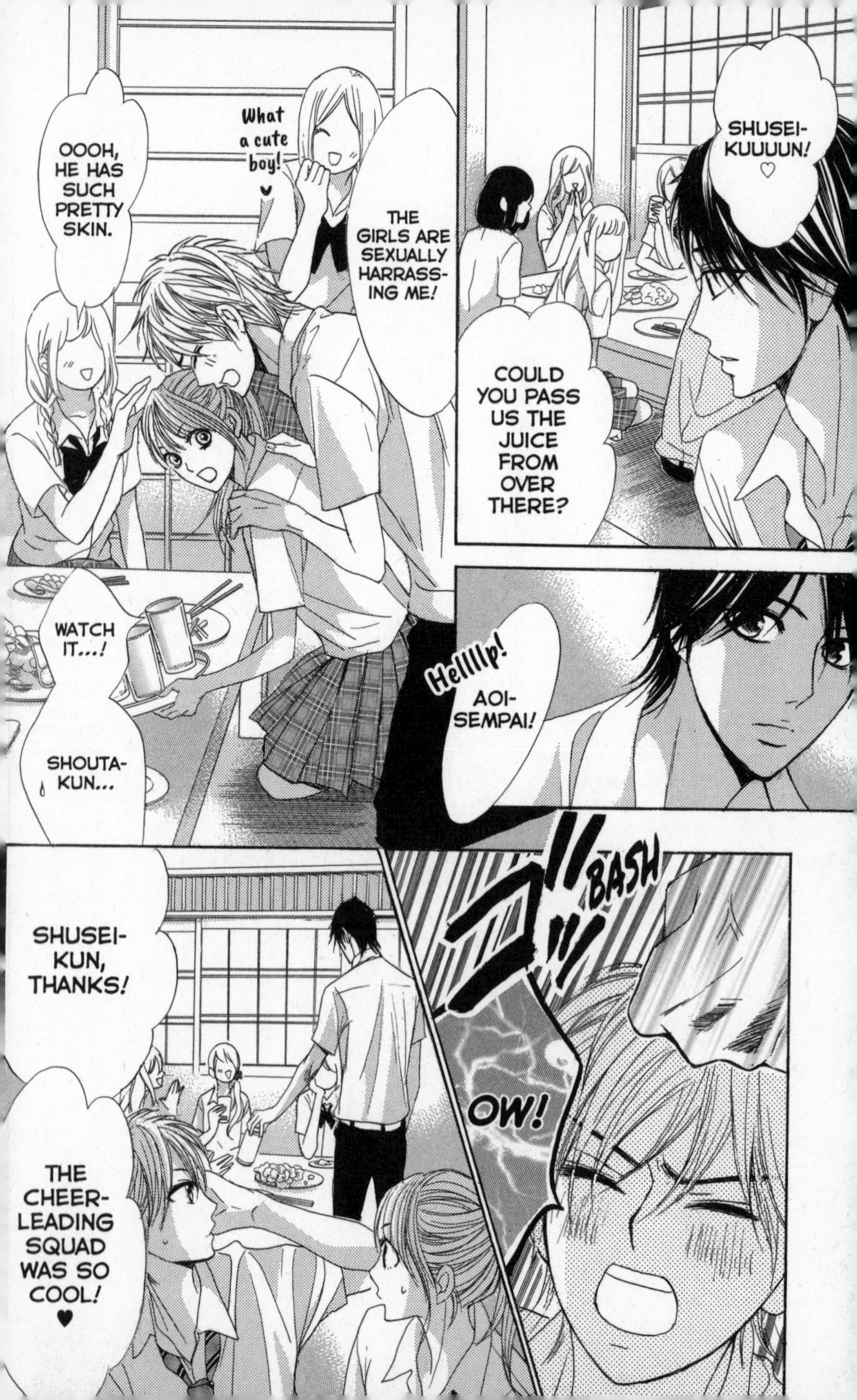
SHUSEI-KUUUUN! ♡
COULD YOU PASS US THE JUICE FROM OVER THERE?
Hellllp!
AOI-SEMPAI!
THE GIRLS ARE SEXUALLY HARRASSING ME!
What a cute boy! ♥
OOOH, HE HAS SUCH PRETTY SKIN.
WATCH IT...!
SHOUTA-KUN...
BASH
OW!
SHUSEI-KUN, THANKS!
THE CHEERLEADING SQUAD WAS SO COOL! ♥

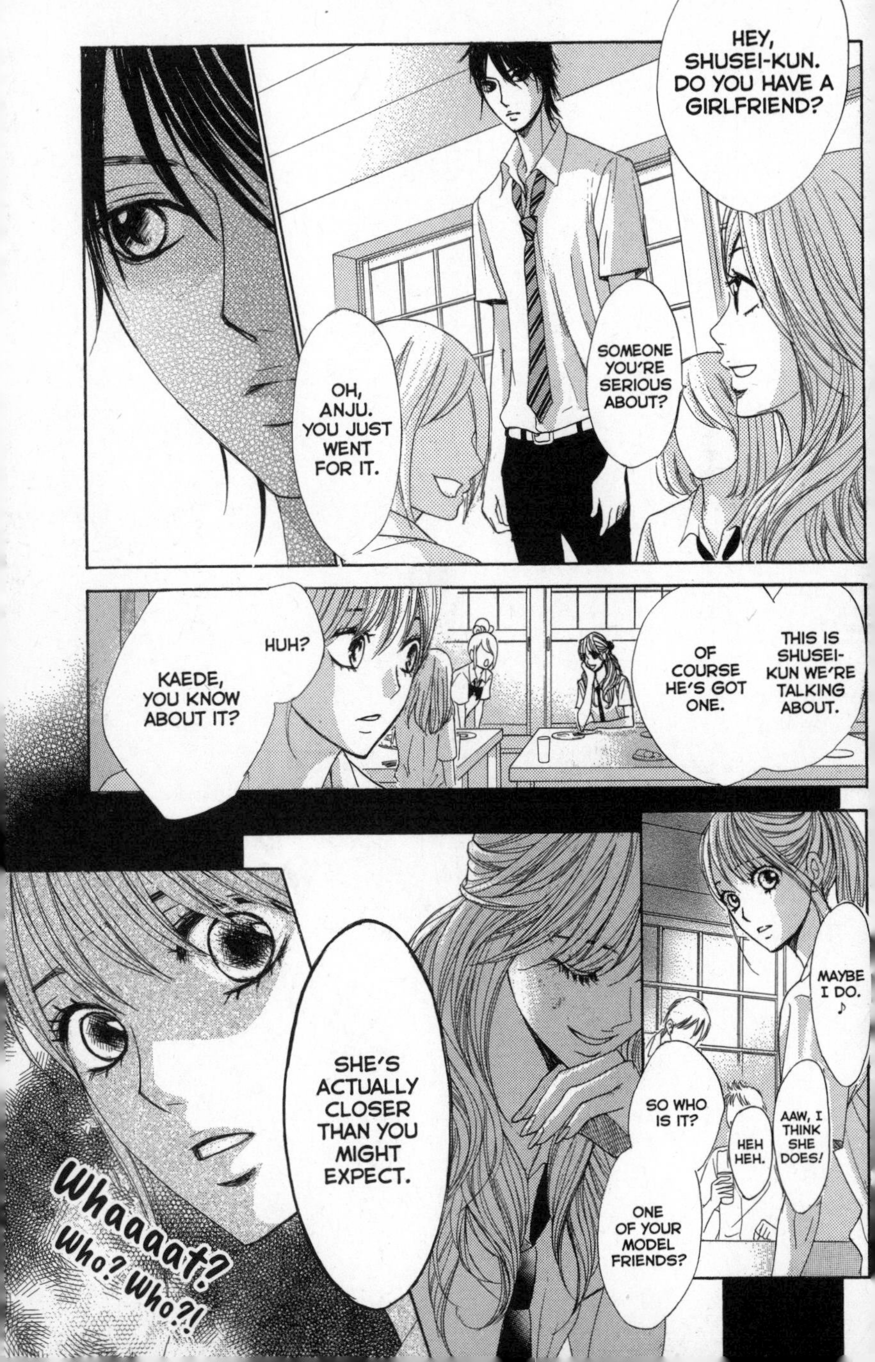
HEY, SHUSEI-KUN. DO YOU HAVE A GIRLFRIEND?
SOMEONE YOU'RE SERIOUS ABOUT?
OH, ANJU. YOU JUST WENT FOR IT.
THIS IS SHUSEI-KUN WE'RE TALKING ABOUT.
OF COURSE HE'S GOT ONE.
HUH?
KAEDE, YOU KNOW ABOUT IT?
MAYBE I DO. ♪
AAW, I THINK SHE DOES!
HEH HEH.
SO WHO IS IT?
ONE OF YOUR MODEL FRIENDS?
SHE'S ACTUALLY CLOSER THAN YOU MIGHT EXPECT.
Whaaaaat?
Who? Who?!

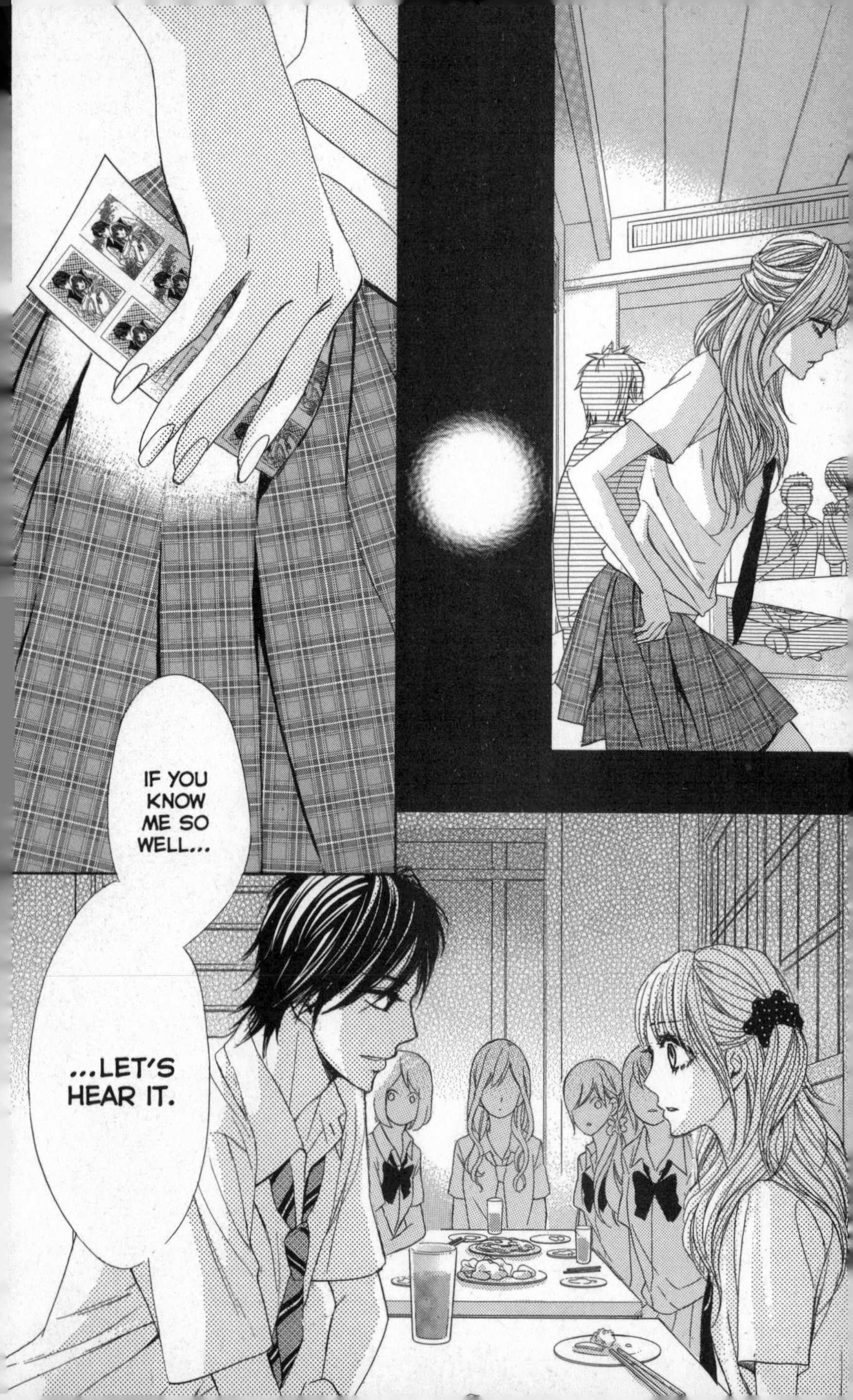
IF YOU KNOW ME SO WELL...
...LET'S HEAR IT.

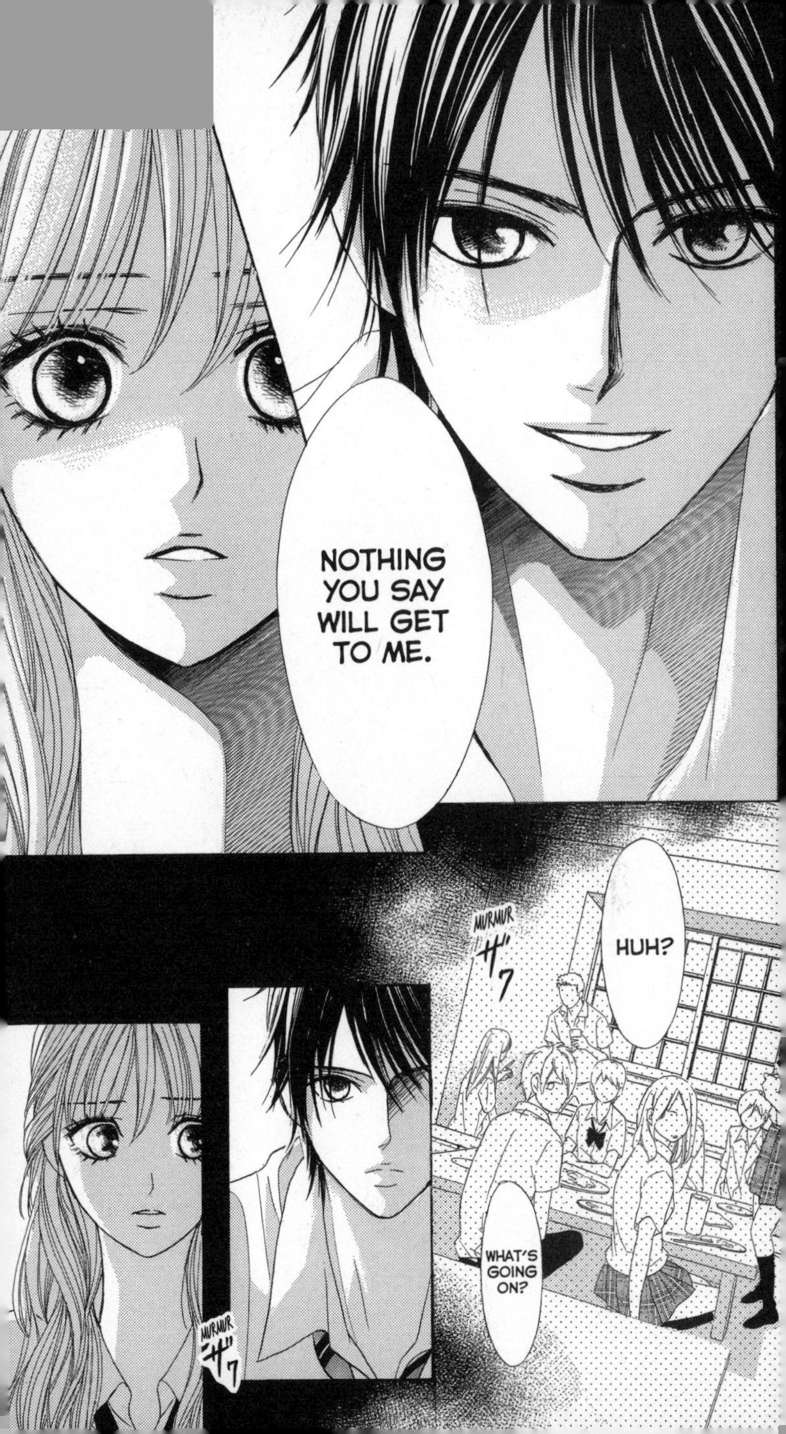
NOTHING YOU SAY WILL GET TO ME.
MURMUR ザワ
HUH?
WHAT'S GOING ON?
MURMUR ザワ

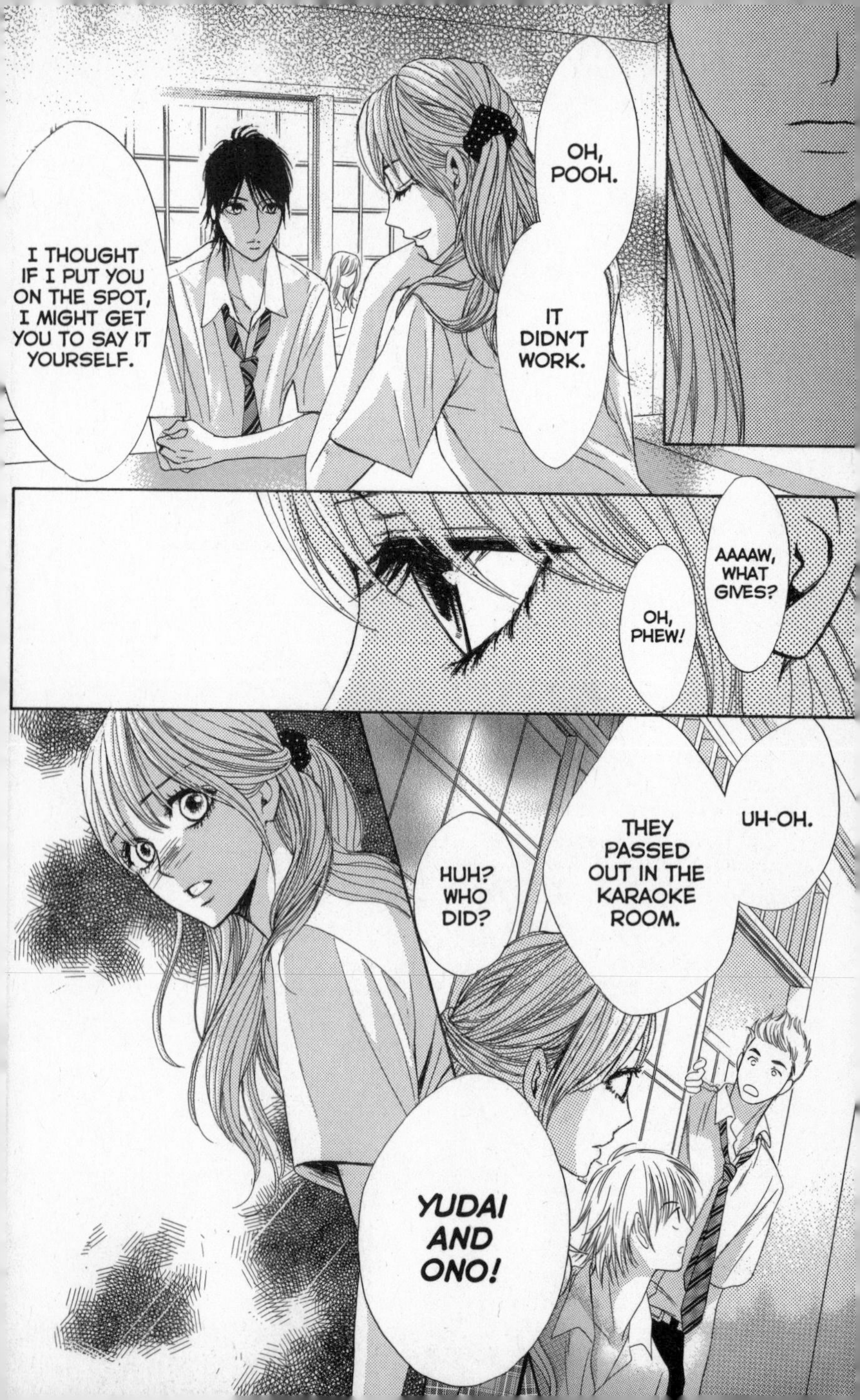
OH, POOH.
IT DIDN'T WORK.
I THOUGHT IF I PUT YOU ON THE SPOT, I MIGHT GET YOU TO SAY IT YOURSELF.
AAAAW, WHAT GIVES?
OH, PHEW!
UH-OH.
THEY PASSED OUT IN THE KARAOKE ROOM.
HUH? WHO DID?
YUDAI AND ONO!

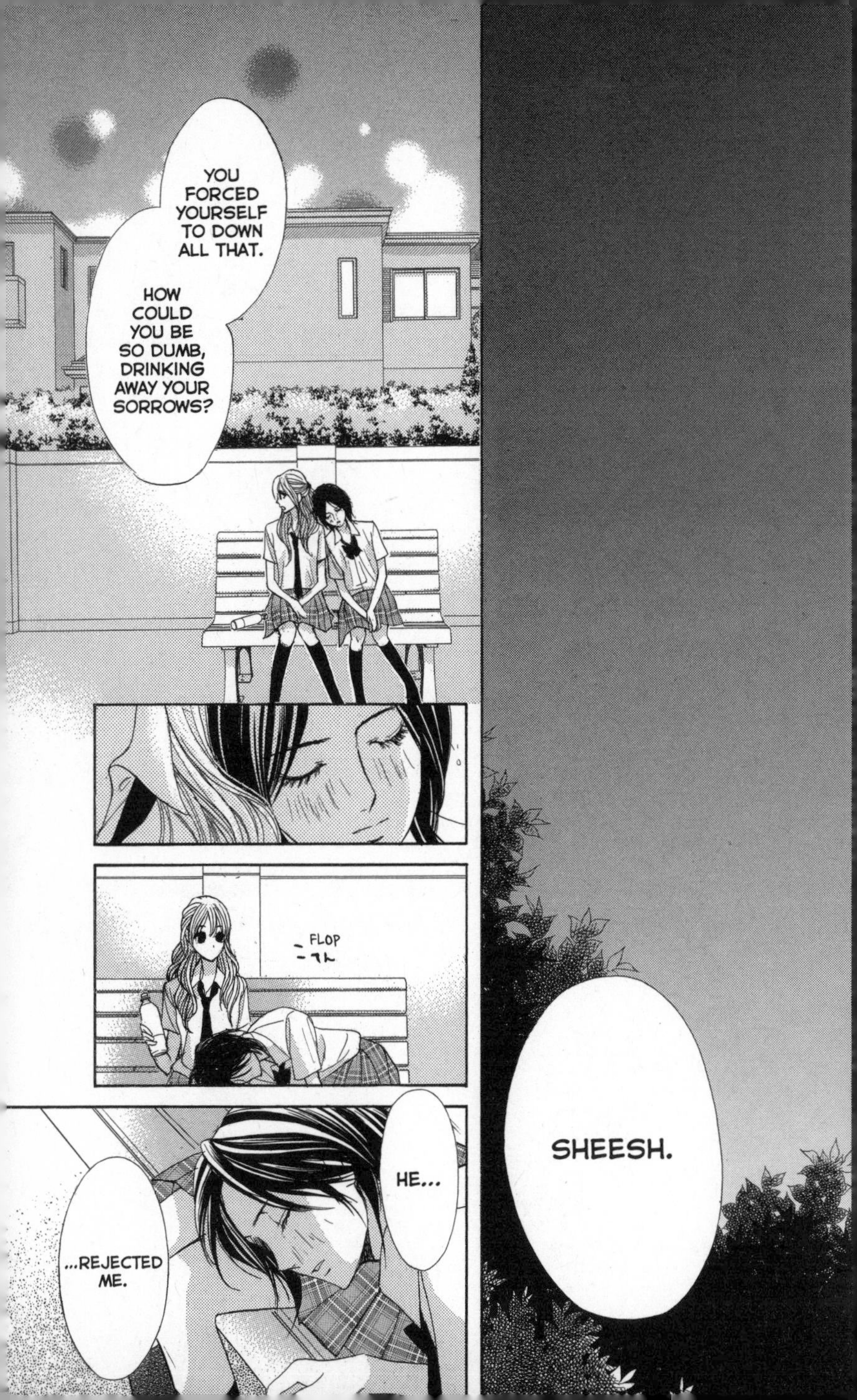
SHEESH.
YOU FORCED YOURSELF TO DOWN ALL THAT.
HOW COULD YOU BE SO DUMB, DRINKING AWAY YOUR SORROWS?
FLOP
HE...
...REJECTED ME.

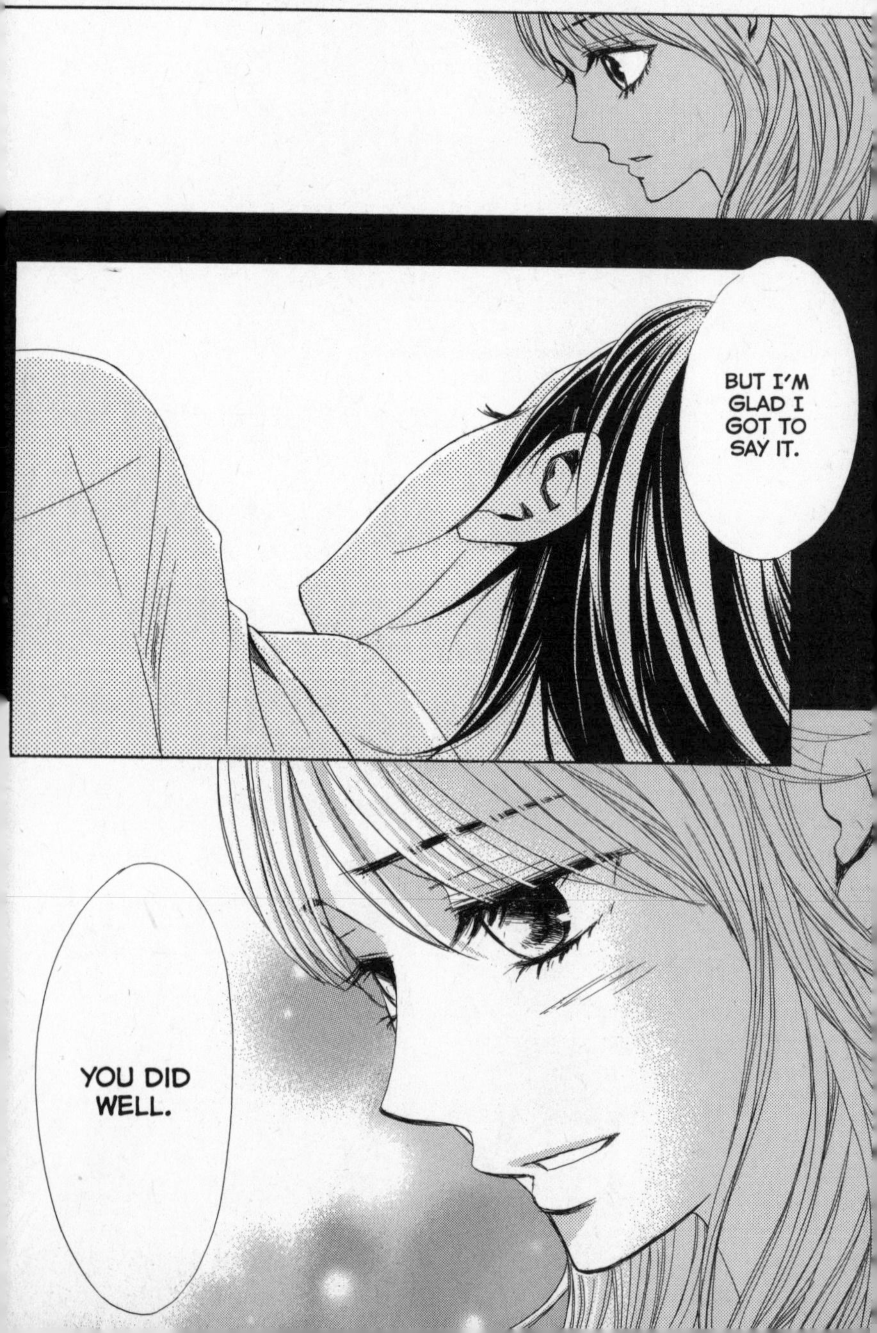
BUT I'M GLAD I GOT TO SAY IT.
YOU DID WELL.

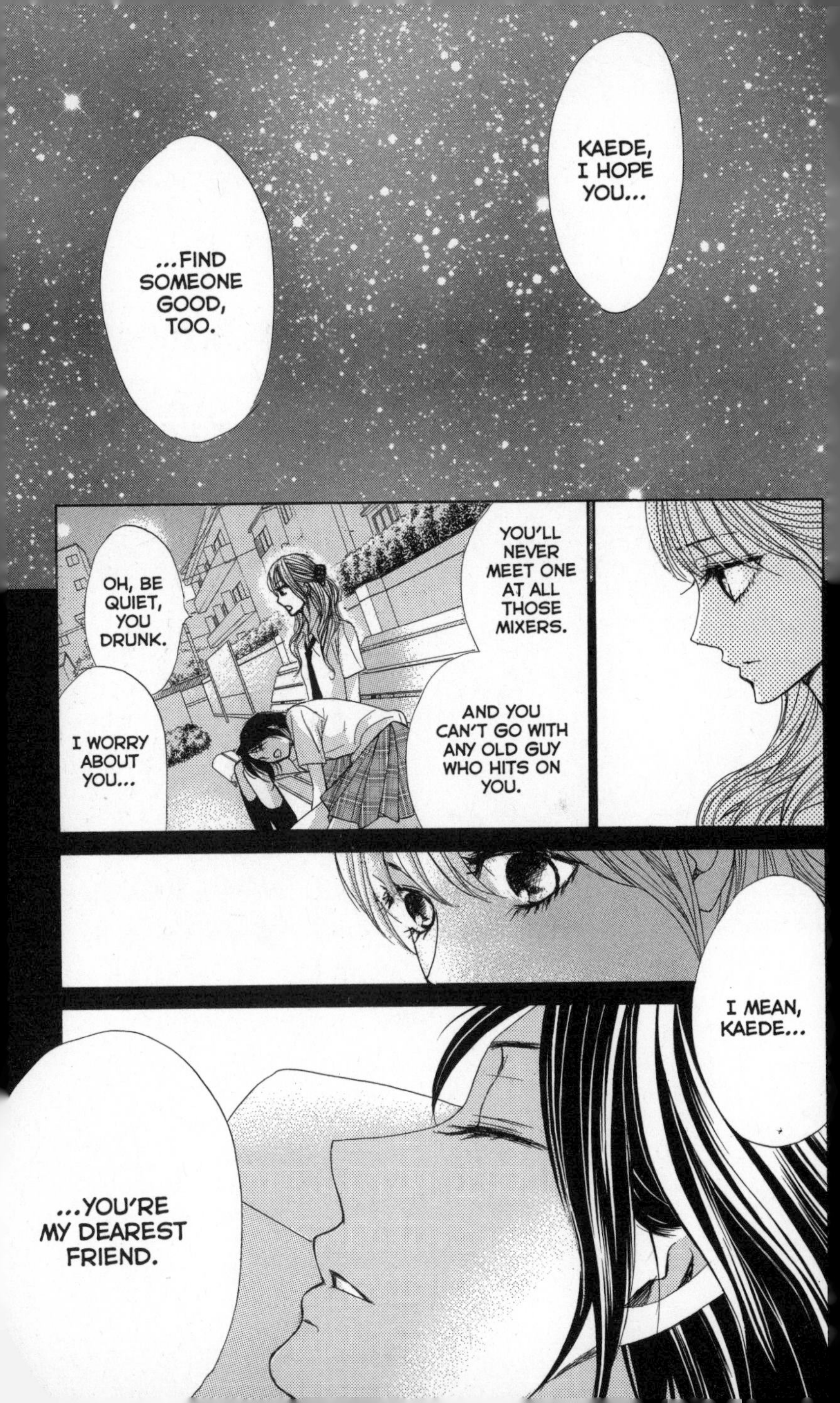
KAEDE, I HOPE YOU...
...FIND SOMEONE GOOD, TOO.
YOU'LL NEVER MEET ONE AT ALL THOSE MIXERS.
AND YOU CAN'T GO WITH ANY OLD GUY WHO HITS ON YOU.
OH, BE QUIET, YOU DRUNK.
I WORRY ABOUT YOU...
I MEAN, KAEDE...
...YOU'RE MY DEAREST FRIEND.

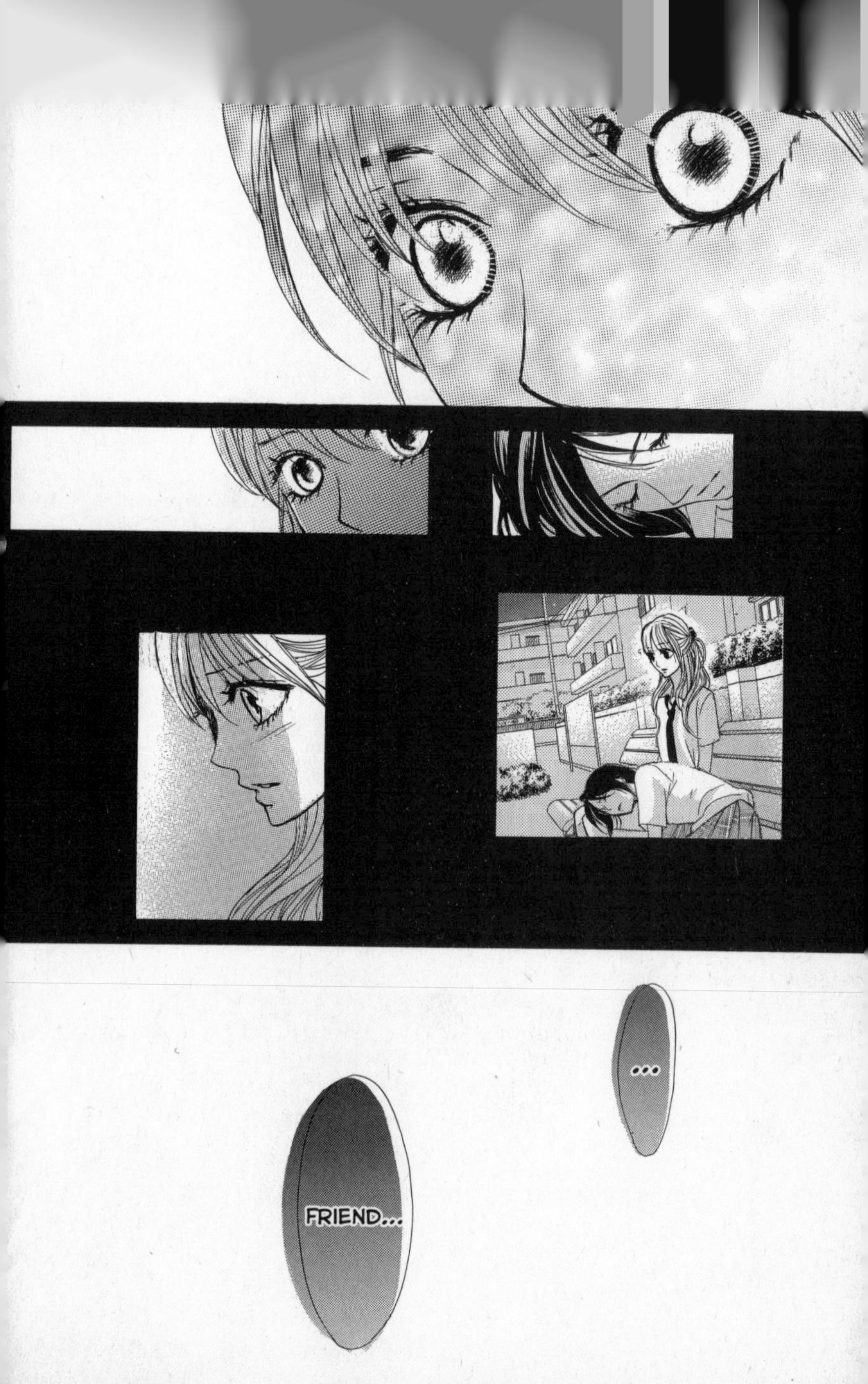
...
FRIEND...

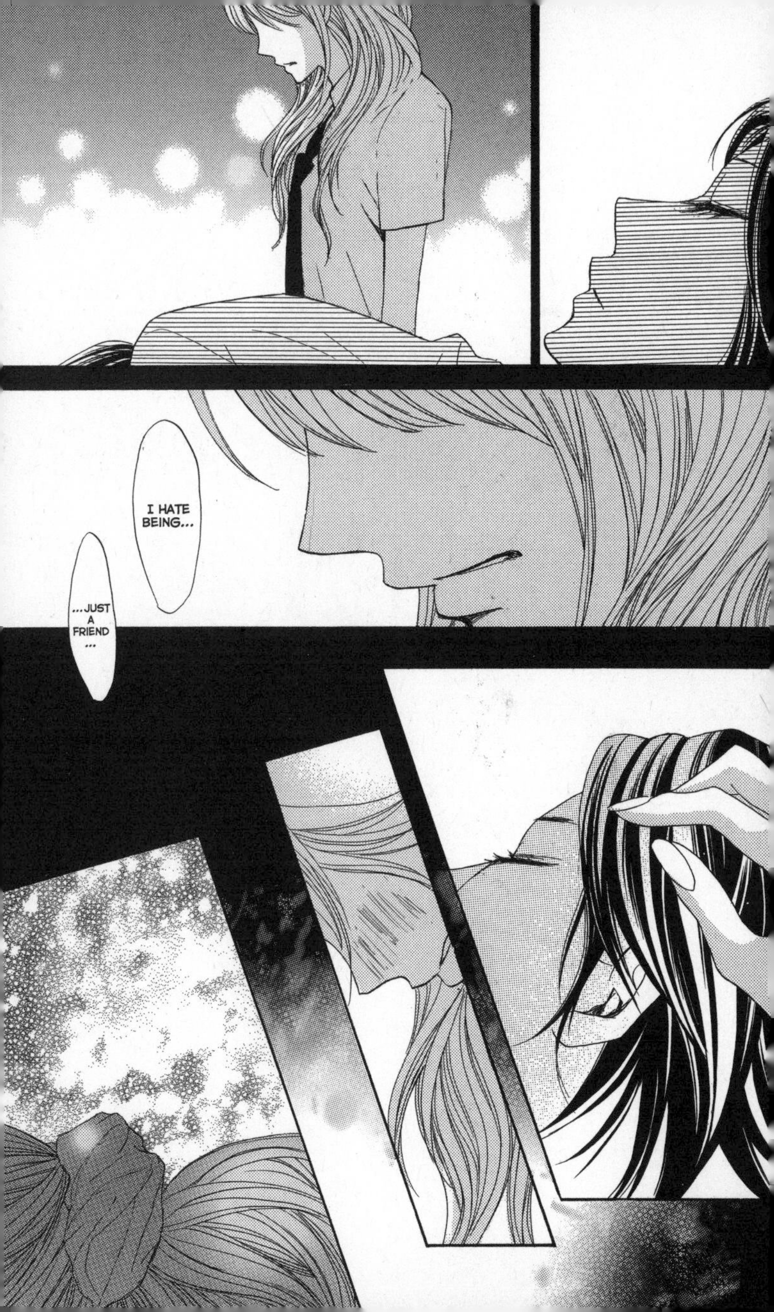
I HATE BEING...
...JUST A FRIEND ...

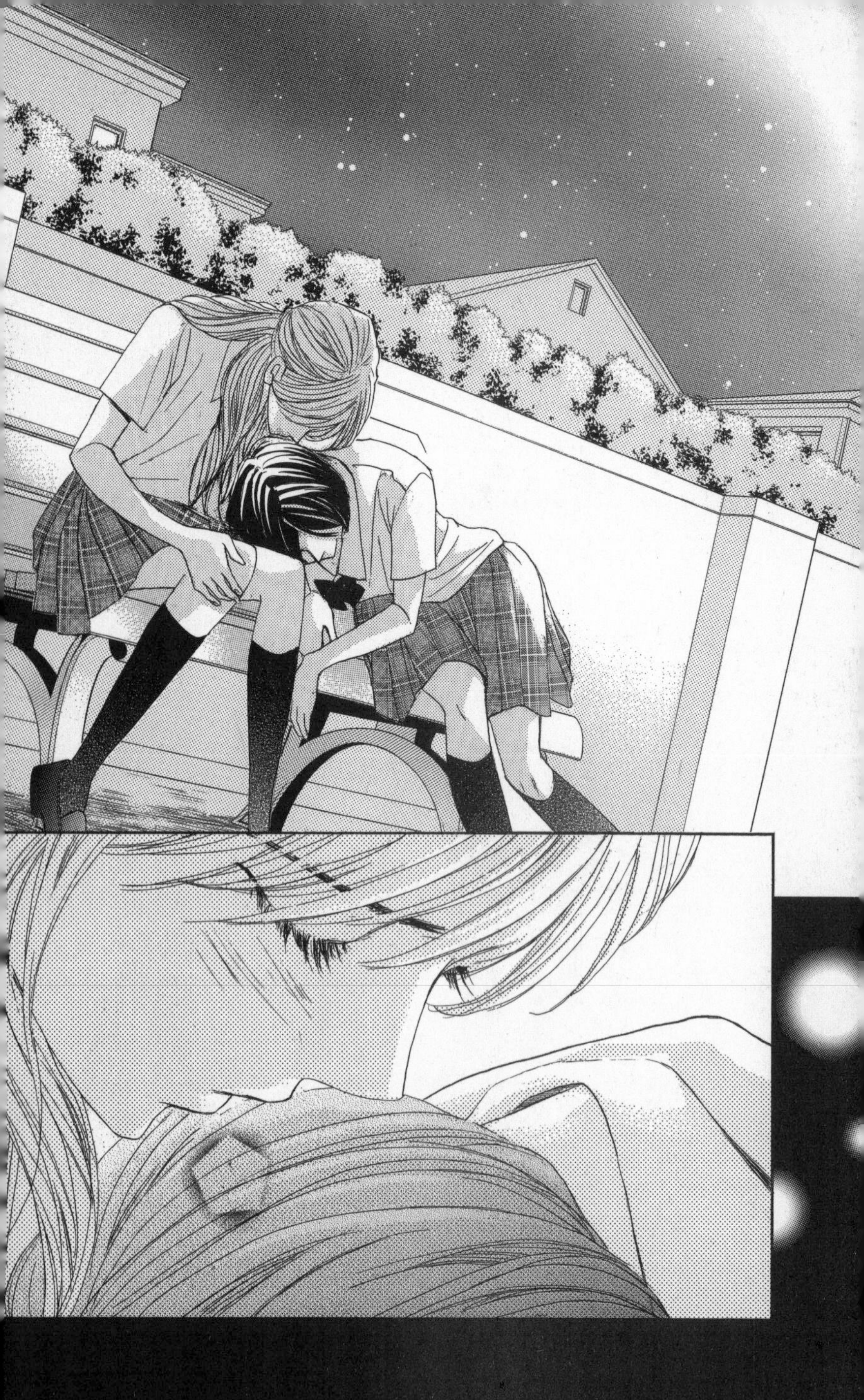

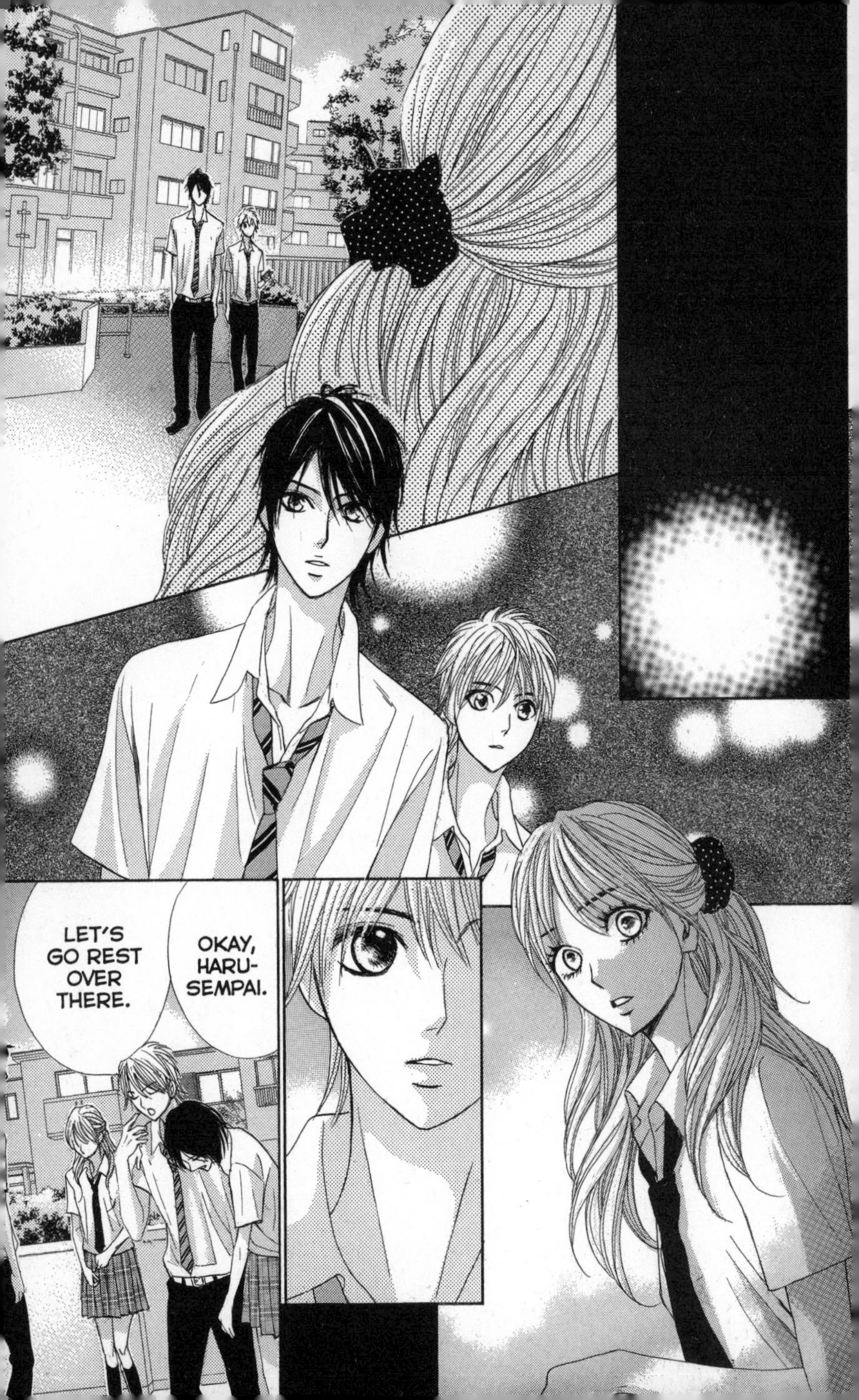
OKAY, HARU-SEMPAI.
LET'S GO REST OVER THERE.

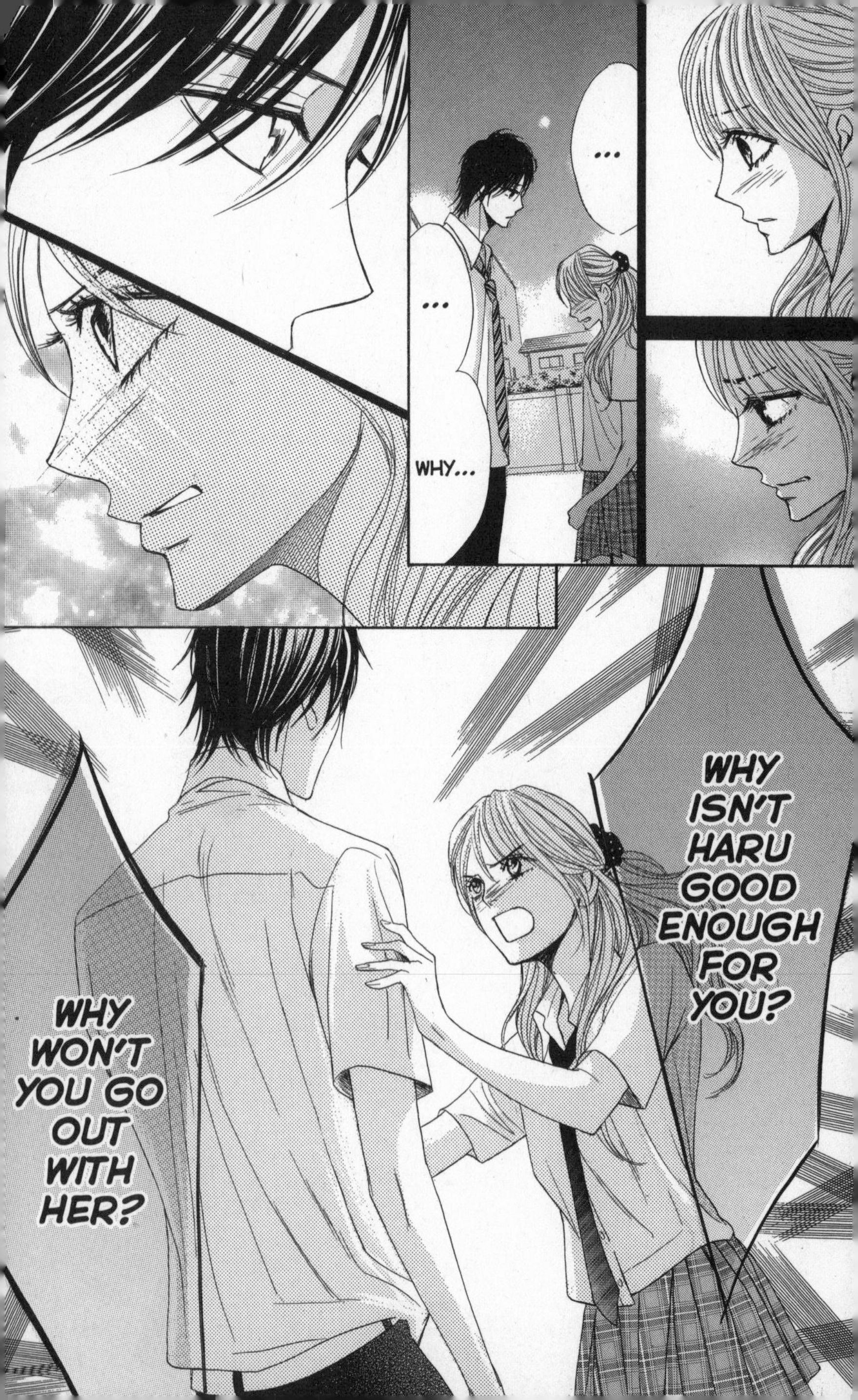
...
...
WHY...
WHY ISN'T HARU GOOD ENOUGH FOR YOU?
WHY WON'T YOU GO OUT WITH HER?

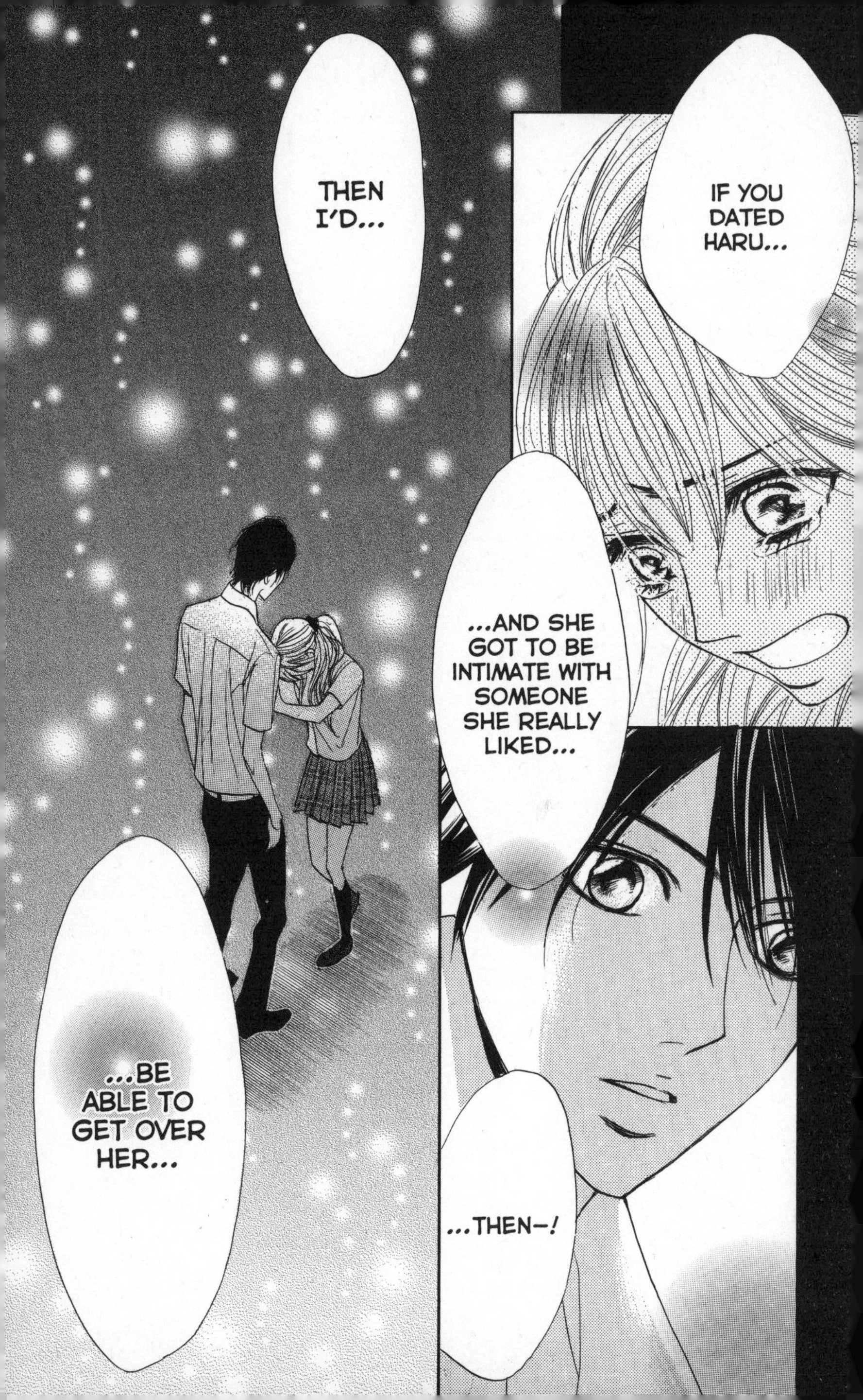
IF YOU DATED HARU...
...AND SHE GOT TO BE INTIMATE WITH SOMEONE SHE REALLY LIKED...
...THEN—!
THEN I'D...
...BE ABLE TO GET OVER HER...

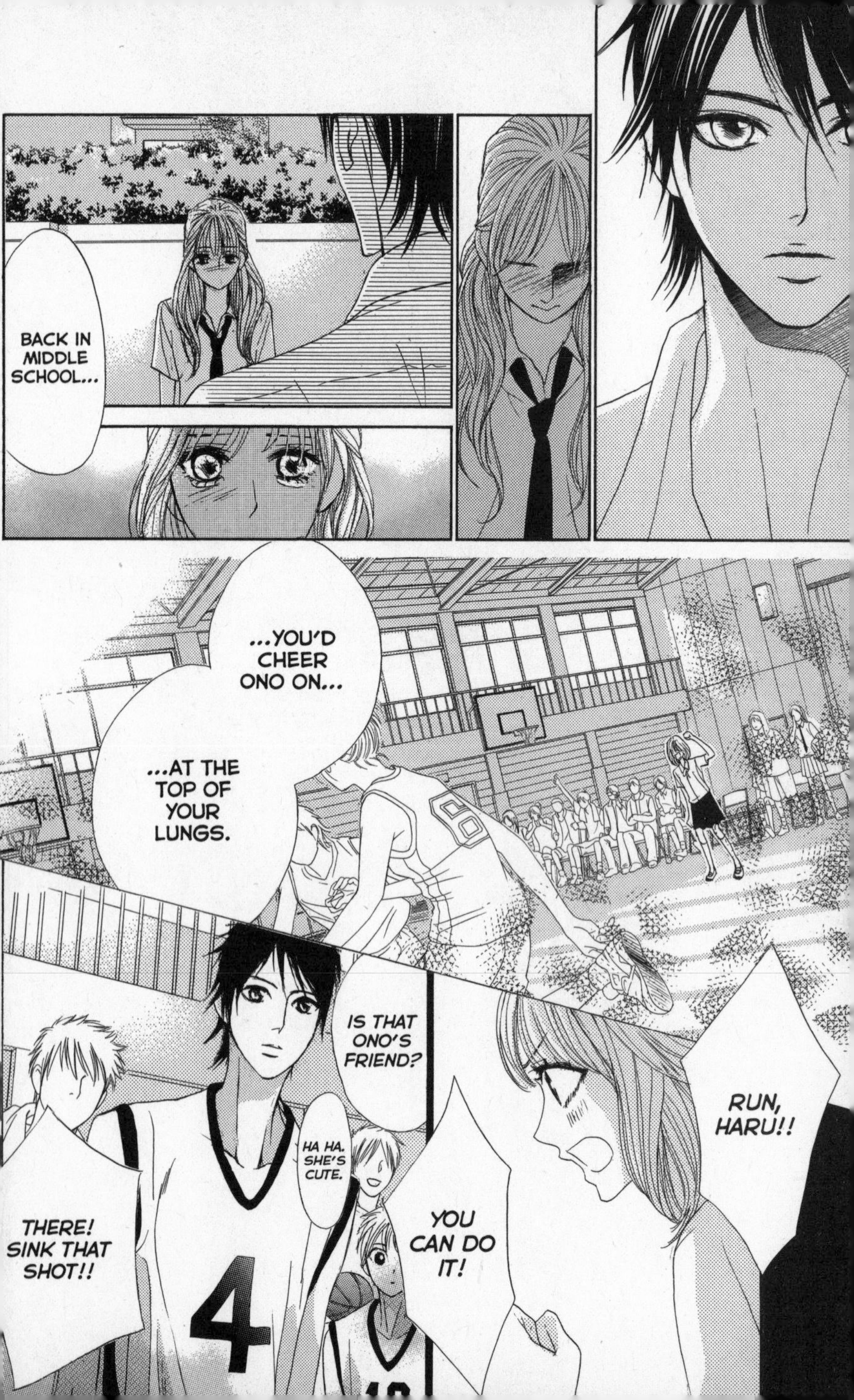
BACK IN MIDDLE SCHOOL...
...YOU'D CHEER ONO ON...
...AT THE TOP OF YOUR LUNGS.
RUN, HARU!!
IS THAT ONO'S FRIEND?
YOU CAN DO IT!
HA HA. SHE'S CUTE.
THERE! SINK THAT SHOT!!

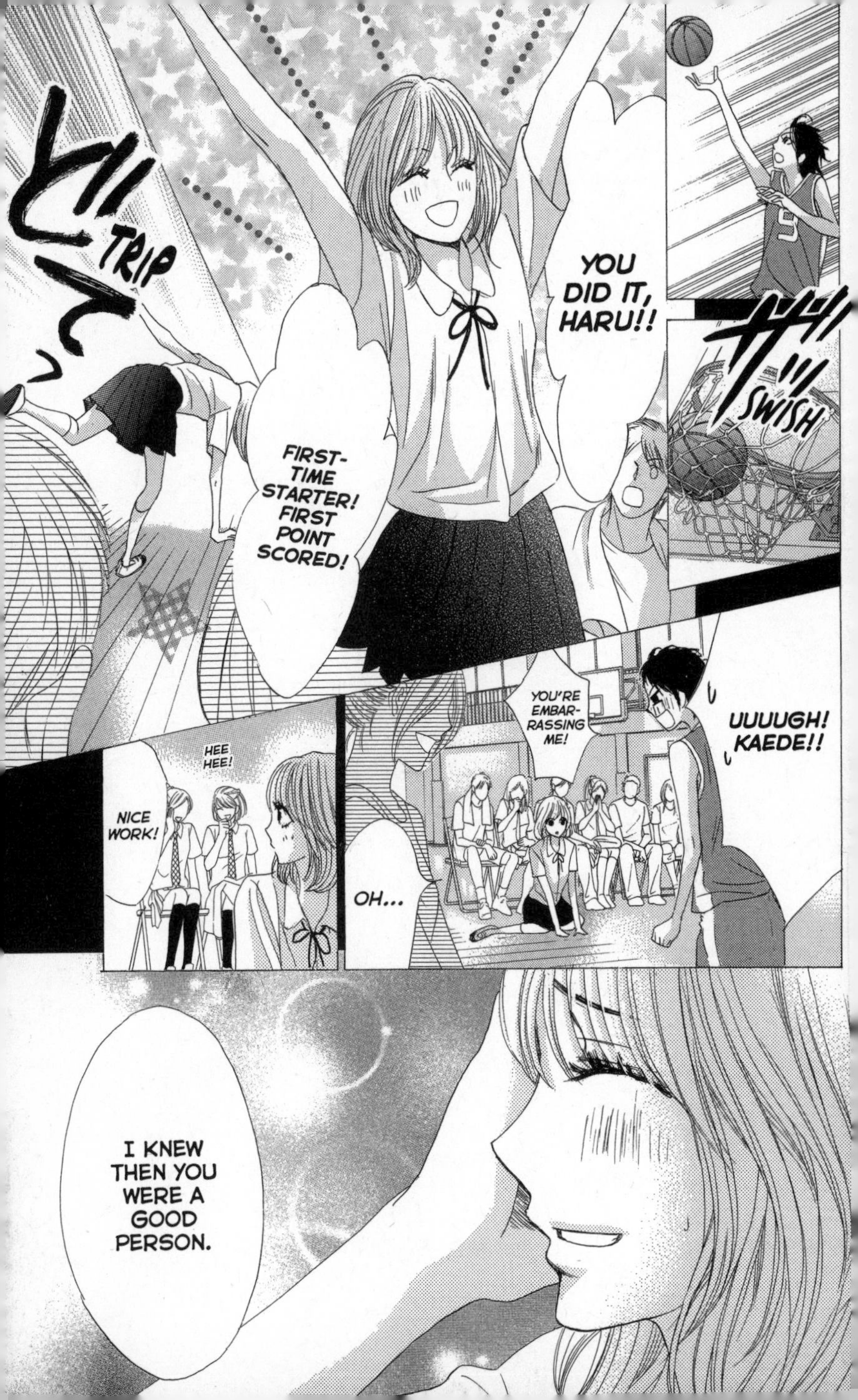
SWISH
YOU DID IT, HARU!!
FIRST-TIME STARTER! FIRST POINT SCORED!
TRIP
UUUUGH! KAEDE!!
YOU'RE EMBARRASSING ME!
OH...
HEE HEE!
NICE WORK!
I KNEW THEN YOU WERE A GOOD PERSON.

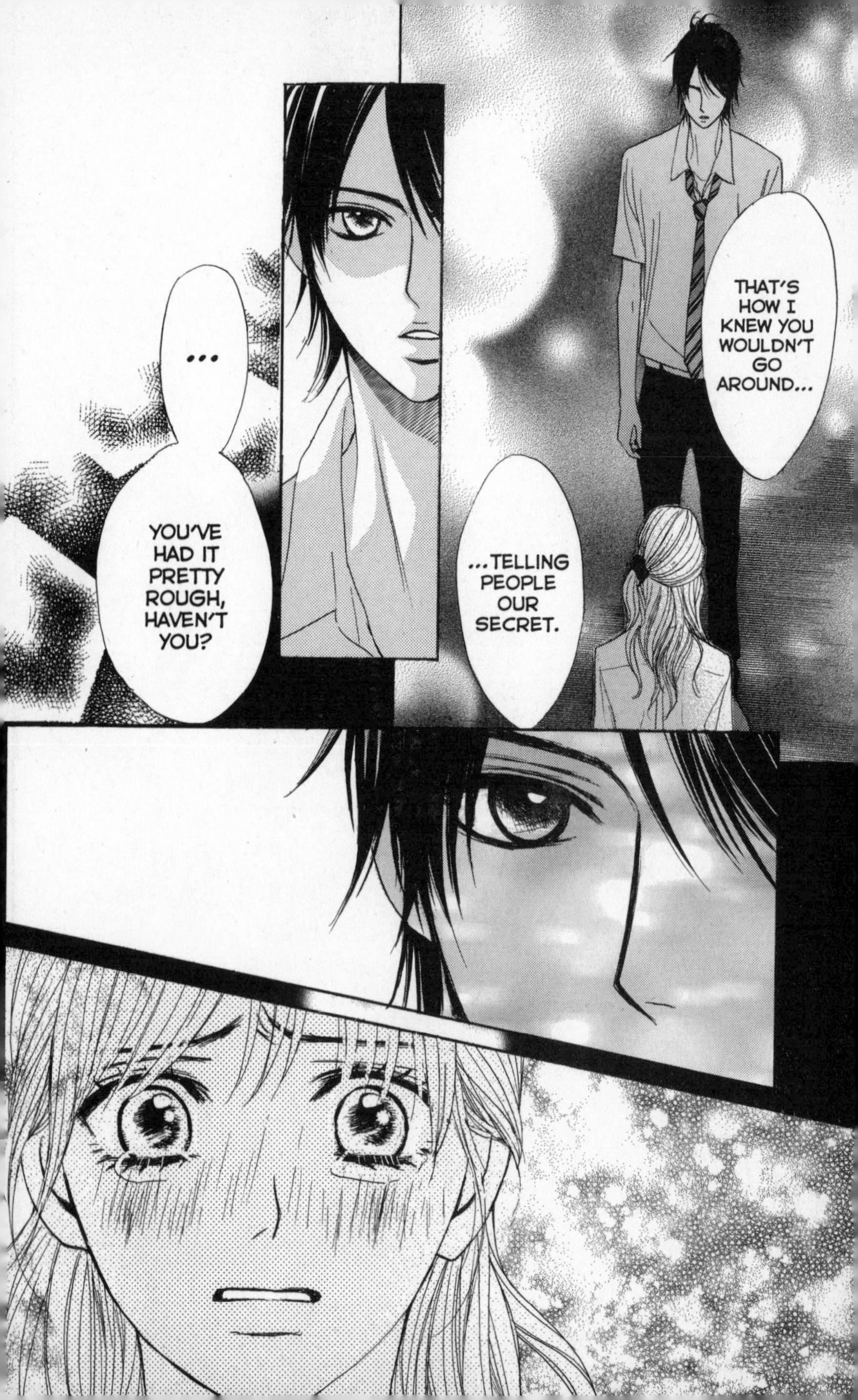
THAT'S HOW I KNEW YOU WOULDN'T GO AROUND...
...TELLING PEOPLE OUR SECRET.
...
YOU'VE HAD IT PRETTY ROUGH, HAVEN'T YOU?

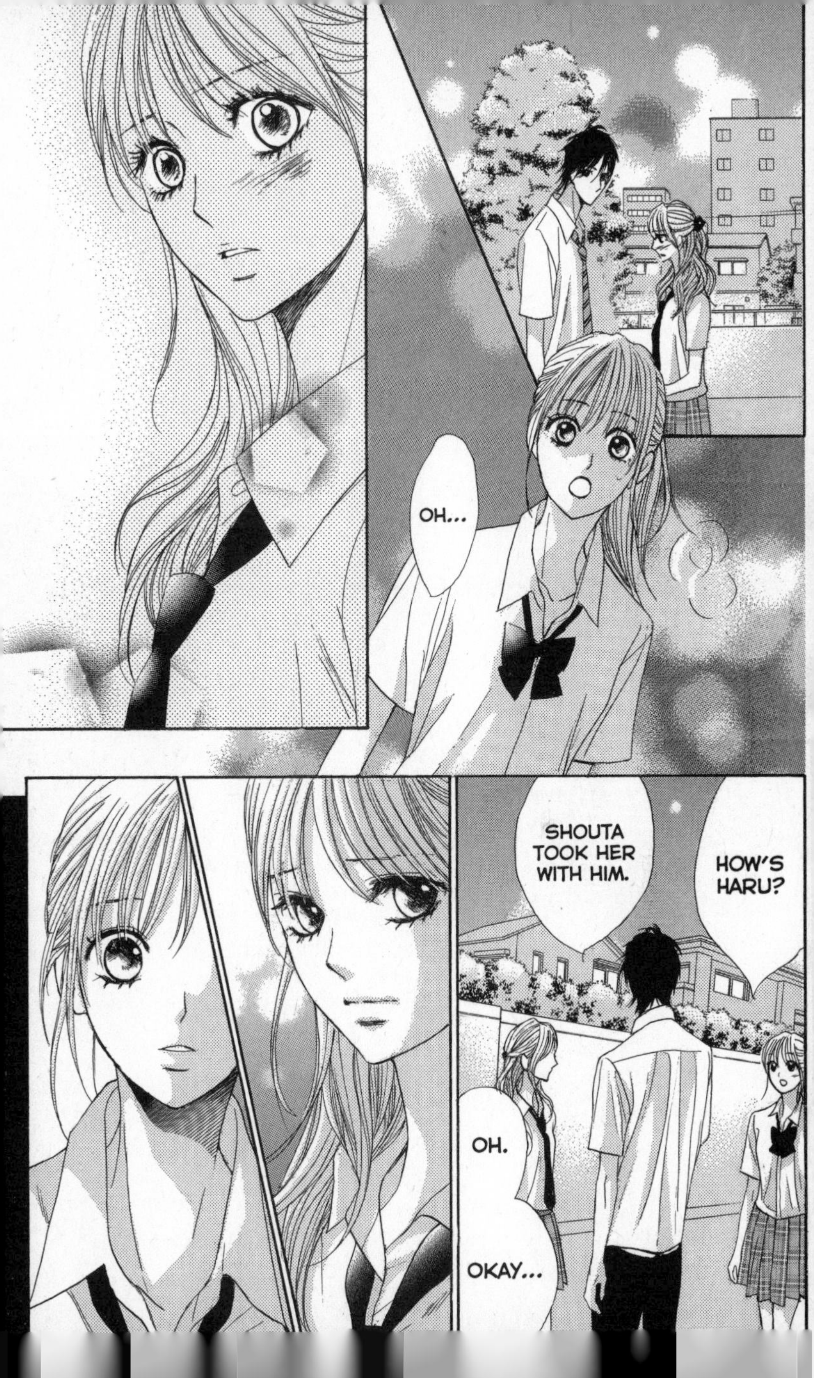
OH...
HOW'S HARU?
SHOUTA TOOK HER WITH HIM.
OH.
OKAY...

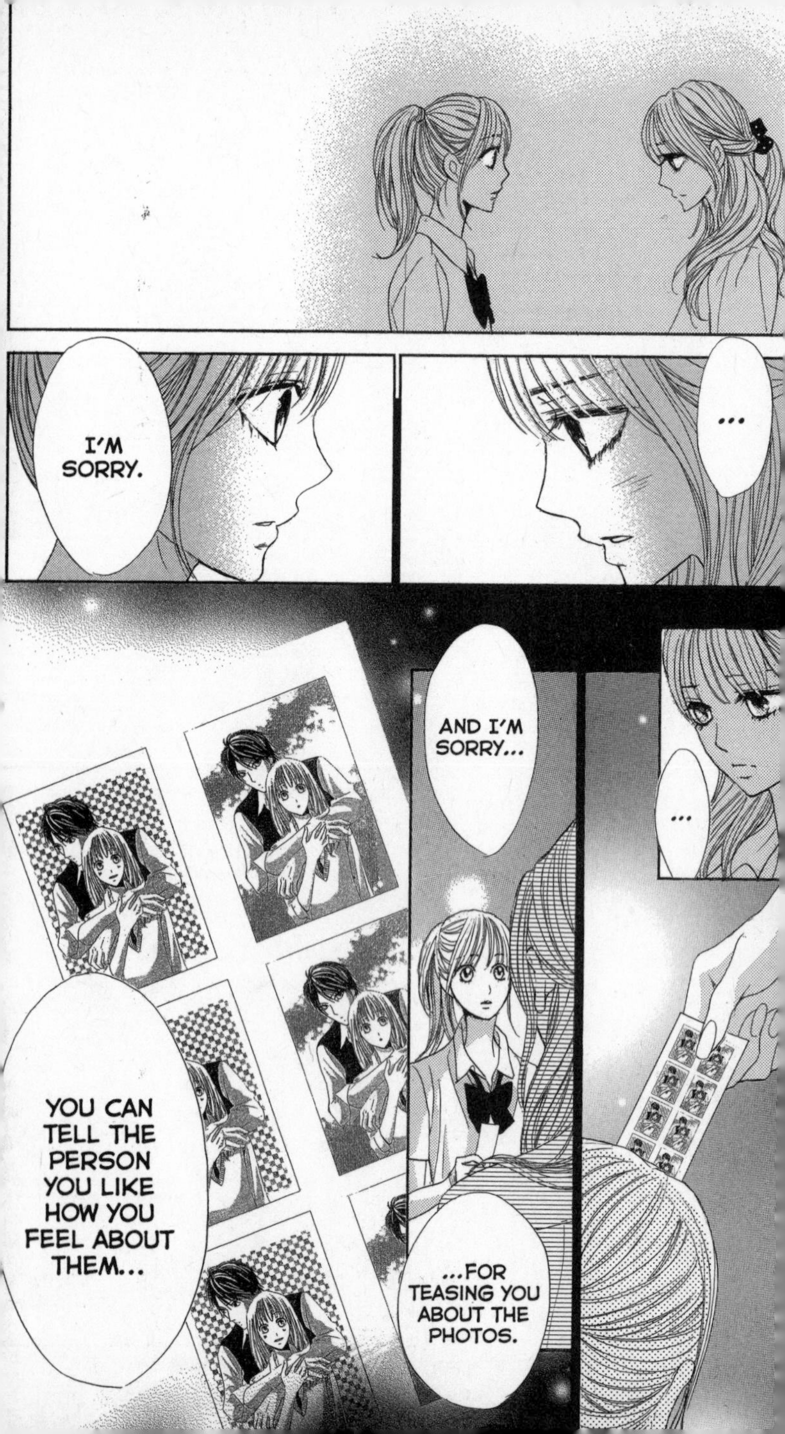
...
I'M SORRY.
...
AND I'M SORRY...
...FOR TEASING YOU ABOUT THE PHOTOS.
YOU CAN TELL THE PERSON YOU LIKE HOW YOU FEEL ABOUT THEM...

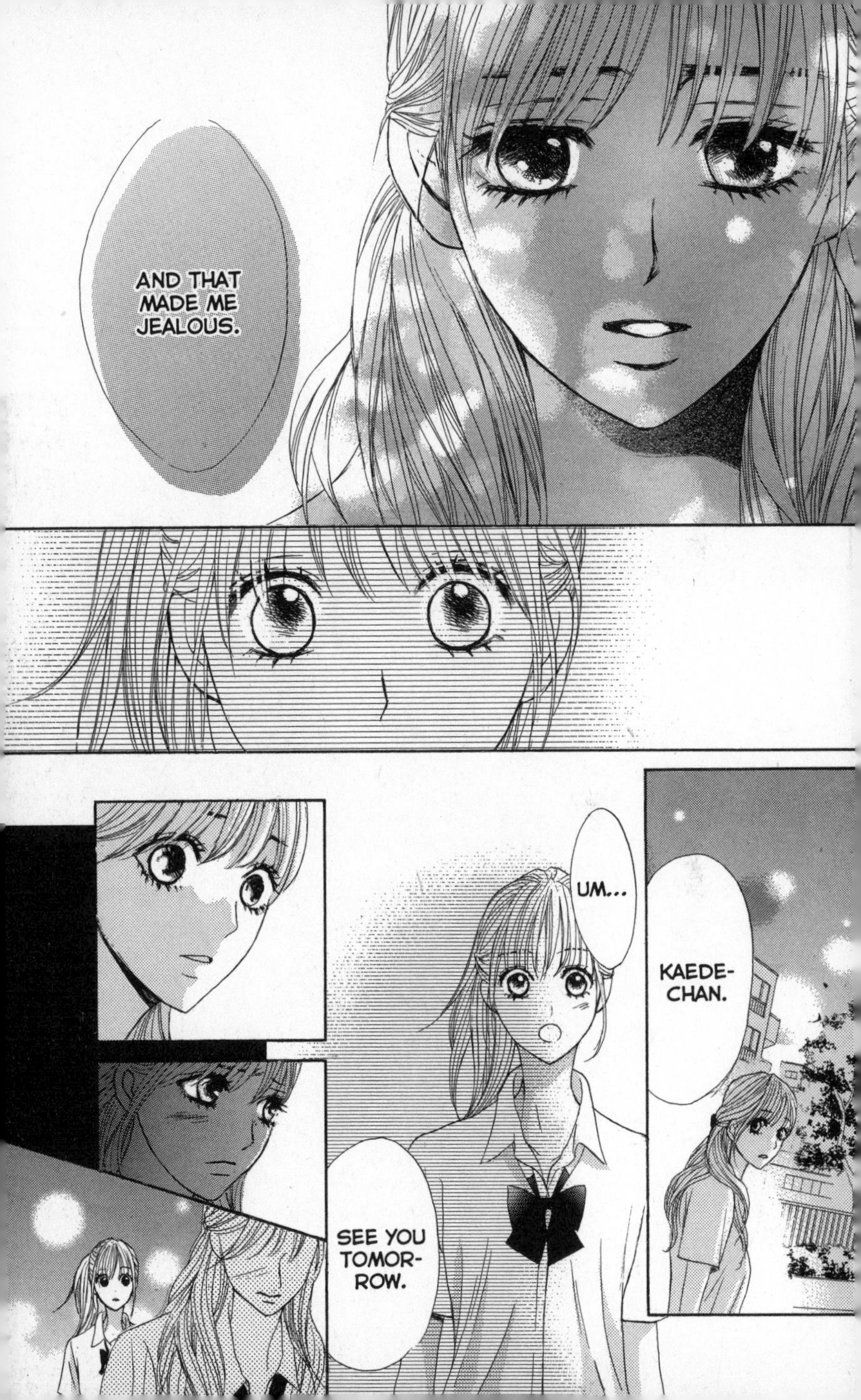
AND THAT MADE ME JEALOUS.
KAEDE-CHAN.
UM...
SEE YOU TOMOR-ROW.

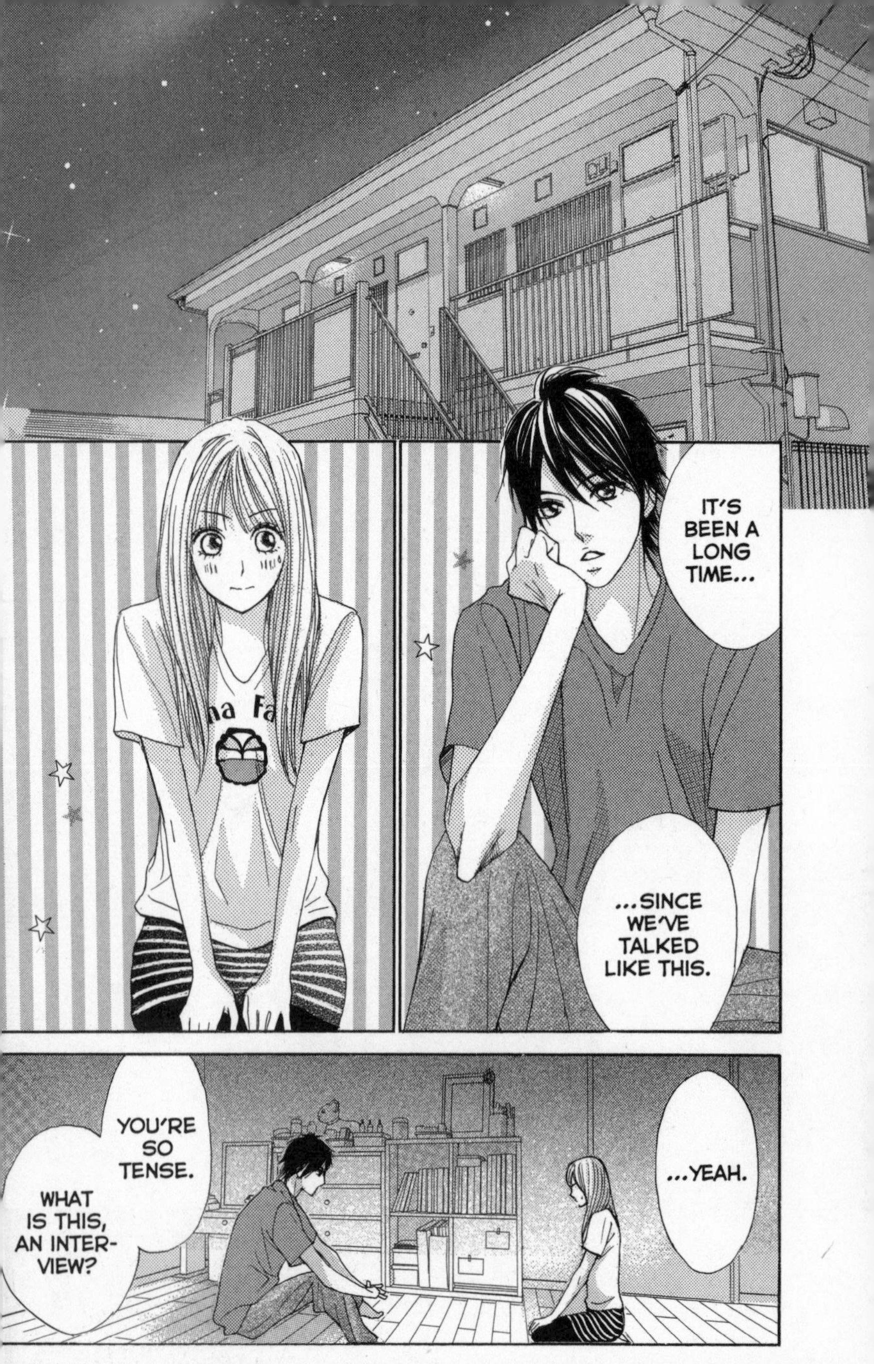
IT'S BEEN A LONG TIME...
...SINCE WE'VE TALKED LIKE THIS.
...YEAH.
YOU'RE SO TENSE.
WHAT IS THIS, AN INTER-VIEW?

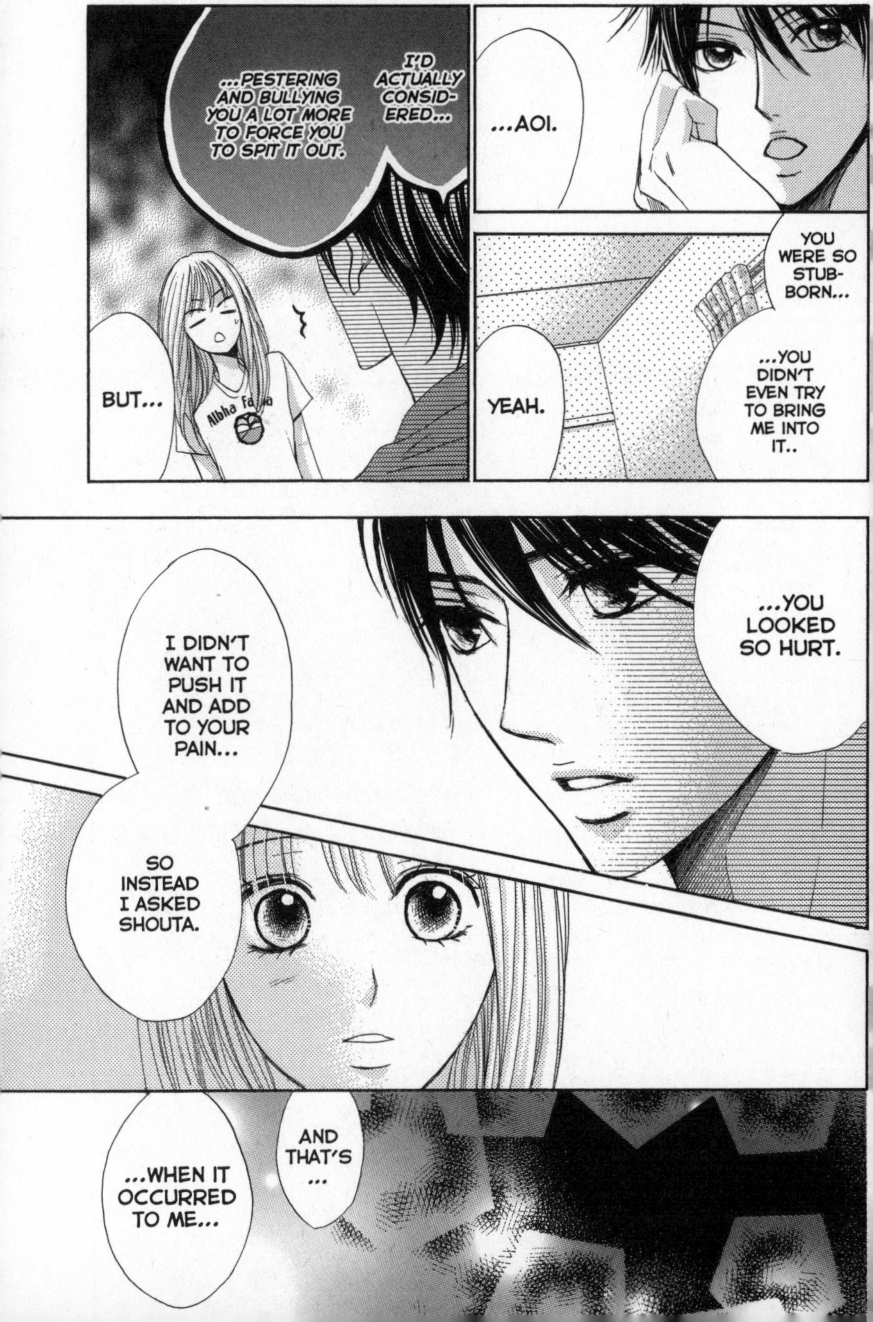
...AOI.
YOU WERE SO STUB-BORN...
...YOU DIDN'T EVEN TRY TO BRING ME INTO IT..
YEAH.
I'D ACTUALLY CONSID-ERED...
...PESTERING AND BULLYING YOU A LOT MORE TO FORCE YOU TO SPIT IT OUT.
BUT...
...YOU LOOKED SO HURT.
I DIDN'T WANT TO PUSH IT AND ADD TO YOUR PAIN...
SO INSTEAD I ASKED SHOUTA.
AND THAT'S ...
...WHEN IT OCCURRED TO ME...

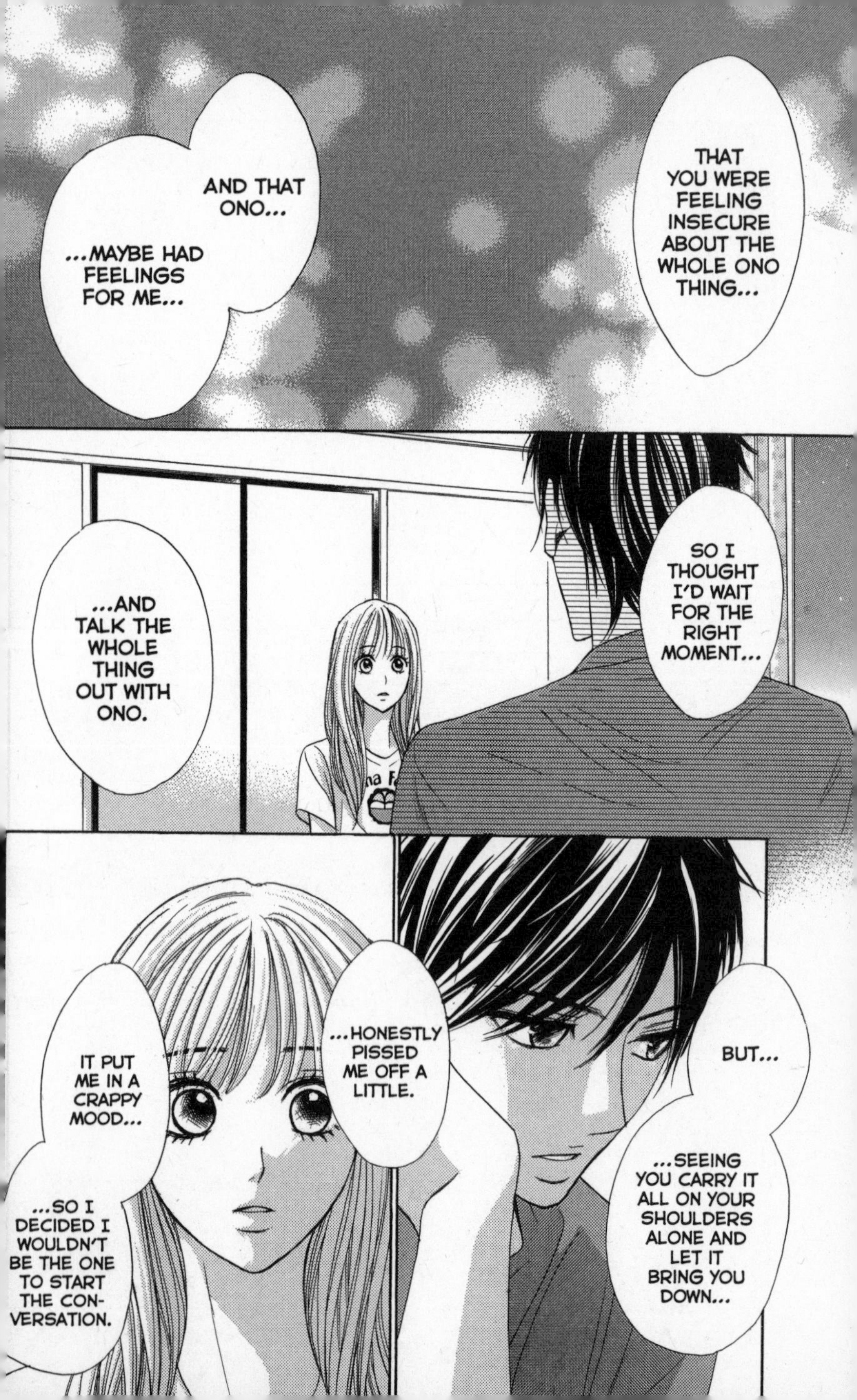
THAT YOU WERE FEELING INSECURE ABOUT THE WHOLE ONO THING...
AND THAT ONO...
...MAYBE HAD FEELINGS FOR ME...
SO I THOUGHT I'D WAIT FOR THE RIGHT MOMENT...
...AND TALK THE WHOLE THING OUT WITH ONO.
BUT...
...SEEING YOU CARRY IT ALL ON YOUR SHOULDERS ALONE AND LET IT BRING YOU DOWN...
...HONESTLY PISSED ME OFF A LITTLE.
IT PUT ME IN A CRAPPY MOOD...
...SO I DECIDED I WOULDN'T BE THE ONE TO START THE CON-VERSATION.

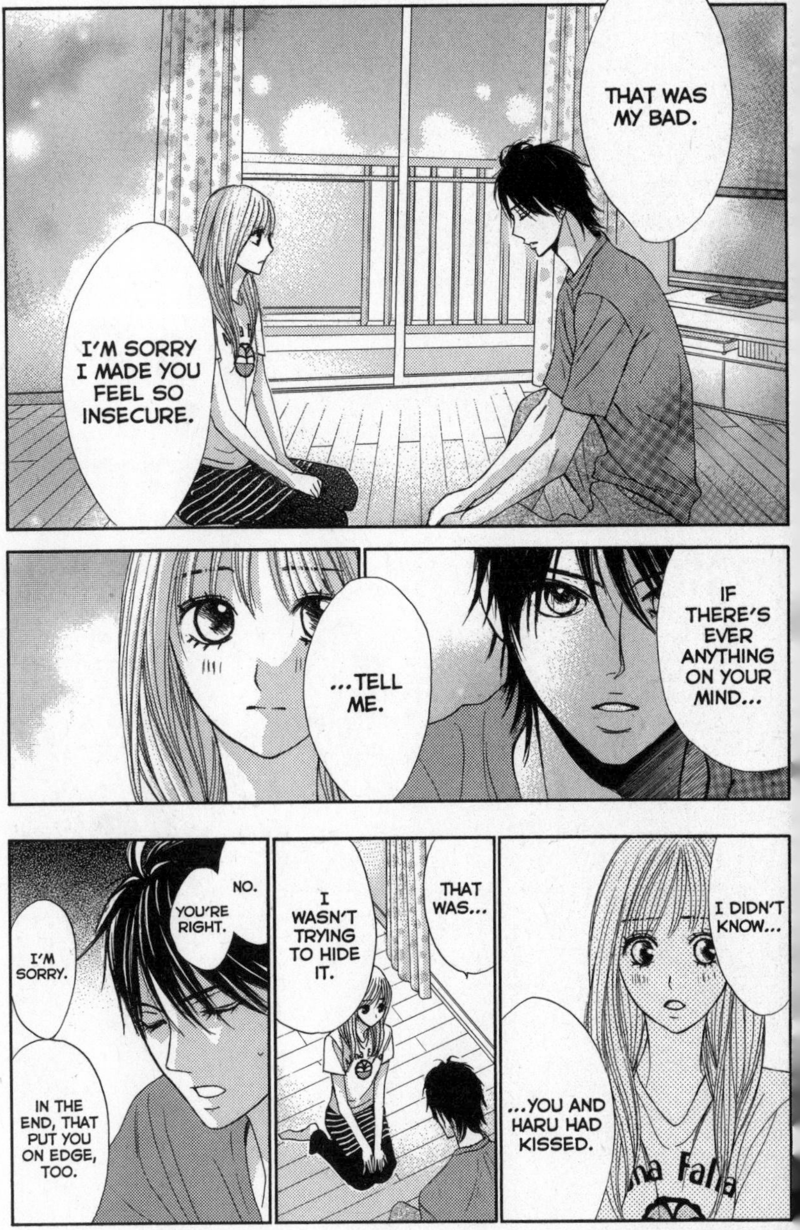
THAT WAS MY BAD.
I'M SORRY I MADE YOU FEEL SO INSECURE.
IF THERE'S EVER ANYTHING ON YOUR MIND...
...TELL ME.
I DIDN'T KNOW...
...YOU AND HARU HAD KISSED.
THAT WAS...
I WASN'T TRYING TO HIDE IT.
NO.
YOU'RE RIGHT.
I'M SORRY.
IN THE END, THAT PUT YOU ON EDGE, TOO.

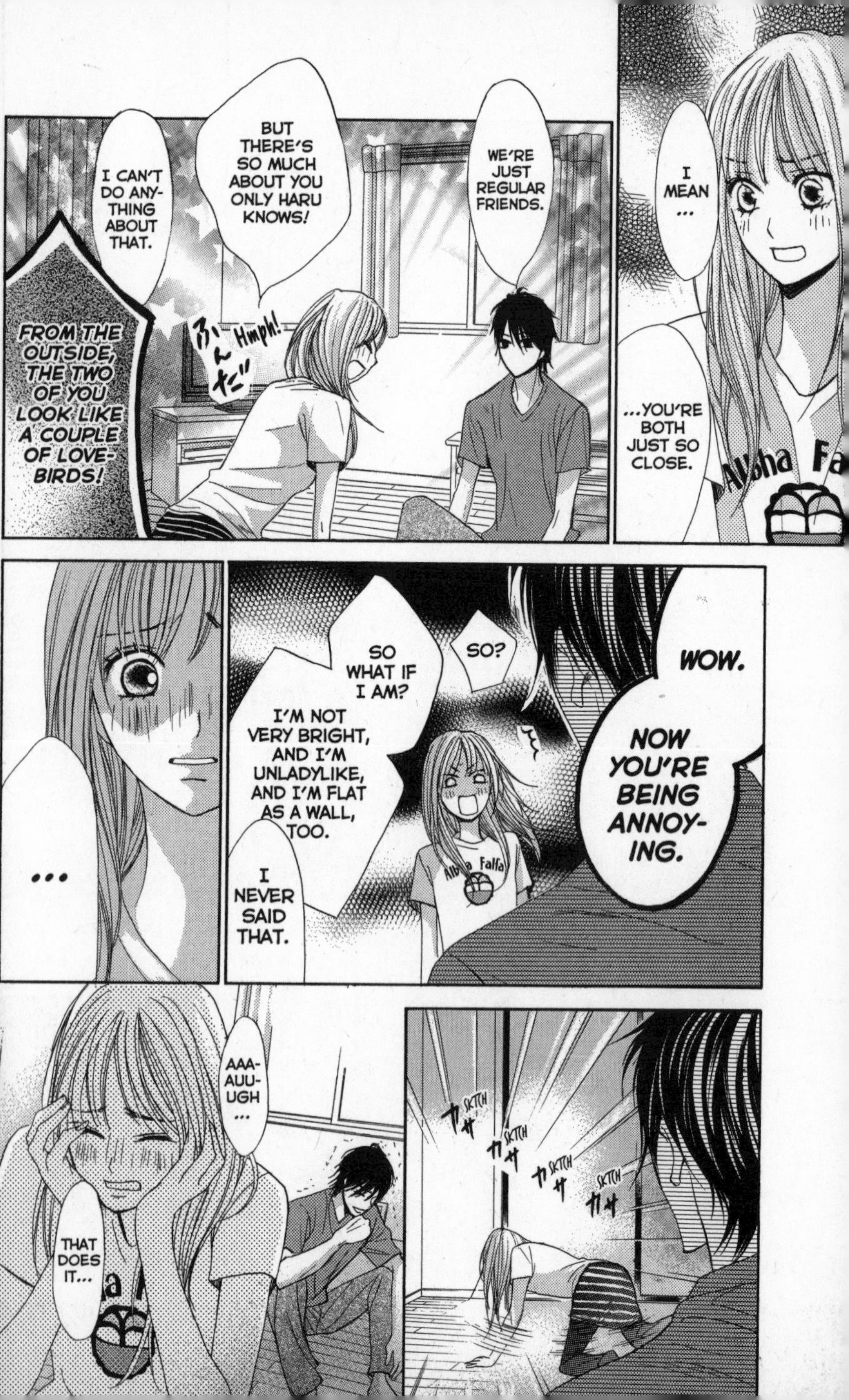
I MEAN...
...YOU'RE BOTH JUST SO CLOSE.
WE'RE JUST REGULAR FRIENDS.
BUT THERE'S SO MUCH ABOUT YOU ONLY HARU KNOWS!
I CAN'T DO ANY-THING ABOUT THAT.
Hmph!
FROM THE OUTSIDE, THE TWO OF YOU LOOK LIKE A COUPLE OF LOVE-BIRDS!
WOW.
NOW YOU'RE BEING ANNOY-ING.
SO?
SO WHAT IF I AM?
I'M NOT VERY BRIGHT, AND I'M UNLADYLIKE, AND I'M FLAT AS A WALL, TOO.
I NEVER SAID THAT.
...
SKTCH
SKTCH
SKTCH
SKTCH
AAA-AUUGH...
THAT DOES IT...

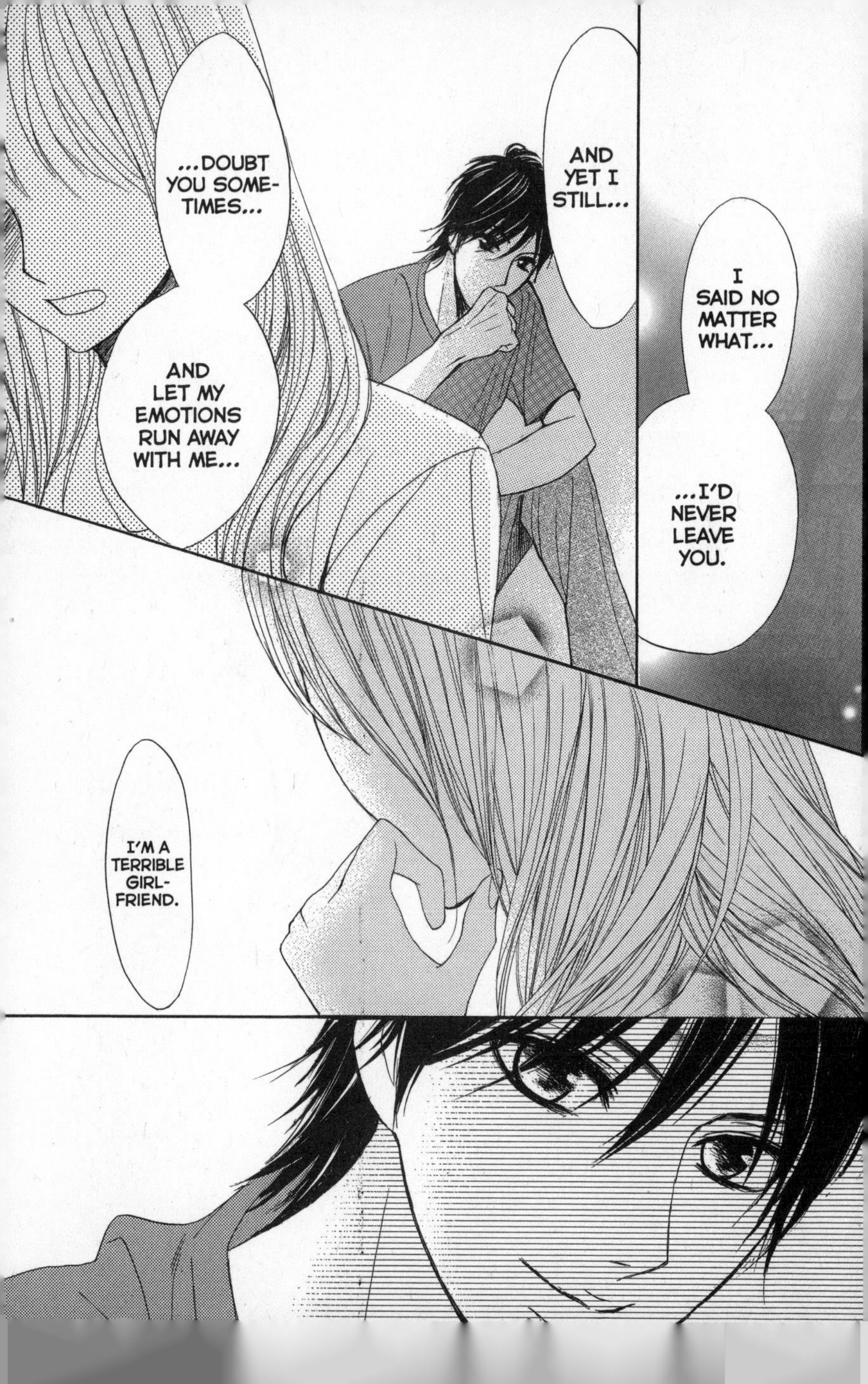
I SAID NO MATTER WHAT...
...I'D NEVER LEAVE YOU.
AND YET I STILL...
...DOUBT YOU SOME-TIMES...
AND LET MY EMOTIONS RUN AWAY WITH ME...
I'M A TERRIBLE GIRL-FRIEND.

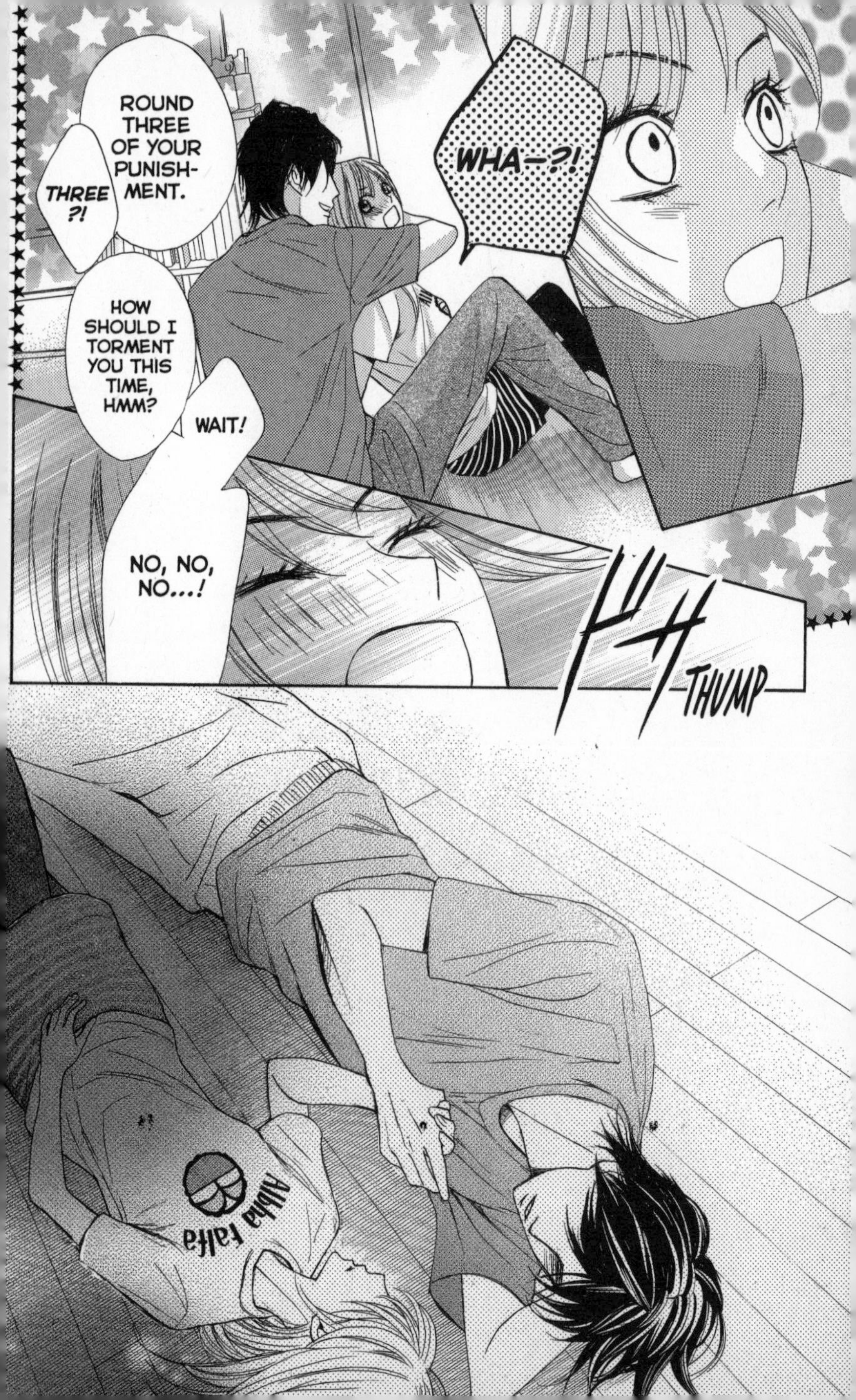
WHA-?!
ROUND THREE OF YOUR PUNISHMENT.
THREE?!
HOW SHOULD I TORMENT YOU THIS TIME, HMM?
WAIT!
NO, NO, NO...!
ドサ
THUMP
Alba falfa

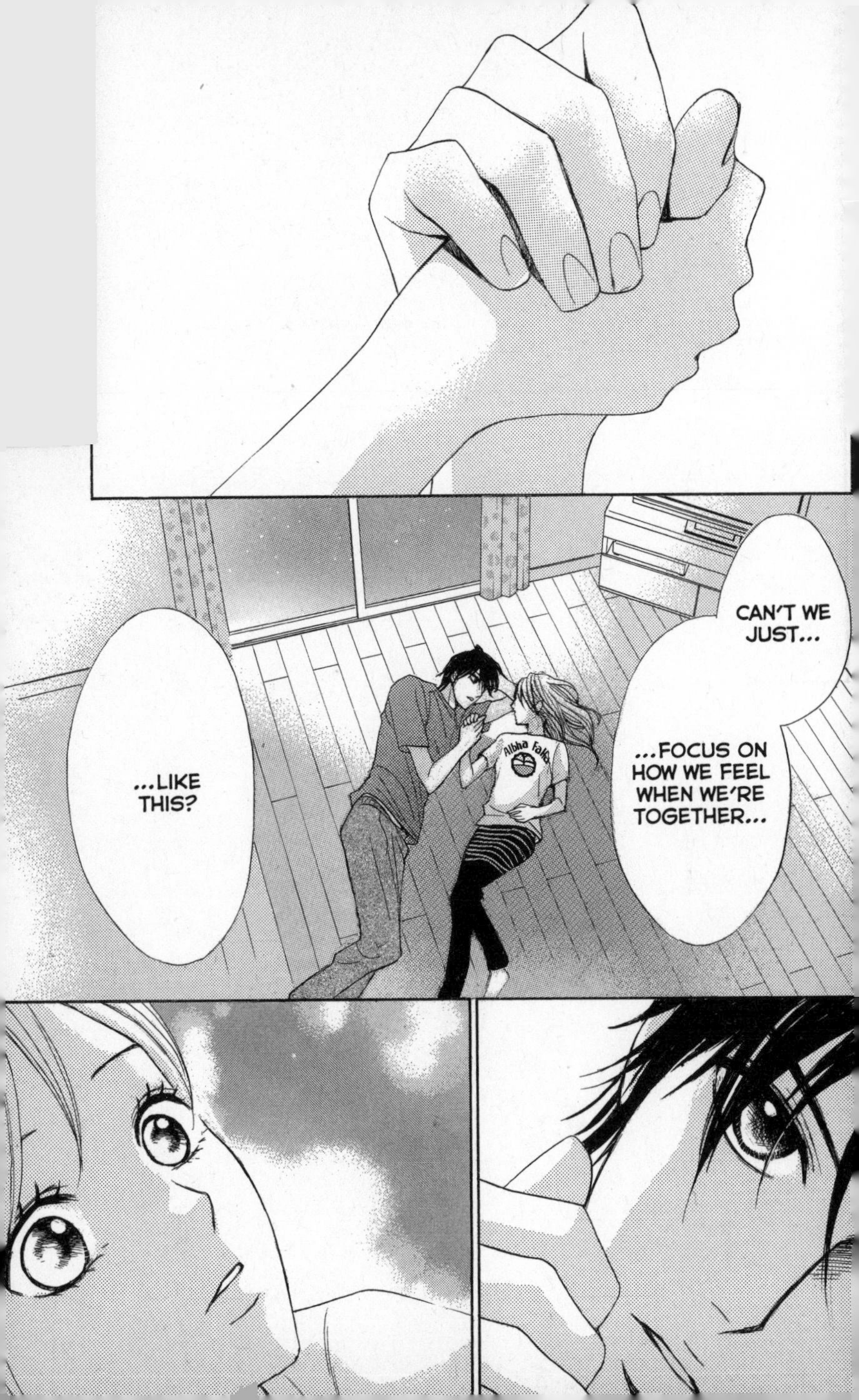
CAN'T WE JUST...
...FOCUS ON HOW WE FEEL WHEN WE'RE TOGETHER...
...LIKE THIS?

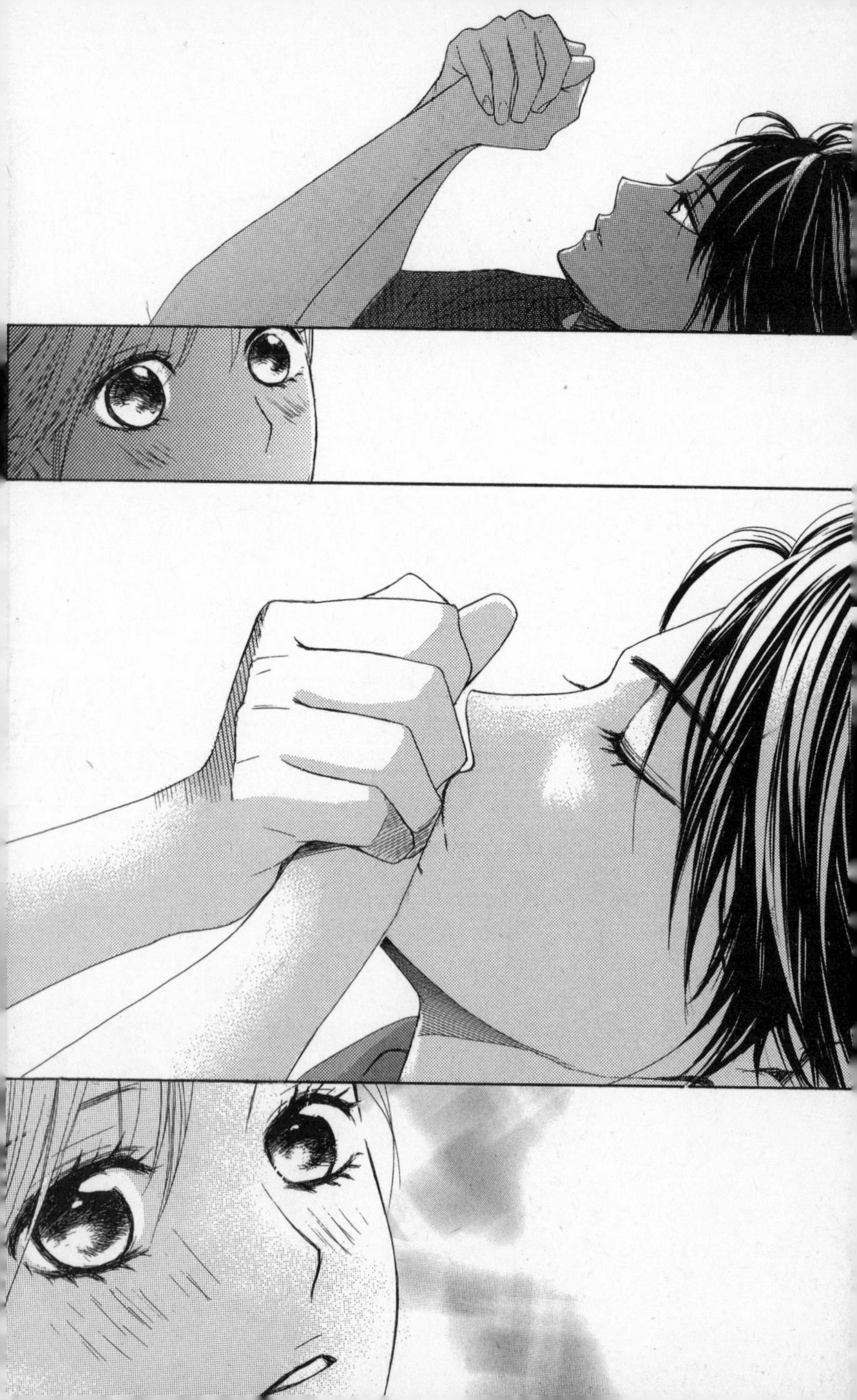

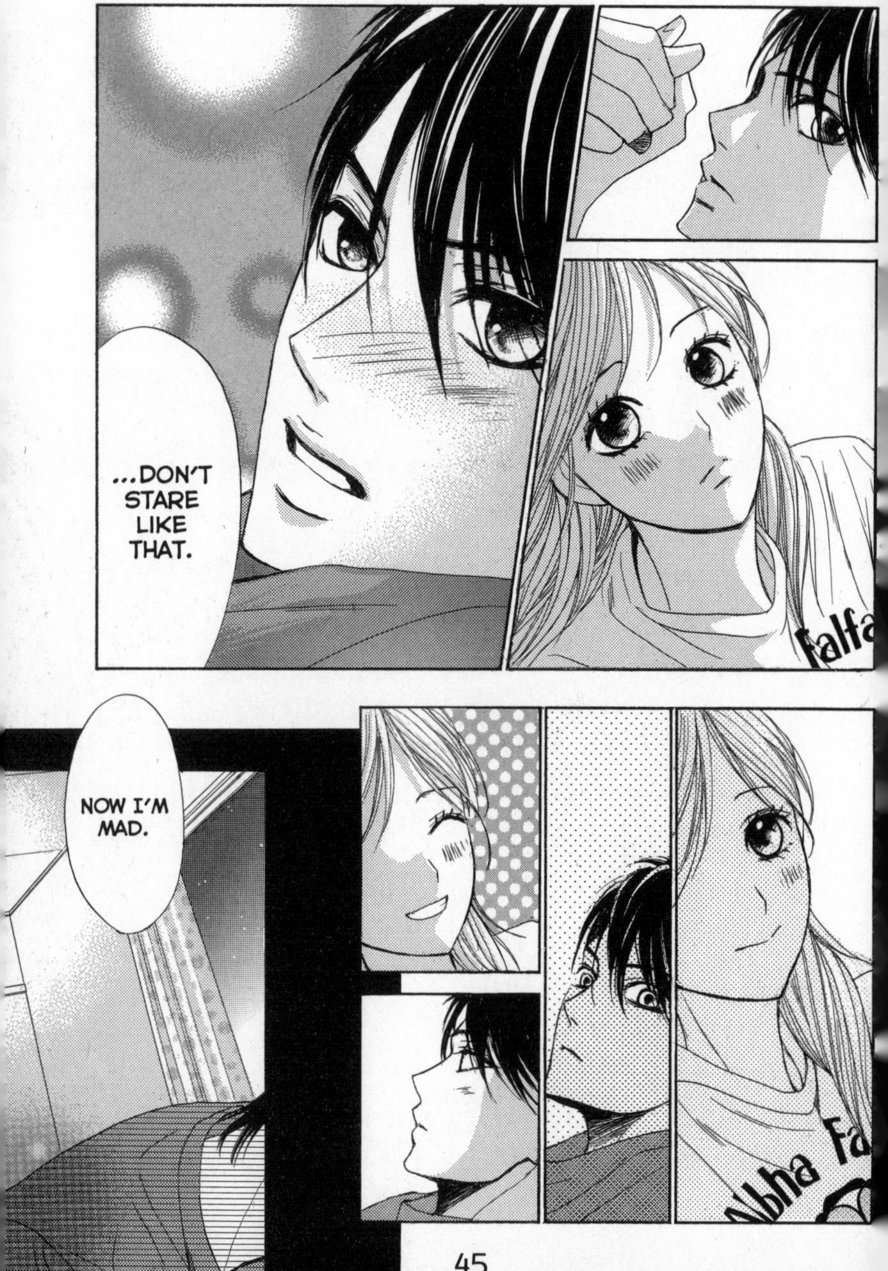
...DON'T STARE LIKE THAT.
NOW I'M MAD.

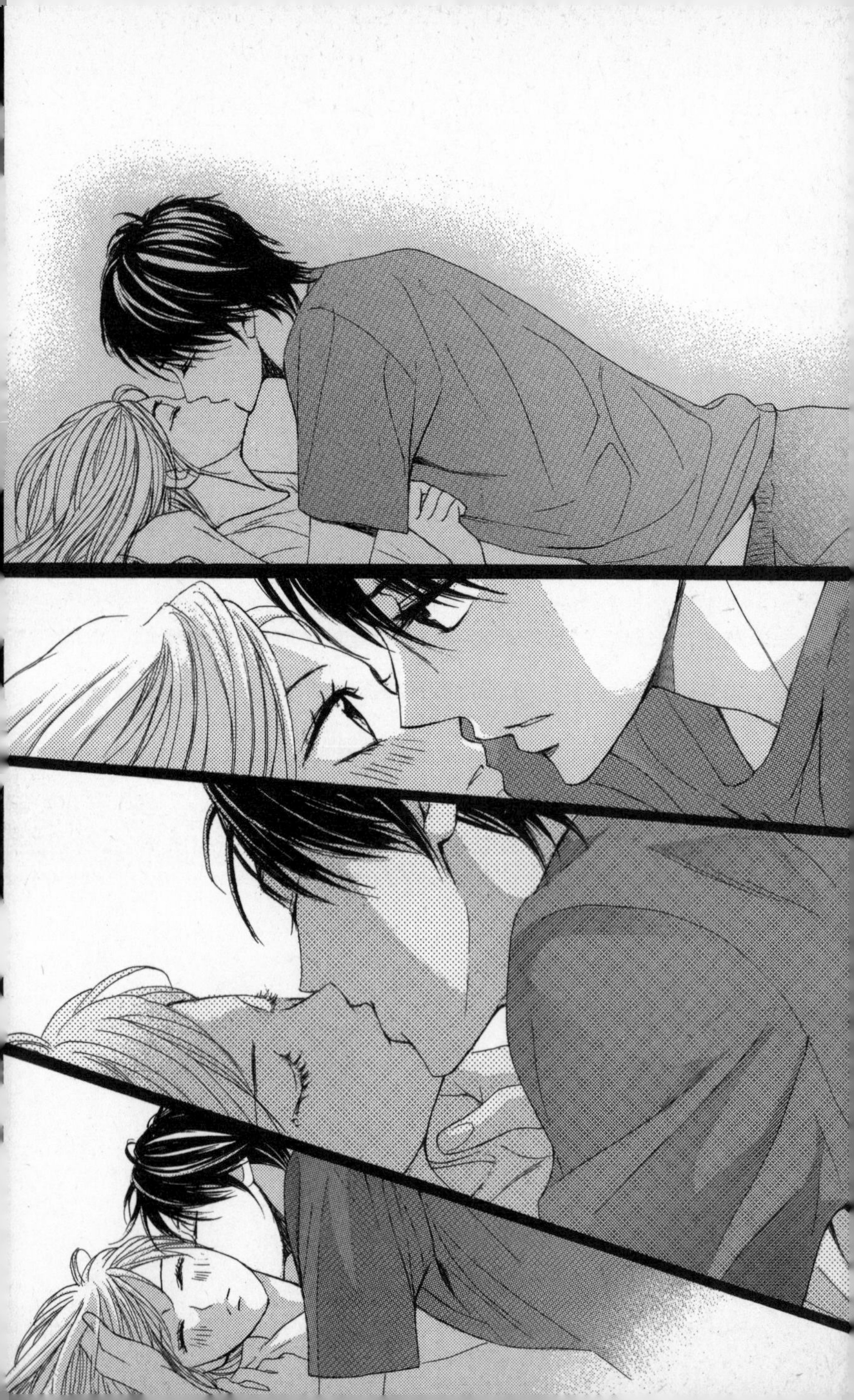

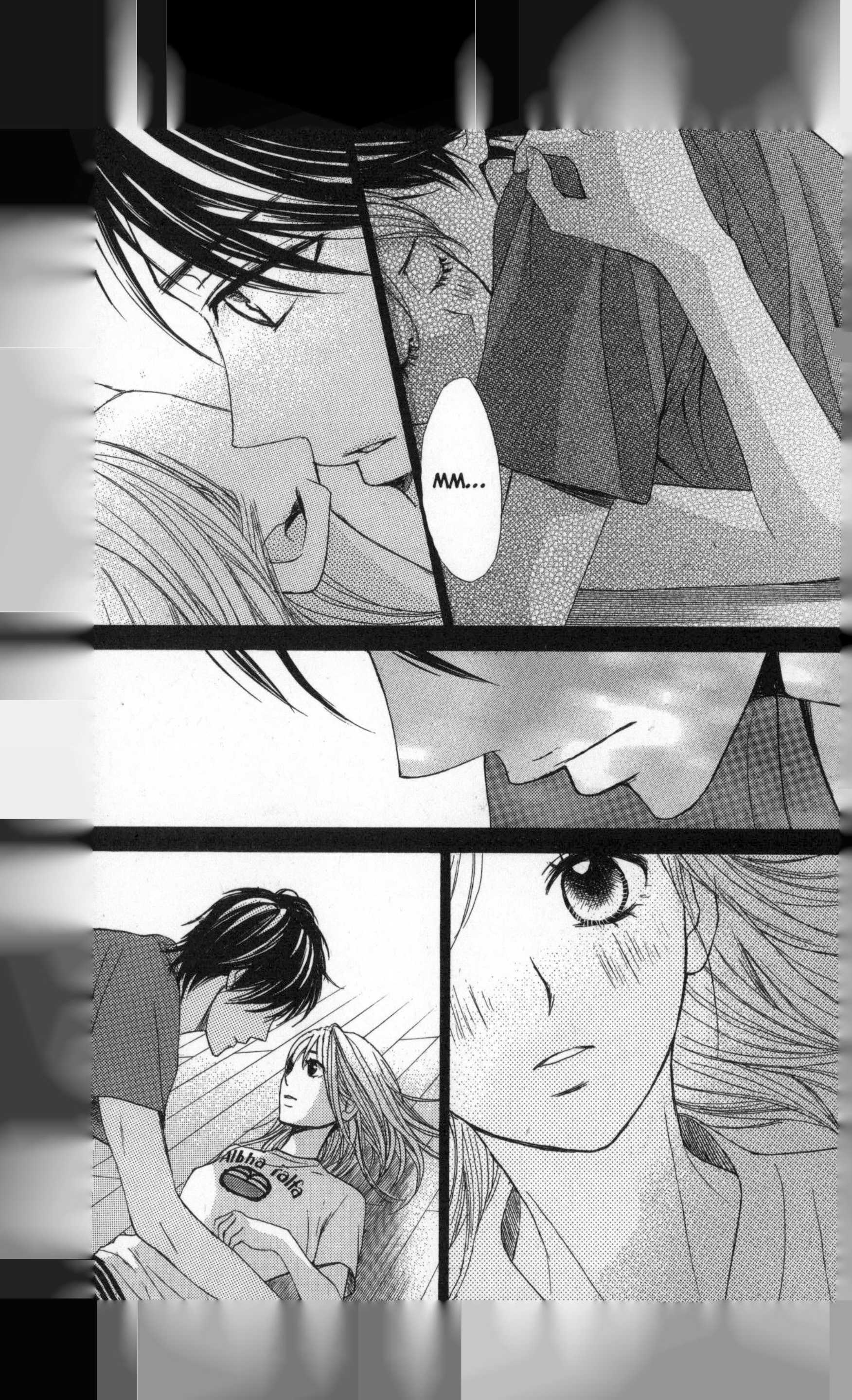
MM...

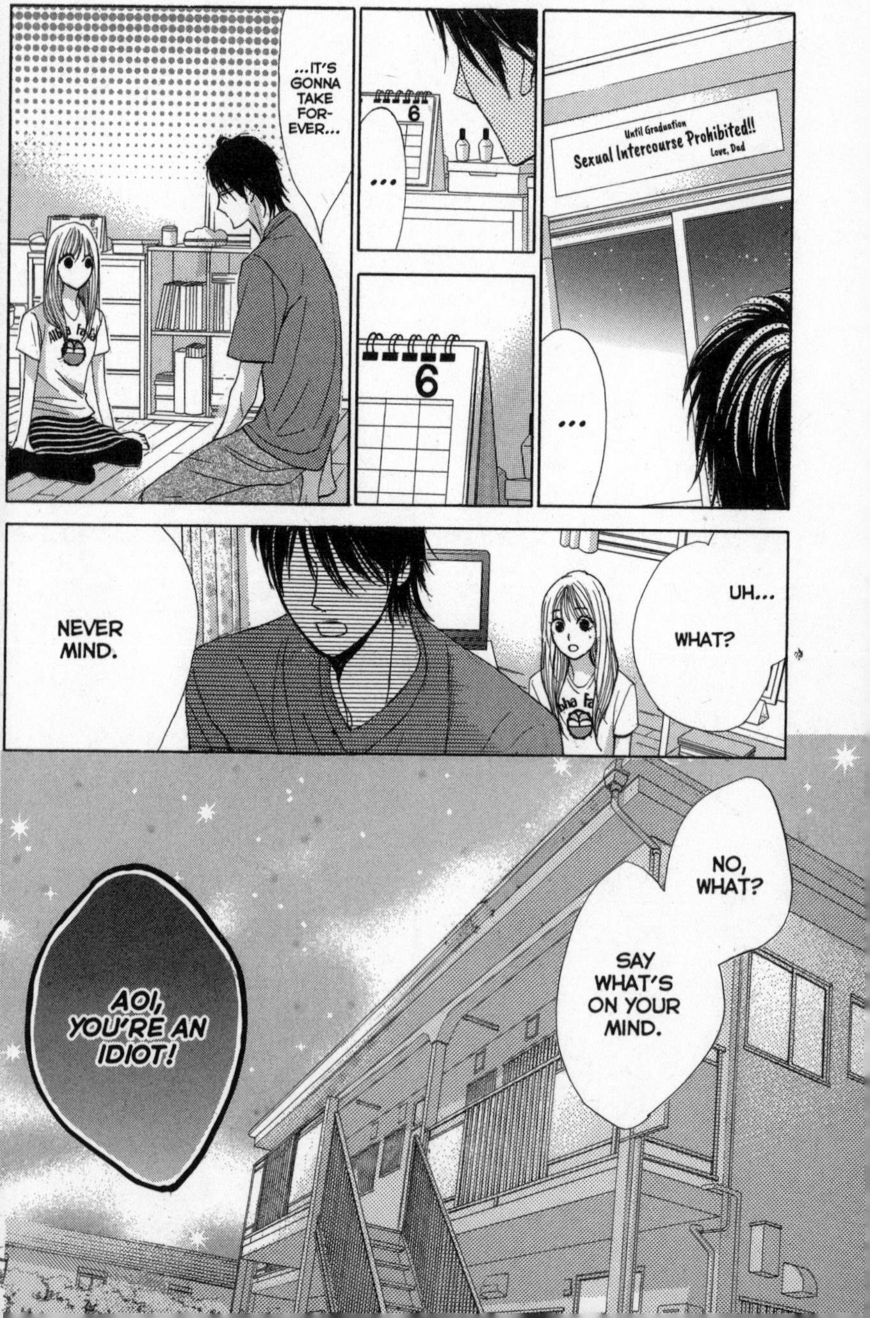
Until Graduation
Sexual Intercourse Prohibited!!
Love, Dad
...
...
...IT'S GONNA TAKE FOR-EVER...
UH...
WHAT?
NEVER MIND.
NO, WHAT?
SAY WHAT'S ON YOUR MIND.
AOI, YOU'RE AN IDIOT!

L♥DK

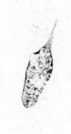

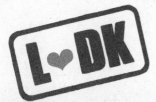

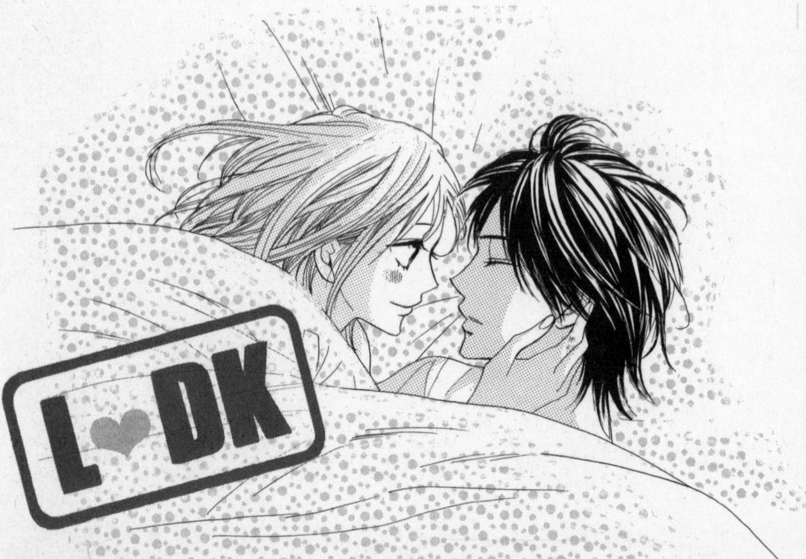
L♥DK

#46 Never-Before-Seen Face

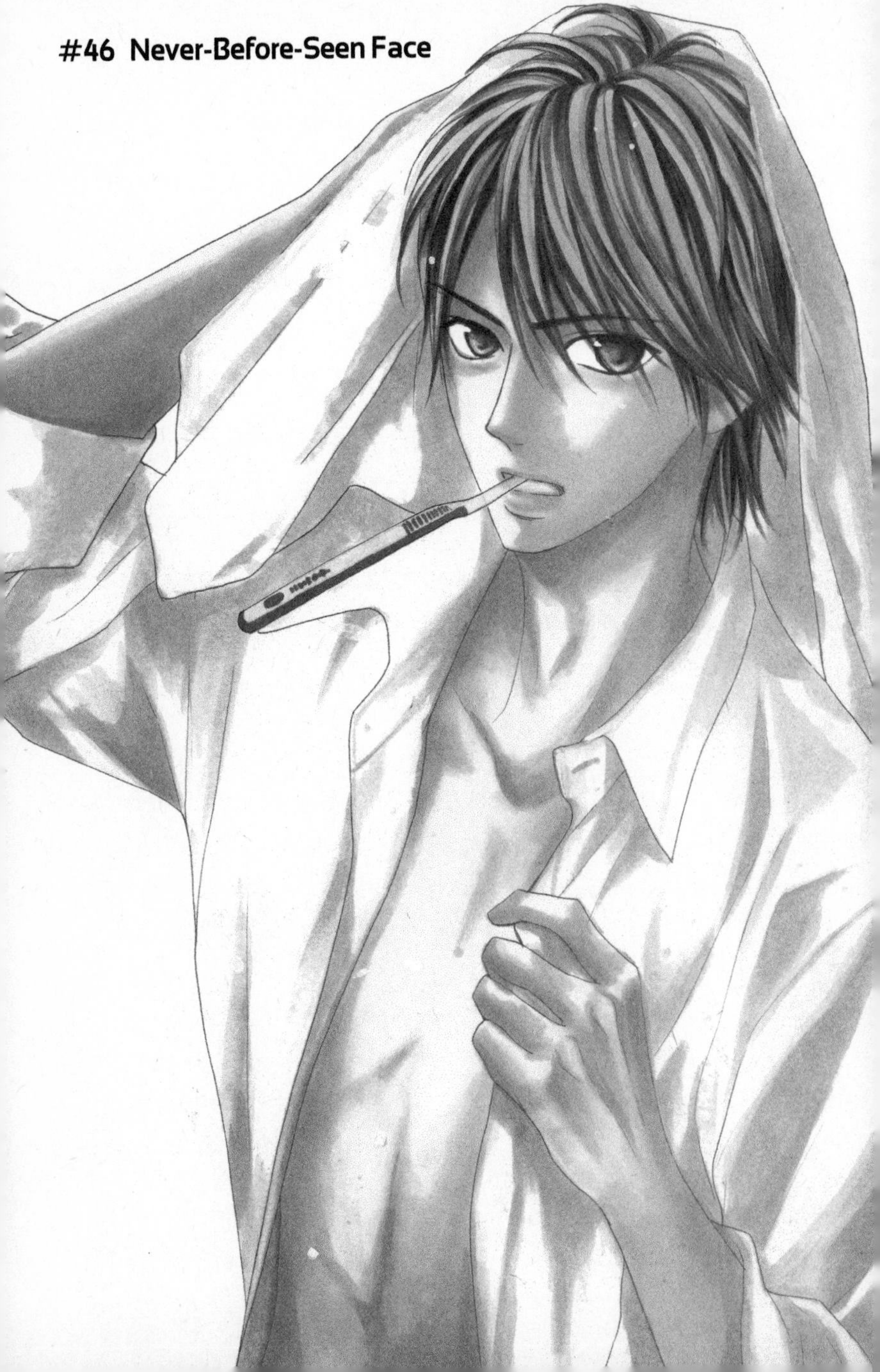

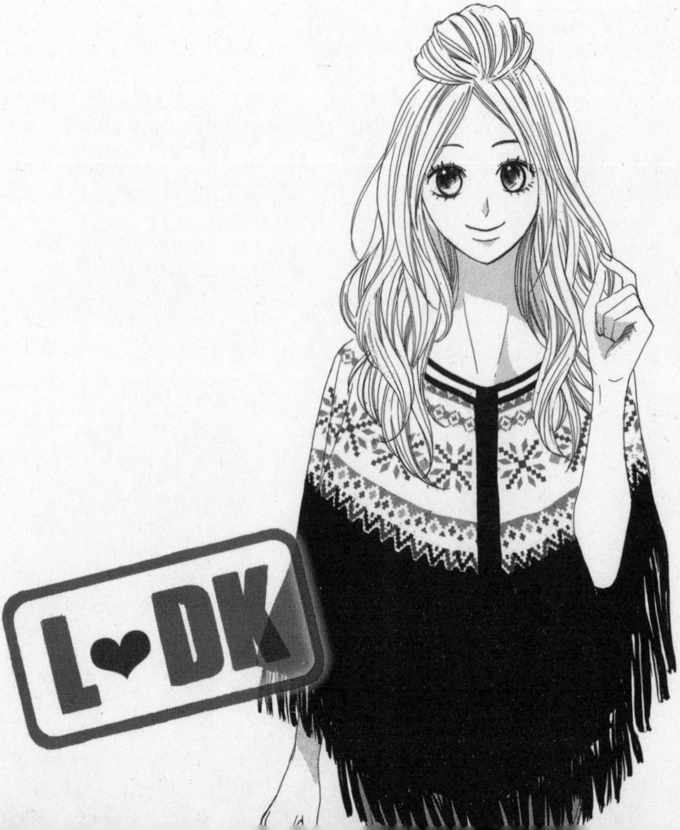
L♥DK

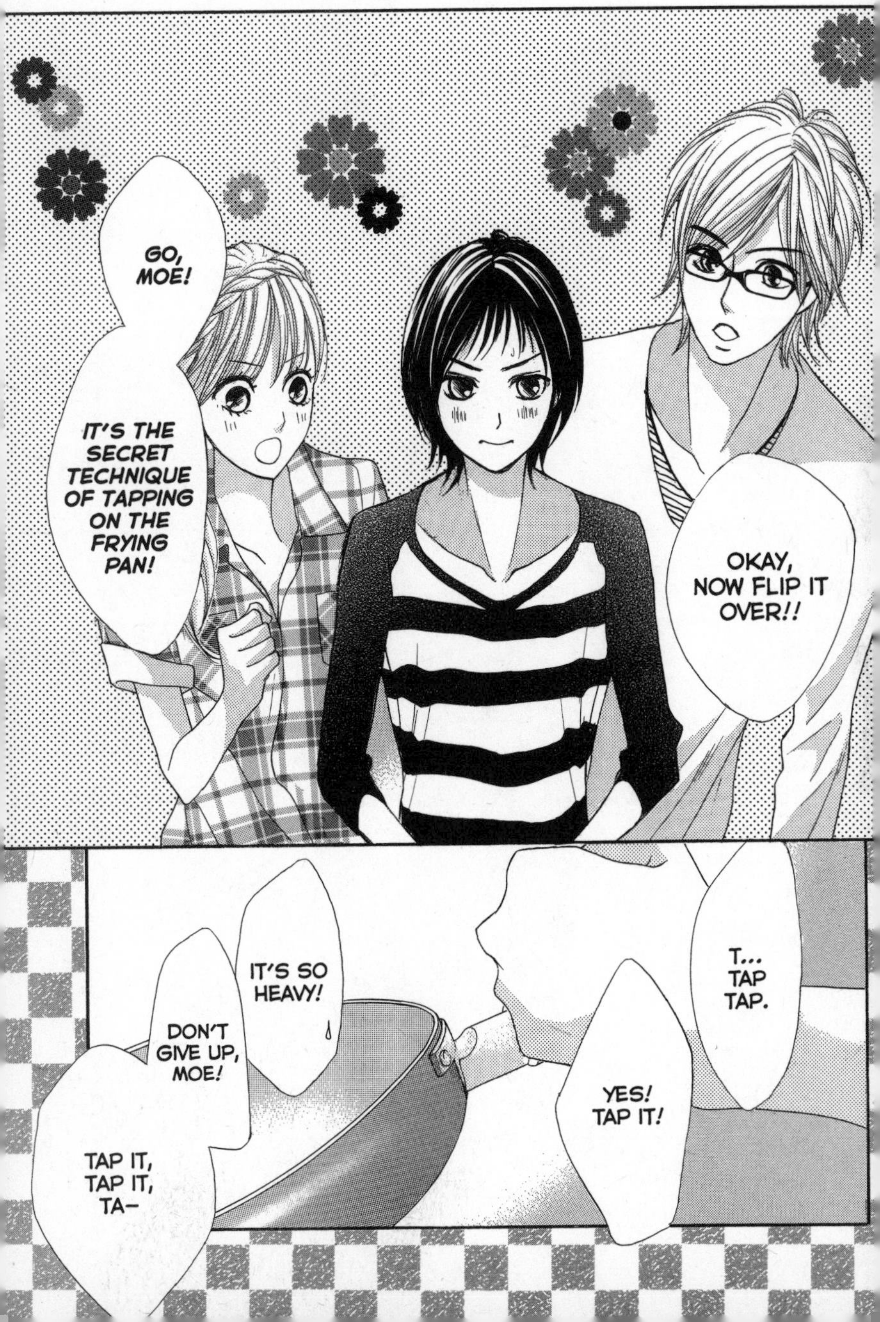
GO, MOE!
IT'S THE SECRET TECHNIQUE OF TAPPING ON THE FRYING PAN!
OKAY, NOW FLIP IT OVER!!
T... TAP TAP.
YES! TAP IT!
IT'S SO HEAVY!
DON'T GIVE UP, MOE!
TAP IT, TAP IT, TA–

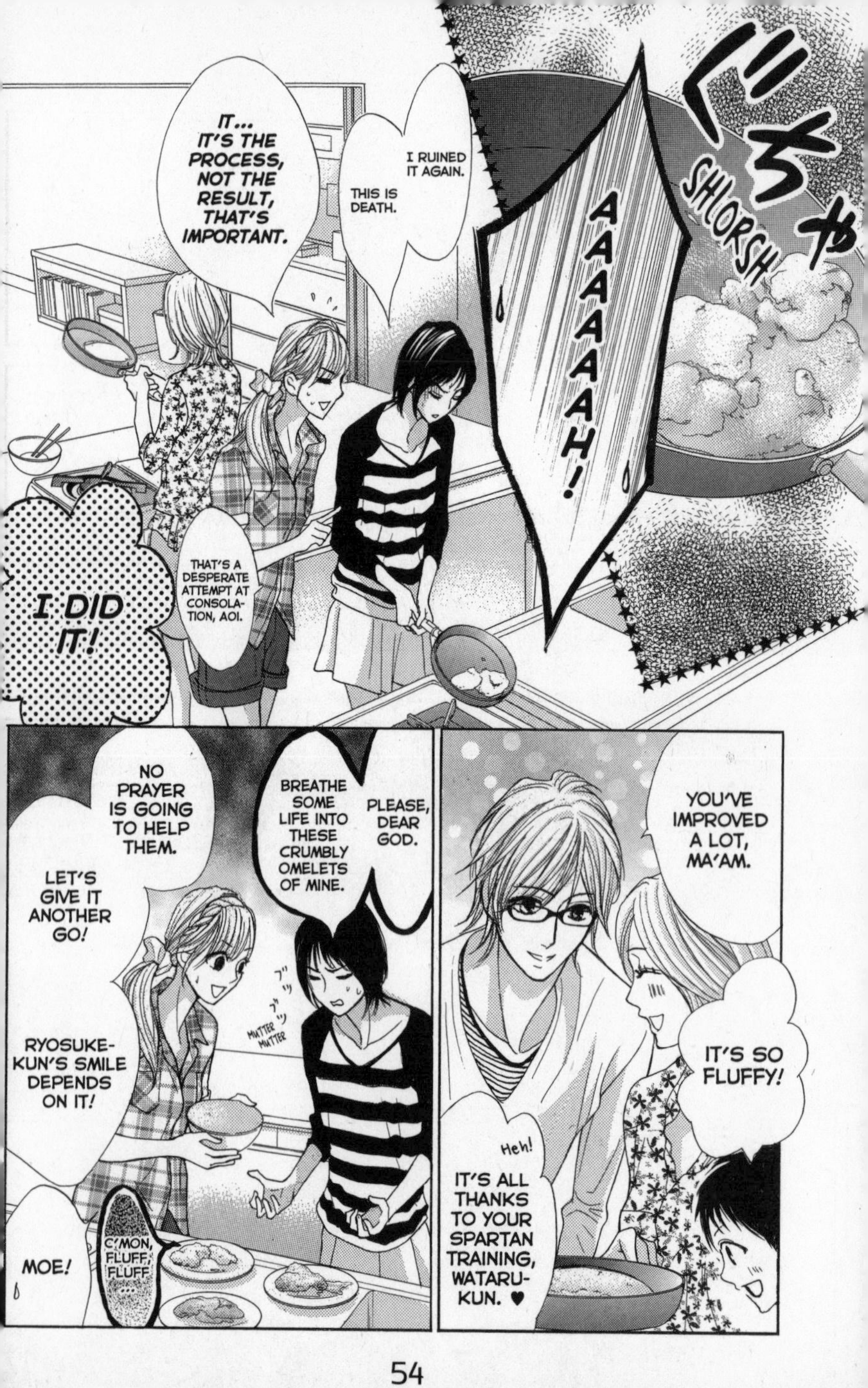
ぐちゃ
SHLORSH
AAAAAAH!
I RUINED IT AGAIN.
THIS IS DEATH.
IT... IT'S THE PROCESS, NOT THE RESULT, THAT'S IMPORTANT.
THAT'S A DESPERATE ATTEMPT AT CONSOLATION, AOI.
I DID IT!
YOU'VE IMPROVED A LOT, MA'AM.
IT'S SO FLUFFY!
Heh!
IT'S ALL THANKS TO YOUR SPARTAN TRAINING, WATARU-KUN. ♥
PLEASE, DEAR GOD.
BREATHE SOME LIFE INTO THESE CRUMBLY OMELETS OF MINE.
NO PRAYER IS GOING TO HELP THEM.
LET'S GIVE IT ANOTHER GO!
RYOSUKE-KUN'S SMILE DEPENDS ON IT!
ブツブツ
MUTTER MUTTER
C'MON, FLUFF, FLUFF...
MOE!

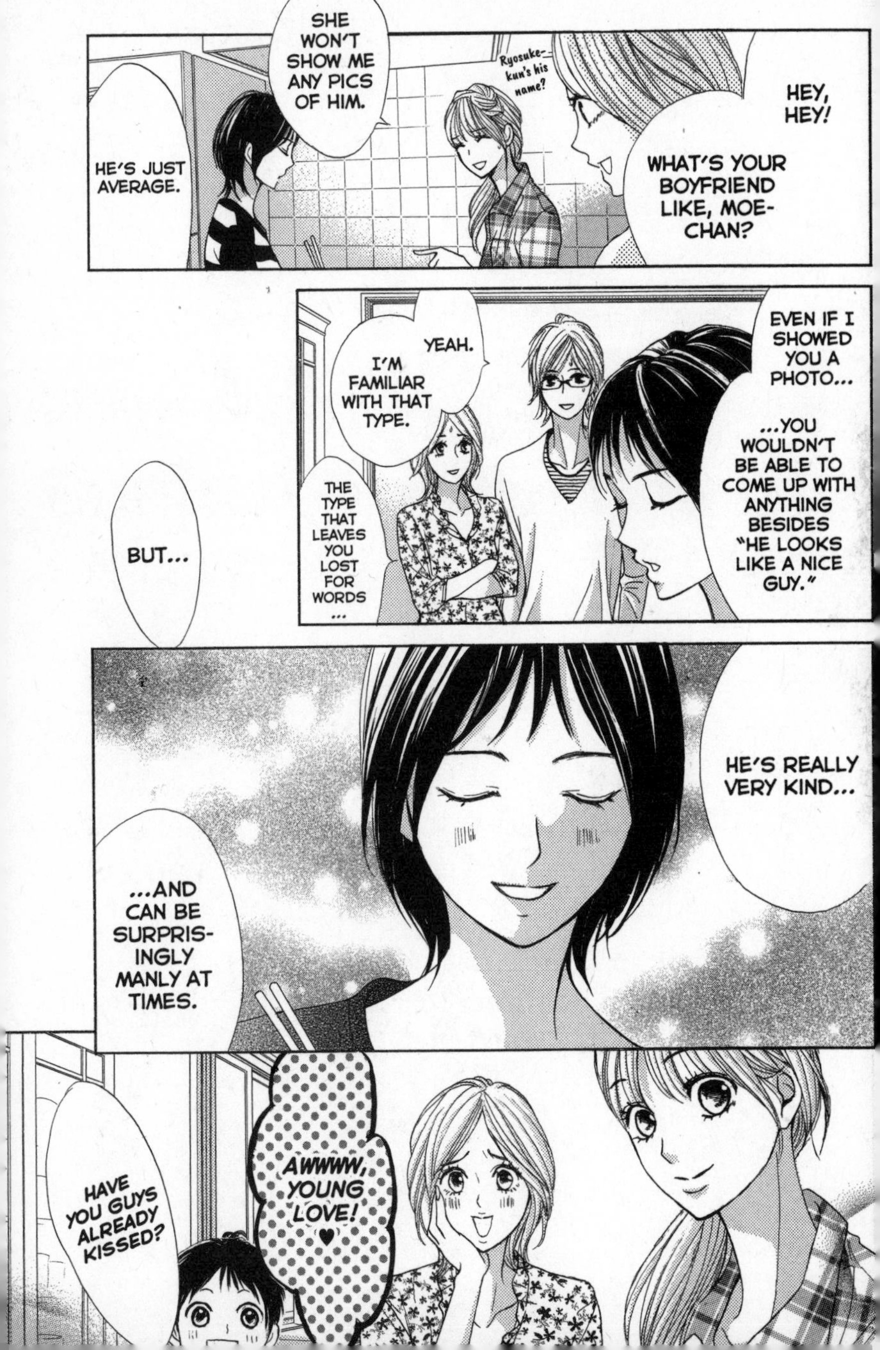

HEY, HEY!
WHAT'S YOUR BOYFRIEND LIKE, MOE-CHAN?
Ryosuke-kun's his name?
SHE WON'T SHOW ME ANY PICS OF HIM.
HE'S JUST AVERAGE.
EVEN IF I SHOWED YOU A PHOTO...
...YOU WOULDN'T BE ABLE TO COME UP WITH ANYTHING BESIDES "HE LOOKS LIKE A NICE GUY."
YEAH.
I'M FAMILIAR WITH THAT TYPE.
THE TYPE THAT LEAVES YOU LOST FOR WORDS...
BUT...
HE'S REALLY VERY KIND...
...AND CAN BE SURPRISINGLY MANLY AT TIMES.
AWWWW, YOUNG LOVE! ♥
HAVE YOU GUYS ALREADY KISSED?

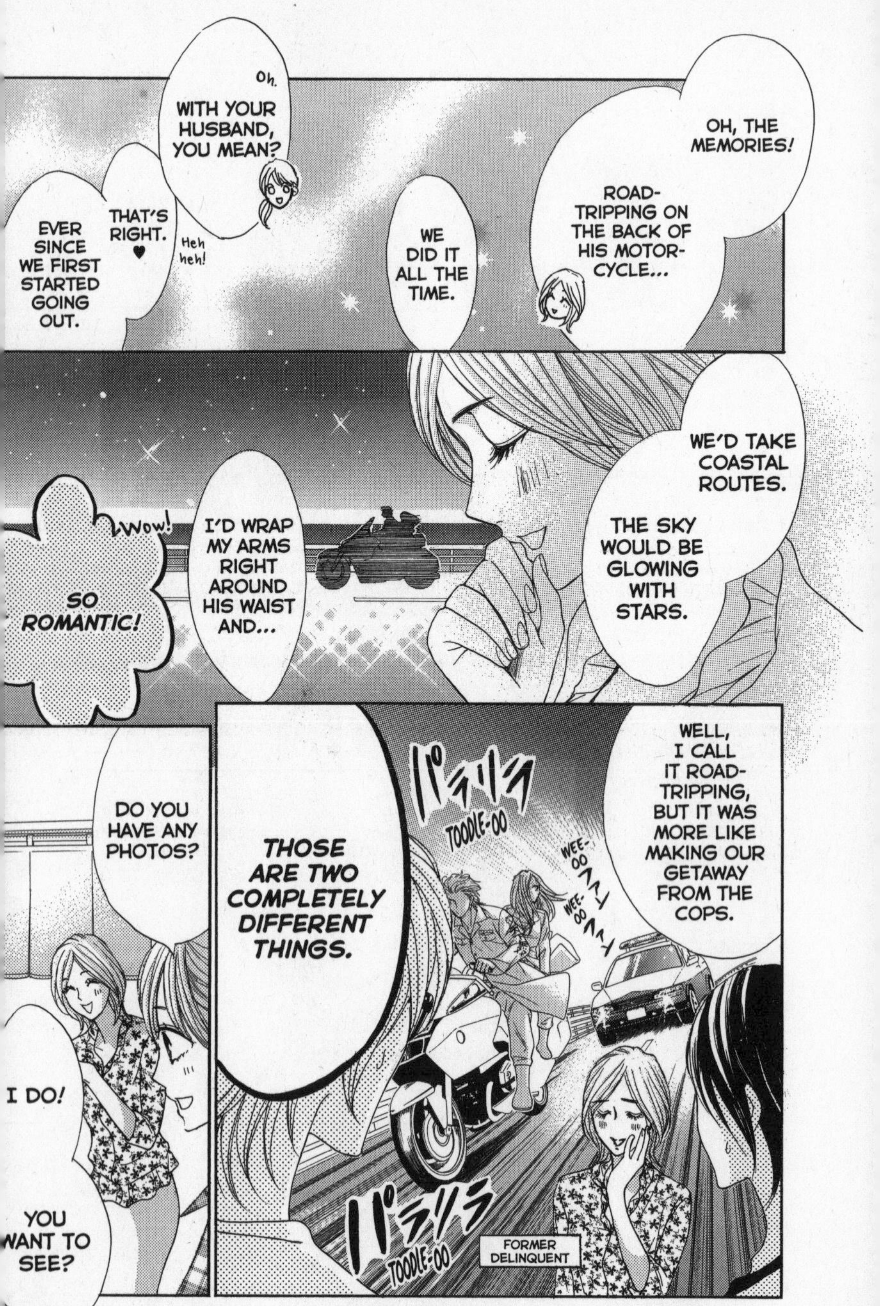
OH, THE MEMORIES!
ROAD-TRIPPING ON THE BACK OF HIS MOTORCYCLE...
WE DID IT ALL THE TIME.
Oh.
WITH YOUR HUSBAND, YOU MEAN?
THAT'S RIGHT. ♥
Heh heh!
EVER SINCE WE FIRST STARTED GOING OUT.
WE'D TAKE COASTAL ROUTES.
THE SKY WOULD BE GLOWING WITH STARS.
I'D WRAP MY ARMS RIGHT AROUND HIS WAIST AND...
Wow!
SO ROMANTIC!
WELL, I CALL IT ROAD-TRIPPING, BUT IT WAS MORE LIKE MAKING OUR GETAWAY FROM THE COPS.
WEE-OO
WEE-OO
パラリラ
TOODLE-OO
THOSE ARE TWO COMPLETELY DIFFERENT THINGS.
パラリラ
TOODLE-OO
FORMER DELINQUENT
DO YOU HAVE ANY PHOTOS?
I DO!
YOU WANT TO SEE?

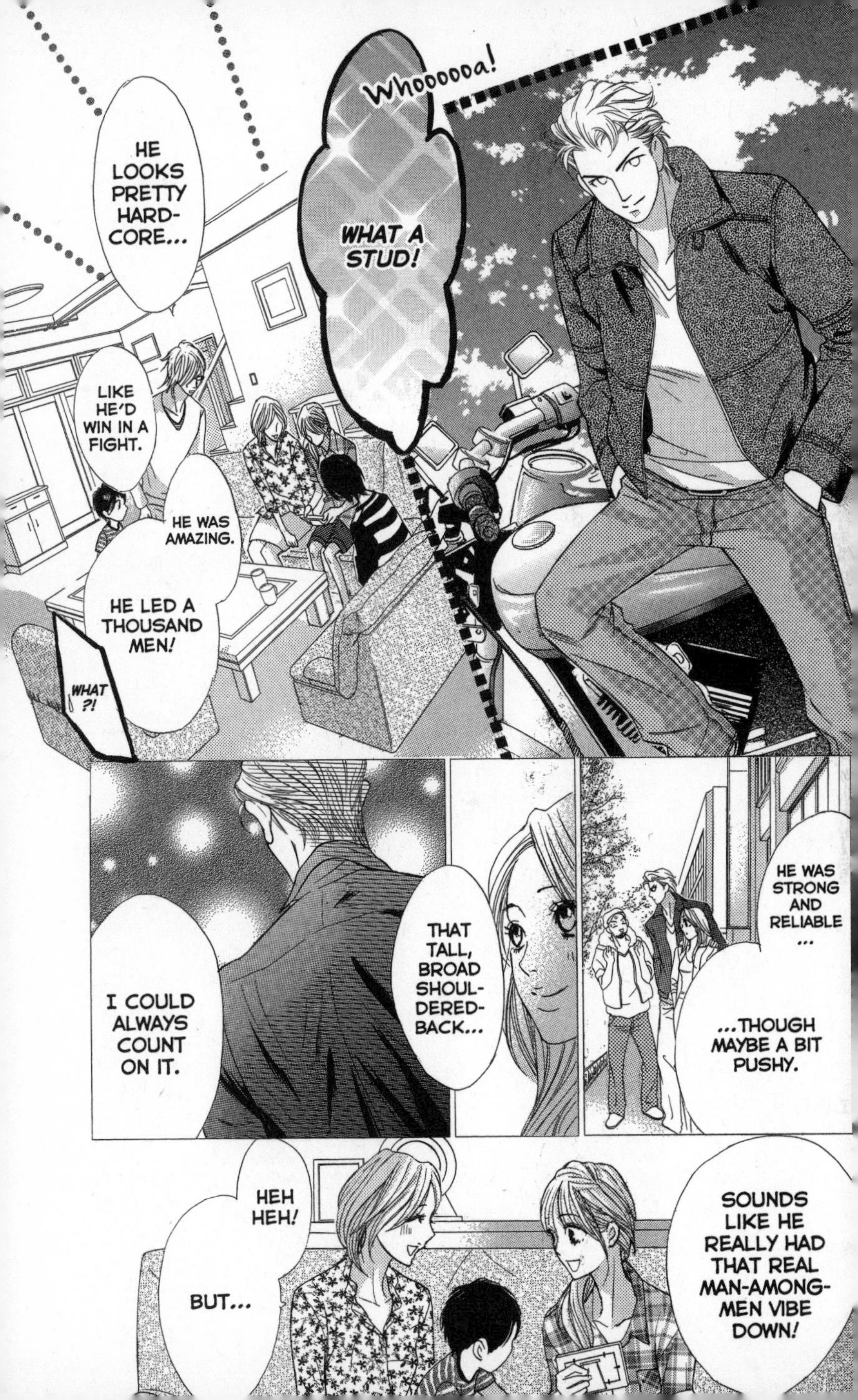
Whoooooa!
WHAT A STUD!
HE LOOKS PRETTY HARD-CORE...
LIKE HE'D WIN IN A FIGHT.
HE WAS AMAZING.
HE LED A THOUSAND MEN!
WHAT ?!
HE WAS STRONG AND RELIABLE...
...THOUGH MAYBE A BIT PUSHY.
THAT TALL, BROAD SHOUL-DERED-BACK...
I COULD ALWAYS COUNT ON IT.
SOUNDS LIKE HE REALLY HAD THAT REAL MAN-AMONG-MEN VIBE DOWN!
HEH HEH!
BUT...

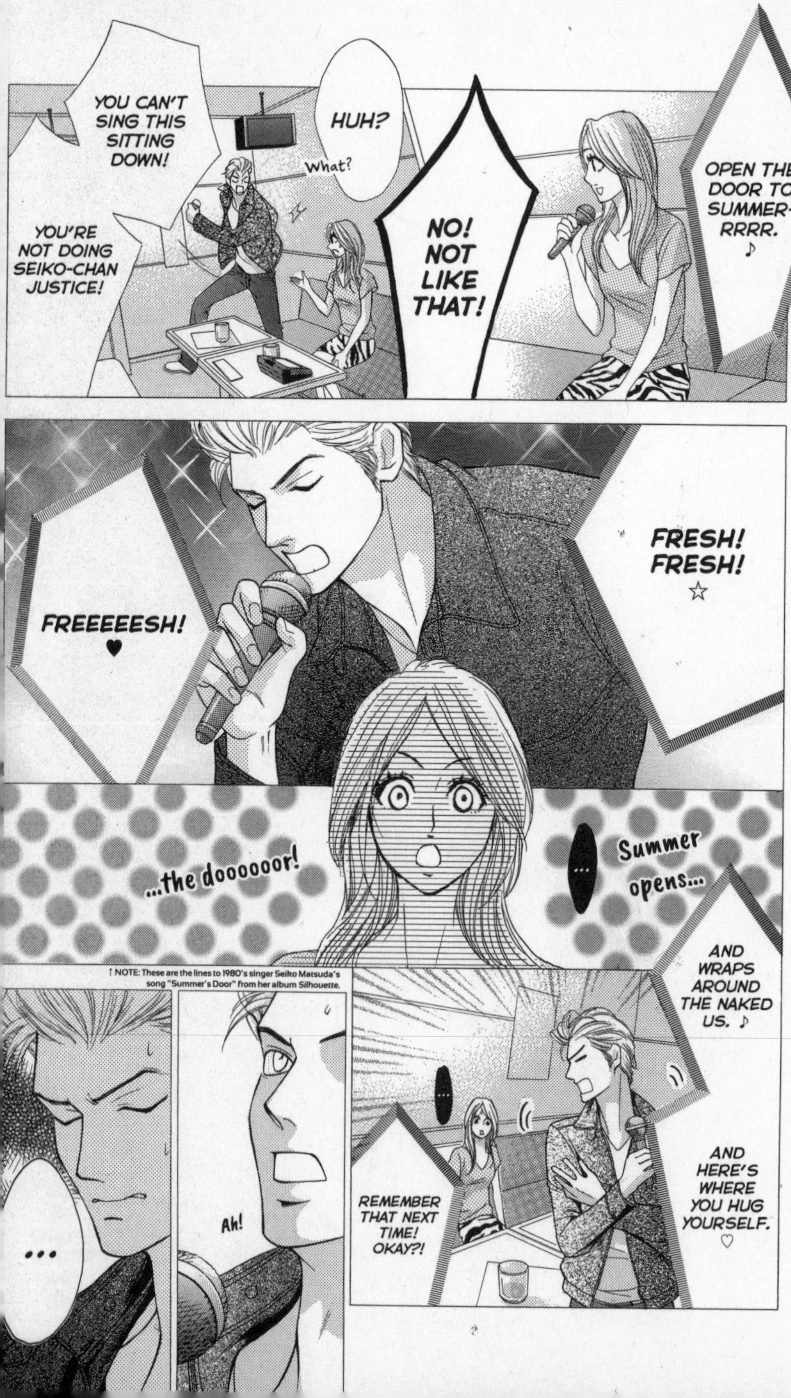
OPEN THE DOOR TO SUMMER-RRRR. ♪
NO! NOT LIKE THAT!
HUH?
What?
YOU CAN'T SING THIS SITTING DOWN!
YOU'RE NOT DOING SEIKO-CHAN JUSTICE!
FRESH! FRESH! ☆
FREEEEEESH! ♥
Summer opens...
...
...the doooooor!
↑ NOTE: These are the lines to 1980's singer Seiko Matsuda's song "Summer's Door" from her album *Silhouette*.
AND WRAPS AROUND THE NAKED US. ♪
AND HERE'S WHERE YOU HUG YOURSELF. ♡
...
REMEMBER THAT NEXT TIME! OKAY?!
Ah!
...

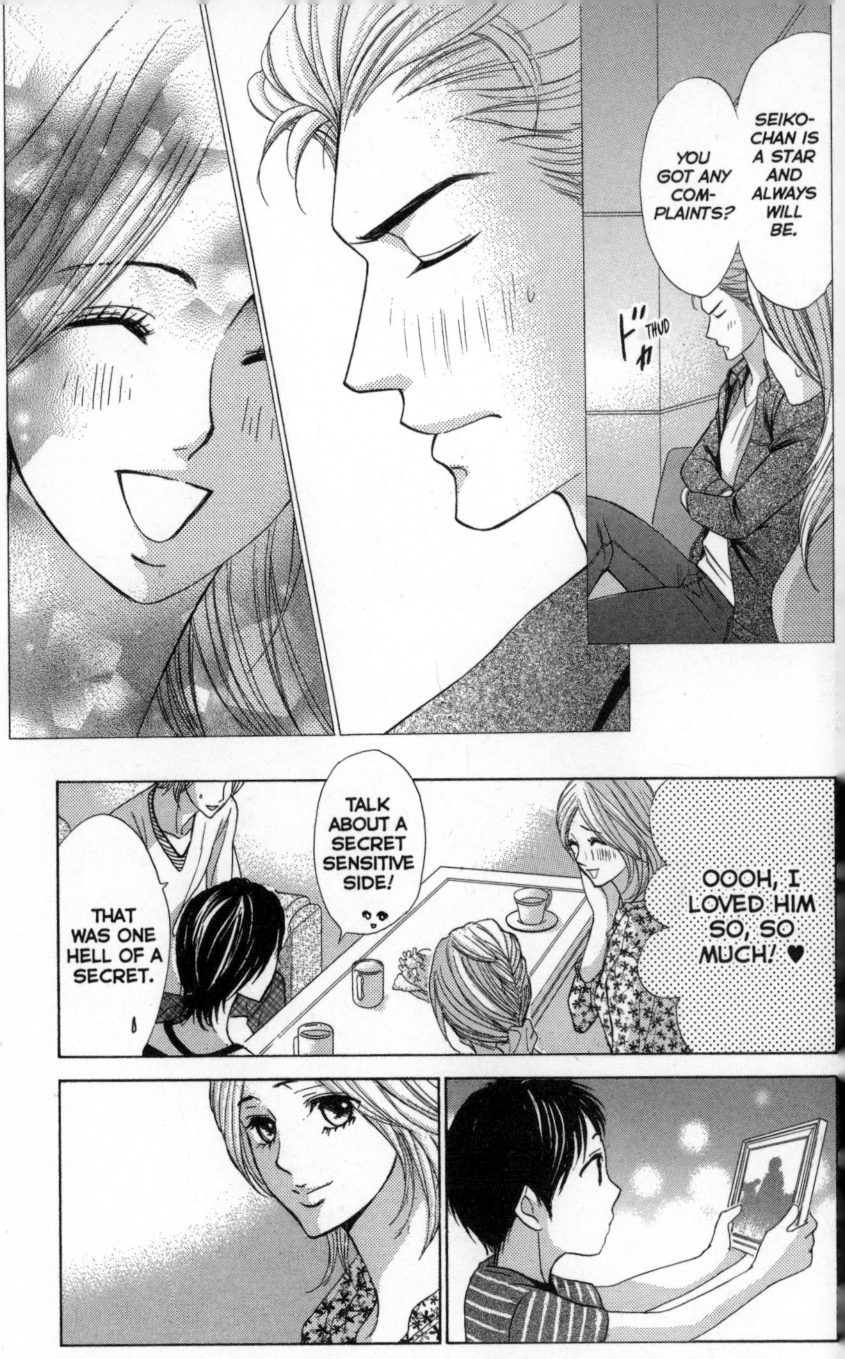
SEIKO-CHAN IS A STAR AND ALWAYS WILL BE.
YOU GOT ANY COM-PLAINTS?
THUD
OOOH, I LOVED HIM SO, SO MUCH! ♥
TALK ABOUT A SECRET SENSITIVE SIDE!
THAT WAS ONE HELL OF A SECRET.

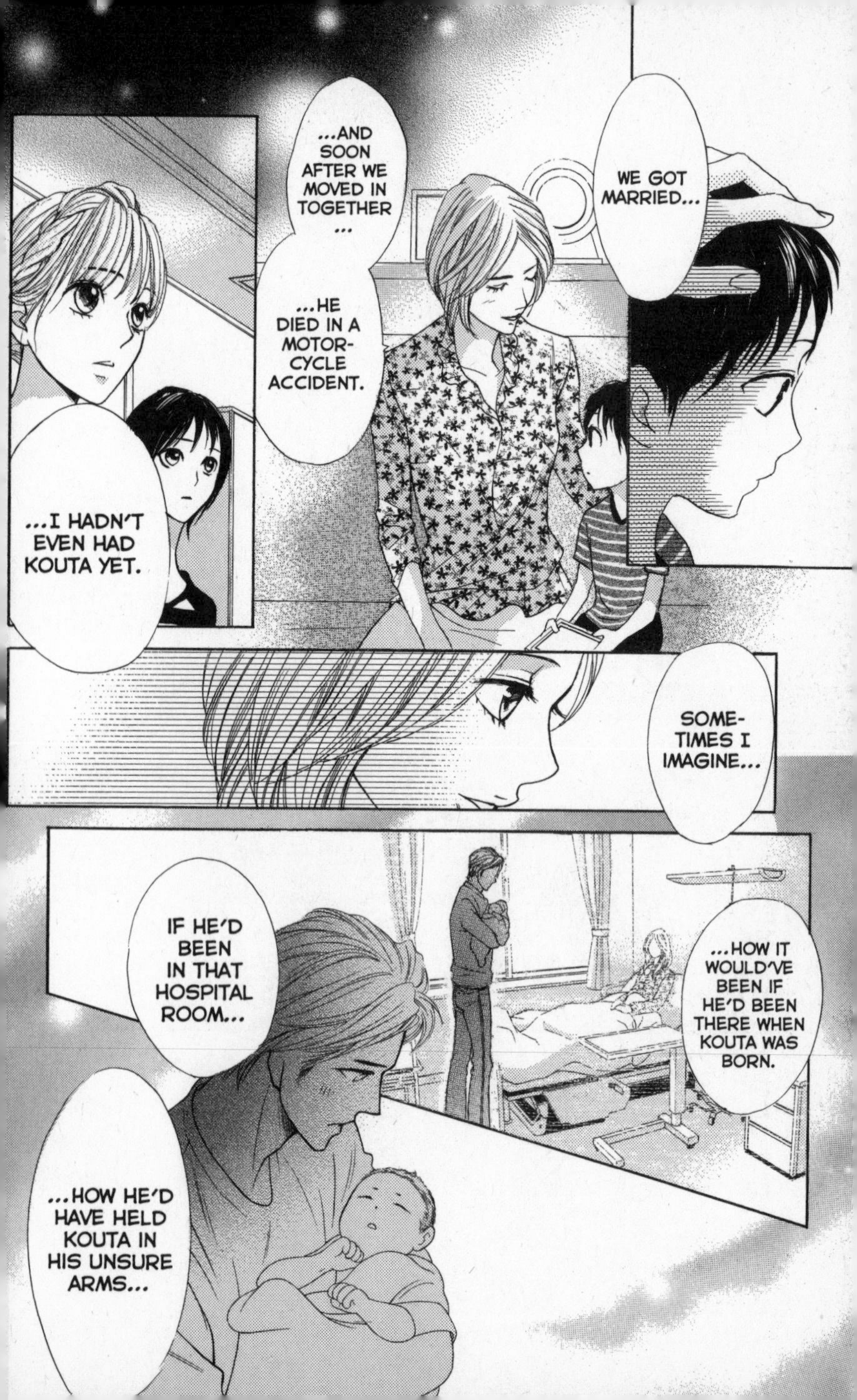
WE GOT MARRIED...
...AND SOON AFTER WE MOVED IN TOGETHER ...
...HE DIED IN A MOTORCYCLE ACCIDENT.
...I HADN'T EVEN HAD KOUTA YET.
SOMETIMES I IMAGINE...
...HOW IT WOULD'VE BEEN IF HE'D BEEN THERE WHEN KOUTA WAS BORN.
IF HE'D BEEN IN THAT HOSPITAL ROOM...
...HOW HE'D HAVE HELD KOUTA IN HIS UNSURE ARMS...

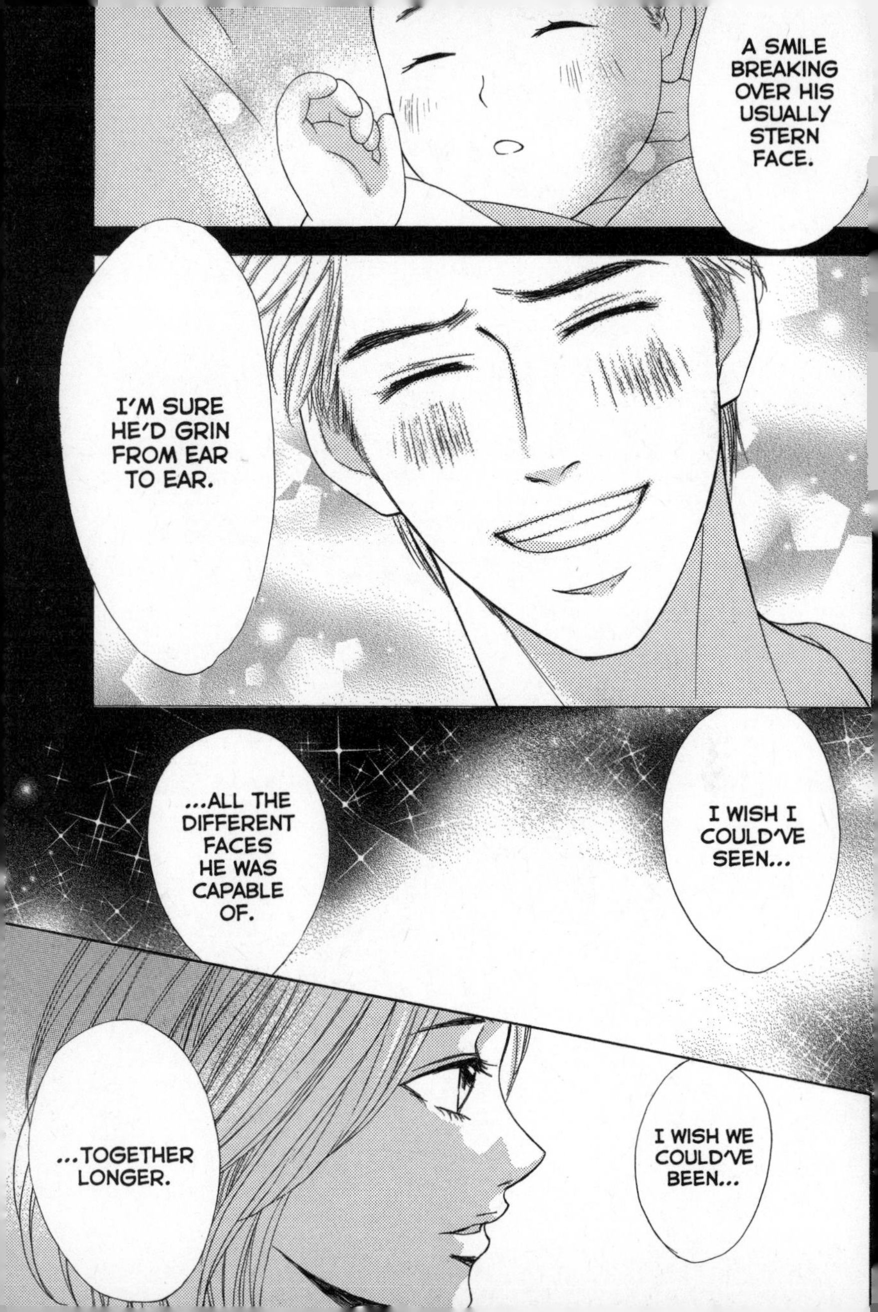
A SMILE BREAKING OVER HIS USUALLY STERN FACE.
I'M SURE HE'D GRIN FROM EAR TO EAR.
I WISH I COULD'VE SEEN...
...ALL THE DIFFERENT FACES HE WAS CAPABLE OF.
I WISH WE COULD'VE BEEN...
...TOGETHER LONGER.

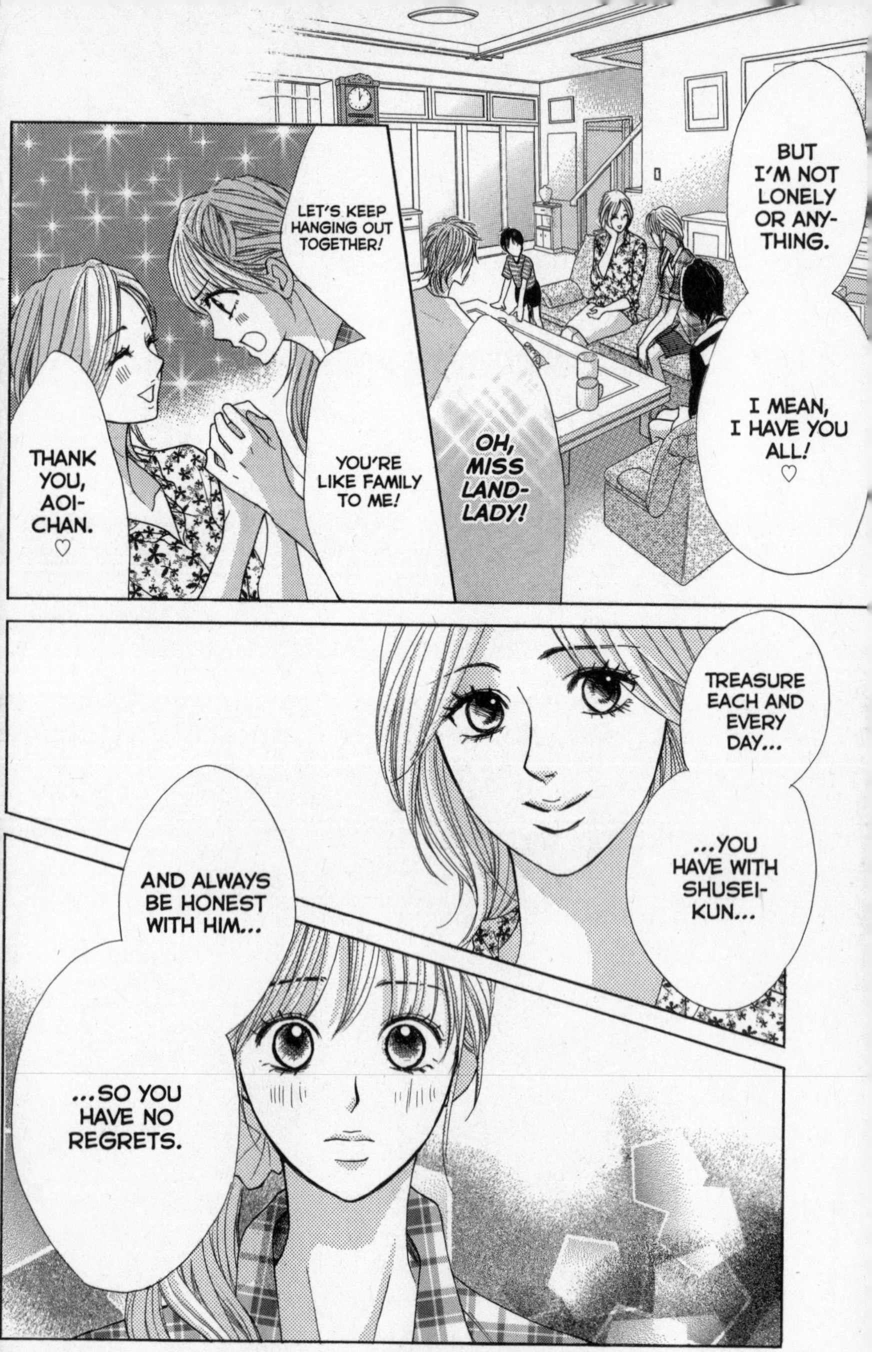
BUT I'M NOT LONELY OR ANYTHING.
I MEAN, I HAVE YOU ALL! ♡
OH, MISS LANDLADY!
LET'S KEEP HANGING OUT TOGETHER!
YOU'RE LIKE FAMILY TO ME!
THANK YOU, AOI-CHAN. ♡
TREASURE EACH AND EVERY DAY...
...YOU HAVE WITH SHUSEI-KUN...
AND ALWAYS BE HONEST WITH HIM...
...SO YOU HAVE NO REGRETS.

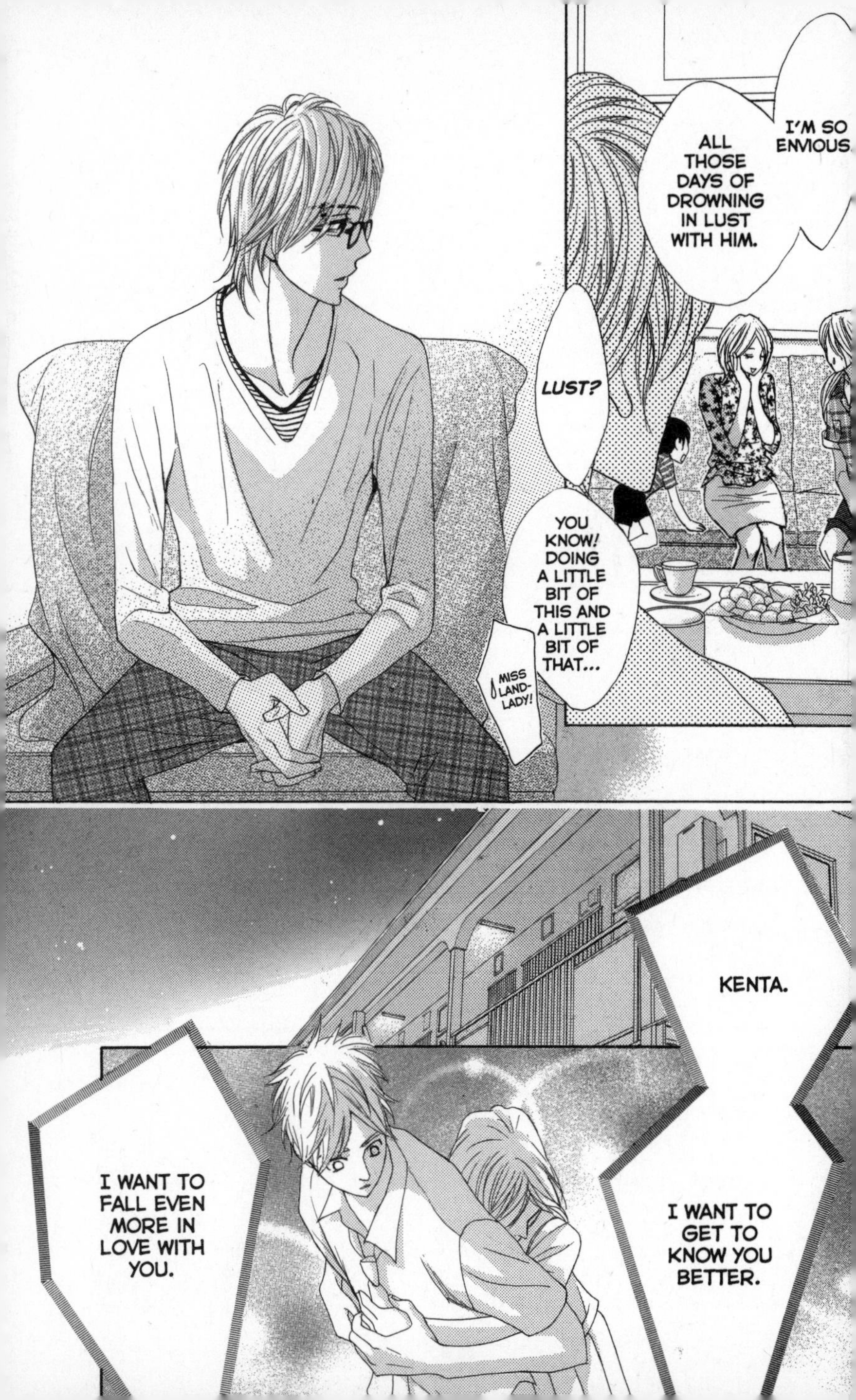
I'M SO ENVIOUS.
ALL THOSE DAYS OF DROWNING IN LUST WITH HIM.
LUST?
YOU KNOW! DOING A LITTLE BIT OF THIS AND A LITTLE BIT OF THAT...
MISS LANDLADY!
KENTA.
I WANT TO GET TO KNOW YOU BETTER.
I WANT TO FALL EVEN MORE IN LOVE WITH YOU.

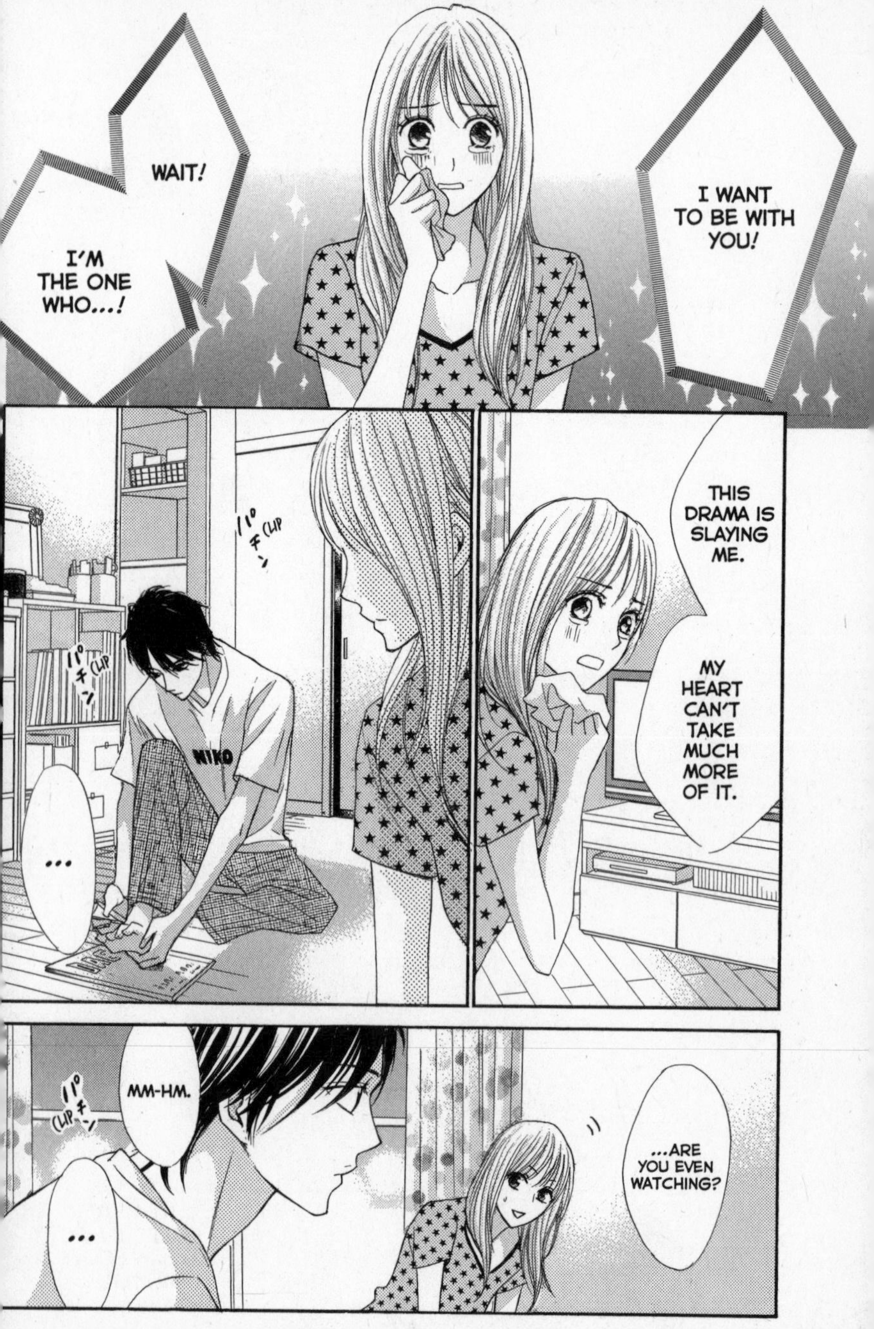
I WANT TO BE WITH YOU!
WAIT!
I'M THE ONE WHO...!
THIS DRAMA IS SLAYING ME.
MY HEART CAN'T TAKE MUCH MORE OF IT.
パチン CLIP
パチン CLIP
...
...ARE YOU EVEN WATCHING?
MM-HM.
パチン CLIP
...

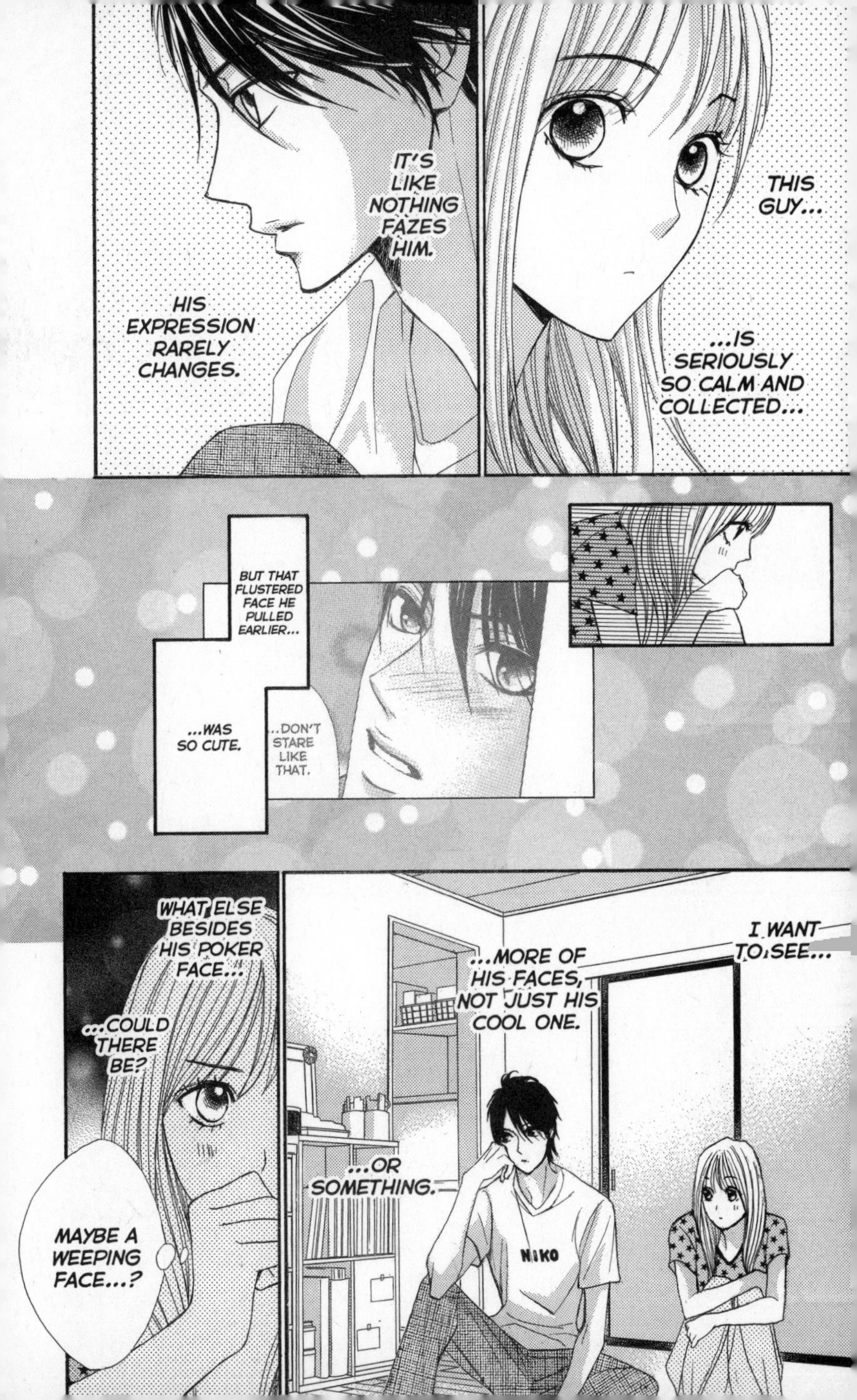
THIS GUY...
...IS SERIOUSLY SO CALM AND COLLECTED...
IT'S LIKE NOTHING FAZES HIM.
HIS EXPRESSION RARELY CHANGES.
BUT THAT FLUSTERED FACE HE PULLED EARLIER...
...DON'T STARE LIKE THAT.
...WAS SO CUTE.
I WANT TO SEE...
...MORE OF HIS FACES, NOT JUST HIS COOL ONE.
...OR SOMETHING.
NIKO
WHAT ELSE BESIDES HIS POKER FACE...
...COULD THERE BE?
MAYBE A WEEPING FACE...?

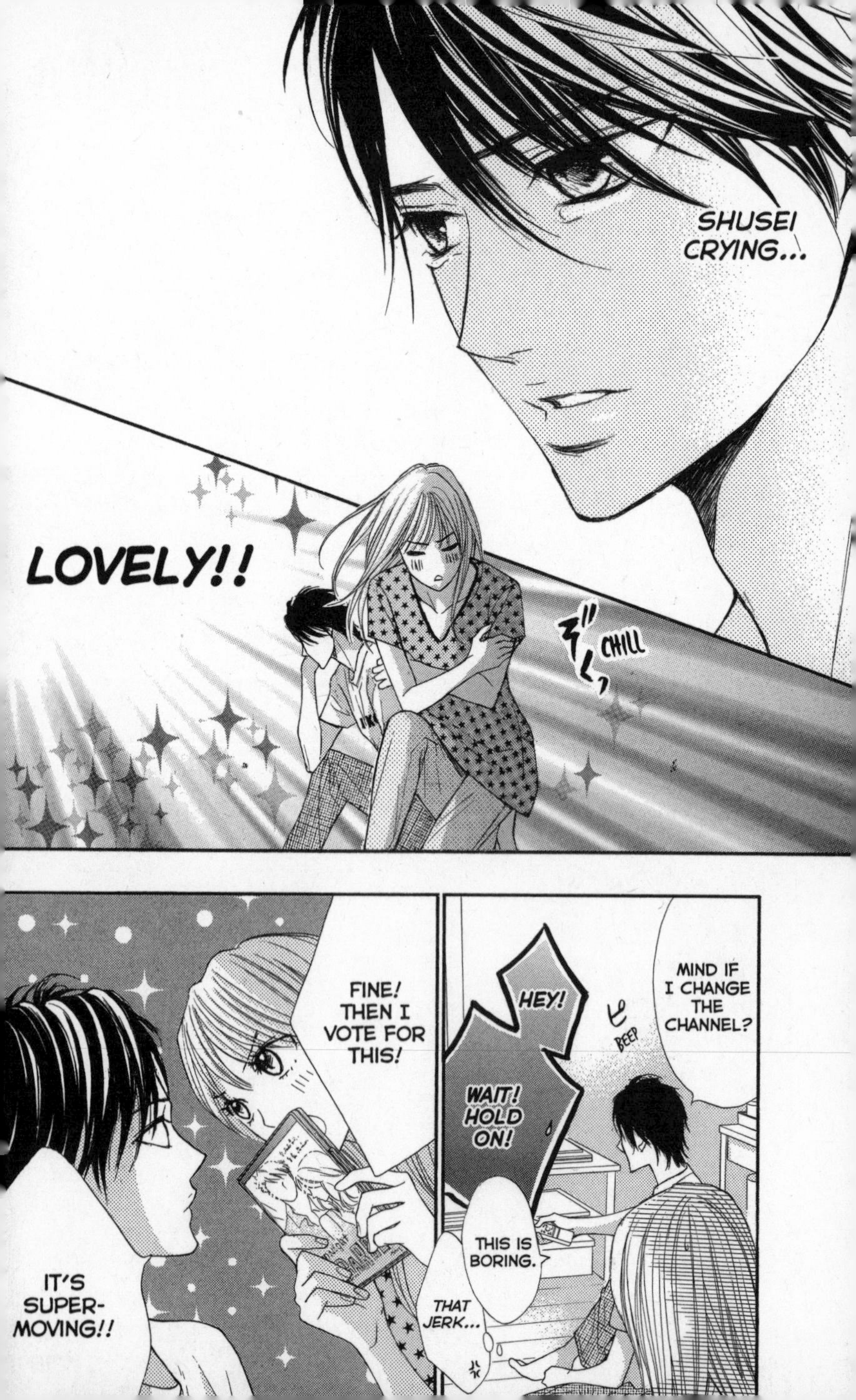
SHUSEI CRYING...
LOVELY!!
CHILL
MIND IF I CHANGE THE CHANNEL?
BEEP
HEY!
WAIT! HOLD ON!
THIS IS BORING.
THAT JERK...
FINE! THEN I VOTE FOR THIS!
IT'S SUPER-MOVING!!

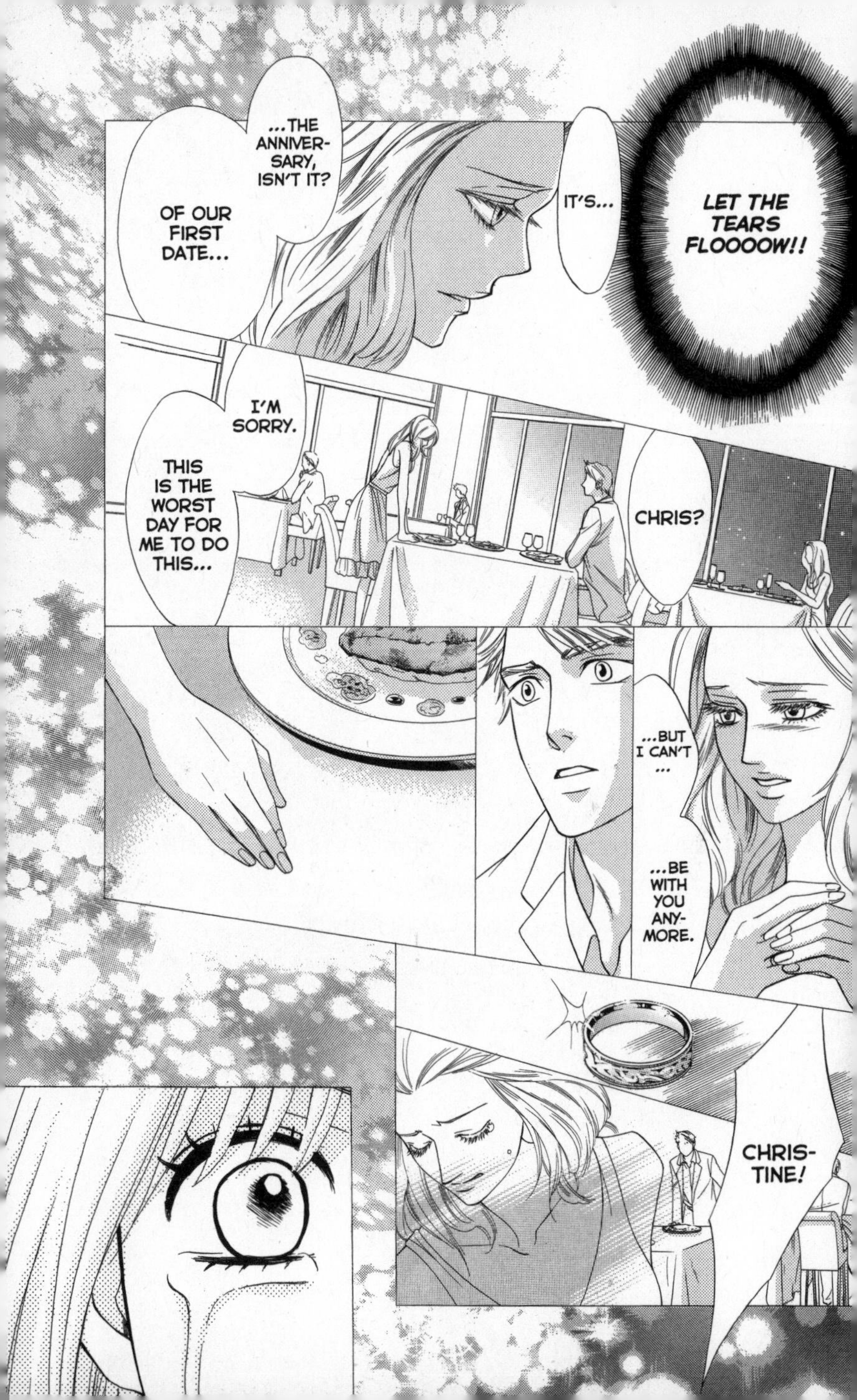
LET THE TEARS FLOOOOW!!
IT'S...
...THE ANNIVERSARY, ISN'T IT?
OF OUR FIRST DATE...
CHRIS?
I'M SORRY.
THIS IS THE WORST DAY FOR ME TO DO THIS...
...BUT I CAN'T ...
...BE WITH YOU ANYMORE.
CHRIS-TINE!

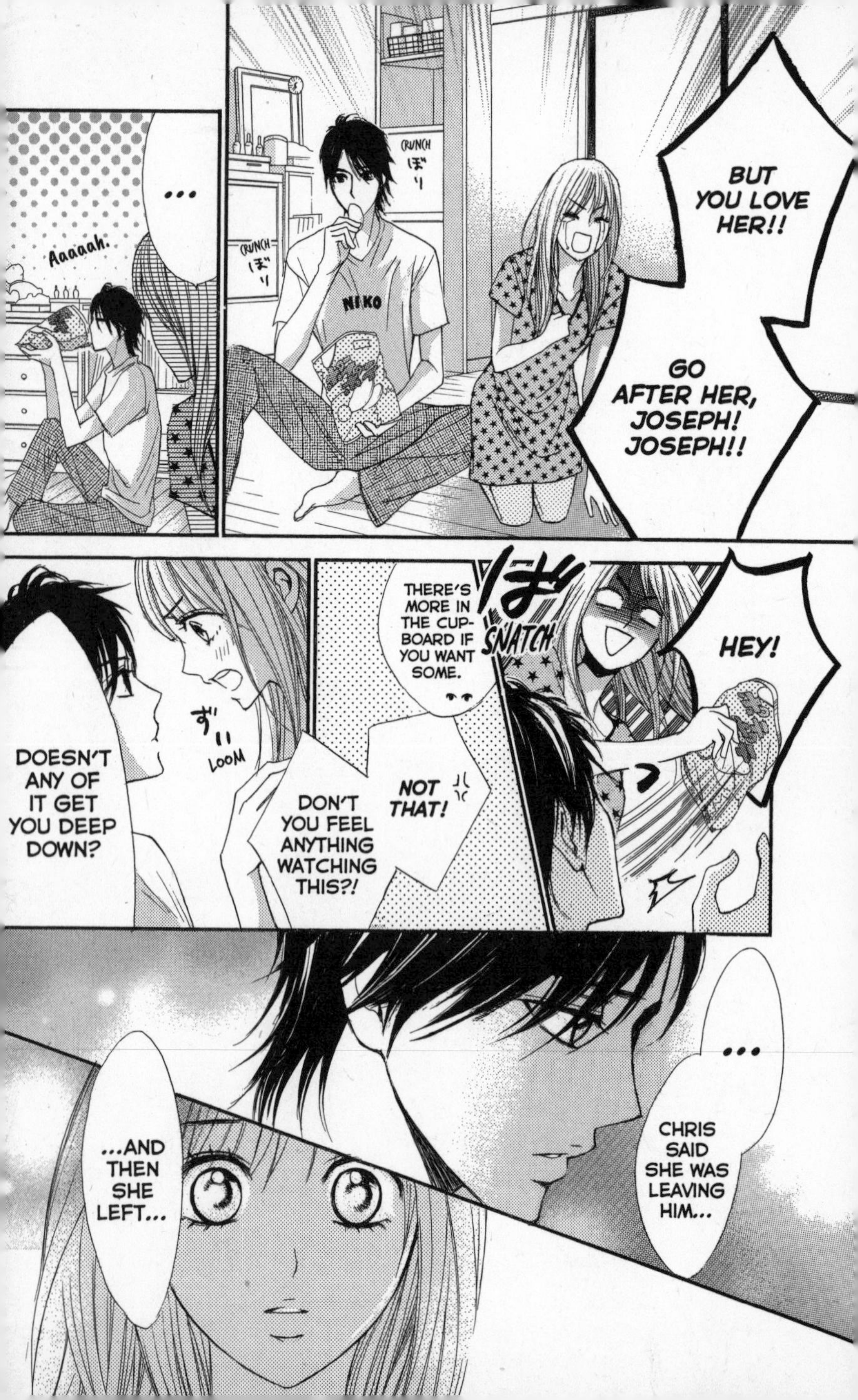
BUT YOU LOVE HER!!
GO AFTER HER, JOSEPH! JOSEPH!!
CRUNCH ぼり
CRUNCH ぼり
...
Aaaaah.
HEY!
ぼ SNATCH
THERE'S MORE IN THE CUPBOARD IF YOU WANT SOME.
NOT THAT!
DON'T YOU FEEL ANYTHING WATCHING THIS?!
ず LOOM
DOESN'T ANY OF IT GET YOU DEEP DOWN?
...
CHRIS SAID SHE WAS LEAVING HIM...
...AND THEN SHE LEFT...

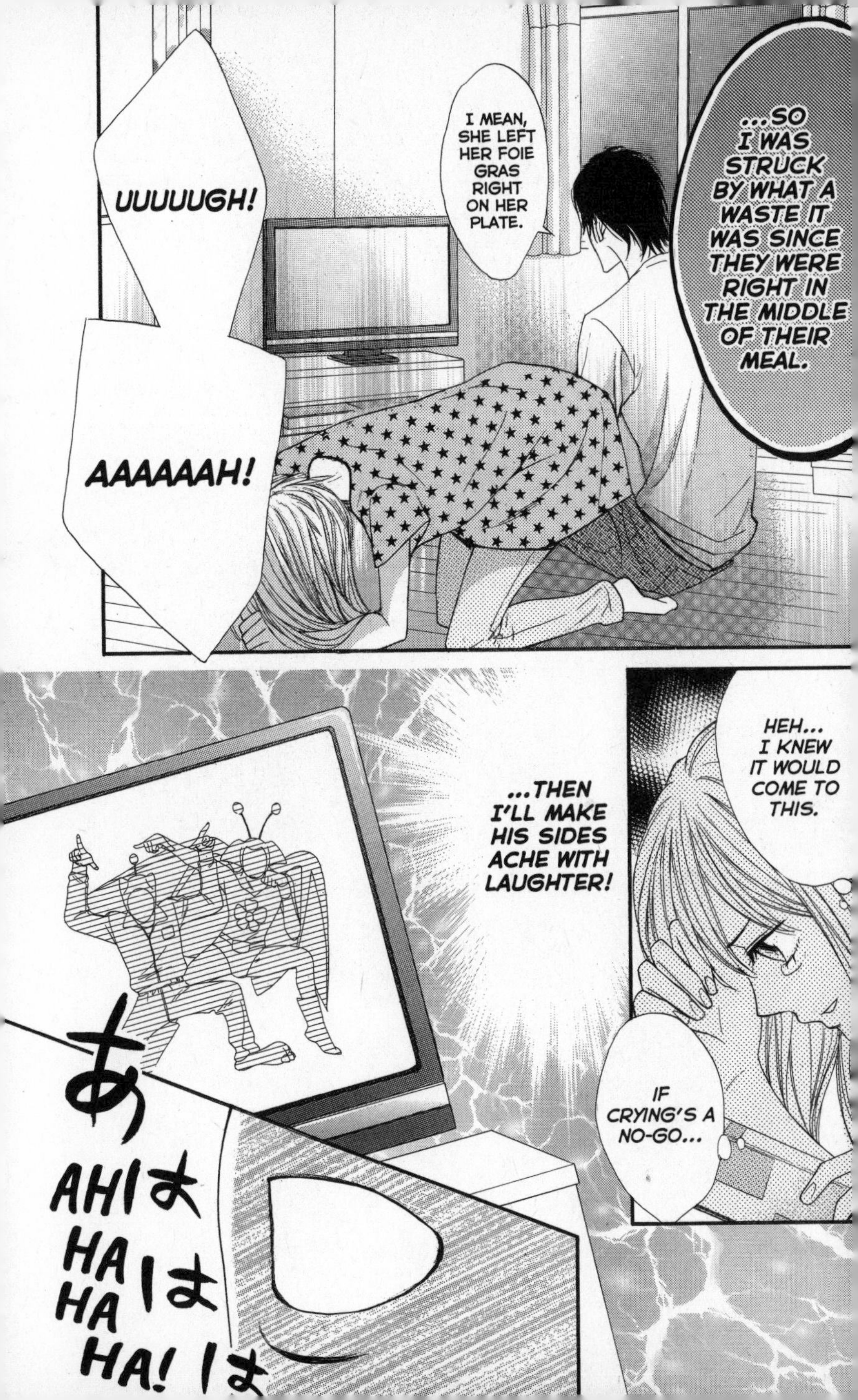
...SO I WAS STRUCK BY WHAT A WASTE IT WAS SINCE THEY WERE RIGHT IN THE MIDDLE OF THEIR MEAL.
I MEAN, SHE LEFT HER FOIE GRAS RIGHT ON HER PLATE.
UUUUUGH!
AAAAAAH!
HEH... I KNEW IT WOULD COME TO THIS.
IF CRYING'S A NO-GO...
...THEN I'LL MAKE HIS SIDES ACHE WITH LAUGHTER!
あははは
AH! HA HA HA!

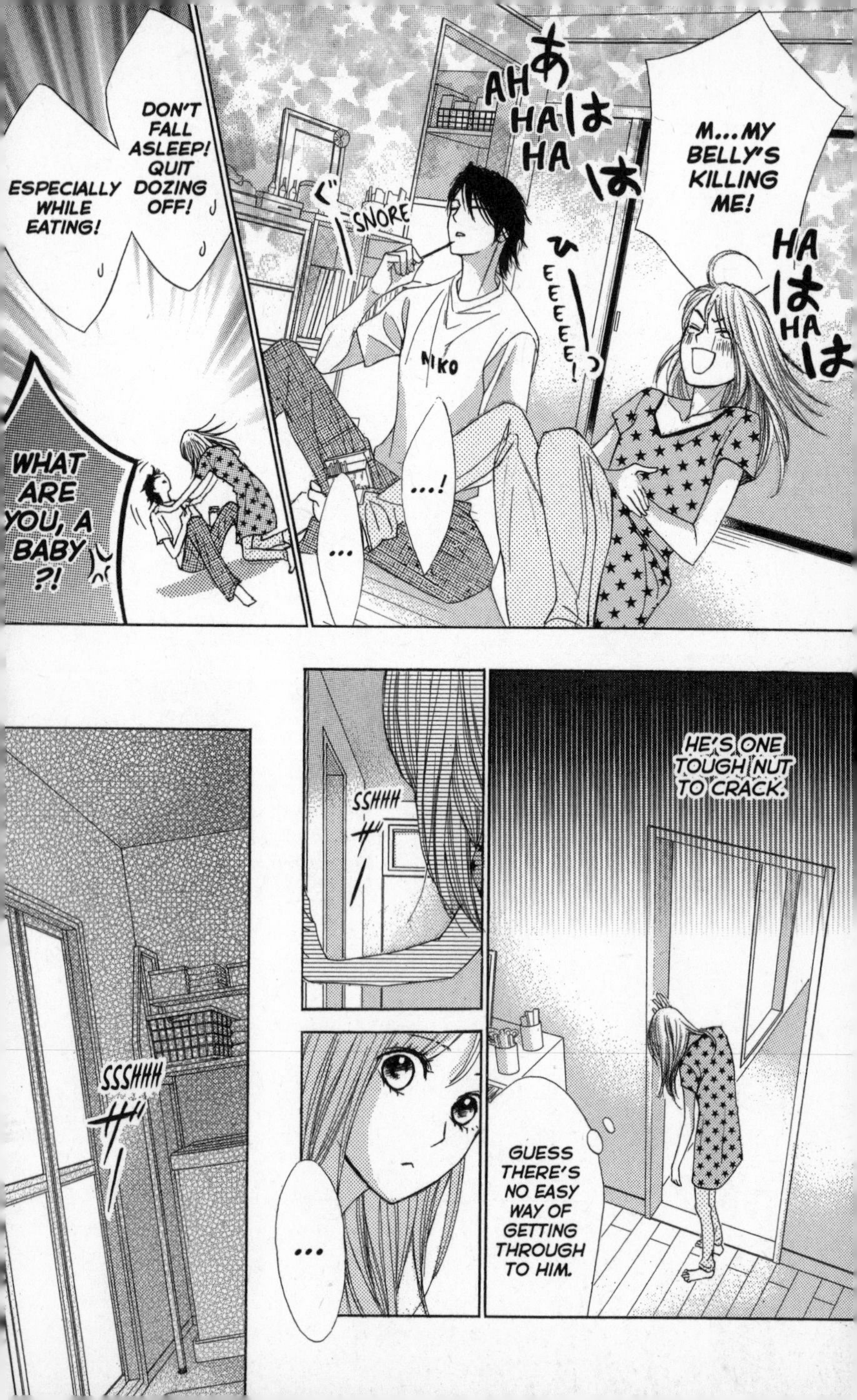
AH HA HA
あはは
M...MY BELLY'S KILLING ME!
HA は HA は
ぐー
SNORE
ひー
EEEEEE!
...!
...
DON'T FALL ASLEEP! QUIT DOZING OFF!
ESPECIALLY WHILE EATING!
WHAT ARE YOU, A BABY?!
HE'S ONE TOUGH NUT TO CRACK.
SSHHH
...
GUESS THERE'S NO EASY WAY OF GETTING THROUGH TO HIM.
SSSHHH

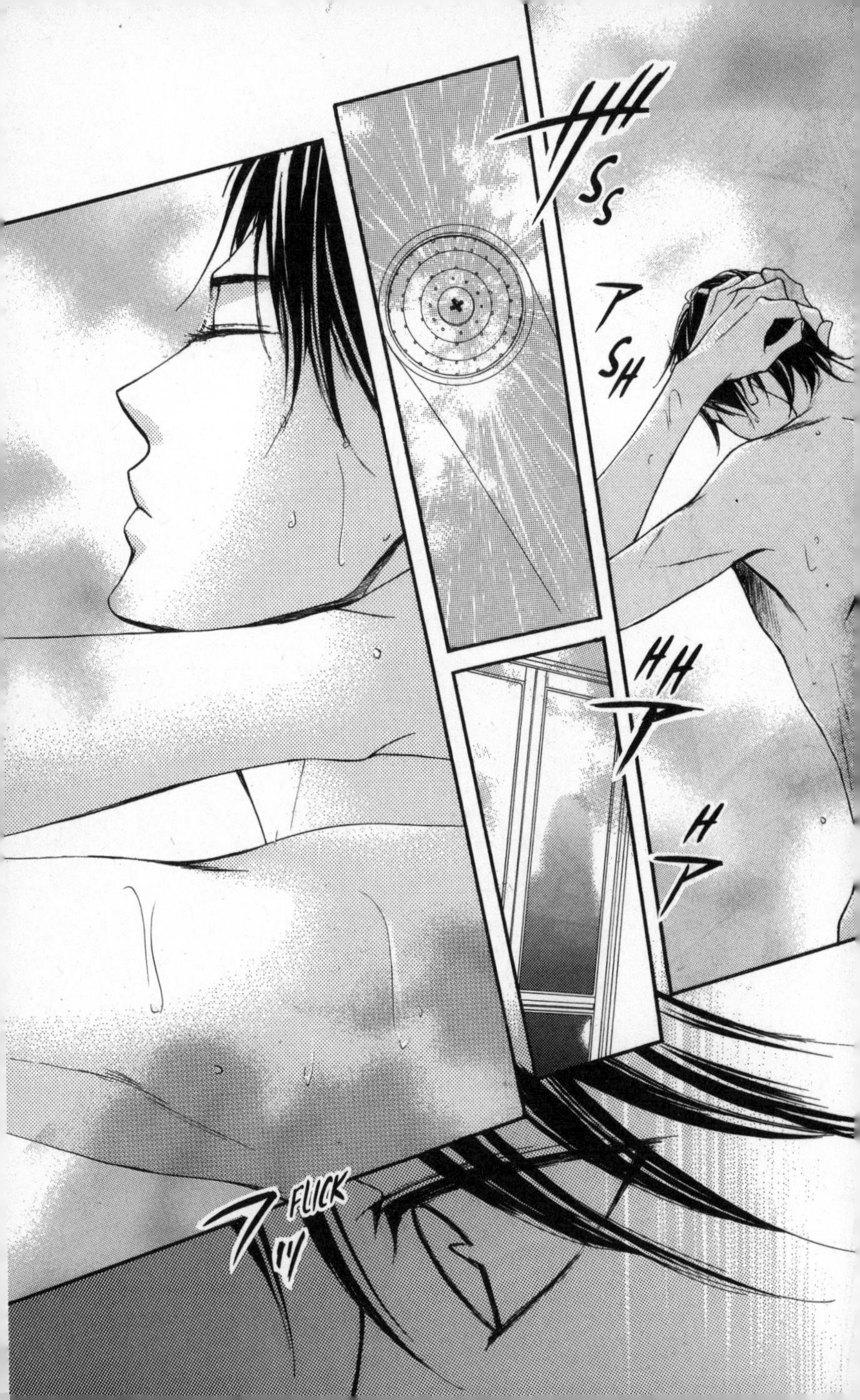
SS
SH
HH
H
FLICK

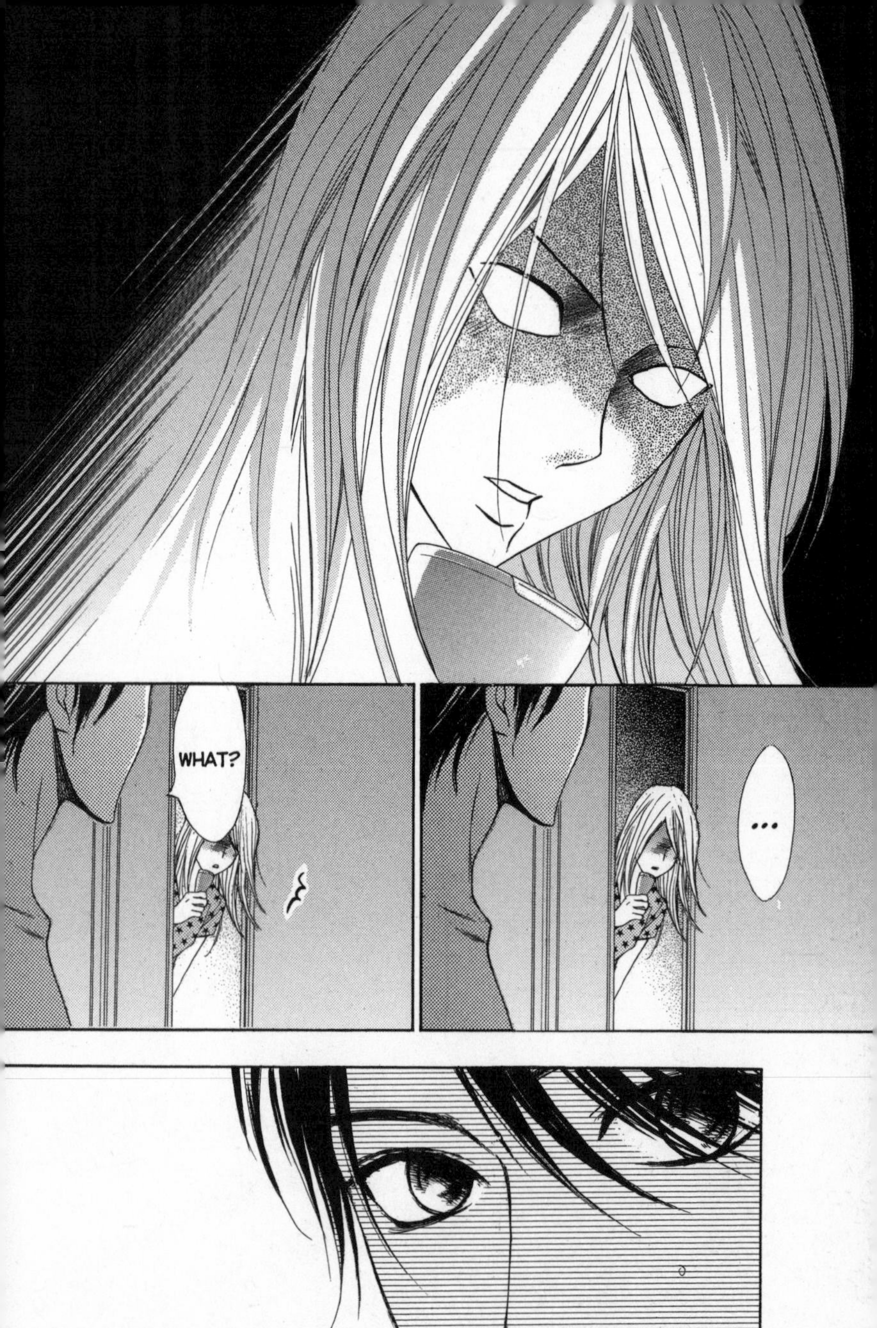
...
WHAT?

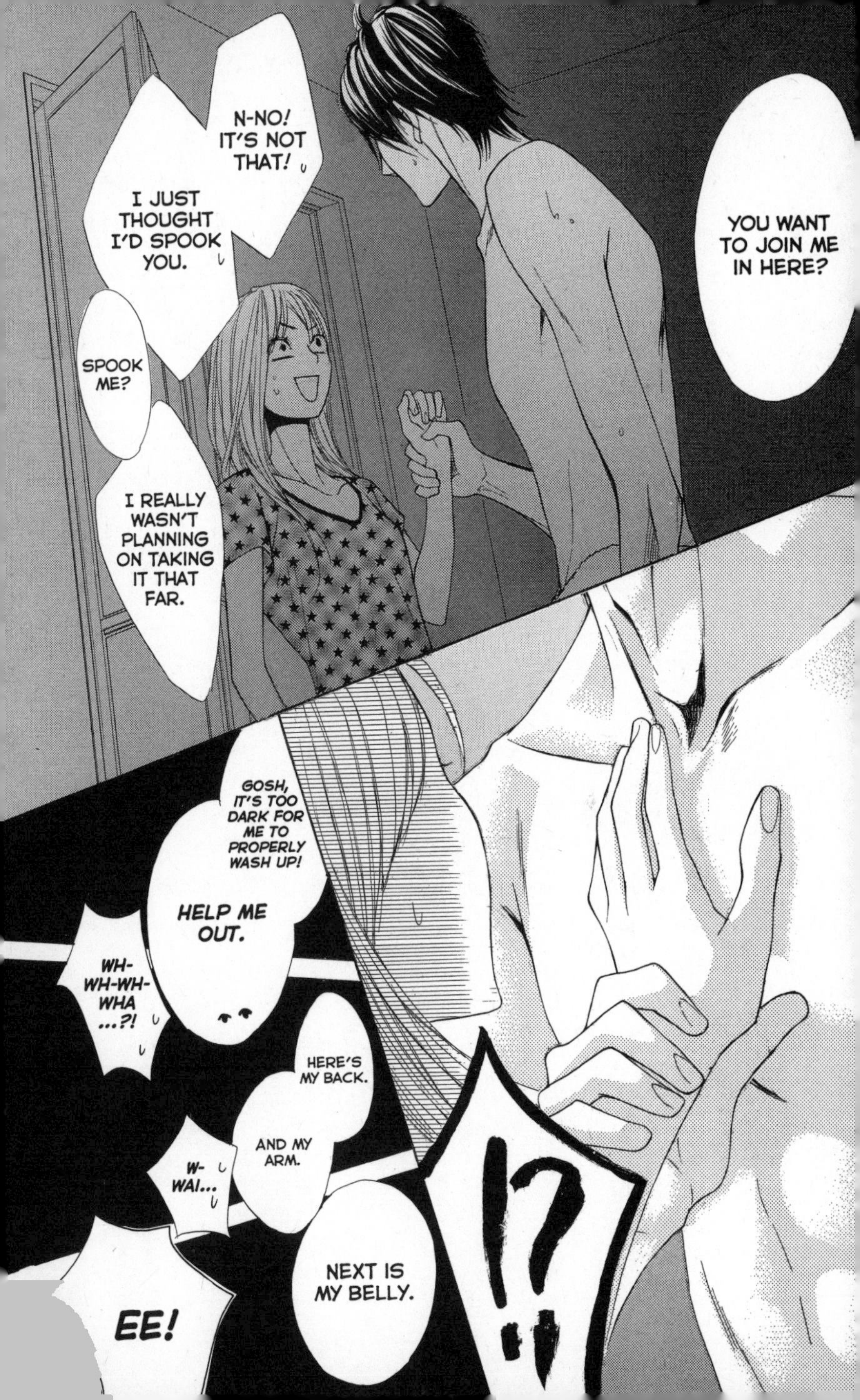
YOU WANT TO JOIN ME IN HERE?
N-NO! IT'S NOT THAT!
I JUST THOUGHT I'D SPOOK YOU.
SPOOK ME?
I REALLY WASN'T PLANNING ON TAKING IT THAT FAR.
GOSH, IT'S TOO DARK FOR ME TO PROPERLY WASH UP!
HELP ME OUT.
WH-WH-WH-WHA...?!
HERE'S MY BACK.
AND MY ARM.
W-WAI...
!?
NEXT IS MY BELLY.
EE!

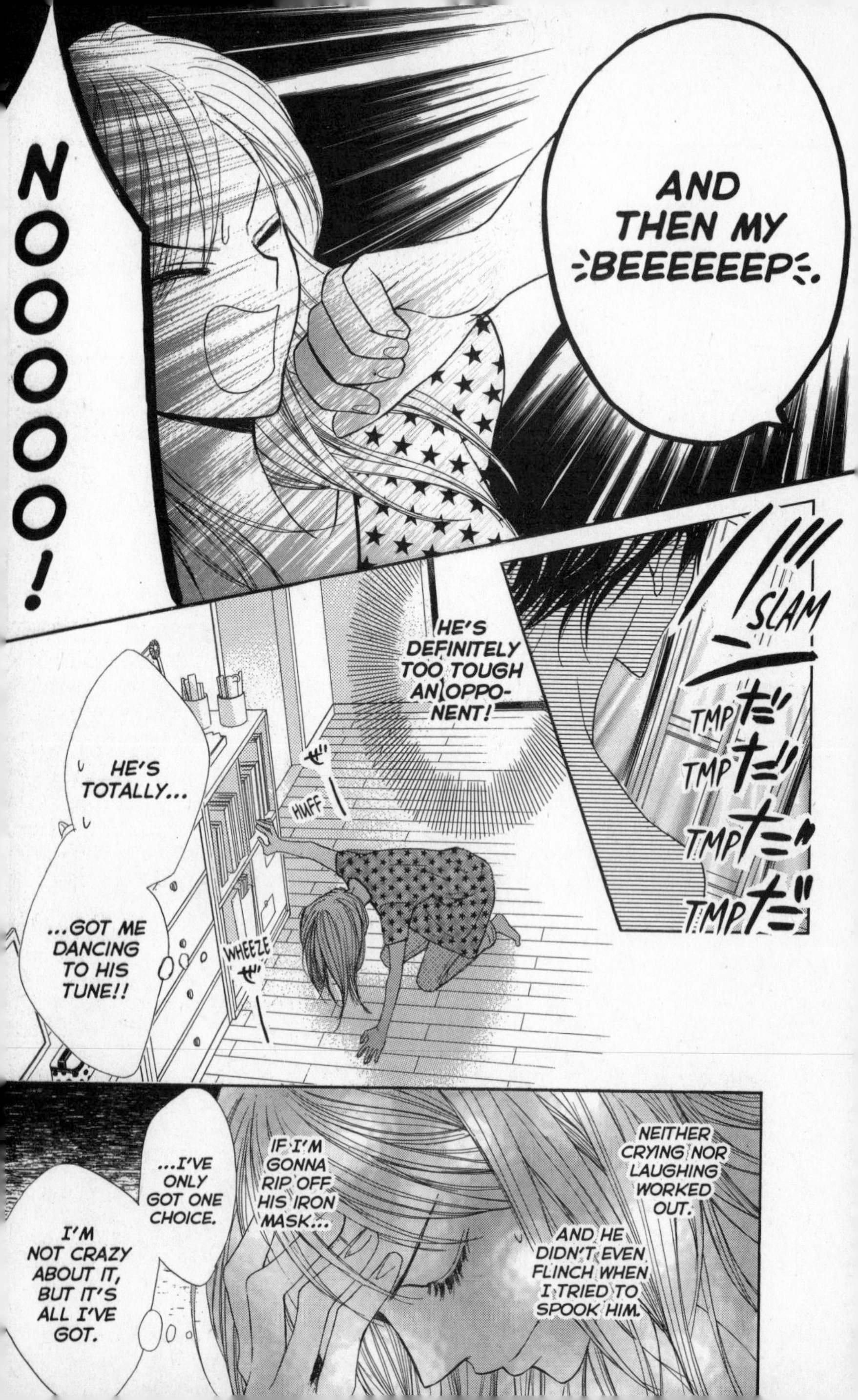
AND THEN MY BEEEEEEP.
NOOOOO!
SLAM
TMP TMP TMP TMP
HE'S DEFINITELY TOO TOUGH AN OPPONENT!
HUFF
WHEEZE
HE'S TOTALLY...
...GOT ME DANCING TO HIS TUNE!!
NEITHER CRYING NOR LAUGHING WORKED OUT.
AND HE DIDN'T EVEN FLINCH WHEN I TRIED TO SPOOK HIM.
IF I'M GONNA RIP OFF HIS IRON MASK...
...I'VE ONLY GOT ONE CHOICE.
I'M NOT CRAZY ABOUT IT, BUT IT'S ALL I'VE GOT.

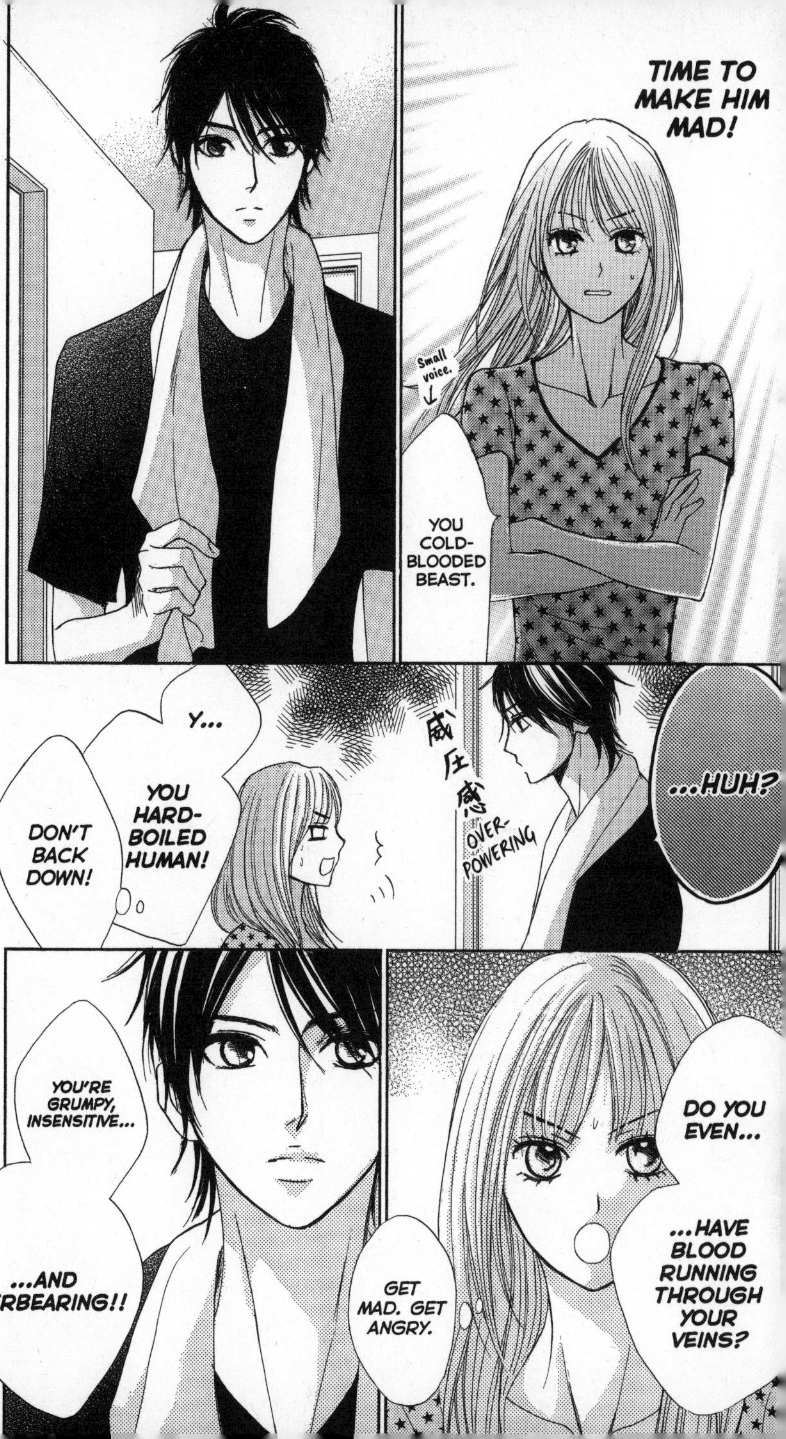
TIME TO MAKE HIM MAD!
Small voice.
YOU COLD-BLOODED BEAST.
...HUH?
威圧感
OVER-POWERING
Y...
YOU HARD-BOILED HUMAN!
DON'T BACK DOWN!
DO YOU EVEN...
...HAVE BLOOD RUNNING THROUGH YOUR VEINS?
GET MAD. GET ANGRY.
YOU'RE GRUMPY, INSENSITIVE...
...AND OVERBEARING!!

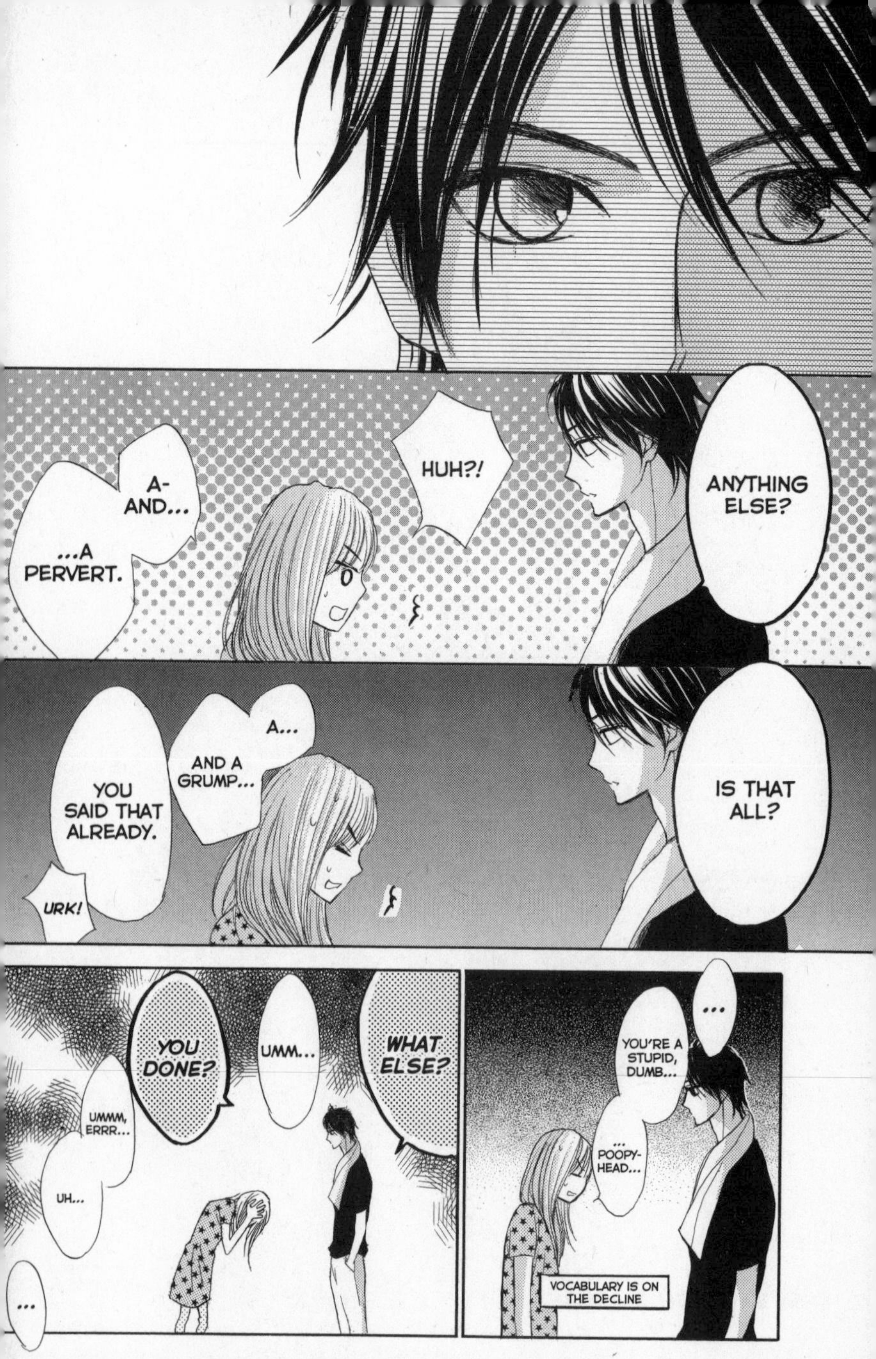
ANYTHING ELSE?
HUH?!
A- AND...
...A PERVERT.
IS THAT ALL?
A...
AND A GRUMP...
YOU SAID THAT ALREADY.
URK!
...
YOU'RE A STUPID, DUMB...
... POOPY-HEAD...
VOCABULARY IS ON THE DECLINE
WHAT ELSE?
UMM...
YOU DONE?
UMMM, ERRR...
UH...
...

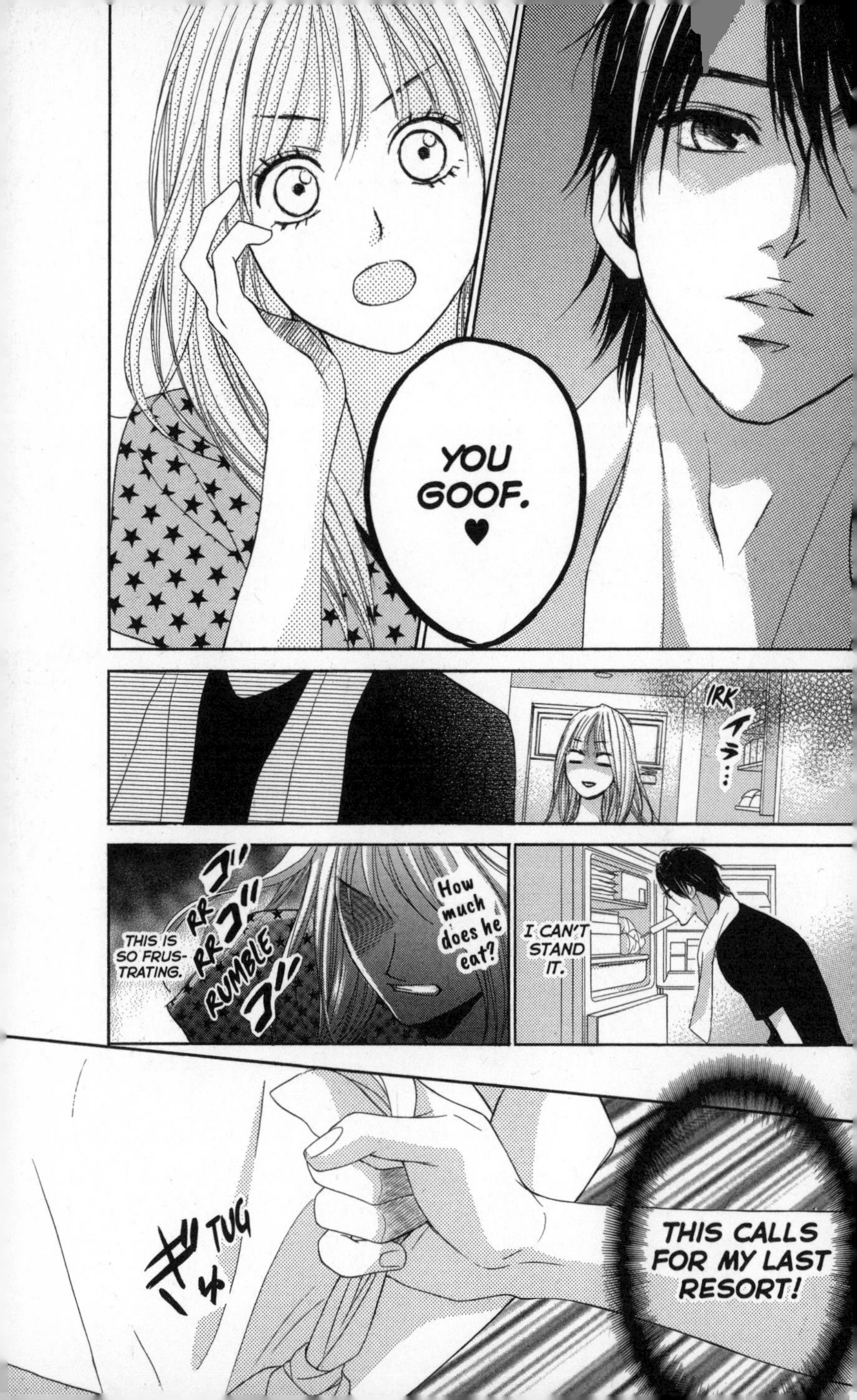
YOU GOOF. ♥
IRK
イラ…
I CAN'T STAND IT.
How much does he eat?
RR ゴ RR ゴ RUMBLE ゴ
THIS IS SO FRUS-TRATING.
THIS CALLS FOR MY LAST RESORT!
TUG
ぎゅ

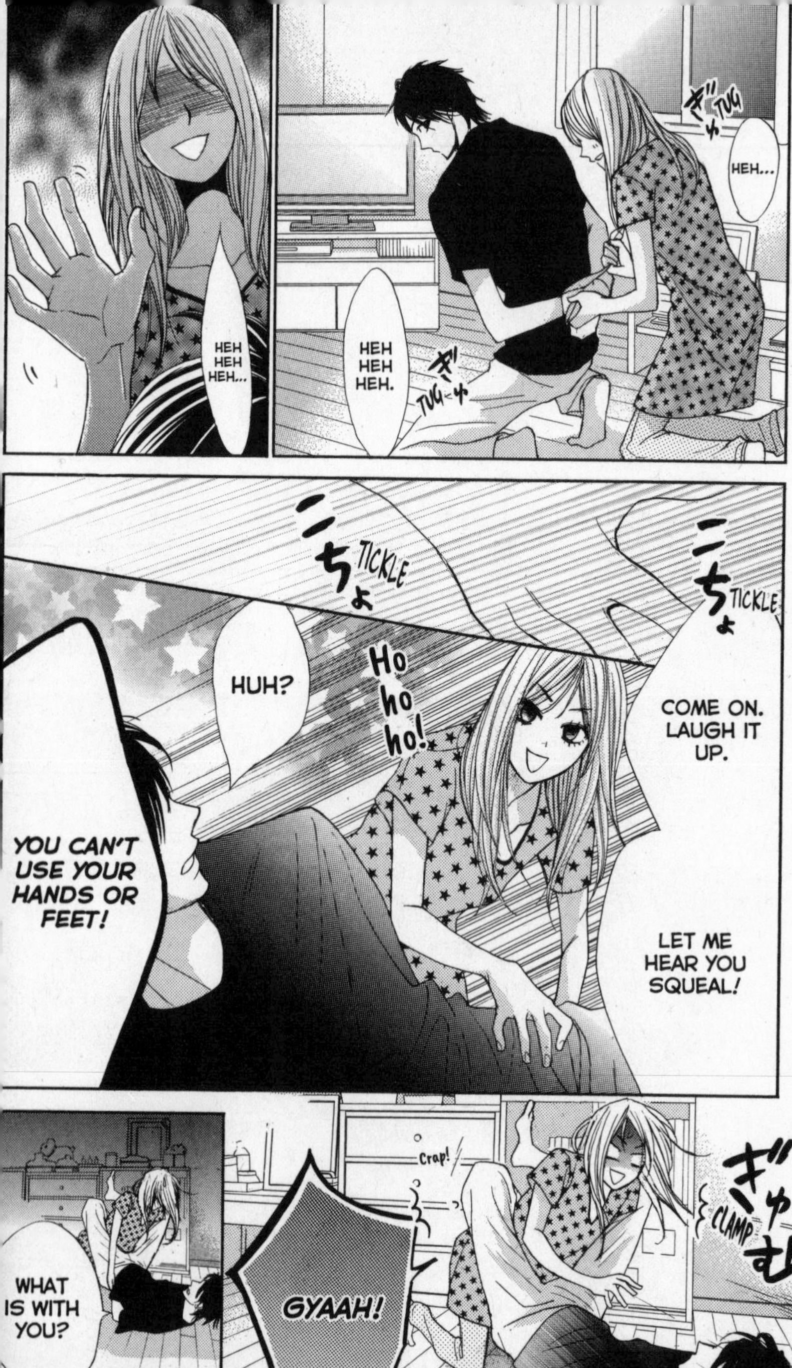
ぎゅ TUG
HEH...
HEH HEH HEH.
ぎゅ TUG
HEH HEH HEH...
こちょ TICKLE
こちょ TICKLE
COME ON. LAUGH IT UP.
Ho ho ho!
HUH?
LET ME HEAR YOU SQUEAL!
YOU CAN'T USE YOUR HANDS OR FEET!
ぎゅむ CLAMP
Crap!
GYAAH!
WHAT IS WITH YOU?

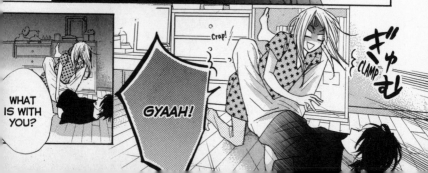

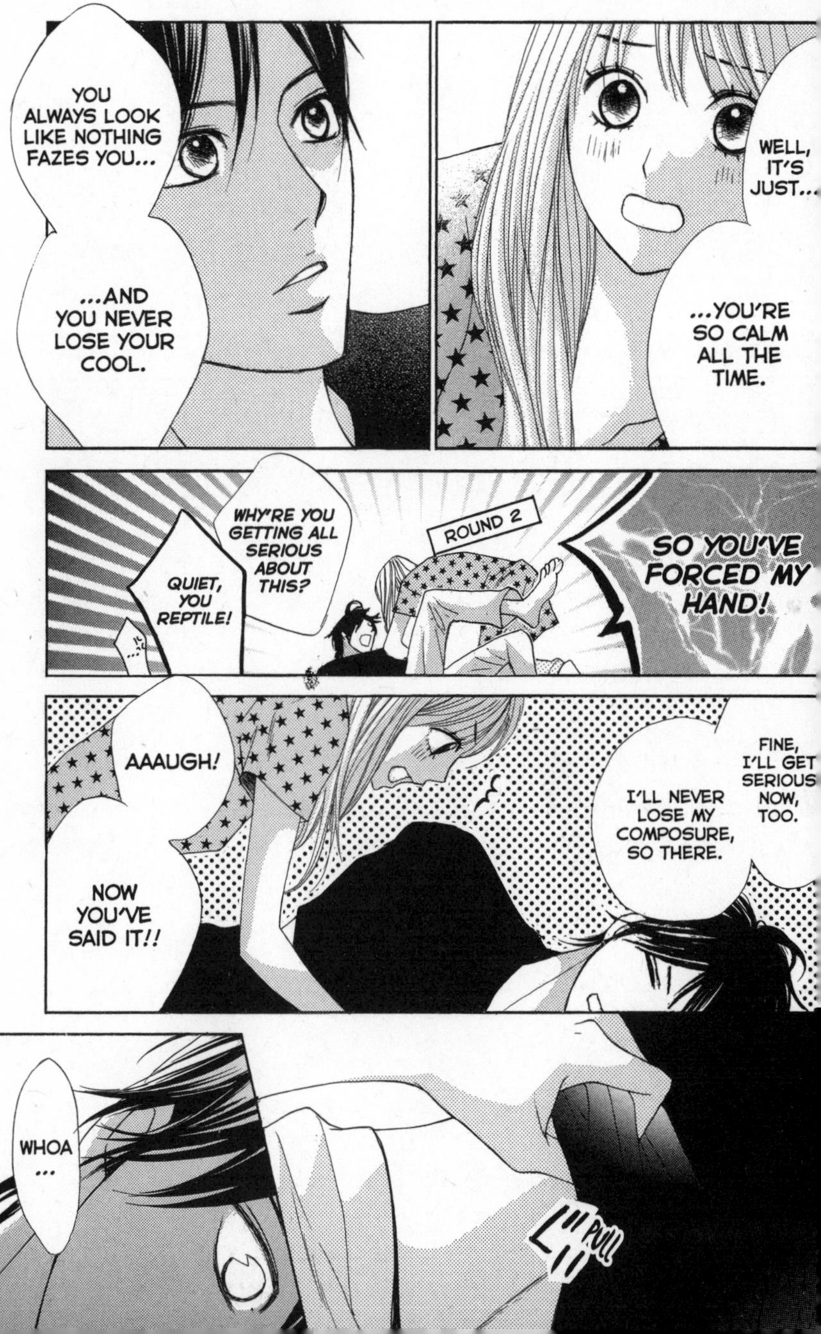

WELL, IT'S JUST...
...YOU'RE SO CALM ALL THE TIME.
YOU ALWAYS LOOK LIKE NOTHING FAZES YOU...
...AND YOU NEVER LOSE YOUR COOL.
SO YOU'VE FORCED MY HAND!
ROUND 2
WHY'RE YOU GETTING ALL SERIOUS ABOUT THIS?
QUIET, YOU REPTILE!
FINE, I'LL GET SERIOUS NOW, TOO.
I'LL NEVER LOSE MY COMPOSURE, SO THERE.
AAAUGH!
NOW YOU'VE SAID IT!!
PULL
WHOA ...

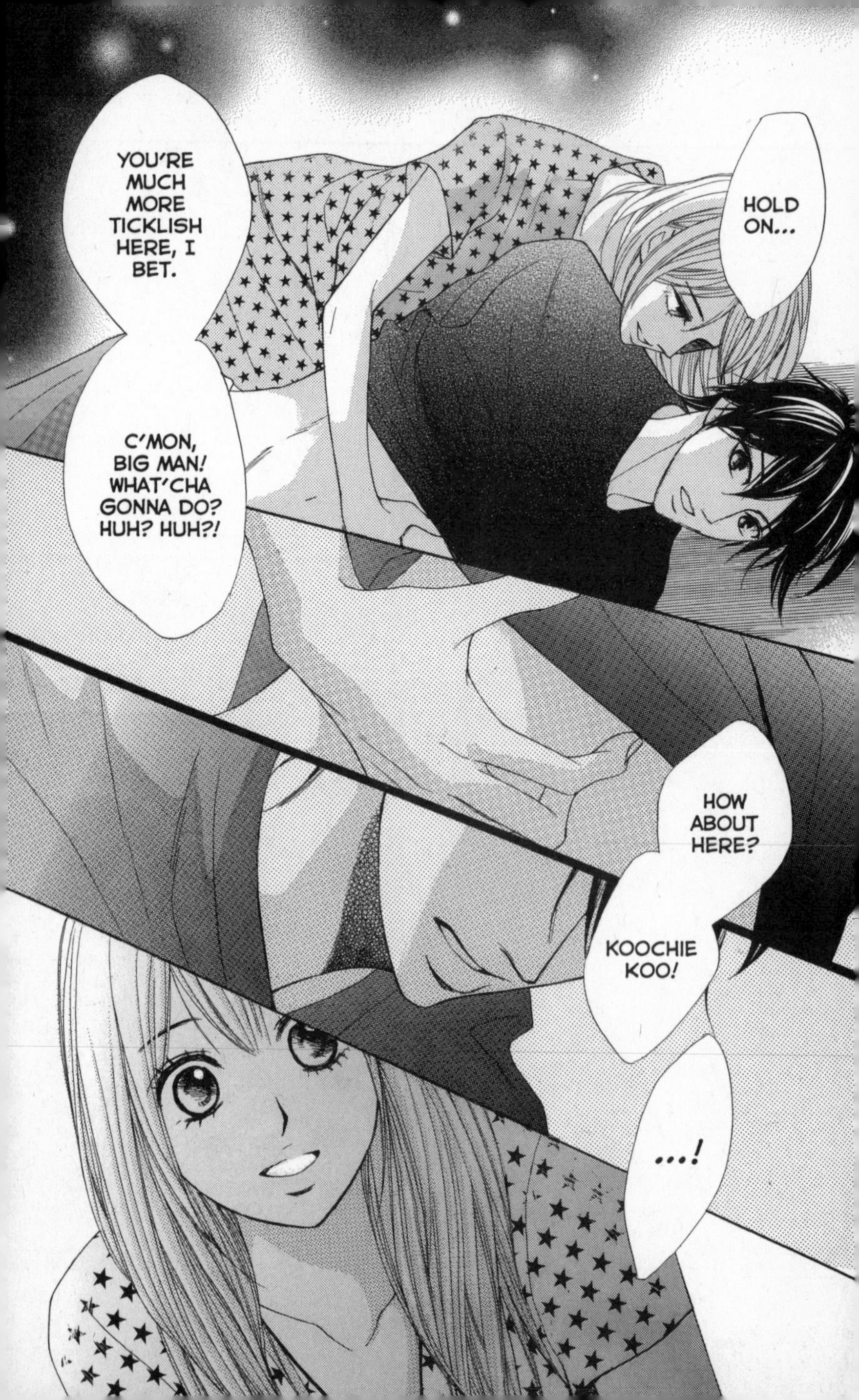
HOLD ON...
YOU'RE MUCH MORE TICKLISH HERE, I BET.
C'MON, BIG MAN! WHAT'CHA GONNA DO? HUH? HUH?!
HOW ABOUT HERE?
KOOCHIE KOO!
...!

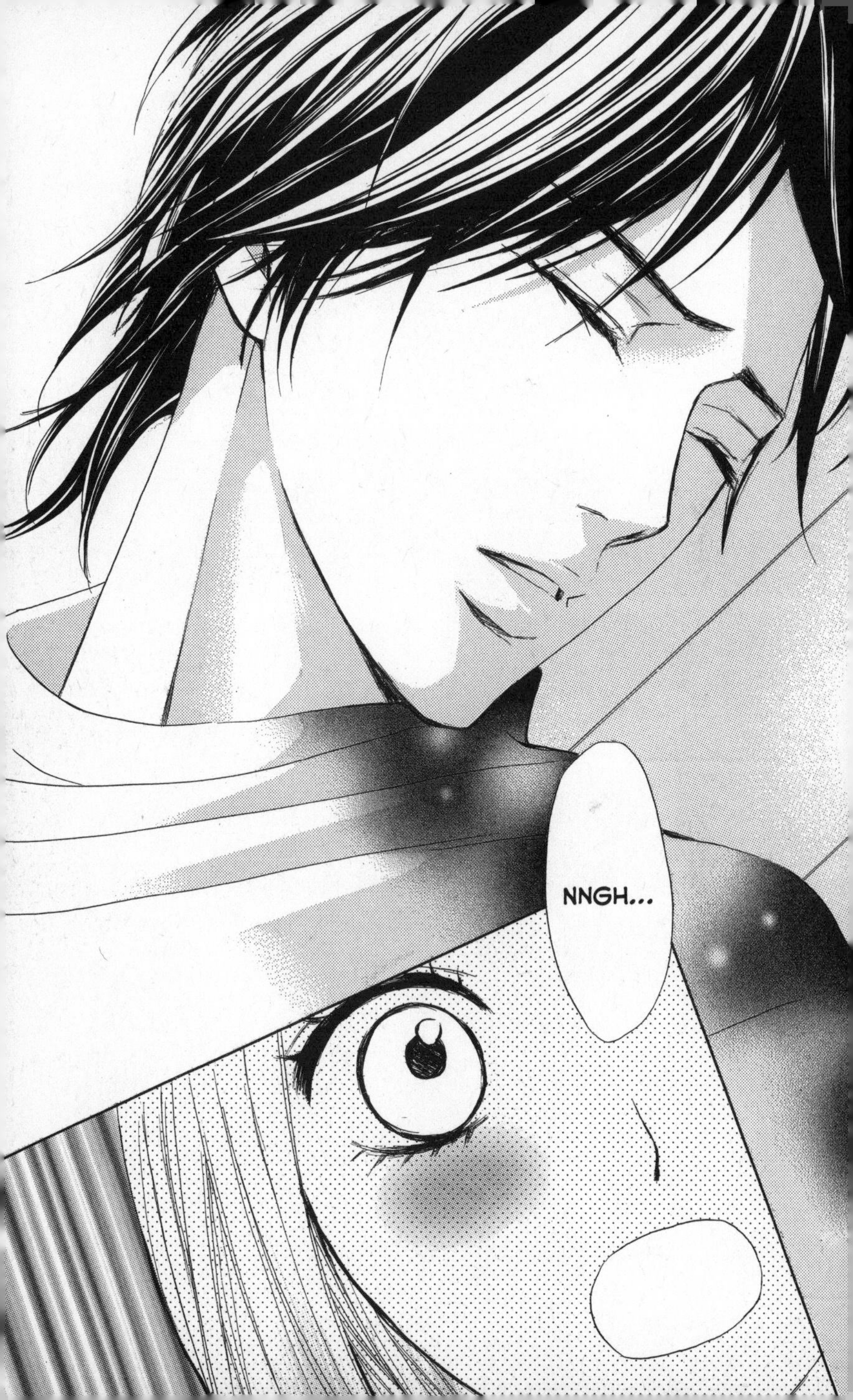
NNGH...

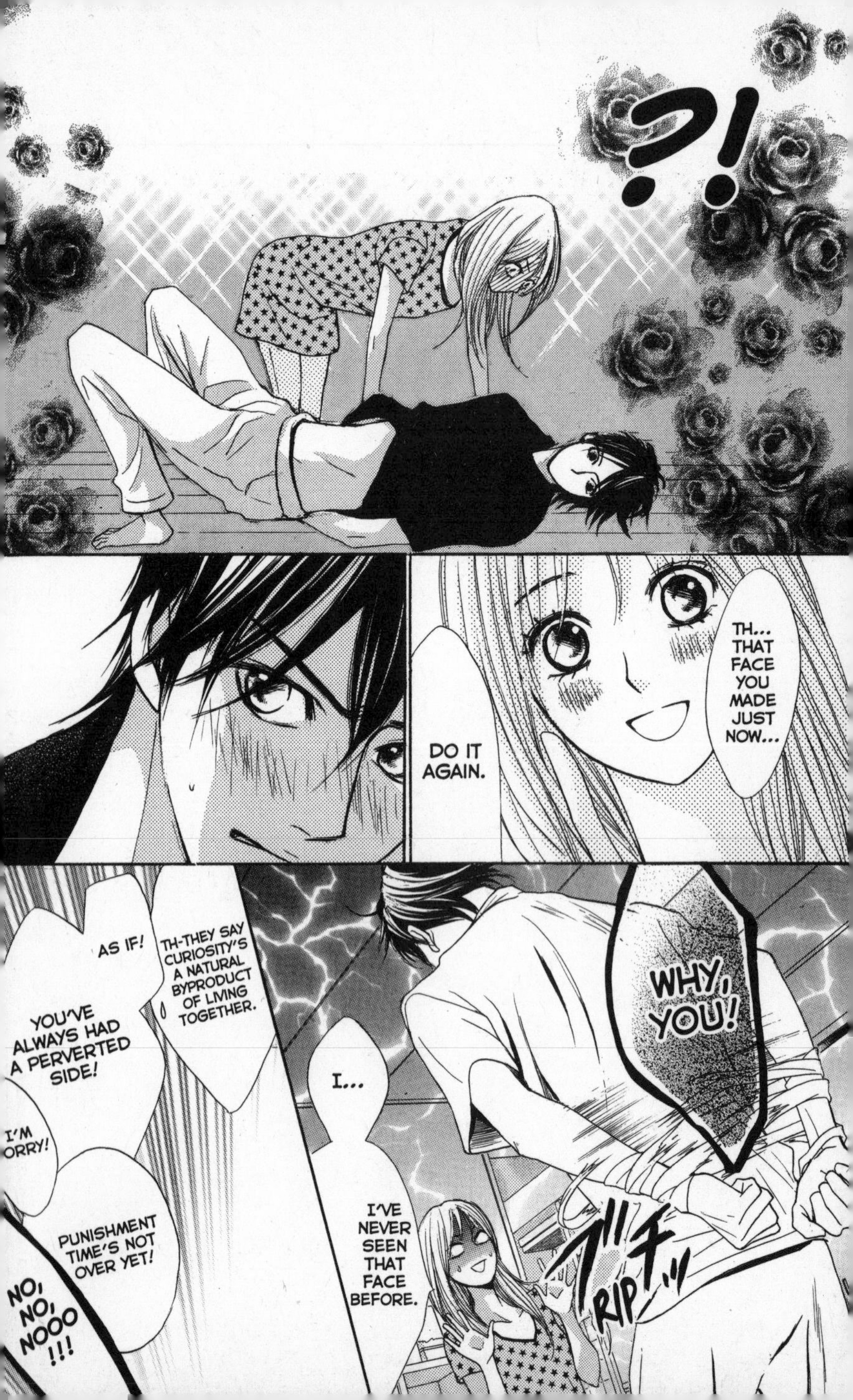

?!
TH... THAT FACE YOU MADE JUST NOW...
DO IT AGAIN.
WHY, YOU!
I...
I'VE NEVER SEEN THAT FACE BEFORE.
RIP
TH-THEY SAY CURIOSITY'S A NATURAL BYPRODUCT OF LIVING TOGETHER.
AS IF!
YOU'VE ALWAYS HAD A PERVERTED SIDE!
I'M ORRY!
PUNISHMENT TIME'S NOT OVER YET!
NO, NO, NOOO!!!

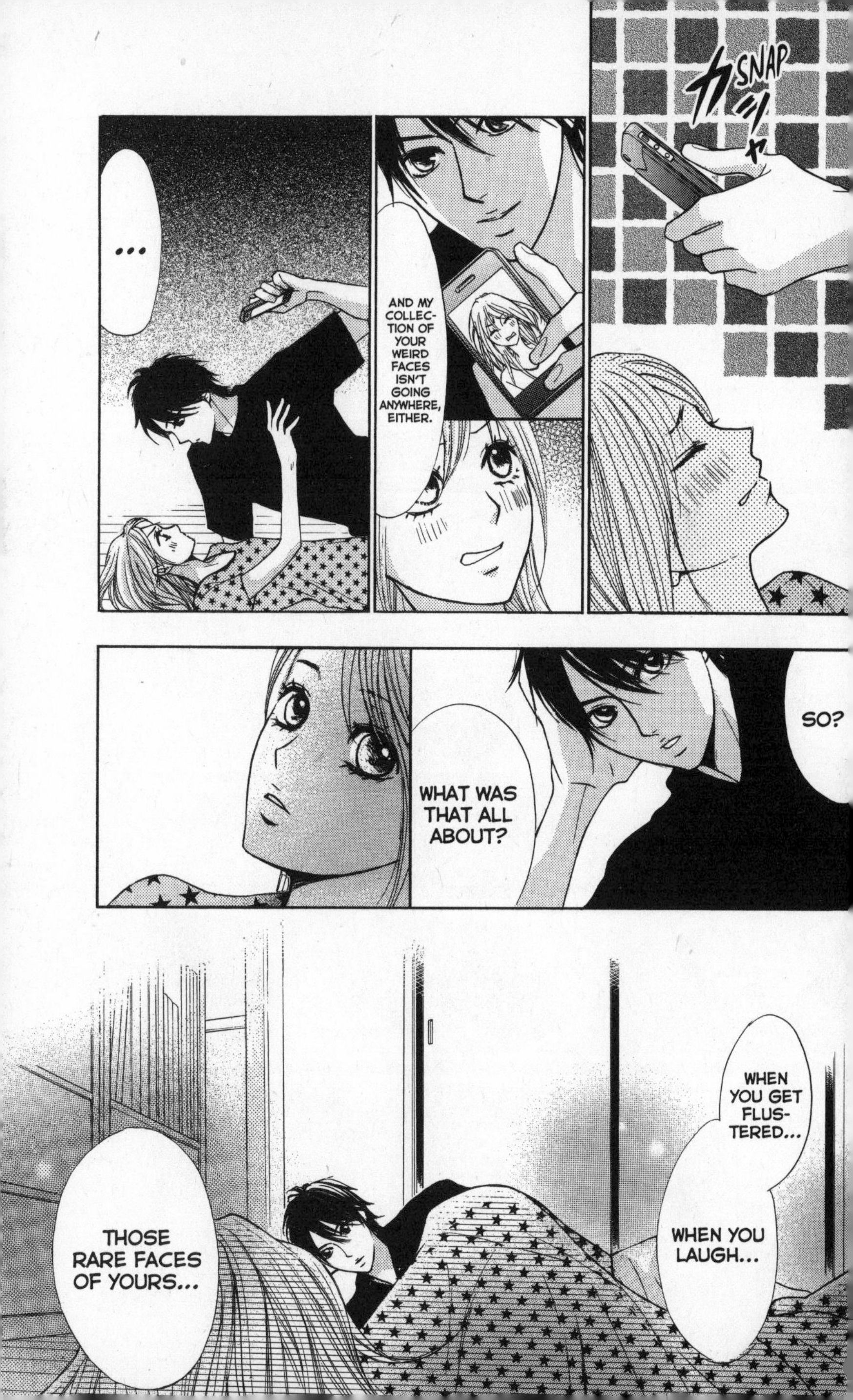
SNAP
AND MY COLLEC-TION OF YOUR WEIRD FACES ISN'T GOING ANYWHERE, EITHER.
...
SO?
WHAT WAS THAT ALL ABOUT?
WHEN YOU GET FLUS-TERED...
WHEN YOU LAUGH...
THOSE RARE FACES OF YOURS...

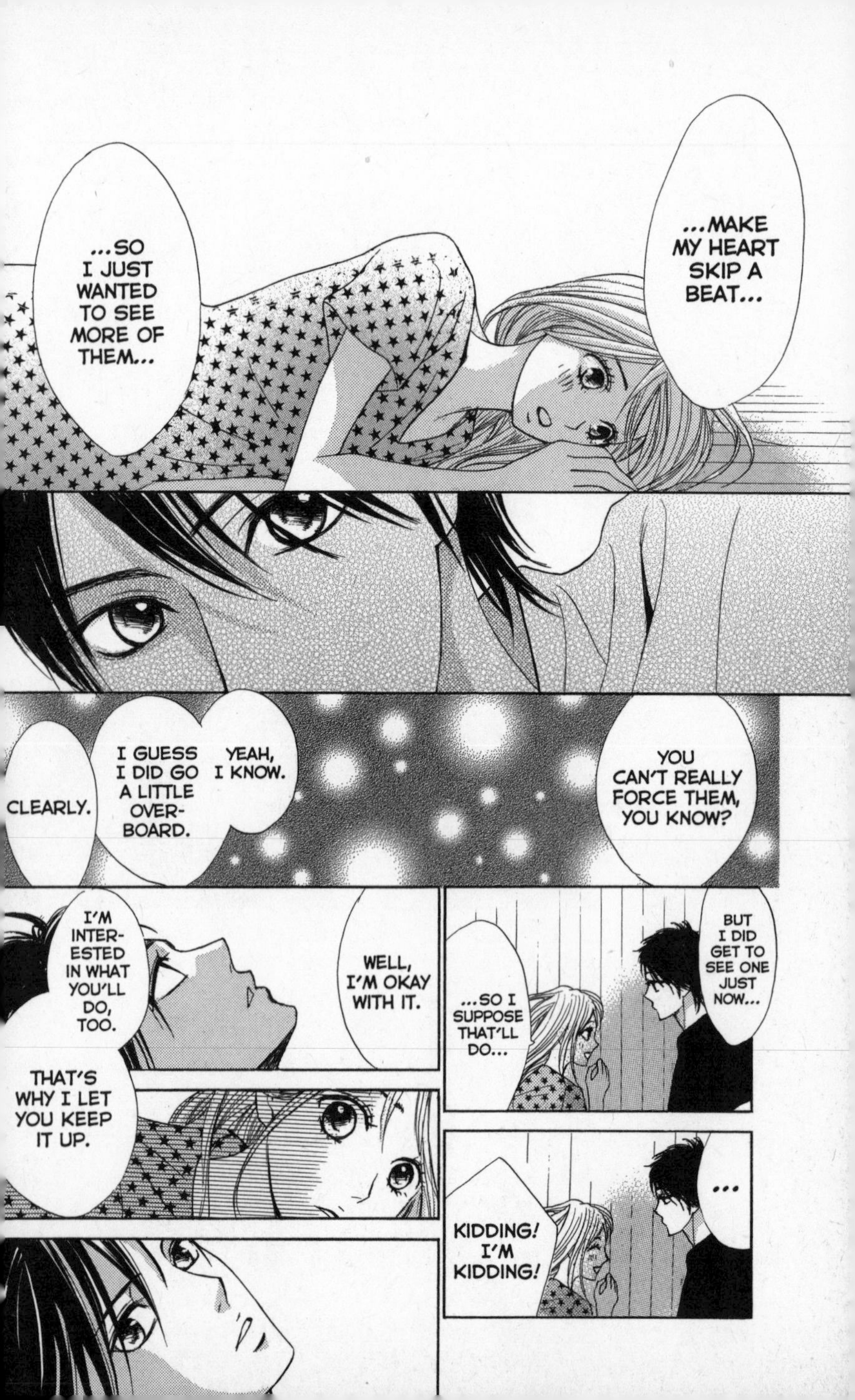
...MAKE MY HEART SKIP A BEAT...
...SO I JUST WANTED TO SEE MORE OF THEM...
YOU CAN'T REALLY FORCE THEM, YOU KNOW?
YEAH, I KNOW.
I GUESS I DID GO A LITTLE OVER-BOARD.
CLEARLY.
BUT I DID GET TO SEE ONE JUST NOW...
...SO I SUPPOSE THAT'LL DO...
...
KIDDING! I'M KIDDING!
WELL, I'M OKAY WITH IT.
I'M INTER-ESTED IN WHAT YOU'LL DO, TOO.
THAT'S WHY I LET YOU KEEP IT UP.

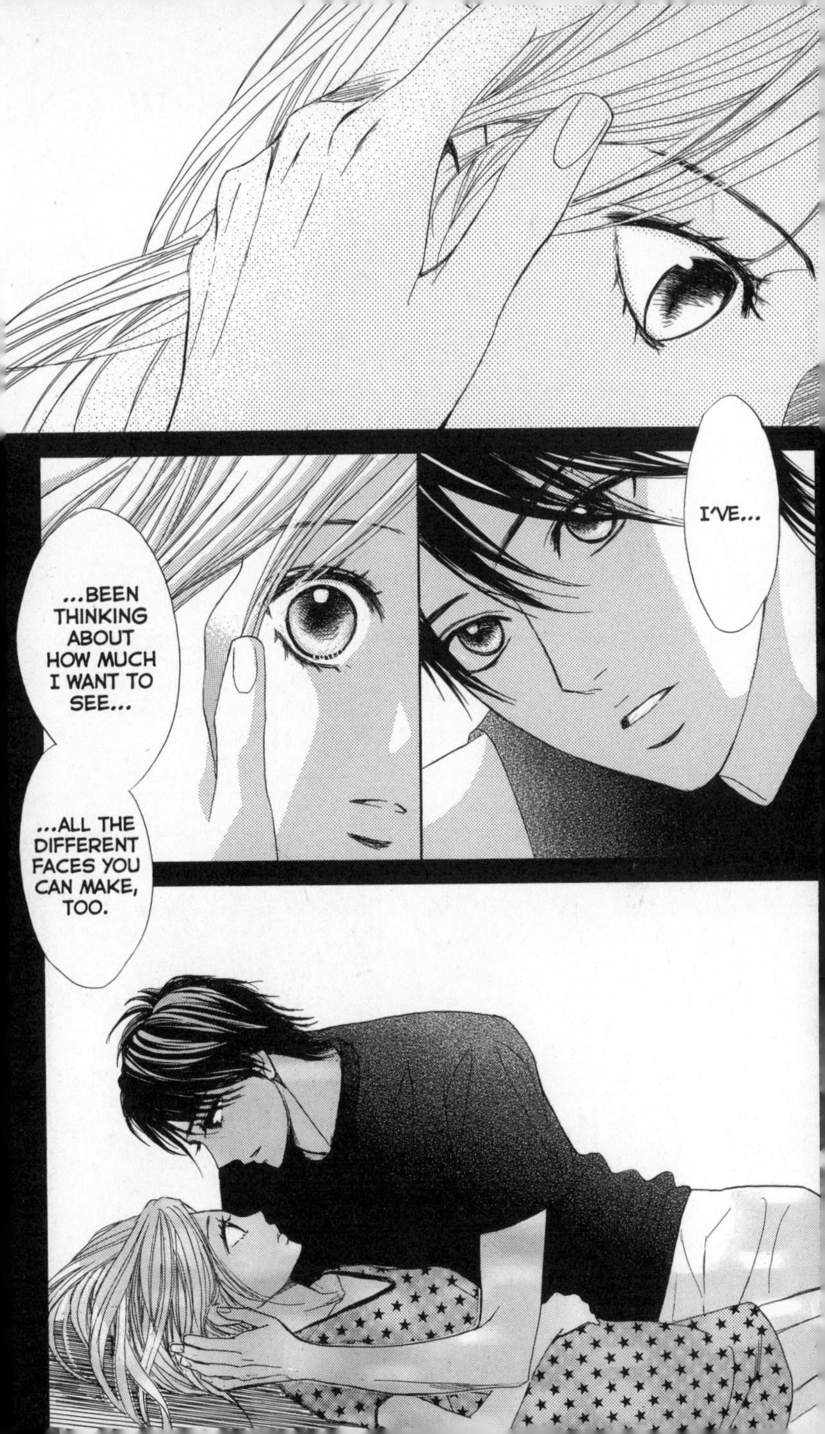
I'VE...
...BEEN THINKING ABOUT HOW MUCH I WANT TO SEE...
...ALL THE DIFFERENT FACES YOU CAN MAKE, TOO.

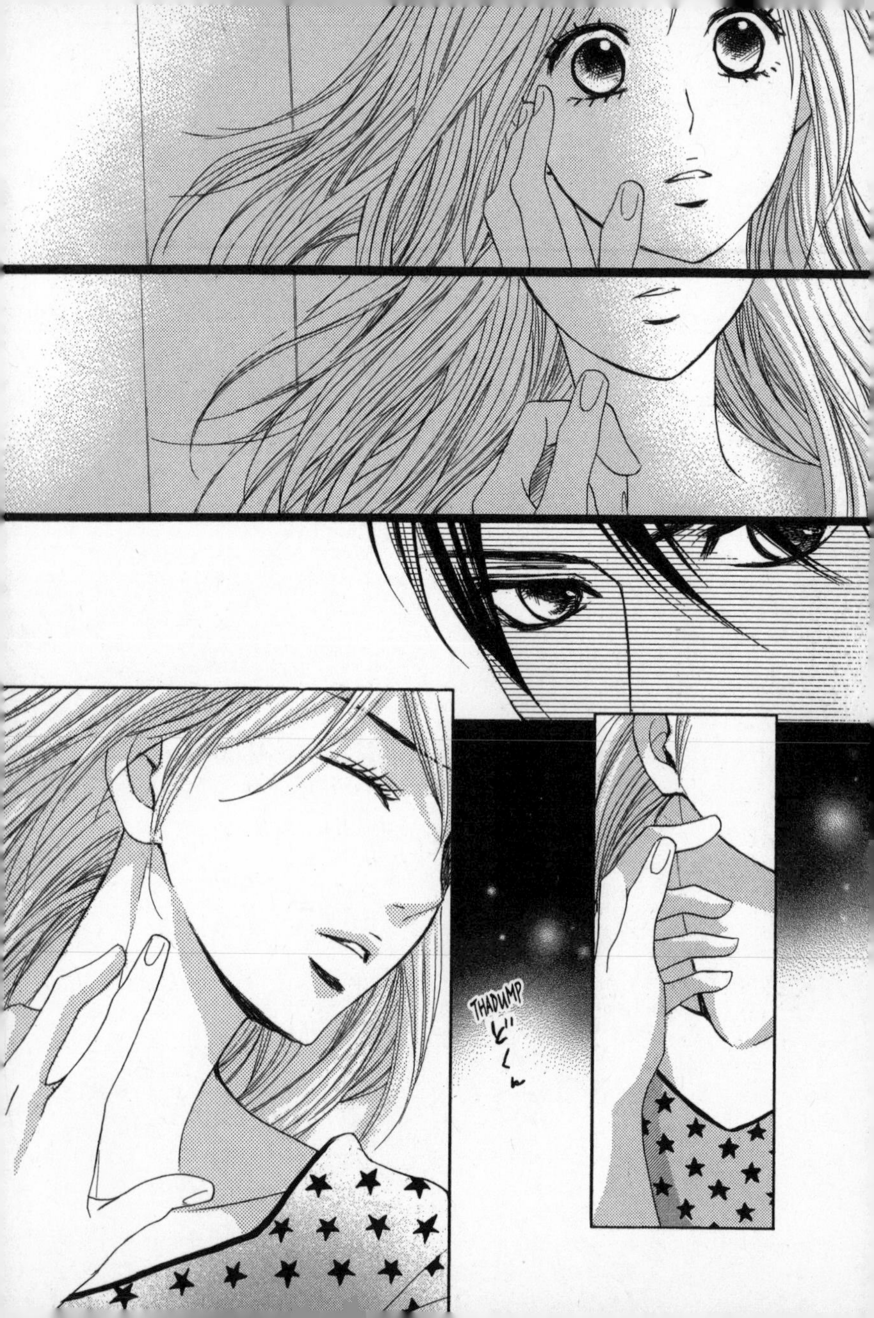
THADUMP
どくん

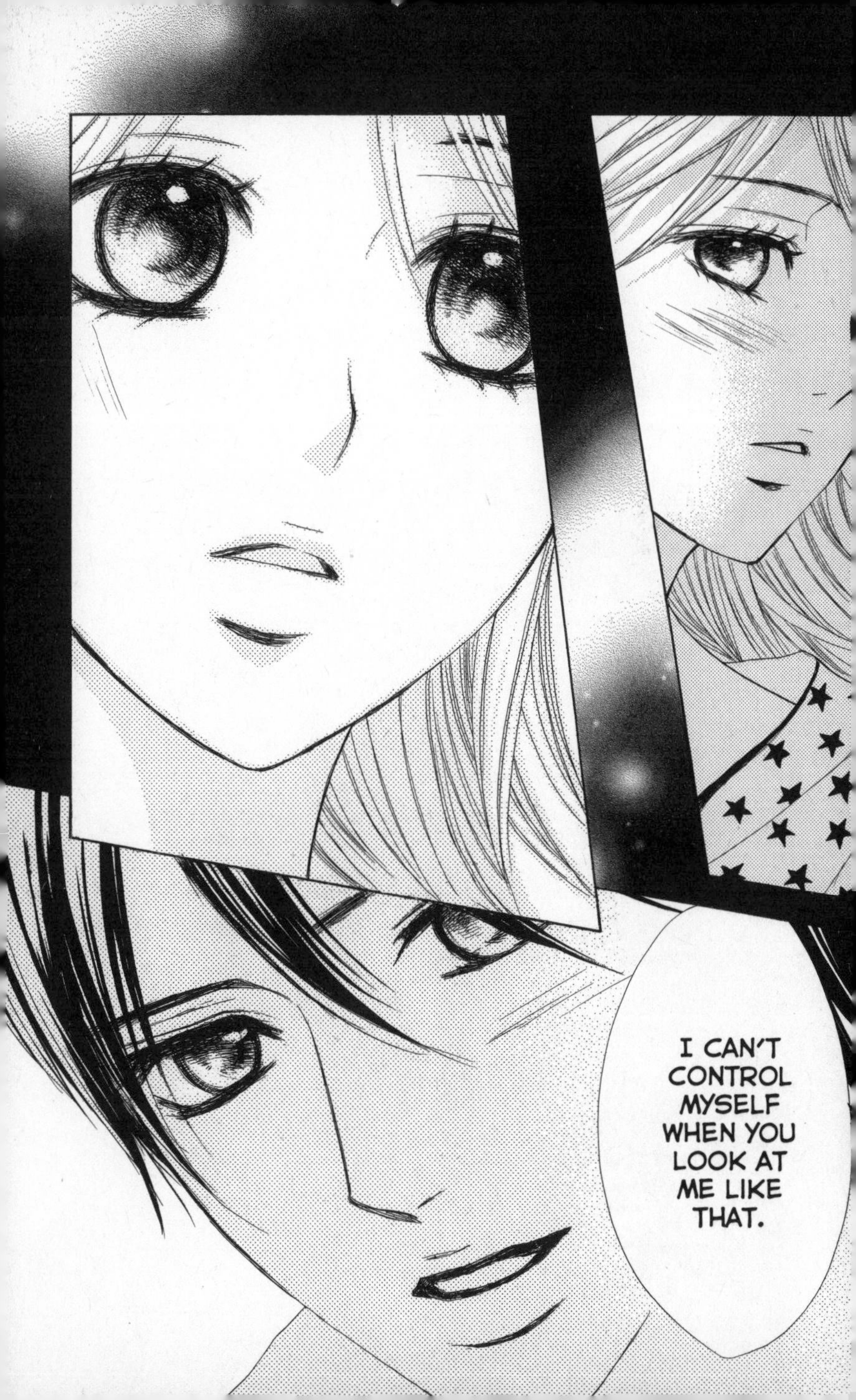
I CAN'T CONTROL MYSELF WHEN YOU LOOK AT ME LIKE THAT.

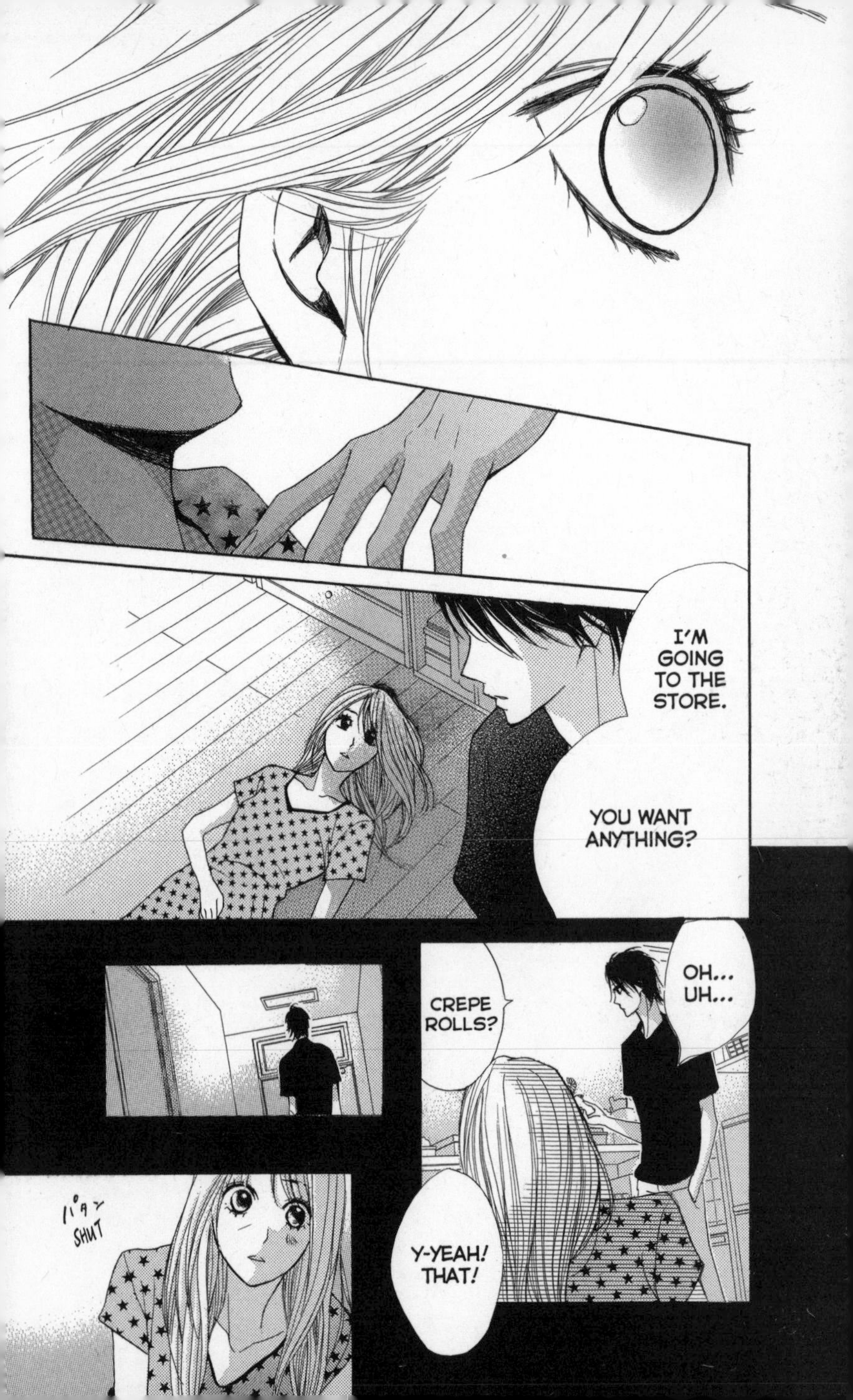
I'M GOING TO THE STORE.
YOU WANT ANYTHING?
OH... UH...
CREPE ROLLS?
Y-YEAH! THAT!
パタン
SHUT

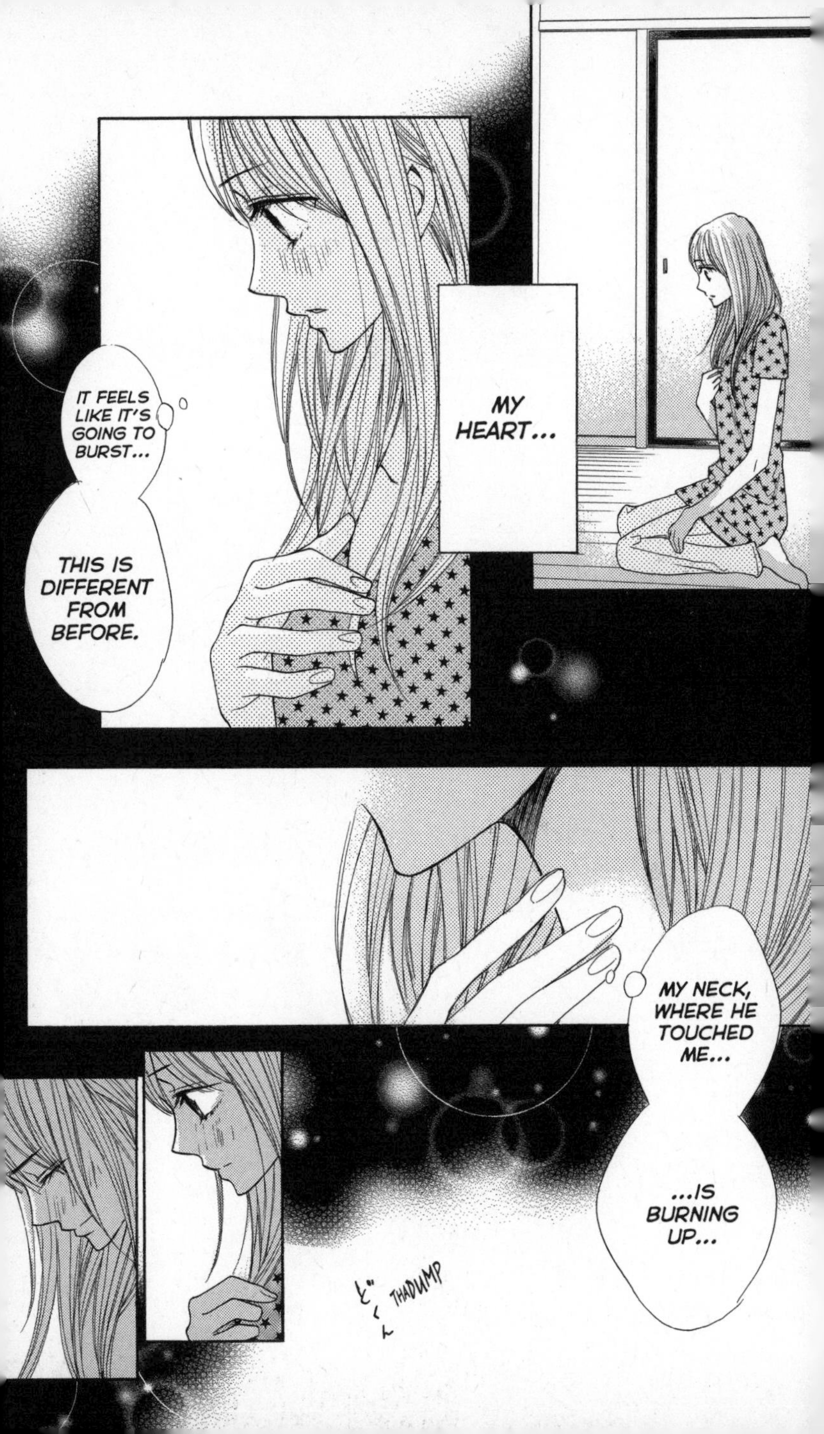
MY HEART...
IT FEELS LIKE IT'S GOING TO BURST...
THIS IS DIFFERENT FROM BEFORE.
MY NECK, WHERE HE TOUCHED ME...
...IS BURNING UP...
どくん THADUMP

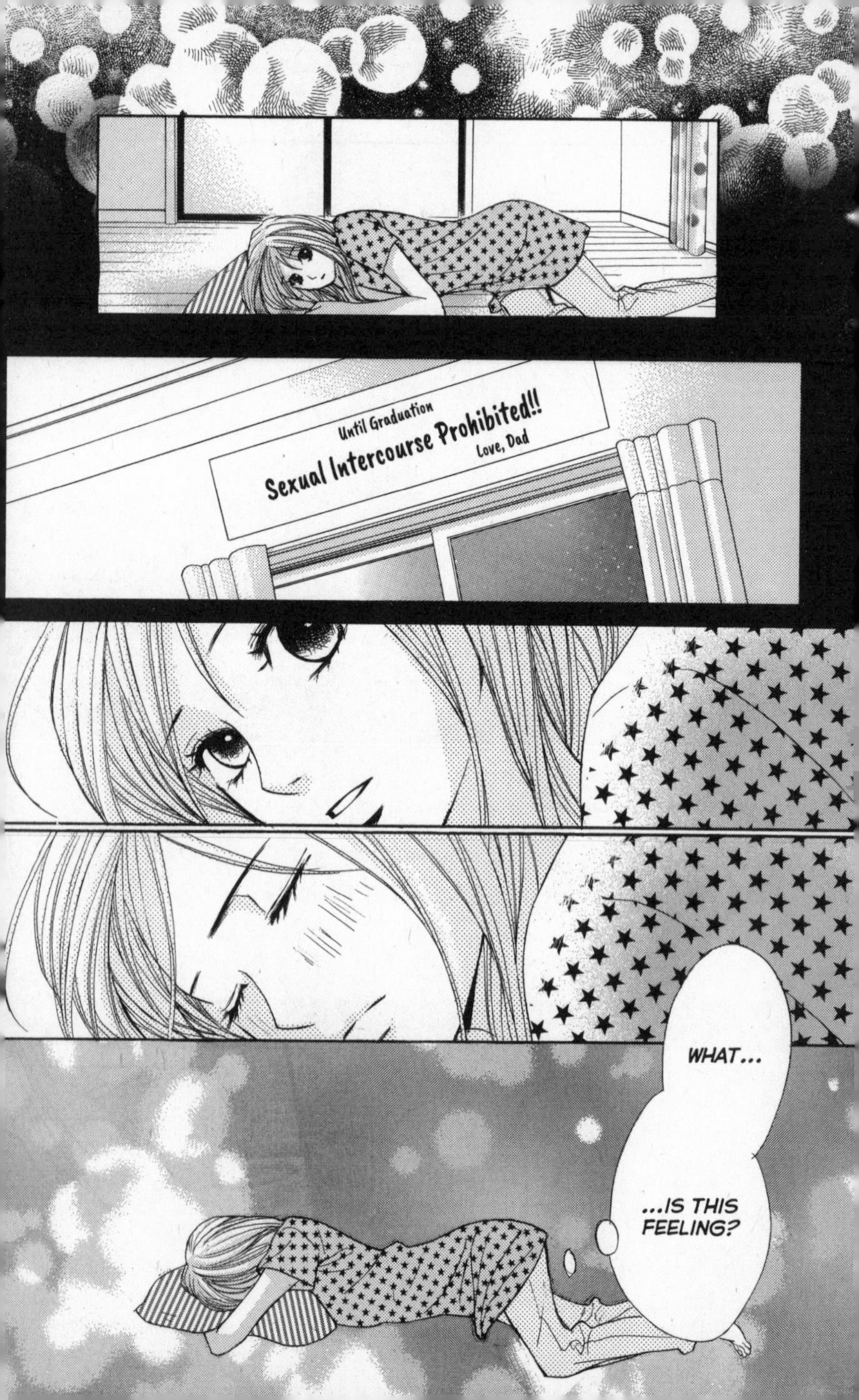
Until Graduation
Sexual Intercourse Prohibited!!
Love, Dad
WHAT...
...IS THIS FEELING?

L♥DK

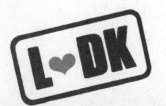

#47 Hot Body

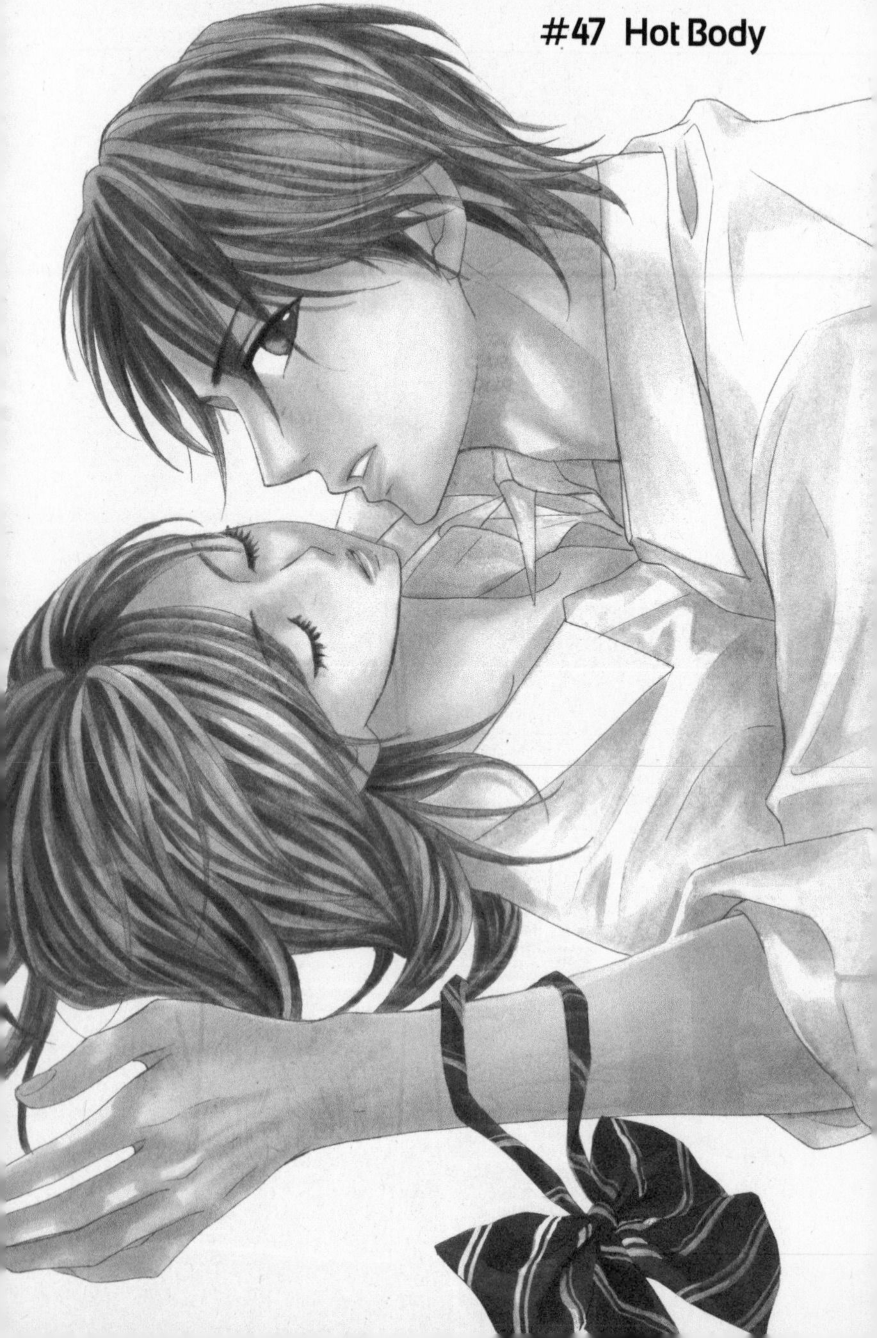

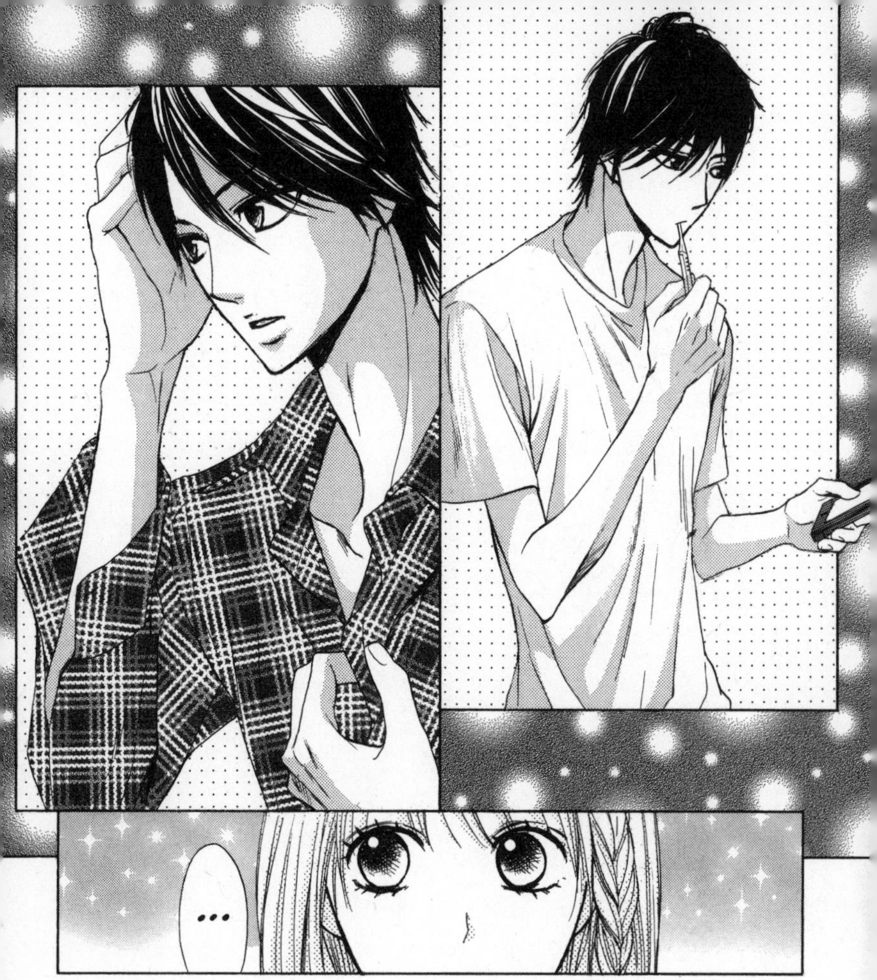
...

L♥DK

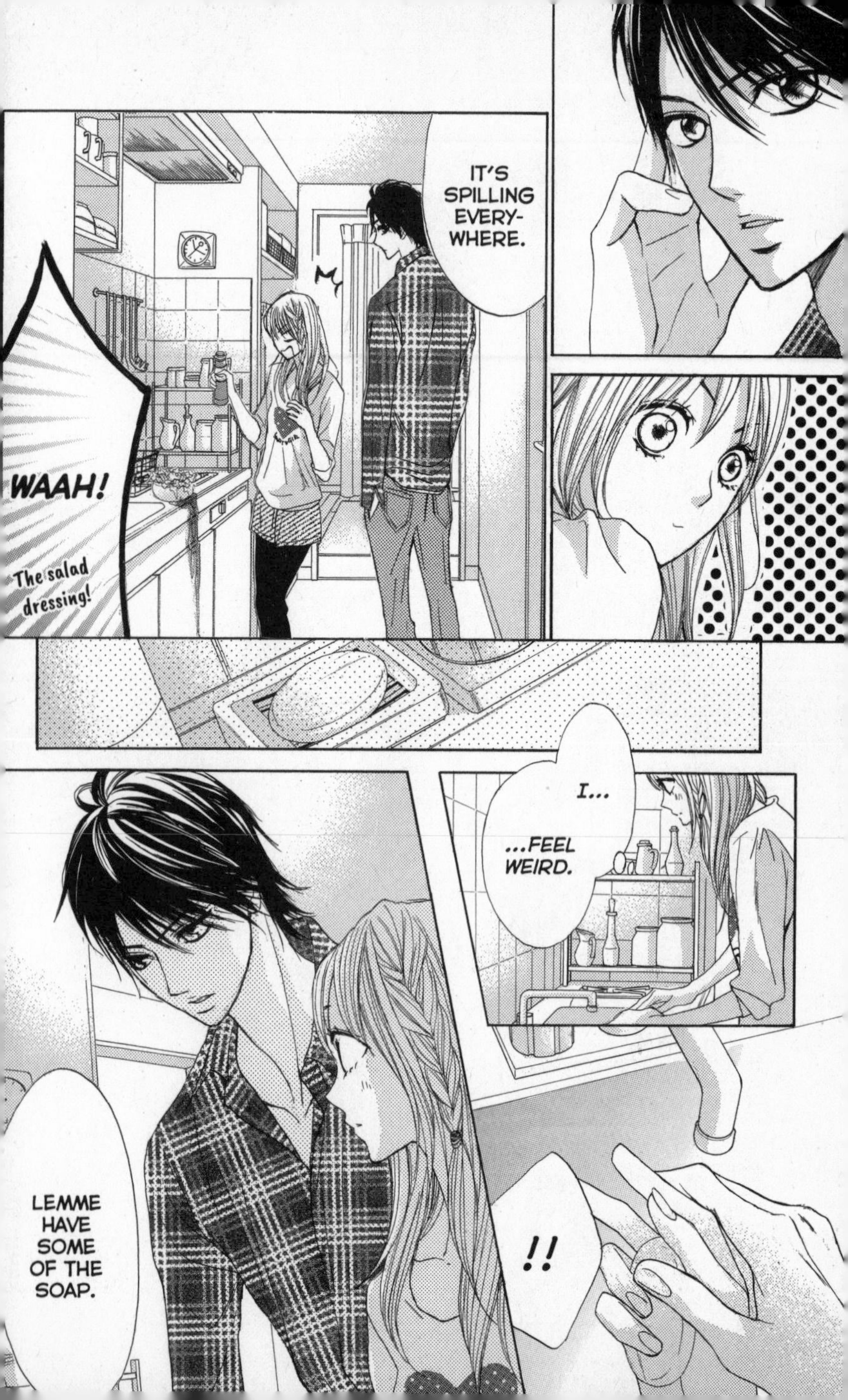
IT'S SPILLING EVERY-WHERE.
WAAH!
The salad dressing!
I...
...FEEL WEIRD.
LEMME HAVE SOME OF THE SOAP.
!!

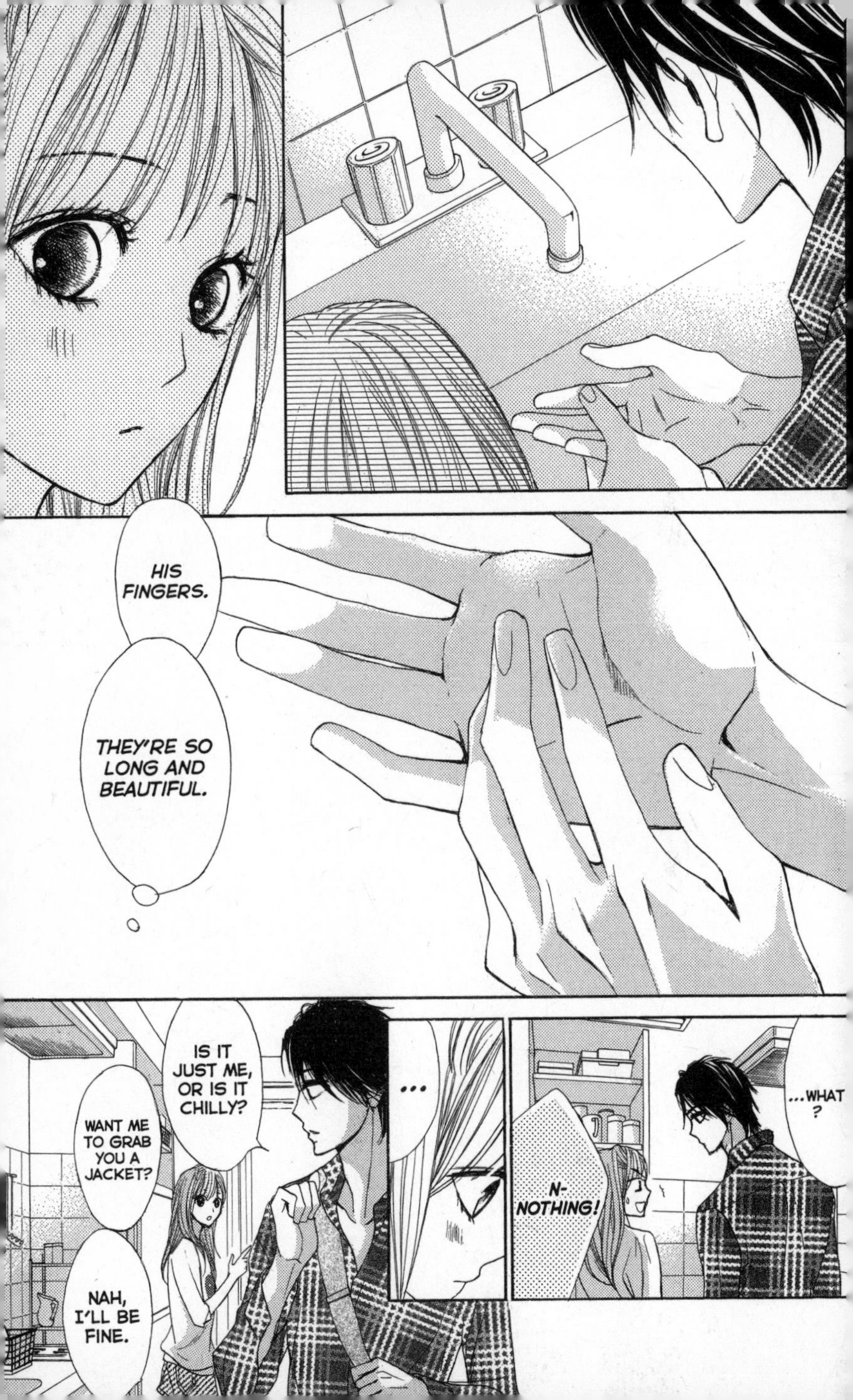
HIS FINGERS.
THEY'RE SO LONG AND BEAUTIFUL.
...WHAT?
N-NOTHING!
...
IS IT JUST ME, OR IS IT CHILLY?
WANT ME TO GRAB YOU A JACKET?
NAH, I'LL BE FINE.

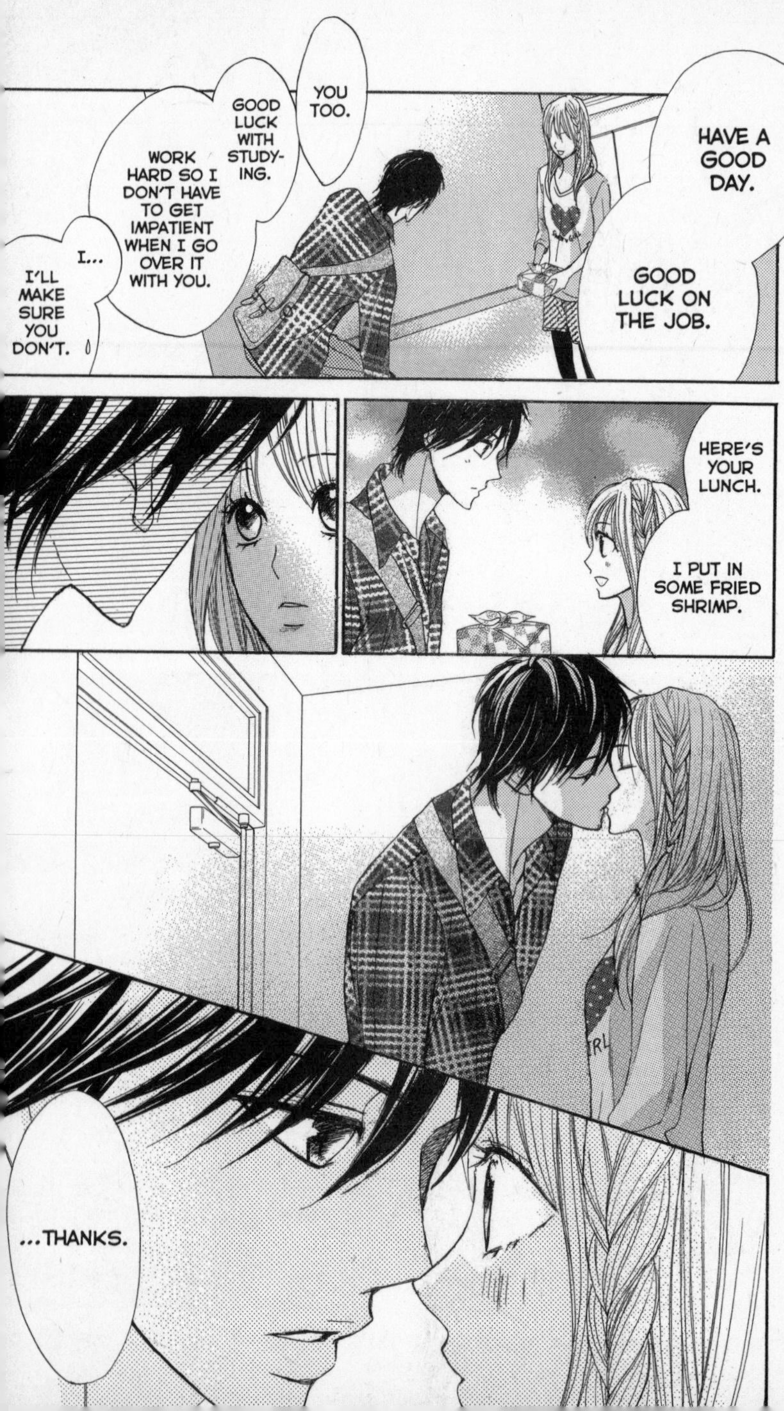

HAVE A GOOD DAY.
GOOD LUCK ON THE JOB.
YOU TOO.
GOOD LUCK WITH STUDY-ING.
WORK HARD SO I DON'T HAVE TO GET IMPATIENT WHEN I GO OVER IT WITH YOU.
I...
I'LL MAKE SURE YOU DON'T.
HERE'S YOUR LUNCH.
I PUT IN SOME FRIED SHRIMP.
...THANKS.

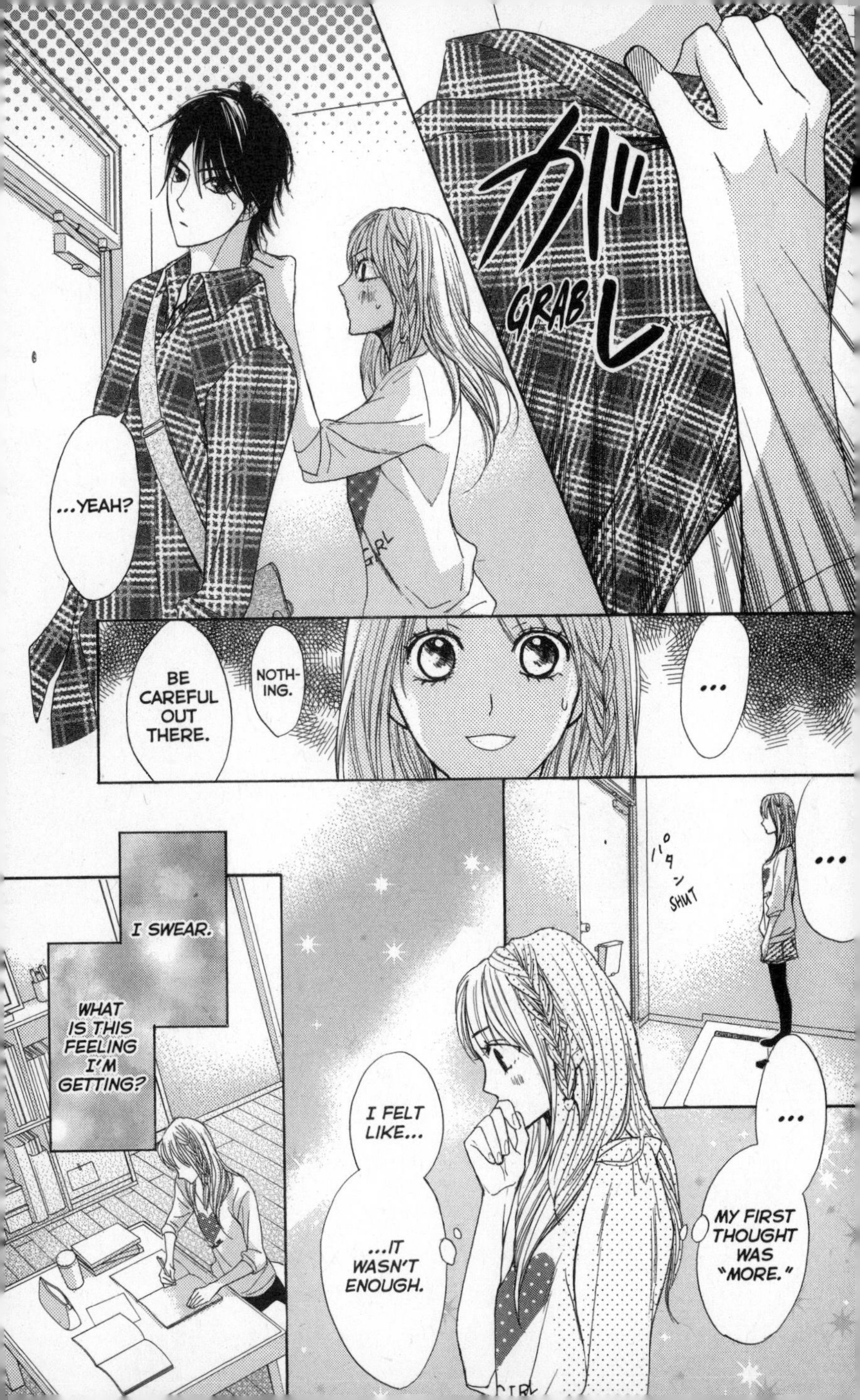
GRAB
...YEAH?
...
NOTH-ING.
BE CAREFUL OUT THERE.
...
パタン
SHUT
...
MY FIRST THOUGHT WAS "MORE."
I FELT LIKE...
...IT WASN'T ENOUGH.
I SWEAR.
WHAT IS THIS FEELING I'M GETTING?

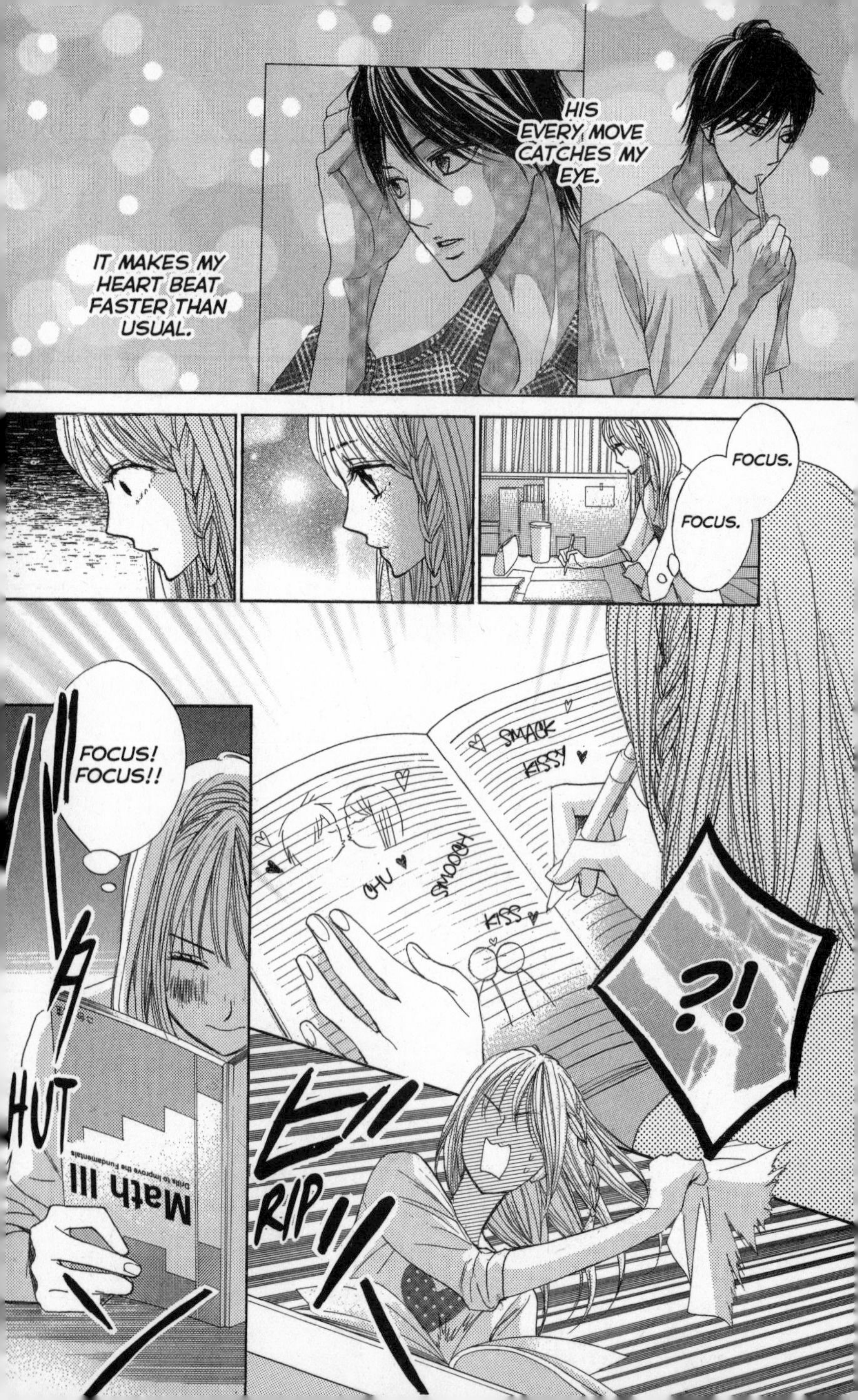
HIS EVERY MOVE CATCHES MY EYE.
IT MAKES MY HEART BEAT FASTER THAN USUAL.
FOCUS.
FOCUS.
SMACK
KISSY
CHU
SMOOCH
KISS
?!
RIP
FOCUS! FOCUS!!
HUT
Math III
Drills to Improve the Fundamentals

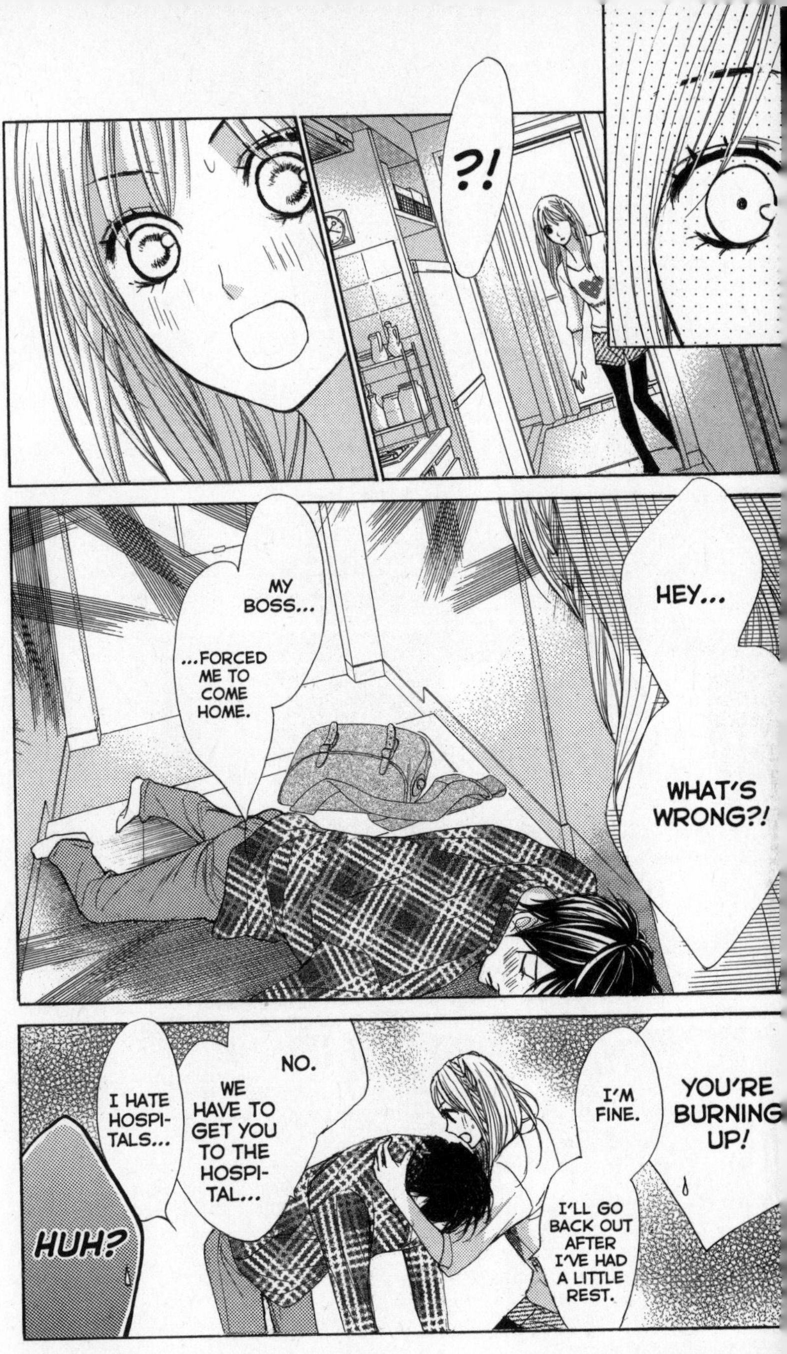
?!
HEY...
WHAT'S WRONG?!
MY BOSS...
...FORCED ME TO COME HOME.
YOU'RE BURNING UP!
I'M FINE.
I'LL GO BACK OUT AFTER I'VE HAD A LITTLE REST.
NO.
WE HAVE TO GET YOU TO THE HOSPITAL...
I HATE HOSPITALS...
HUH?

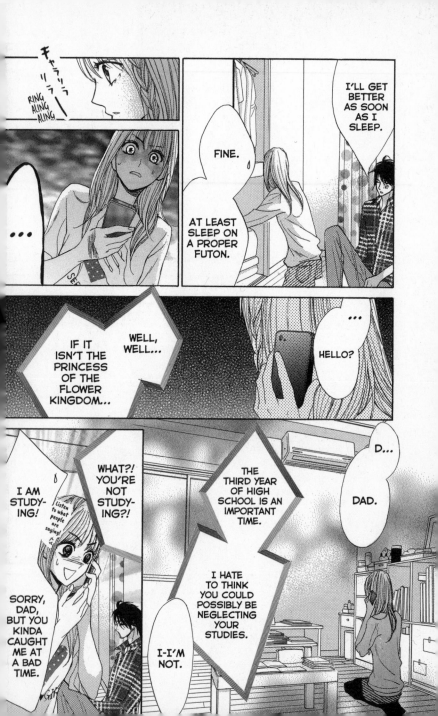

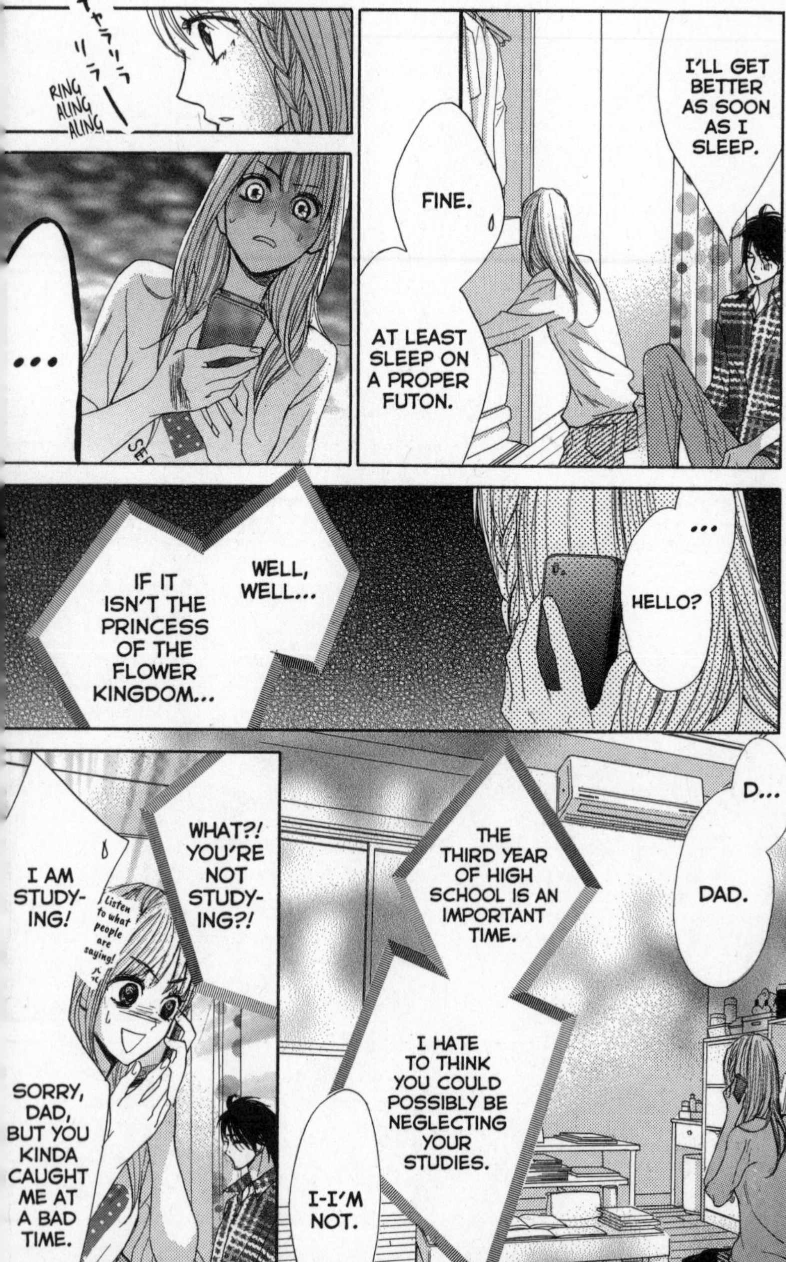
I'LL GET BETTER AS SOON AS I SLEEP.
FINE.
AT LEAST SLEEP ON A PROPER FUTON.
キャラリラリラ
RING ALING ALING
...
...
HELLO?
WELL, WELL...
IF IT ISN'T THE PRINCESS OF THE FLOWER KINGDOM...
D...
DAD.
THE THIRD YEAR OF HIGH SCHOOL IS AN IMPORTANT TIME.
I HATE TO THINK YOU COULD POSSIBLY BE NEGLECTING YOUR STUDIES.
I-I'M NOT.
WHAT?! YOU'RE NOT STUDYING?!
I AM STUDYING!
Listen to what people are saying!
SORRY, DAD, BUT YOU KINDA CAUGHT ME AT A BAD TIME.

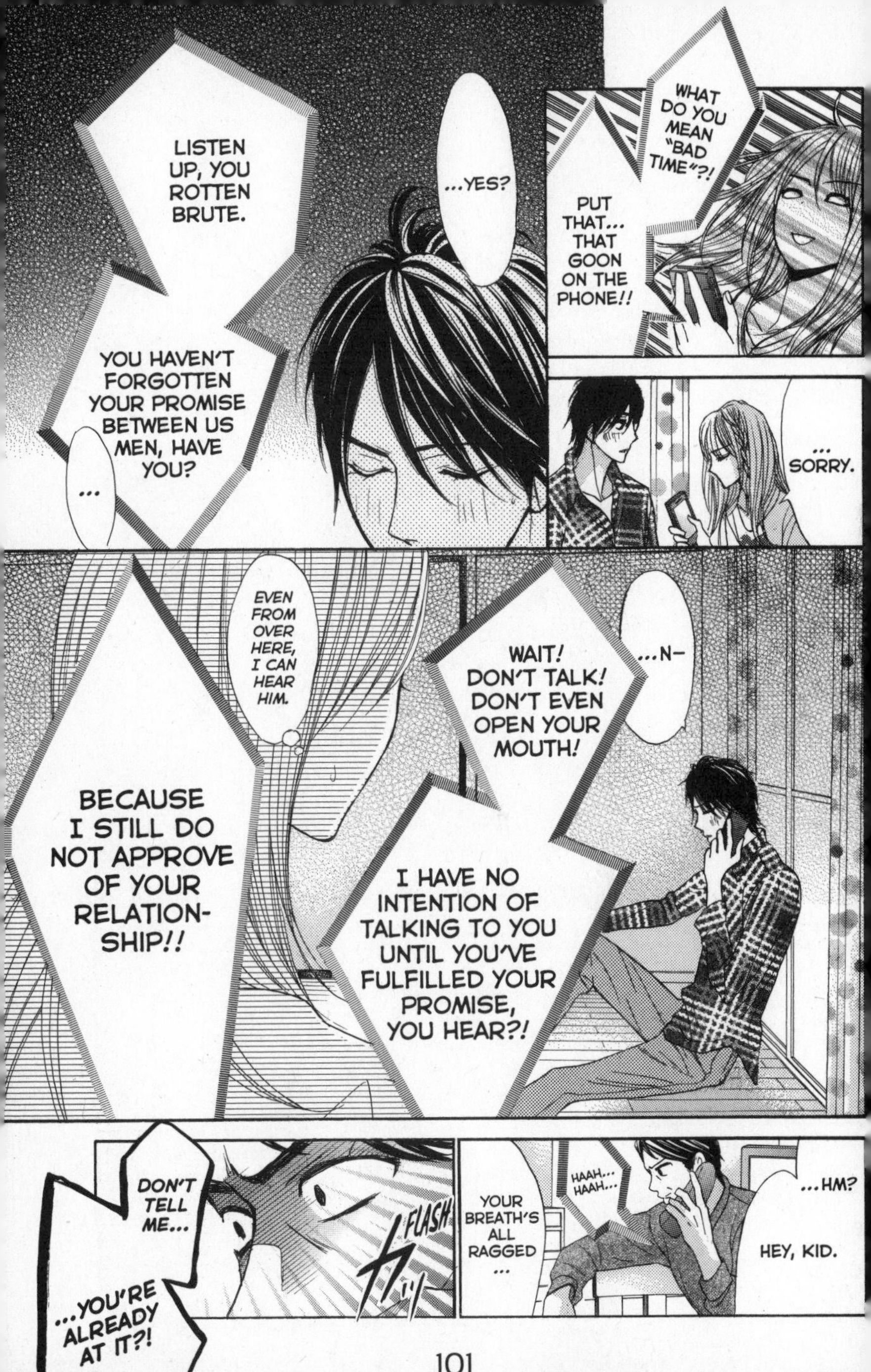
WHAT DO YOU MEAN "BAD TIME"?!
PUT THAT... THAT GOON ON THE PHONE!!
... SORRY.
...YES?
LISTEN UP, YOU ROTTEN BRUTE.
YOU HAVEN'T FORGOTTEN YOUR PROMISE BETWEEN US MEN, HAVE YOU?
...
...N-
WAIT! DON'T TALK! DON'T EVEN OPEN YOUR MOUTH!
EVEN FROM OVER HERE, I CAN HEAR HIM.
I HAVE NO INTENTION OF TALKING TO YOU UNTIL YOU'VE FULFILLED YOUR PROMISE, YOU HEAR?!
BECAUSE I STILL DO NOT APPROVE OF YOUR RELATION-SHIP!!
...HM?
HEY, KID.
HAAH... HAAH...
YOUR BREATH'S ALL RAGGED ...
FLASH
DON'T TELL ME...
...YOU'RE ALREADY AT IT?!

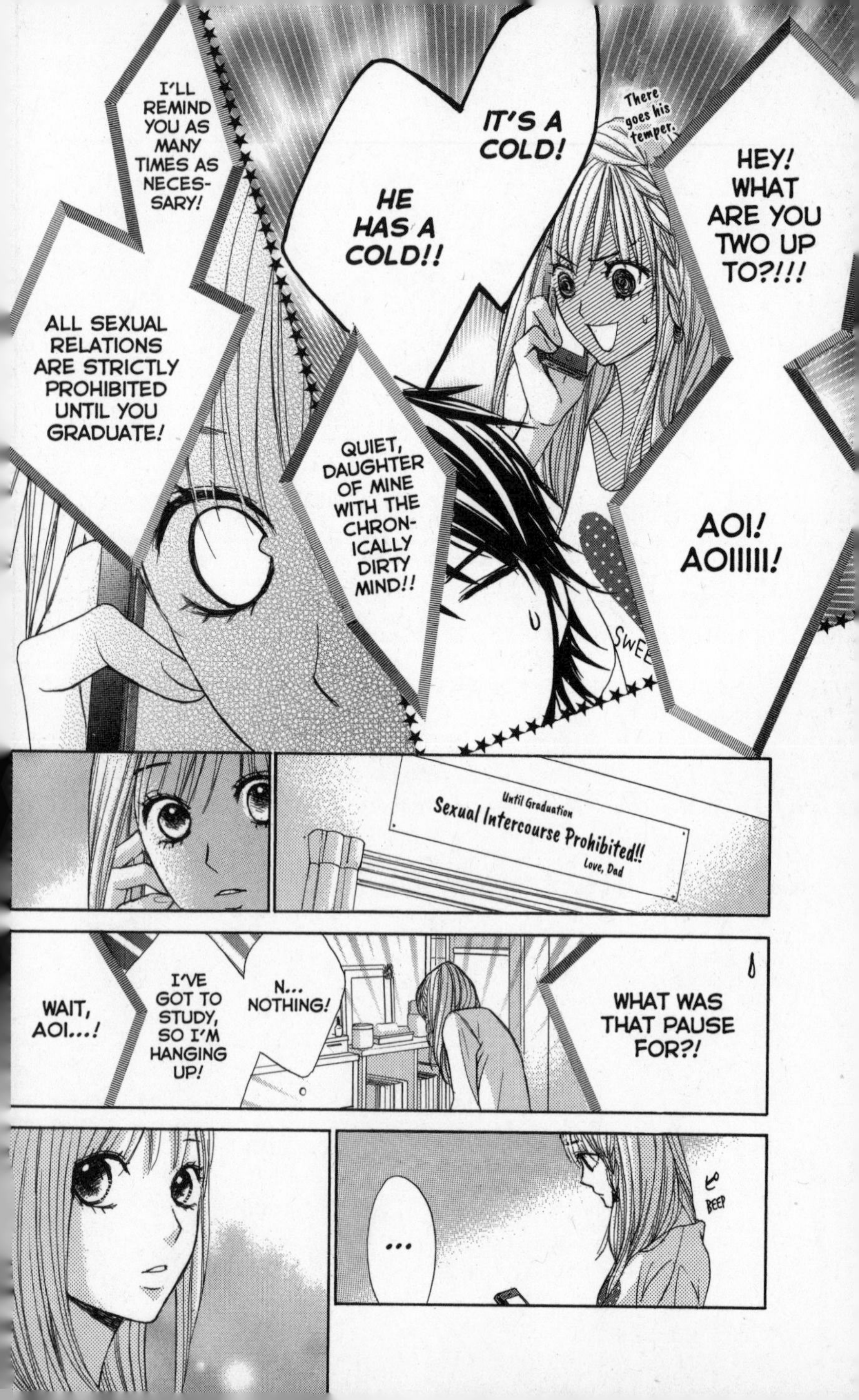
HEY! WHAT ARE YOU TWO UP TO?!!!
There goes his temper.
IT'S A COLD!
HE HAS A COLD!!
I'LL REMIND YOU AS MANY TIMES AS NECES-SARY!
AOI! AOIIIII!
SWEE
QUIET, DAUGHTER OF MINE WITH THE CHRON-ICALLY DIRTY MIND!!
ALL SEXUAL RELATIONS ARE STRICTLY PROHIBITED UNTIL YOU GRADUATE!
Until Graduation
Sexual Intercourse Prohibited!!
Love, Dad
WHAT WAS THAT PAUSE FOR?!
N... NOTHING!
I'VE GOT TO STUDY, SO I'M HANGING UP!
WAIT, AOI...!
BEEP
...

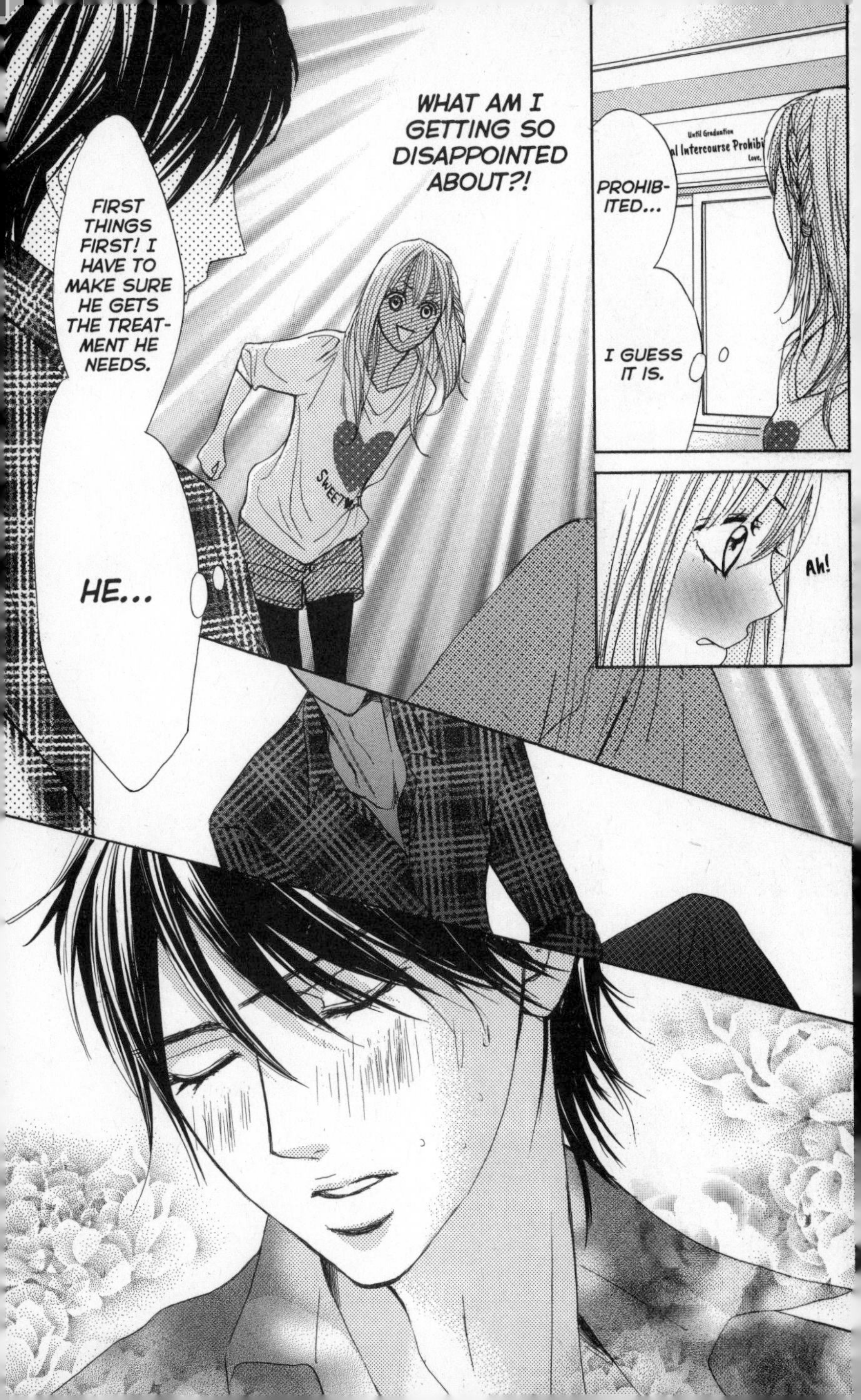
Until Graduation
al Intercourse Prohibi
Love,
PROHIB- ITED...
I GUESS IT IS.
Ah!
WHAT AM I GETTING SO DISAPPOINTED ABOUT?!
FIRST THINGS FIRST! I HAVE TO MAKE SURE HE GETS THE TREATMENT HE NEEDS.
SWEET
HE...

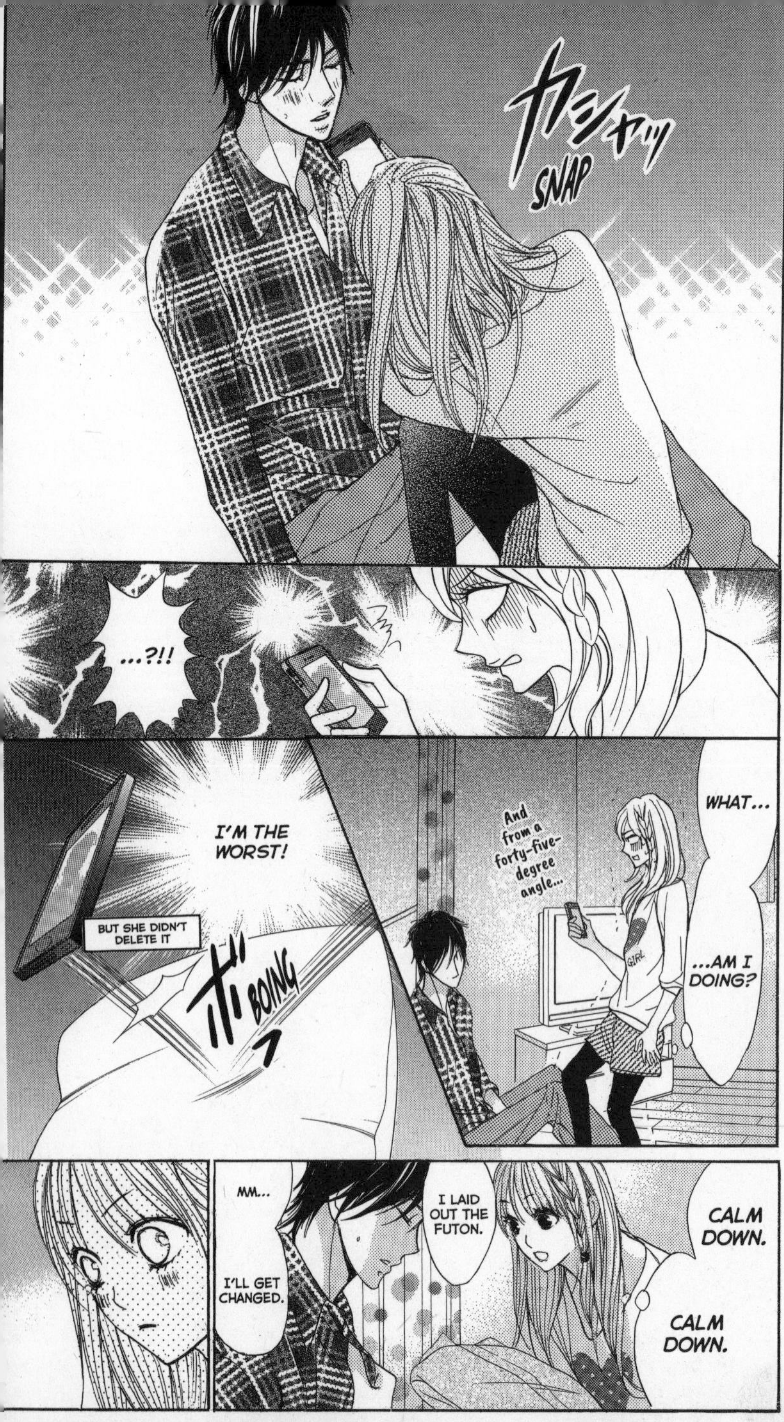
カシャッ
SNAP
...?!!
WHAT...
...AM I DOING?
And from a forty-five-degree angle...
I'M THE WORST!
BUT SHE DIDN'T DELETE IT
BOING
CALM DOWN.
CALM DOWN.
I LAID OUT THE FUTON.
MM...
I'LL GET CHANGED.

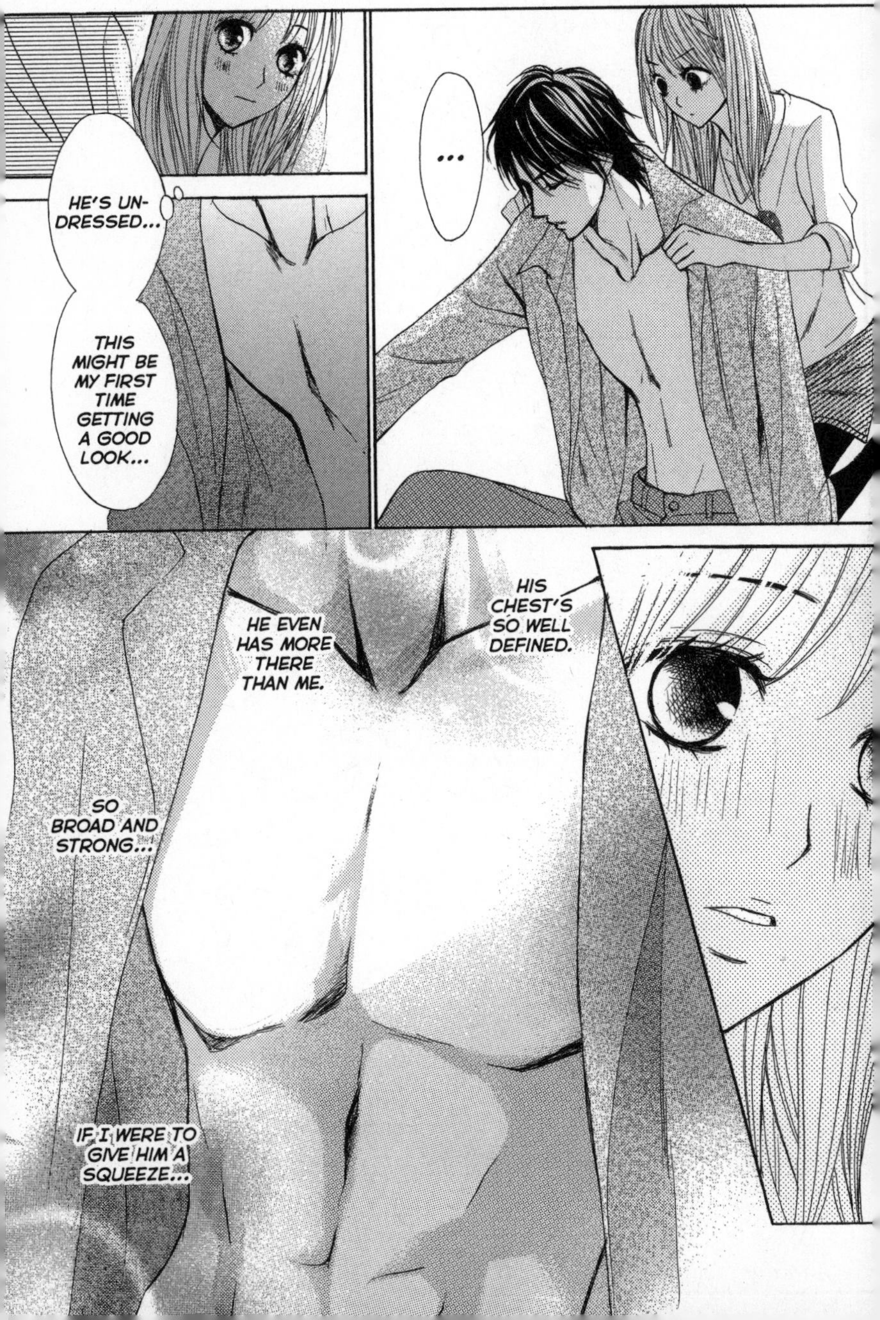
...
HE'S UNDRESSED...
THIS MIGHT BE MY FIRST TIME GETTING A GOOD LOOK...
HIS CHEST'S SO WELL DEFINED.
HE EVEN HAS MORE THERE THAN ME.
SO BROAD AND STRONG...
IF I WERE TO GIVE HIM A SQUEEZE...

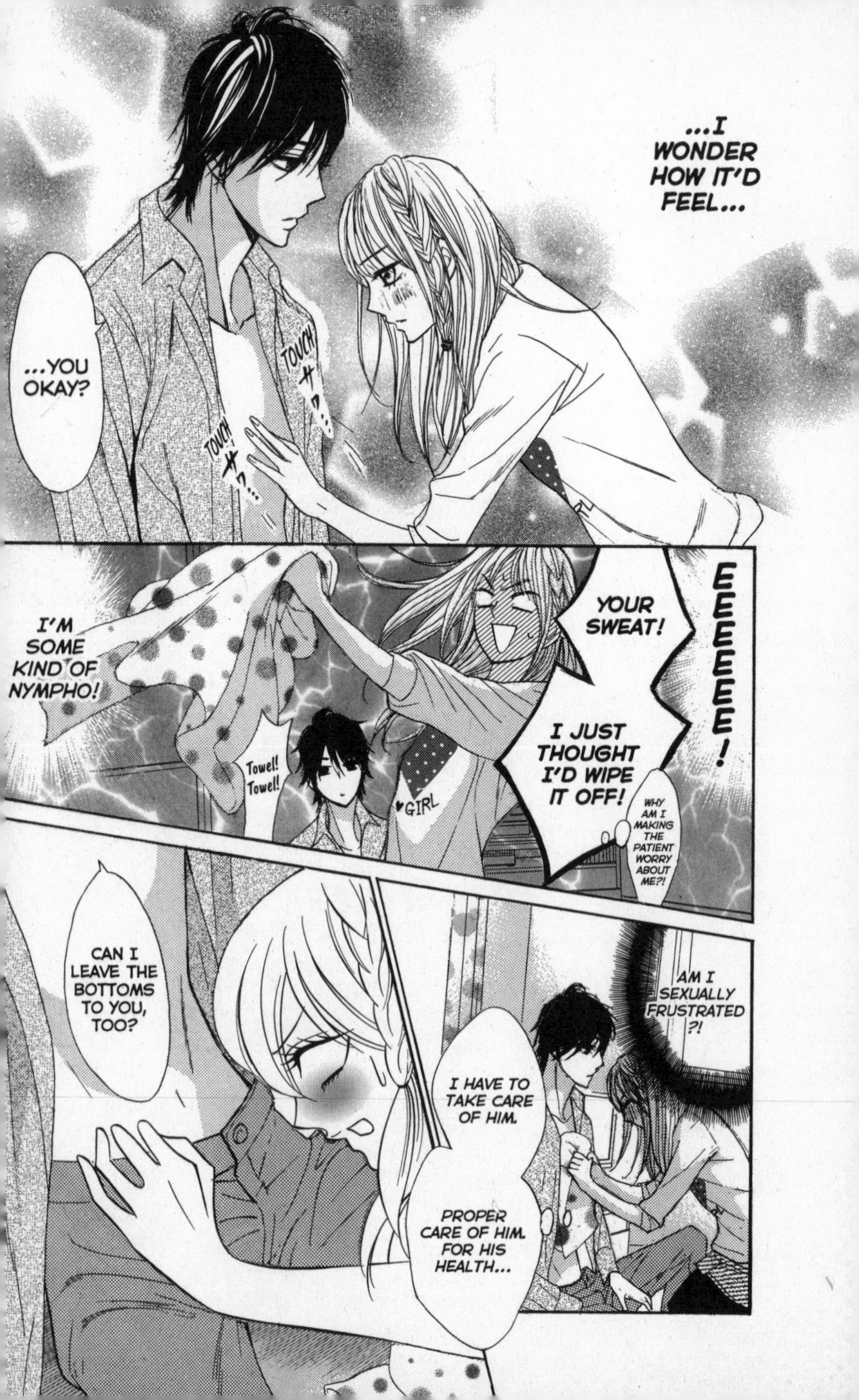
...I WONDER HOW IT'D FEEL...
TOUCH
TOUCH
...YOU OKAY?
EEEEEEE!
YOUR SWEAT!
I JUST THOUGHT I'D WIPE IT OFF!
WHY AM I MAKING THE PATIENT WORRY ABOUT ME?!
Towel! Towel!
GIRL
I'M SOME KIND OF NYMPHO!
AM I SEXUALLY FRUSTRATED?!
I HAVE TO TAKE CARE OF HIM.
PROPER CARE OF HIM. FOR HIS HEALTH...
CAN I LEAVE THE BOTTOMS TO YOU, TOO?

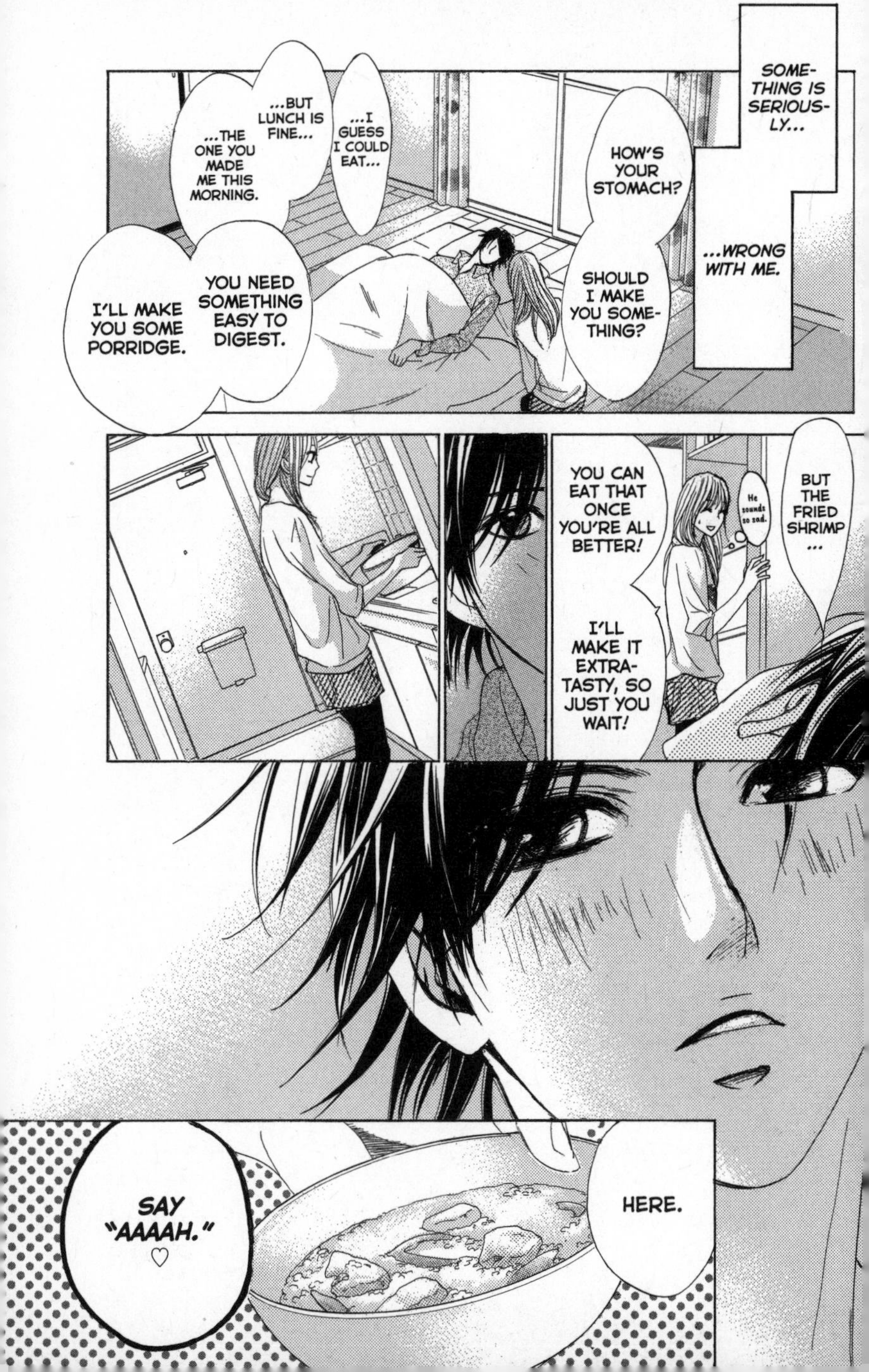
SOME-THING IS SERIOUS-LY...
...WRONG WITH ME.
HOW'S YOUR STOMACH?
SHOULD I MAKE YOU SOME-THING?
...I GUESS I COULD EAT...
...BUT LUNCH IS FINE...
...THE ONE YOU MADE ME THIS MORNING.
YOU NEED SOMETHING EASY TO DIGEST.
I'LL MAKE YOU SOME PORRIDGE.
BUT THE FRIED SHRIMP ...
He sounds so sad.
YOU CAN EAT THAT ONCE YOU'RE ALL BETTER!
I'LL MAKE IT EXTRA-TASTY, SO JUST YOU WAIT!
HERE.
SAY "AAAAH." ♡

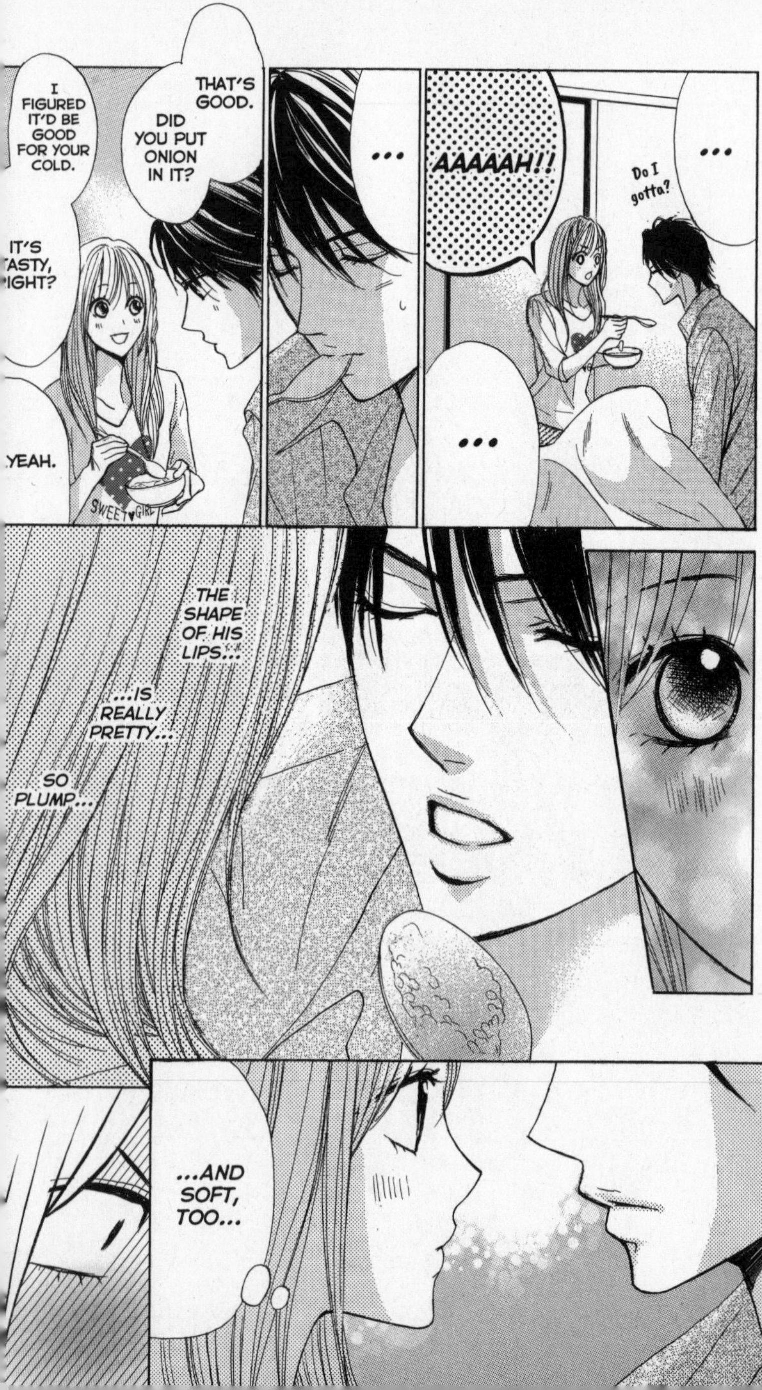
...
Do I gotta?
AAAAAH!!
...
...
THAT'S GOOD. DID YOU PUT ONION IN IT?
I FIGURED IT'D BE GOOD FOR YOUR COLD.
IT'S TASTY, RIGHT?
YEAH.
THE SHAPE OF HIS LIPS...
...IS REALLY PRETTY...
SO PLUMP...
...AND SOFT, TOO...

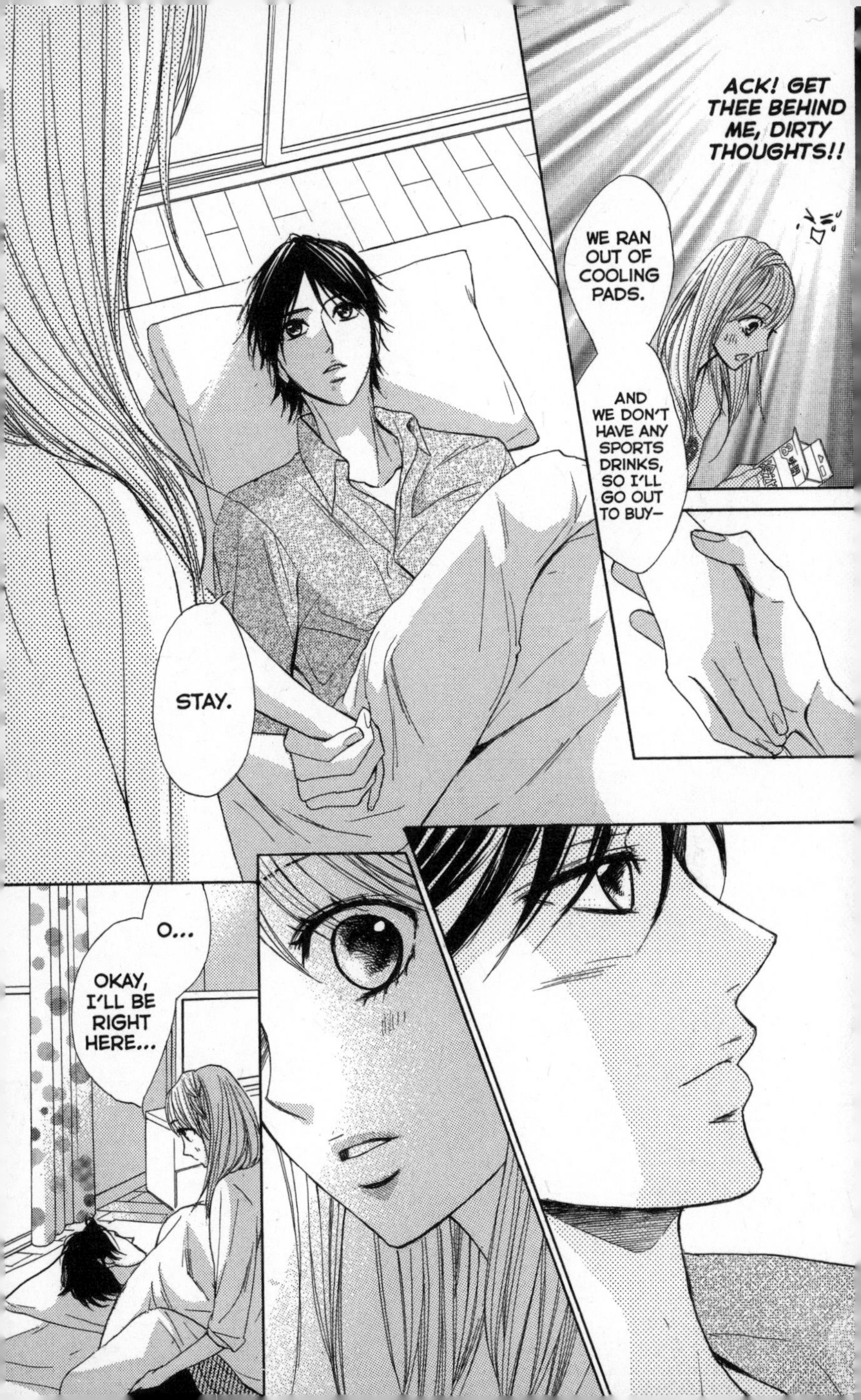
ACK! GET THEE BEHIND ME, DIRTY THOUGHTS!!
WE RAN OUT OF COOLING PADS.
AND WE DON'T HAVE ANY SPORTS DRINKS, SO I'LL GO OUT TO BUY–
STAY.
O...
OKAY, I'LL BE RIGHT HERE...

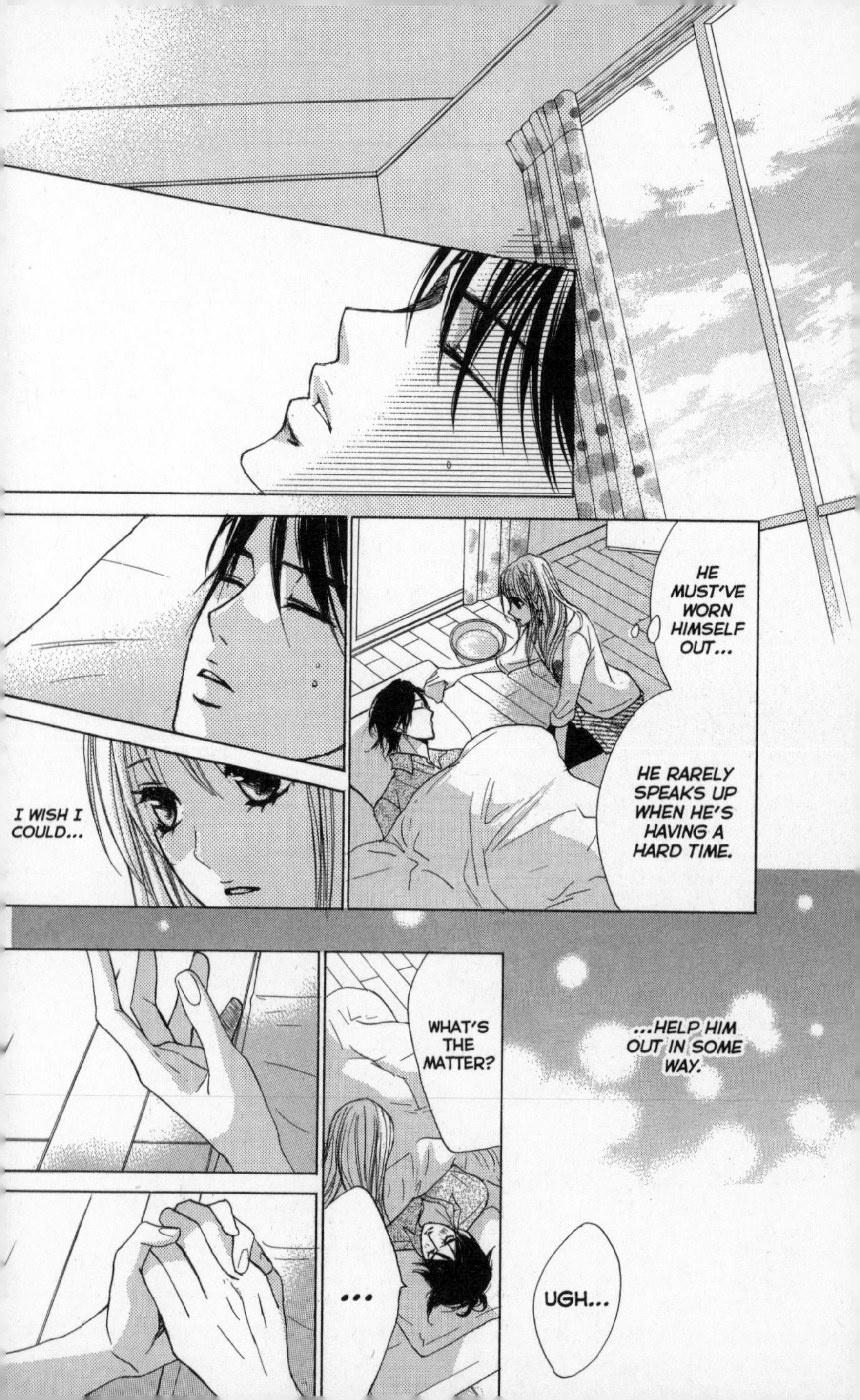
HE MUST'VE WORN HIMSELF OUT...
HE RARELY SPEAKS UP WHEN HE'S HAVING A HARD TIME.
I WISH I COULD...
...HELP HIM OUT IN SOME WAY.
WHAT'S THE MATTER?
UGH...
...

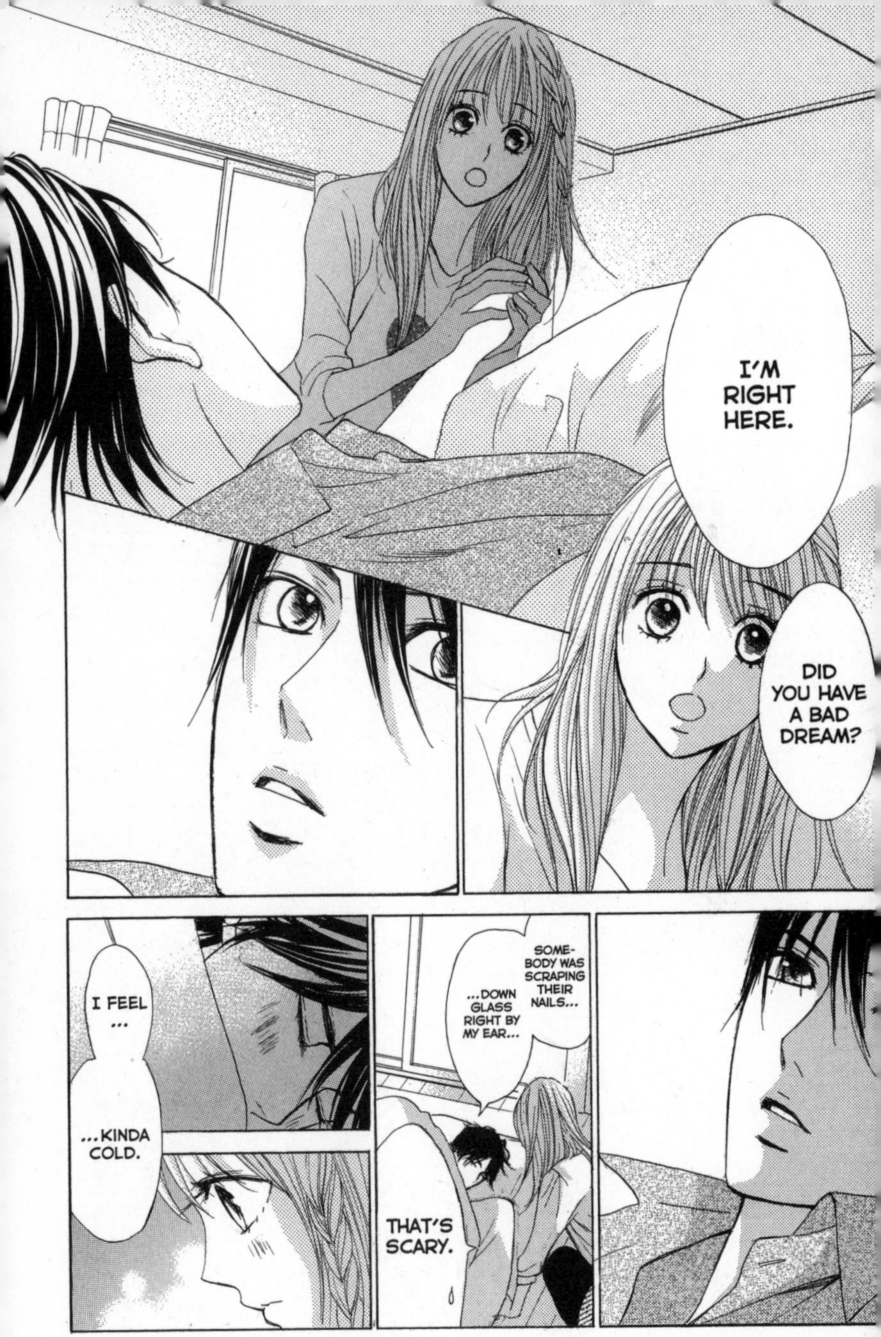
I'M RIGHT HERE.
DID YOU HAVE A BAD DREAM?
SOMEBODY WAS SCRAPING THEIR NAILS...
...DOWN GLASS RIGHT BY MY EAR...
THAT'S SCARY.
I FEEL ...
...KINDA COLD.

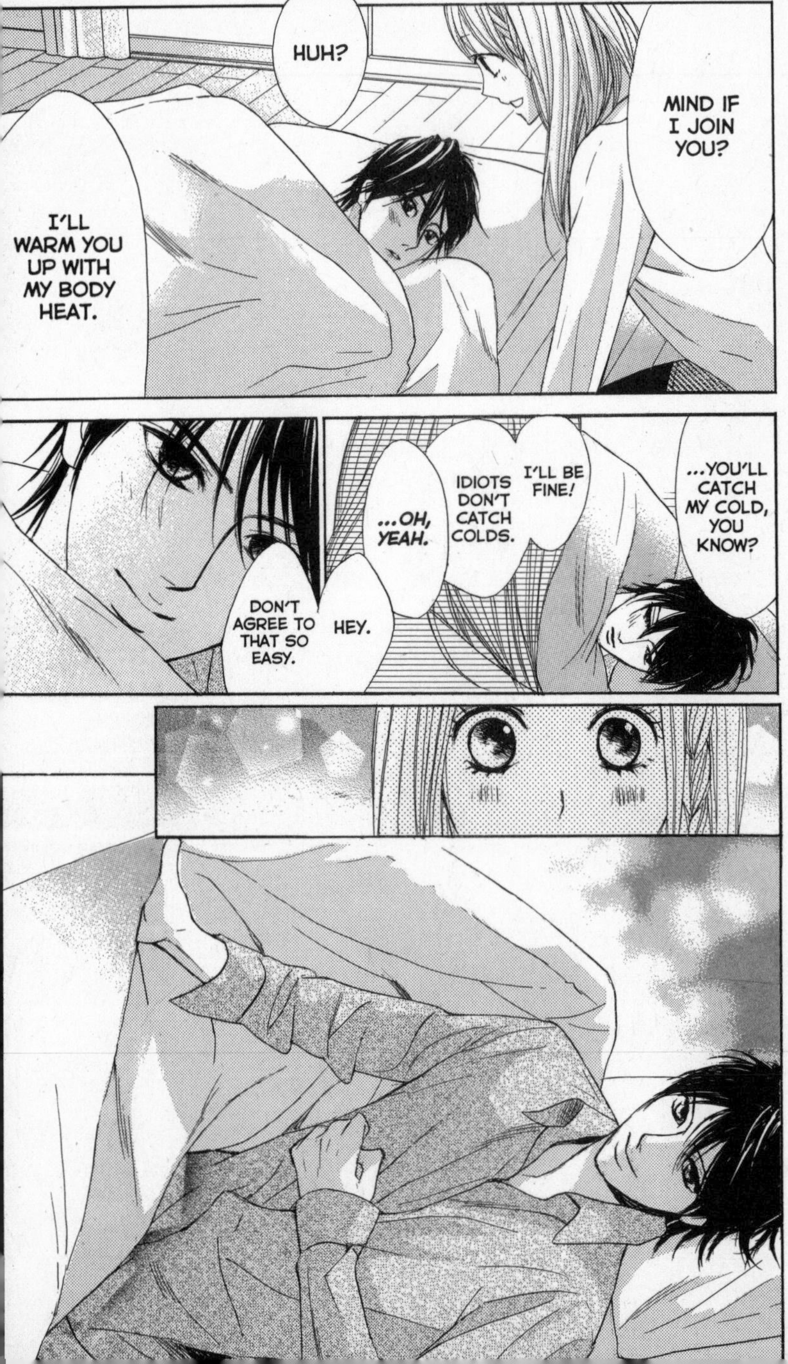

MIND IF I JOIN YOU?
HUH?
I'LL WARM YOU UP WITH MY BODY HEAT.
...YOU'LL CATCH MY COLD, YOU KNOW?
I'LL BE FINE!
IDIOTS DON'T CATCH COLDS.
...OH, YEAH.
HEY.
DON'T AGREE TO THAT SO EASY.

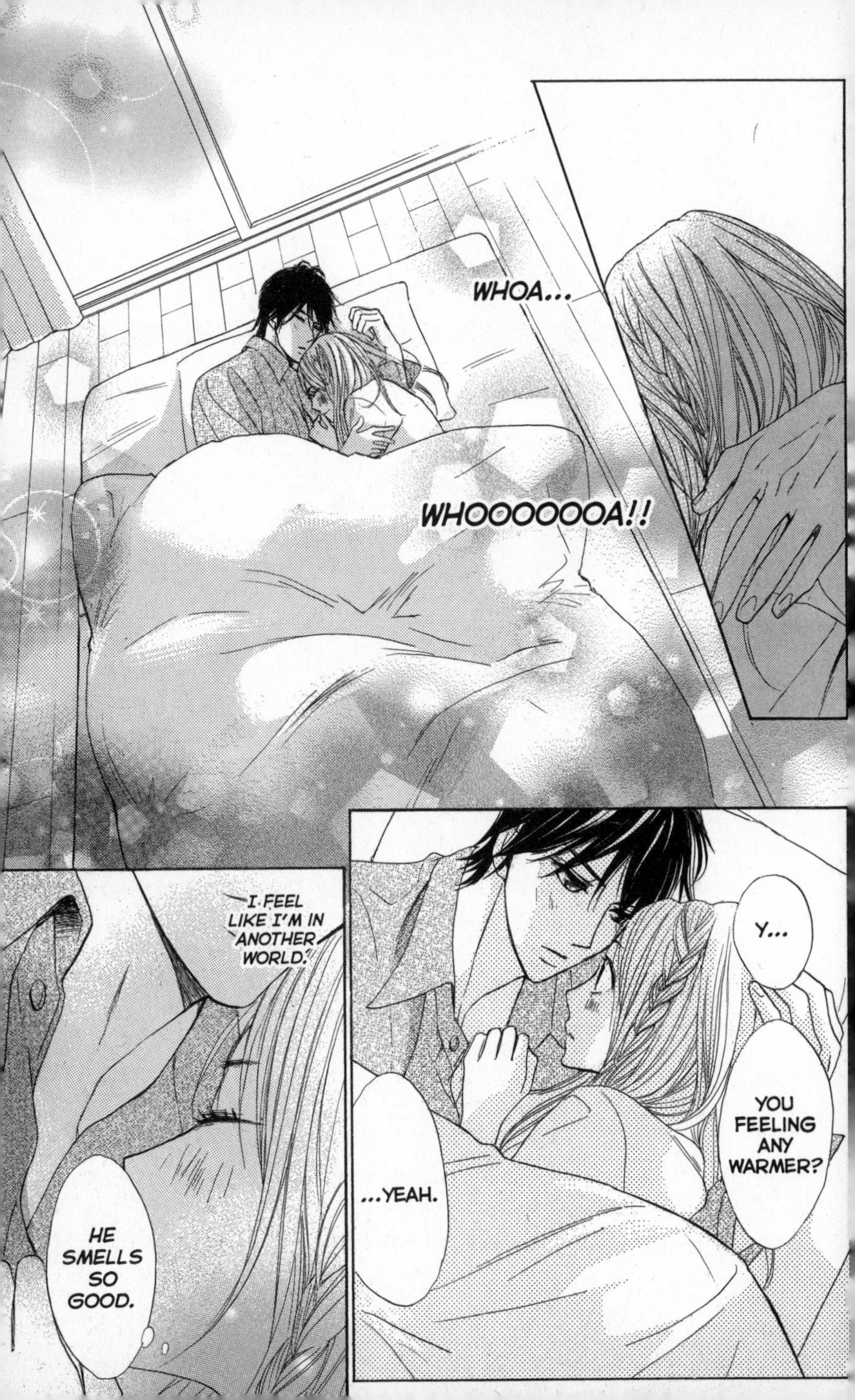
WHOA...
WHOOOOOOA!!
Y...
YOU FEELING ANY WARMER?
...YEAH.
I FEEL LIKE I'M IN ANOTHER WORLD.
HE SMELLS SO GOOD.

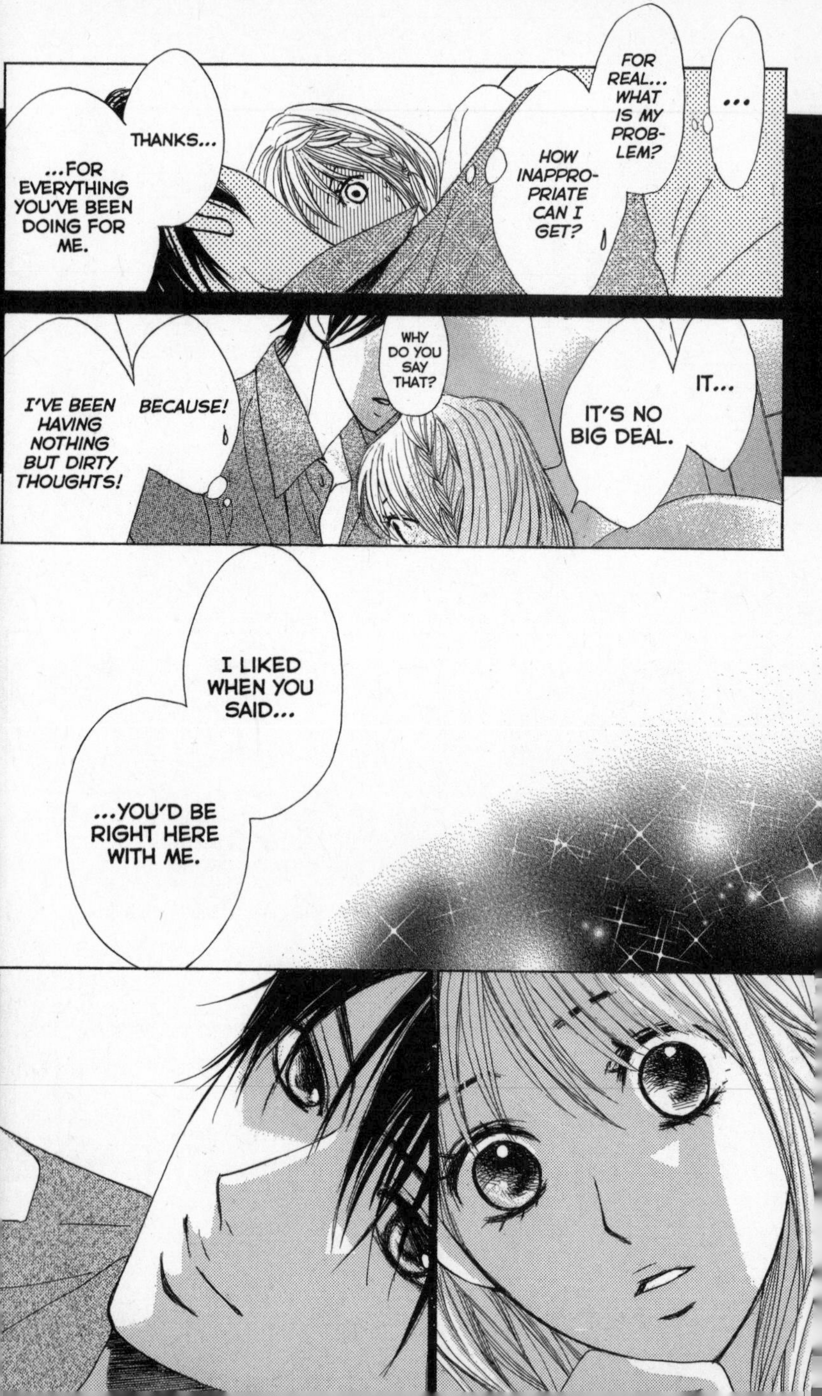
...
FOR REAL... WHAT IS MY PROB-LEM?
HOW INAPPRO-PRIATE CAN I GET?
THANKS...
...FOR EVERYTHING YOU'VE BEEN DOING FOR ME.
IT...
IT'S NO BIG DEAL.
WHY DO YOU SAY THAT?
BECAUSE!
I'VE BEEN HAVING NOTHING BUT DIRTY THOUGHTS!
I LIKED WHEN YOU SAID...
...YOU'D BE RIGHT HERE WITH ME.

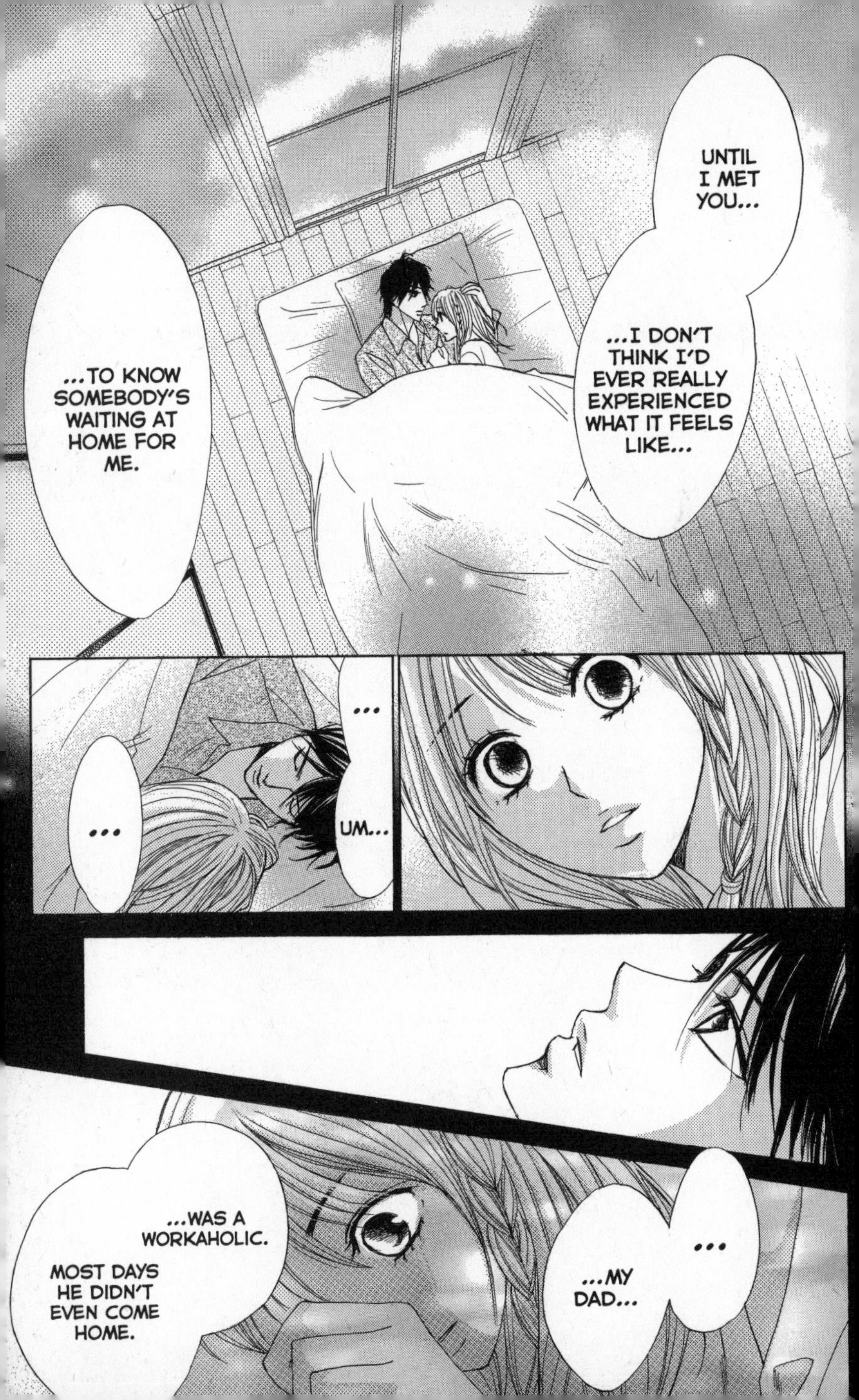
UNTIL I MET YOU...
...I DON'T THINK I'D EVER REALLY EXPERIENCED WHAT IT FEELS LIKE...
...TO KNOW SOMEBODY'S WAITING AT HOME FOR ME.
...
UM...
...
...
...MY DAD...
...WAS A WORKAHOLIC.
MOST DAYS HE DIDN'T EVEN COME HOME.

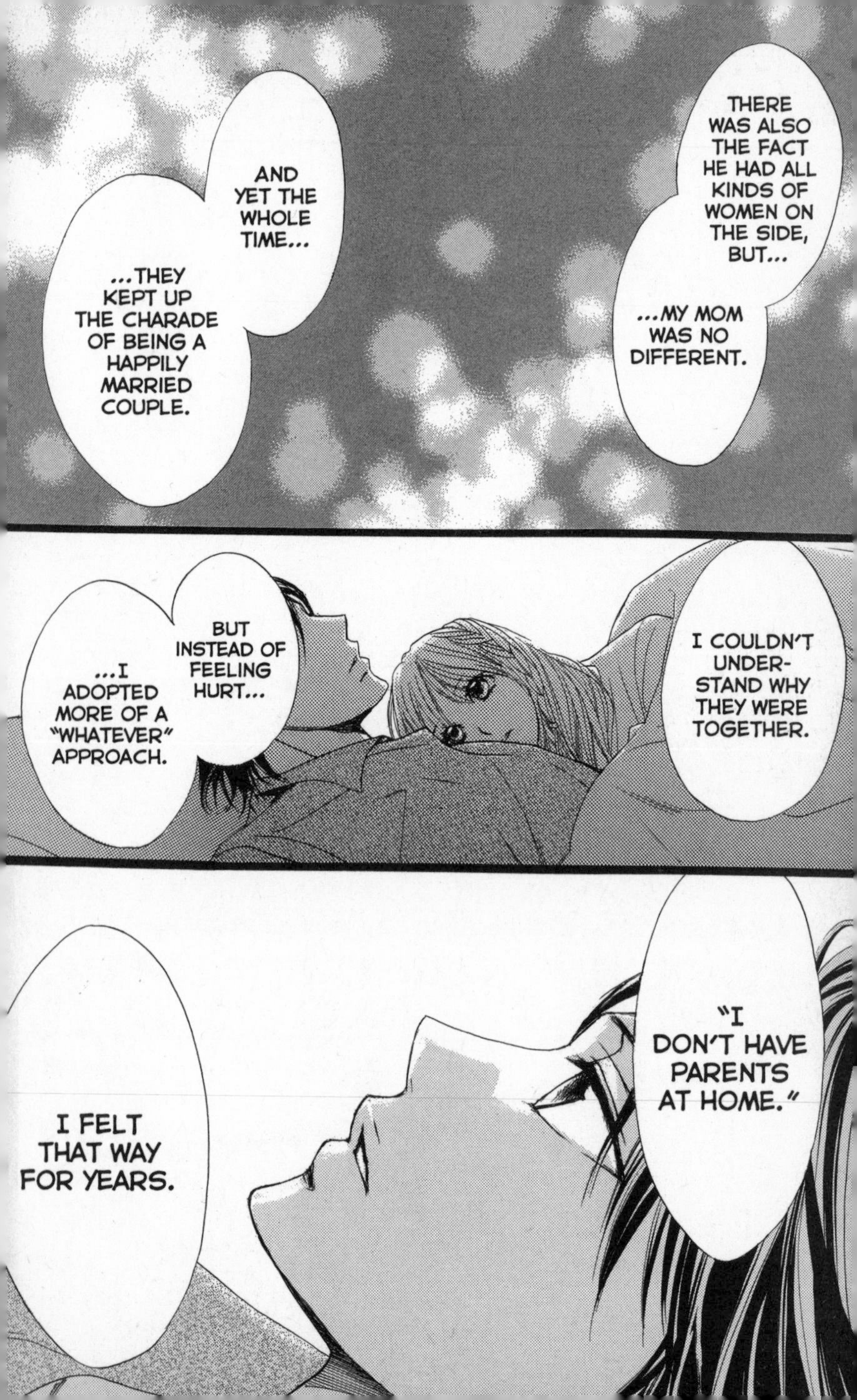
THERE WAS ALSO THE FACT HE HAD ALL KINDS OF WOMEN ON THE SIDE, BUT...
...MY MOM WAS NO DIFFERENT.
AND YET THE WHOLE TIME...
...THEY KEPT UP THE CHARADE OF BEING A HAPPILY MARRIED COUPLE.
I COULDN'T UNDER-STAND WHY THEY WERE TOGETHER.
BUT INSTEAD OF FEELING HURT...
...I ADOPTED MORE OF A "WHATEVER" APPROACH.
"I DON'T HAVE PARENTS AT HOME."
I FELT THAT WAY FOR YEARS.

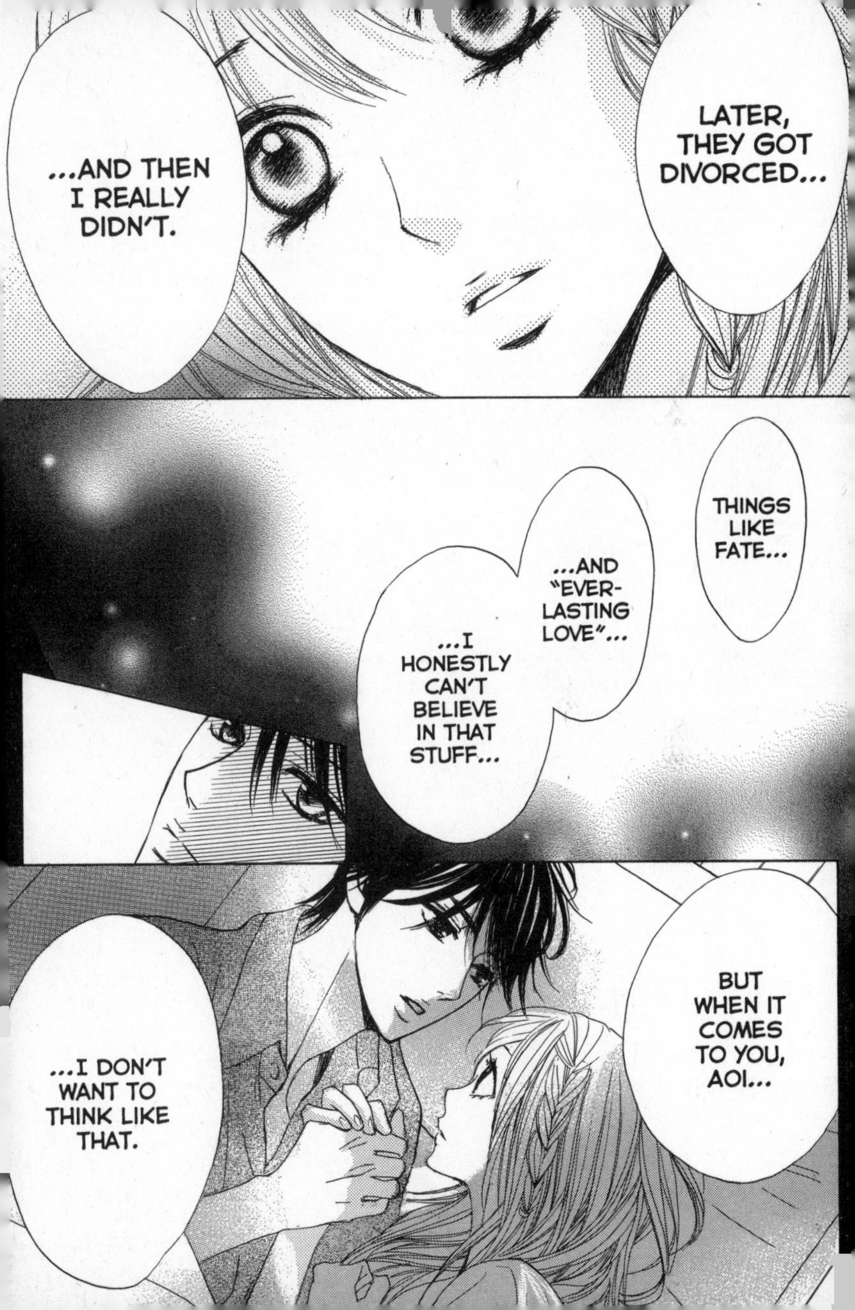
LATER, THEY GOT DIVORCED...
...AND THEN I REALLY DIDN'T.
THINGS LIKE FATE...
...AND "EVER-LASTING LOVE"...
...I HONESTLY CAN'T BELIEVE IN THAT STUFF...
BUT WHEN IT COMES TO YOU, AOI...
...I DON'T WANT TO THINK LIKE THAT.

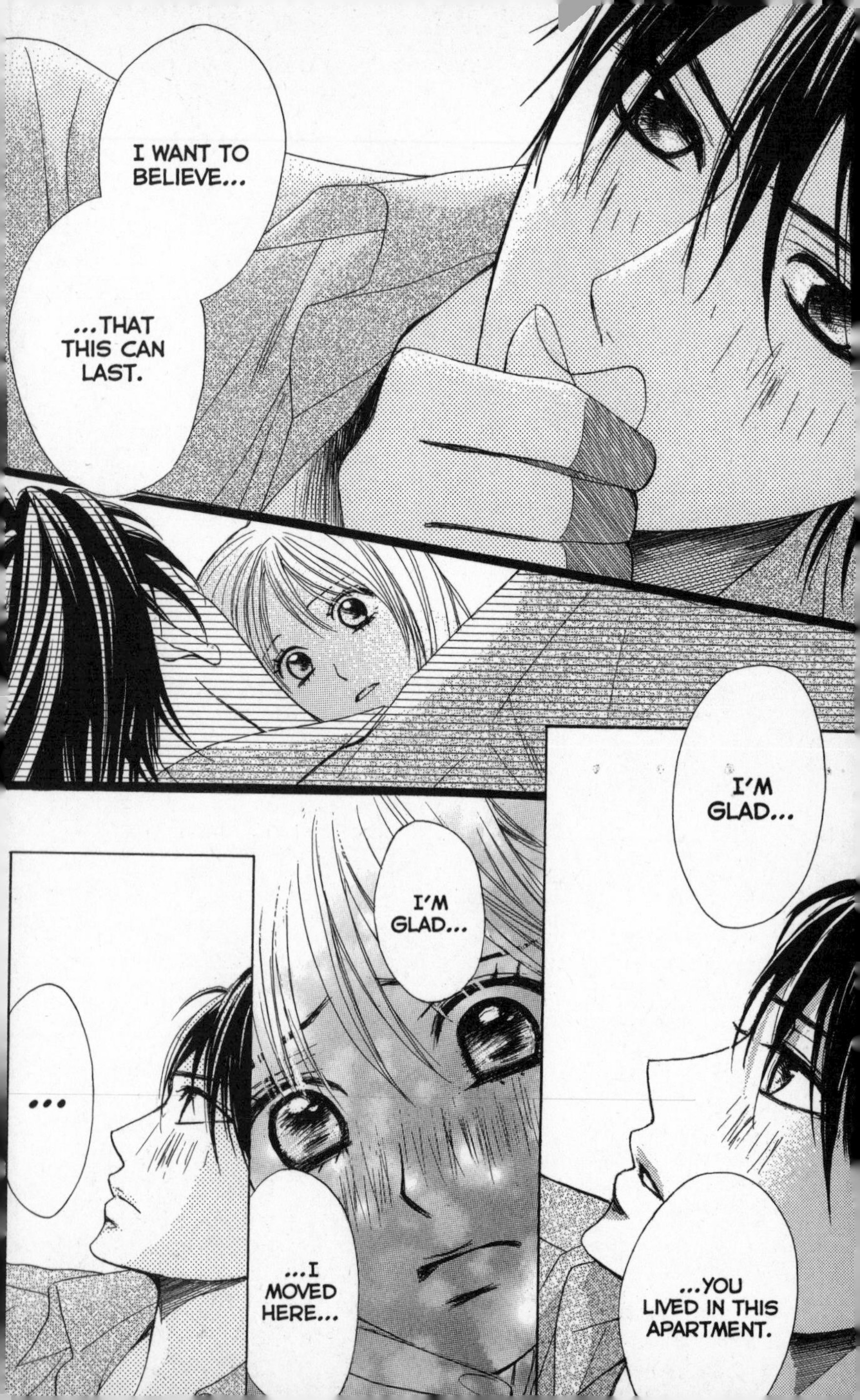
I WANT TO BELIEVE...
...THAT THIS CAN LAST.
I'M GLAD...
...YOU LIVED IN THIS APARTMENT.
I'M GLAD...
...I MOVED HERE...
...

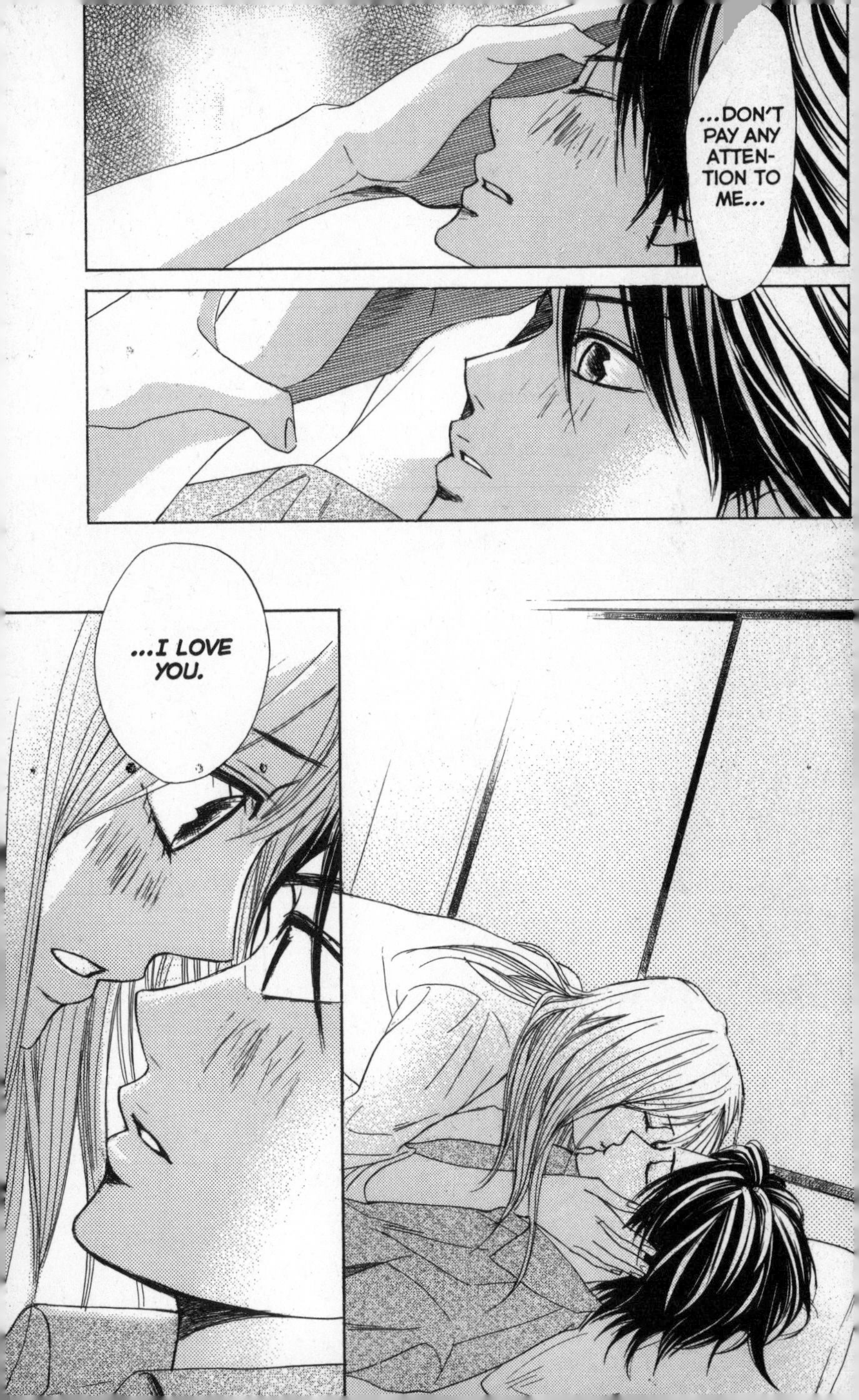
...DON'T PAY ANY ATTENTION TO ME...
...I LOVE YOU.

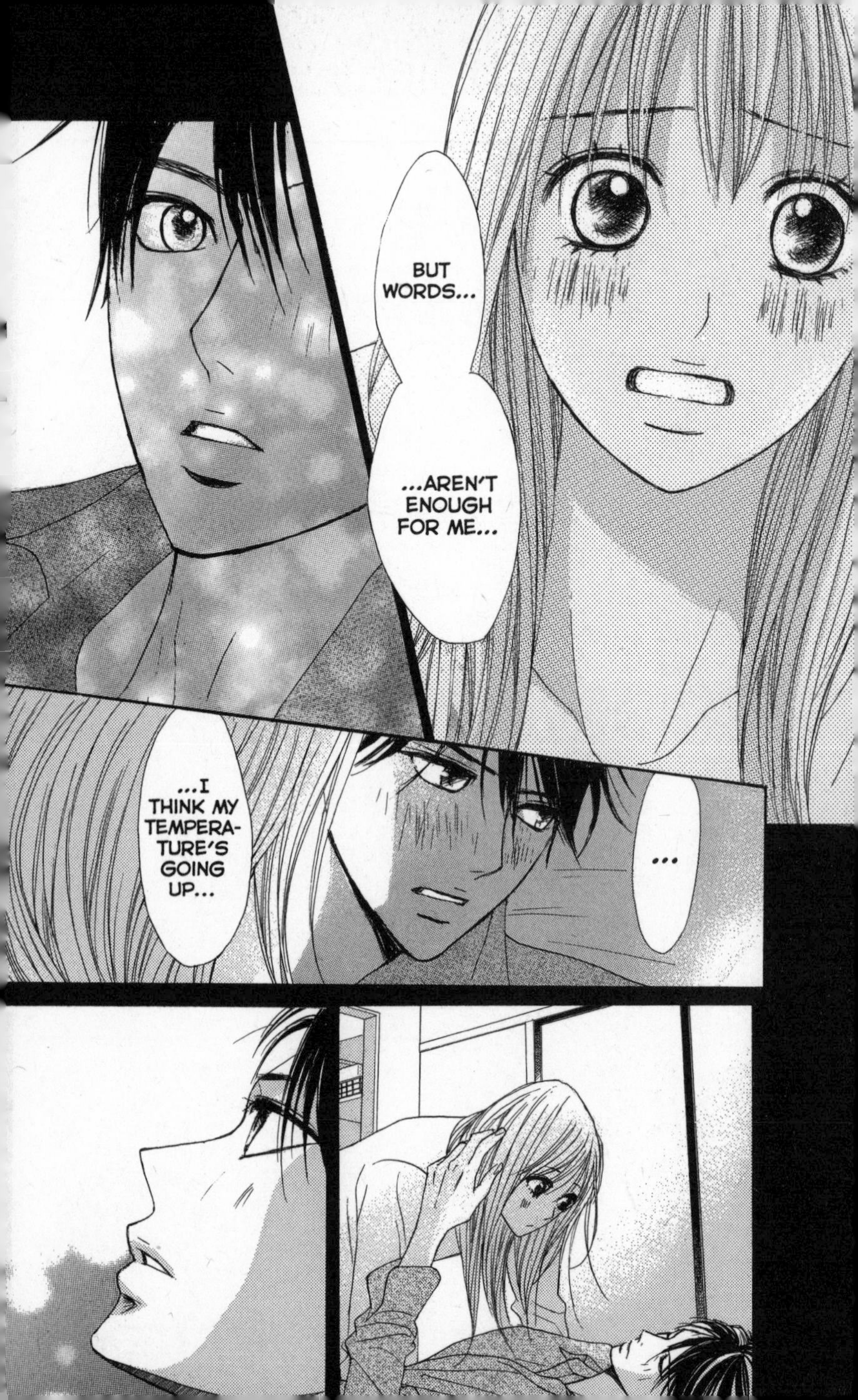
BUT WORDS...
...AREN'T ENOUGH FOR ME...
...
...I THINK MY TEMPERA-TURE'S GOING UP...

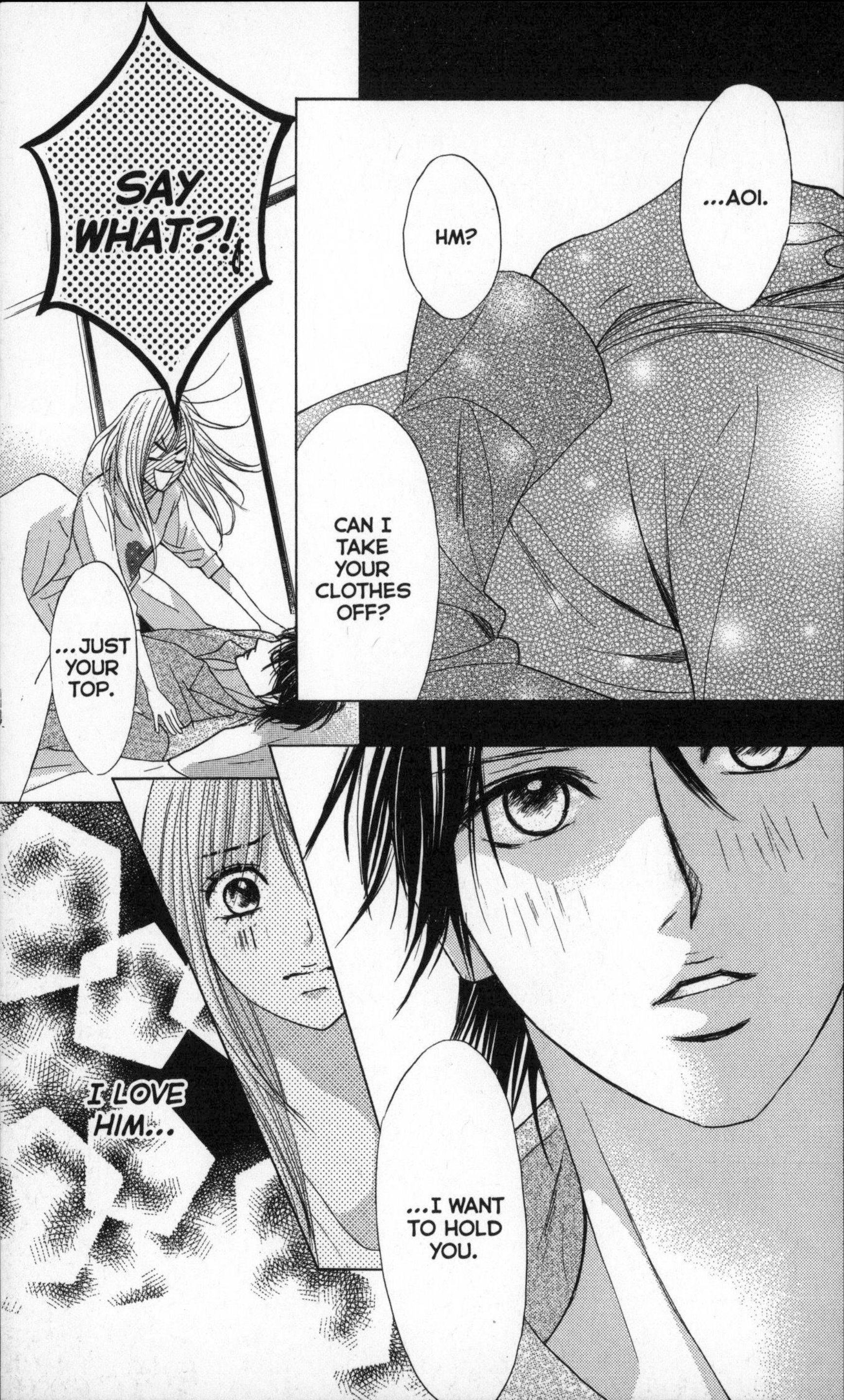
...AOI.
HM?
CAN I TAKE YOUR CLOTHES OFF?
SAY WHAT?!
...JUST YOUR TOP.
...I WANT TO HOLD YOU.
I LOVE HIM...

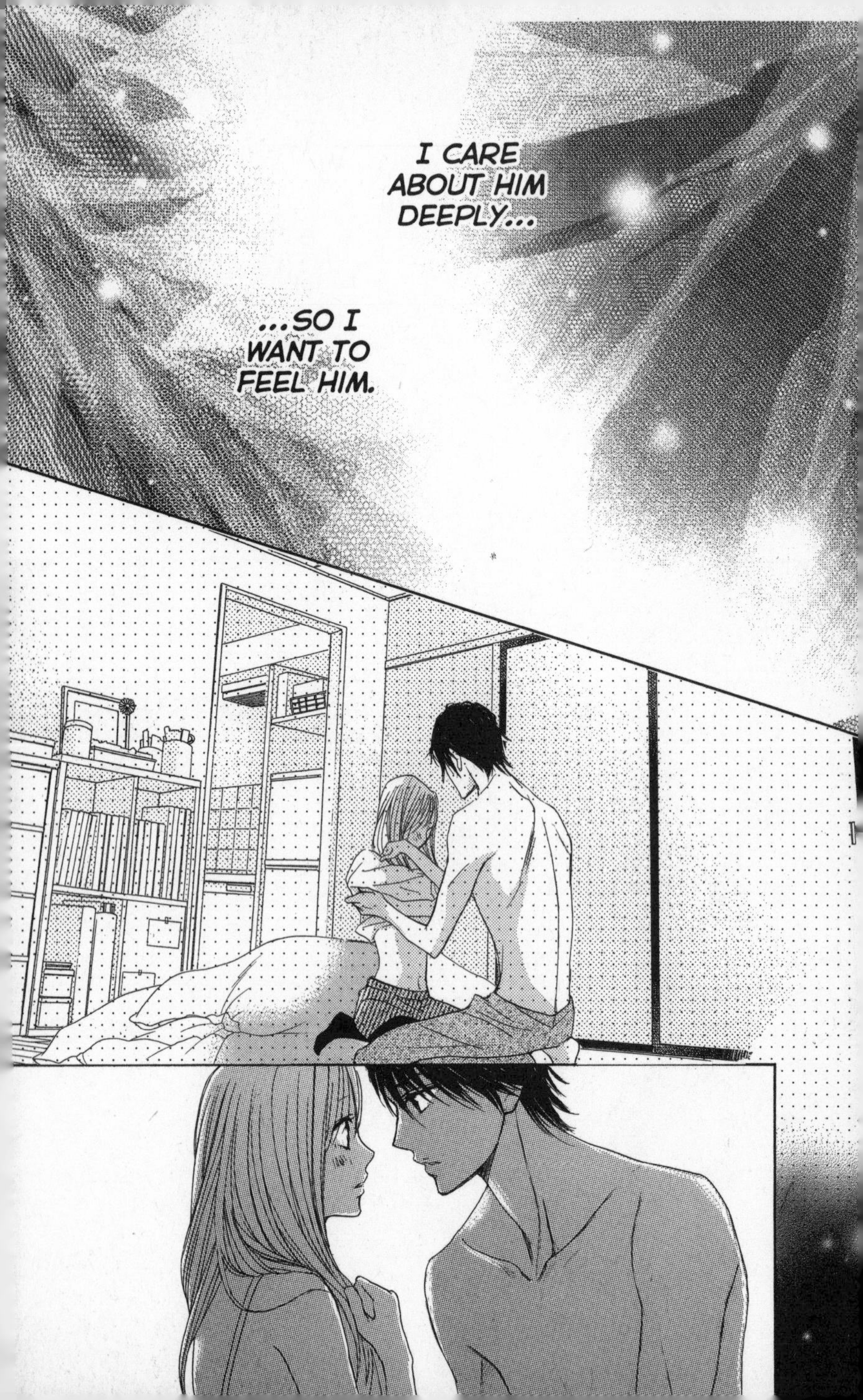
I CARE ABOUT HIM DEEPLY...
...SO I WANT TO FEEL HIM.

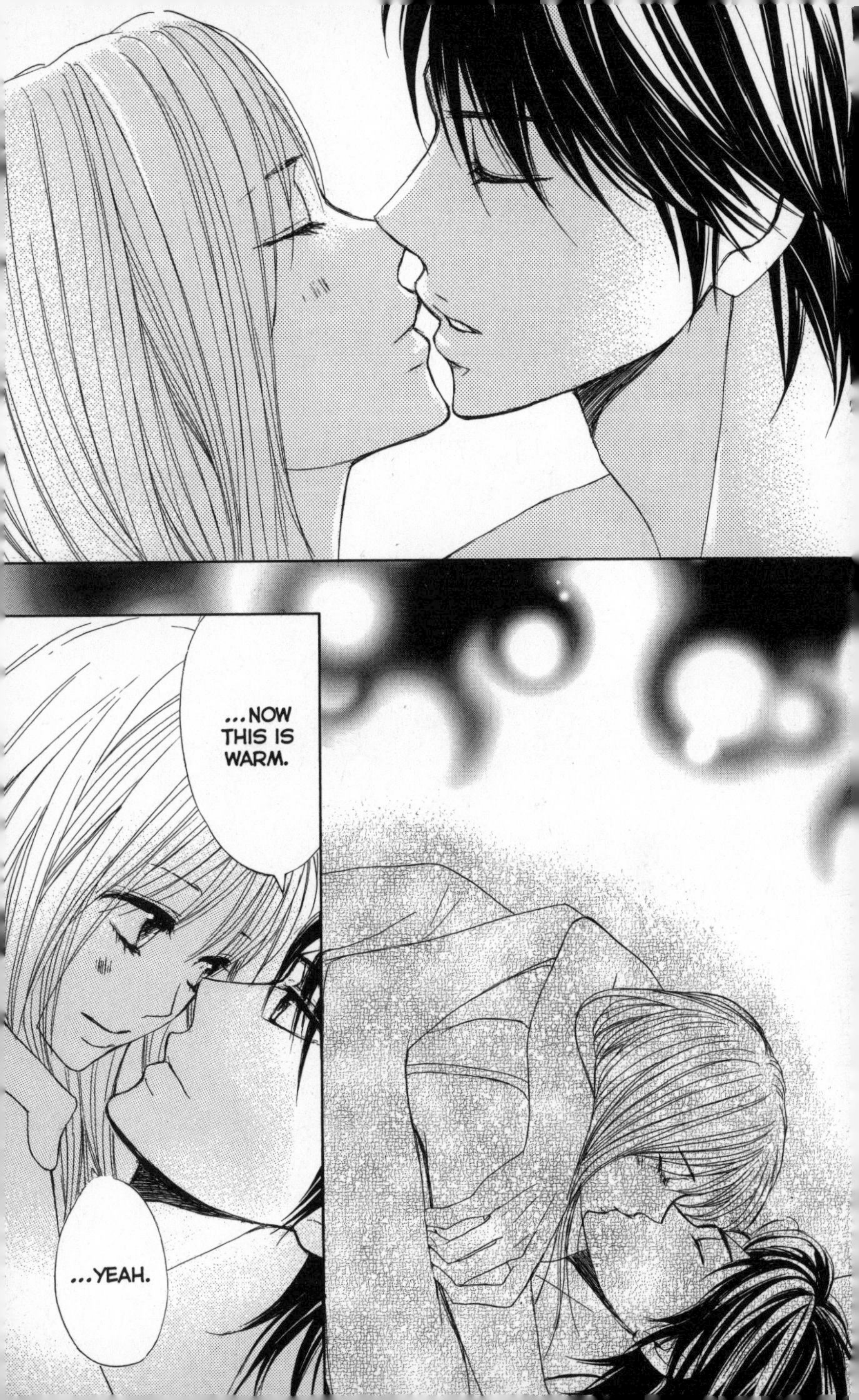
...NOW THIS IS WARM.
...YEAH.

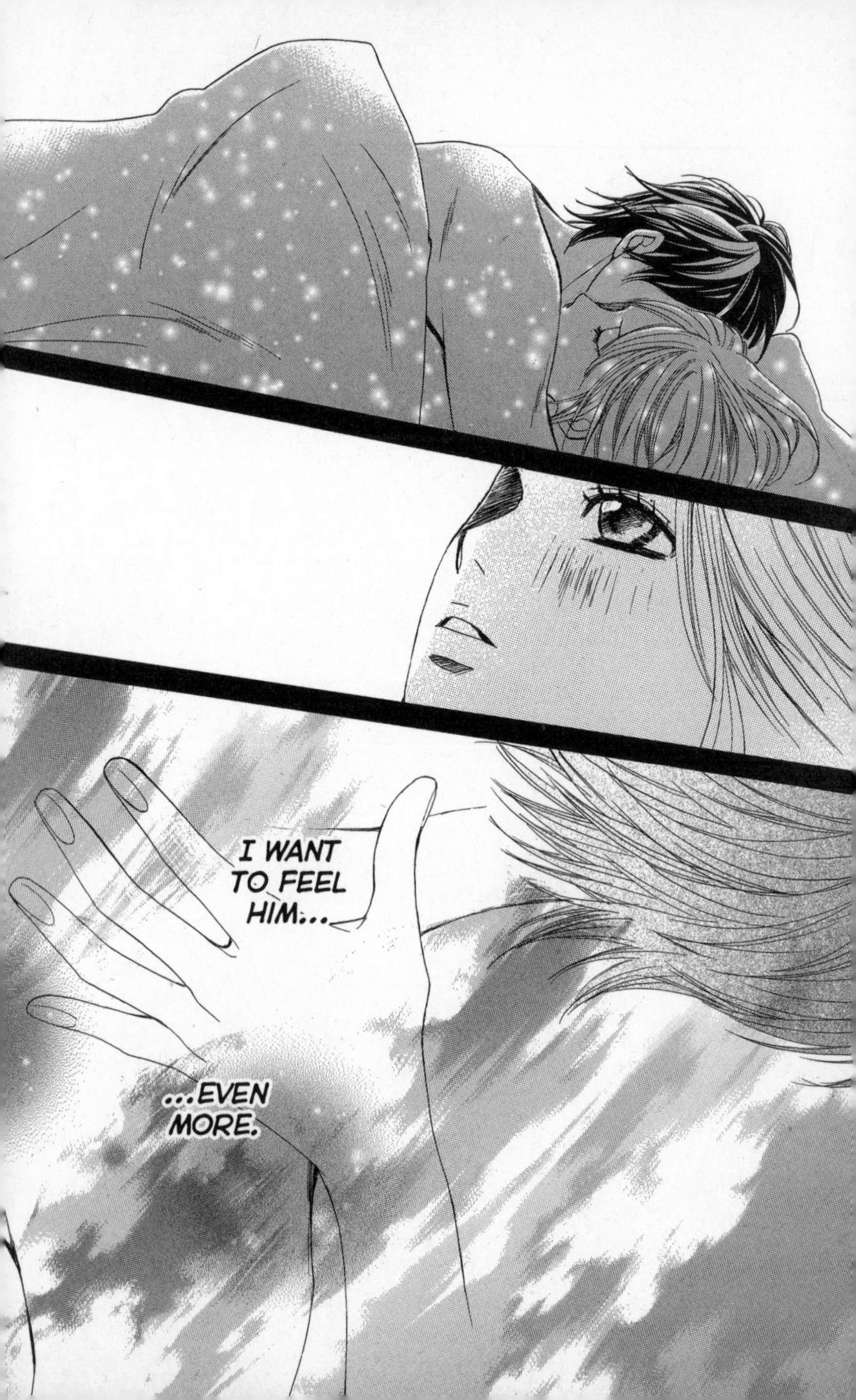
I WANT TO FEEL HIM...
...EVEN MORE.

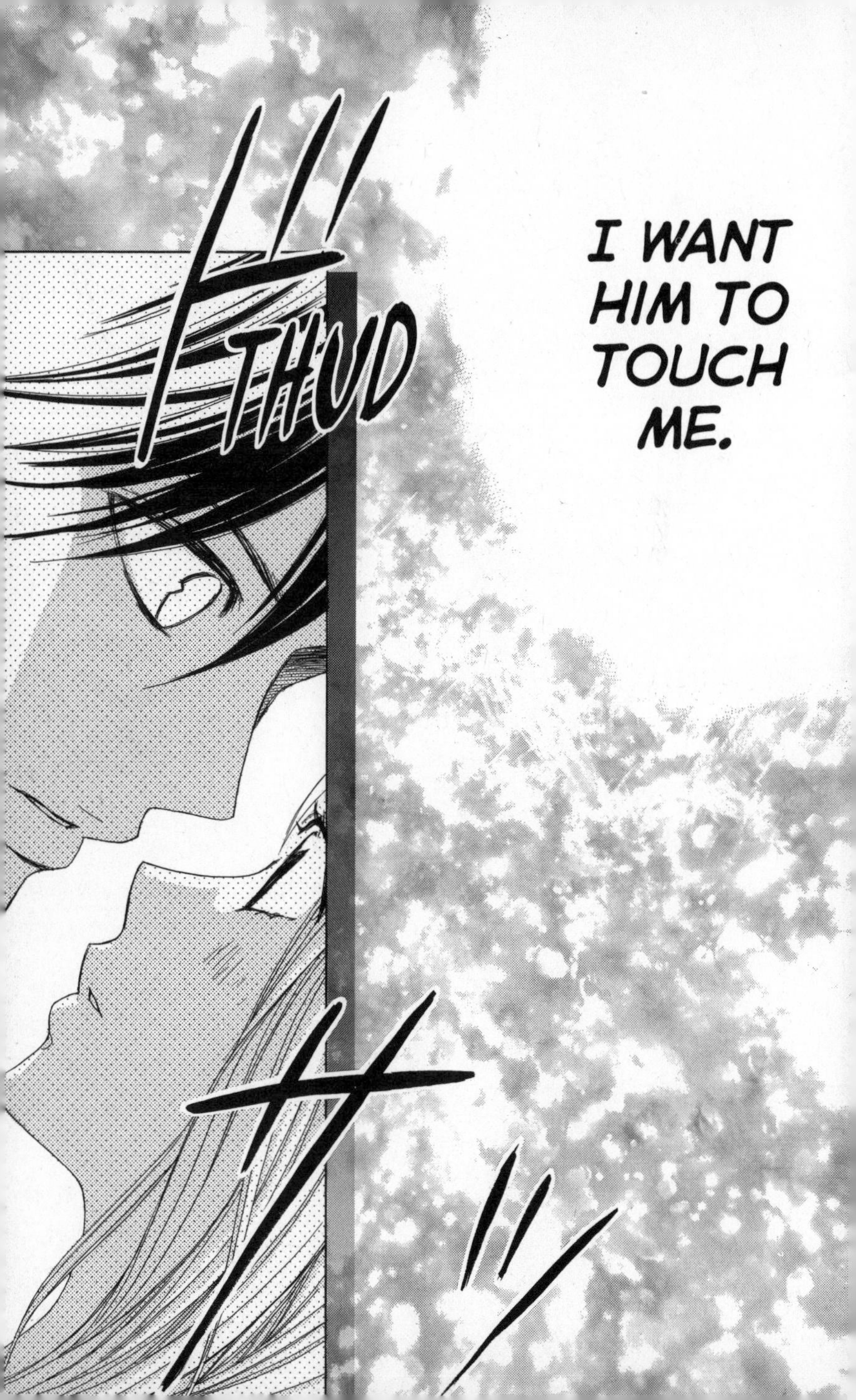
I WANT HIM TO TOUCH ME.
THUD

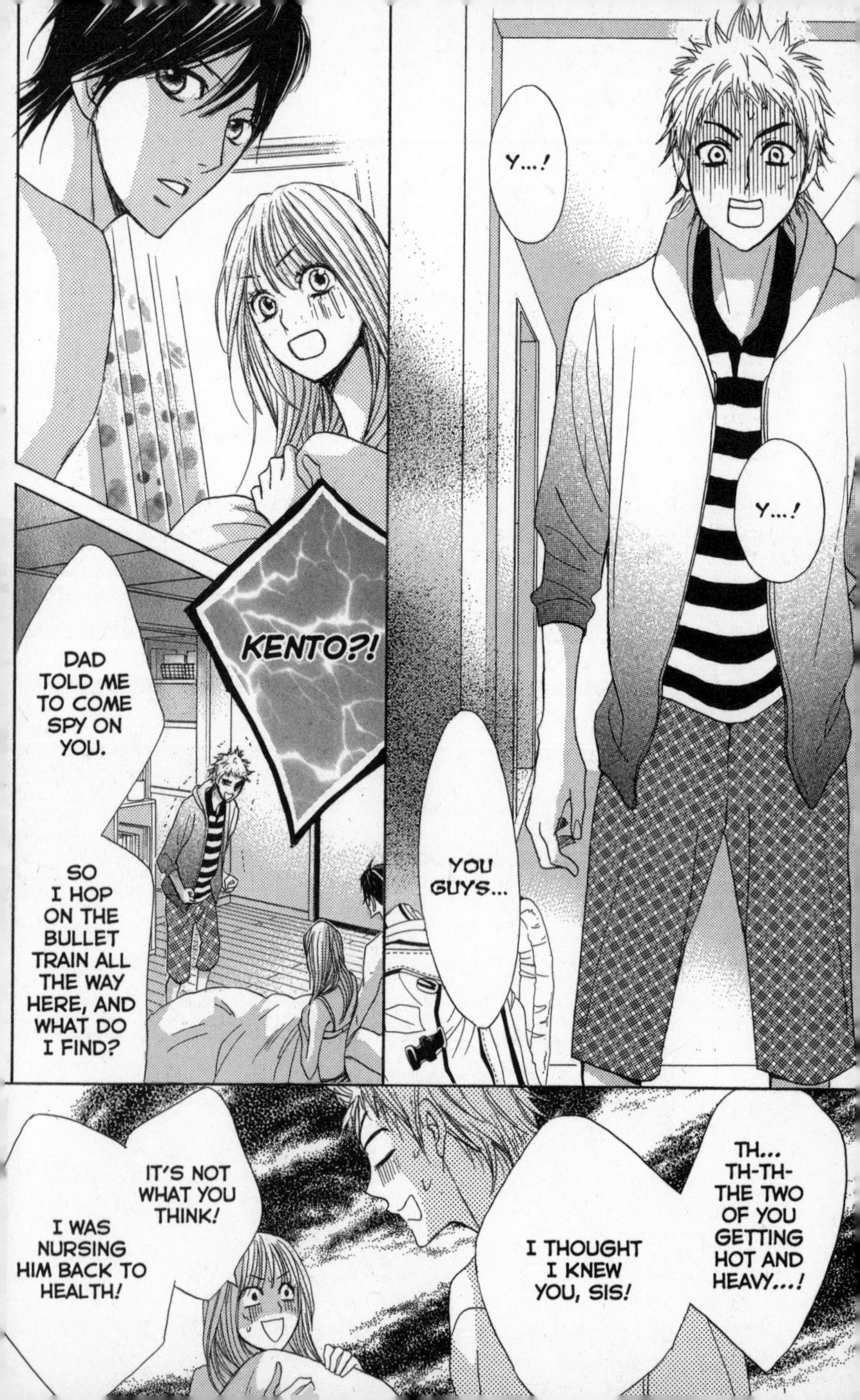
Y...!
Y...!
YOU GUYS...
KENTO?!
DAD TOLD ME TO COME SPY ON YOU.
SO I HOP ON THE BULLET TRAIN ALL THE WAY HERE, AND WHAT DO I FIND?
TH... TH-TH-THE TWO OF YOU GETTING HOT AND HEAVY...!
I THOUGHT I KNEW YOU, SIS!
IT'S NOT WHAT YOU THINK!
I WAS NURSING HIM BACK TO HEALTH!

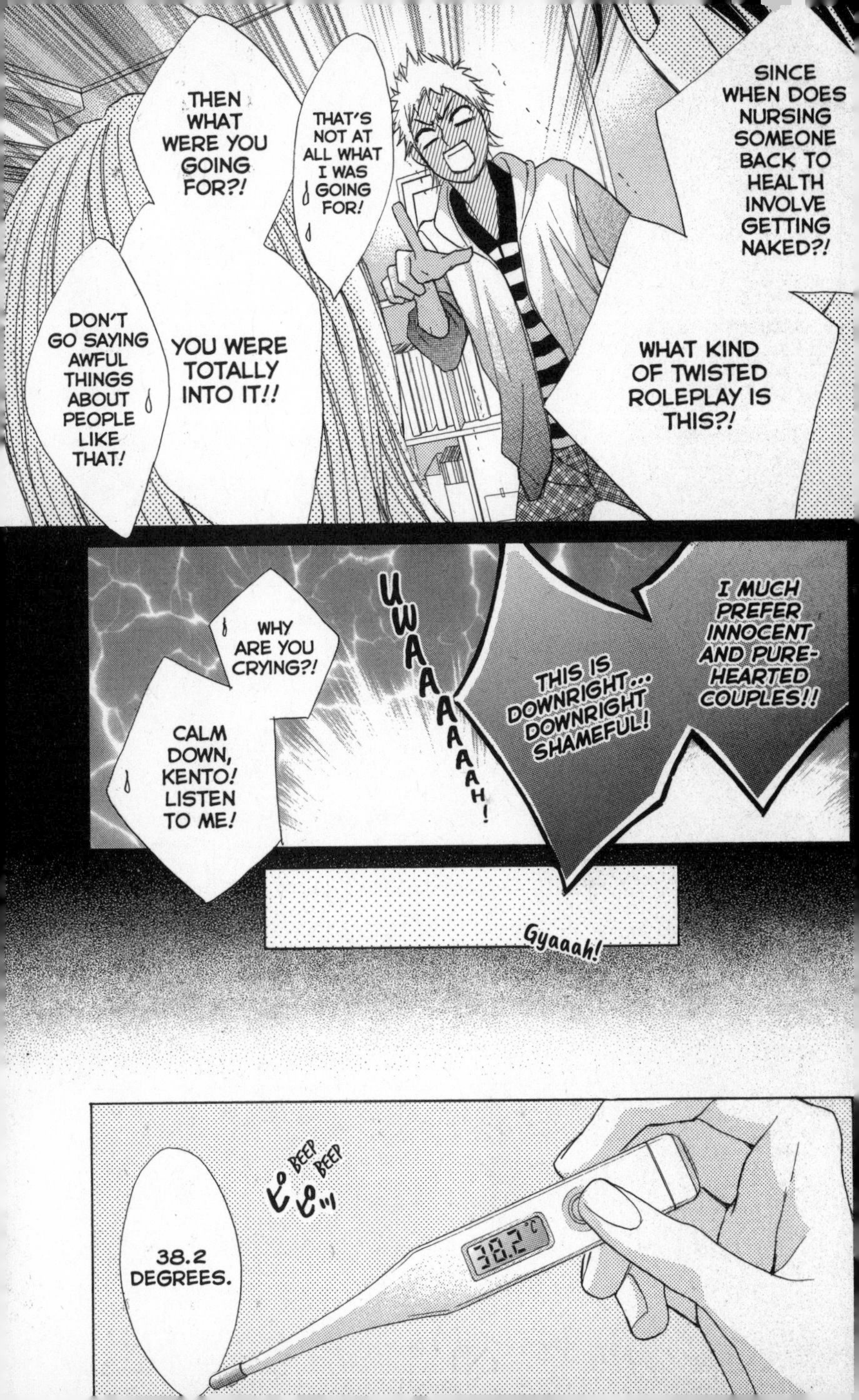
SINCE WHEN DOES NURSING SOMEONE BACK TO HEALTH INVOLVE GETTING NAKED?!
WHAT KIND OF TWISTED ROLEPLAY IS THIS?!
THAT'S NOT AT ALL WHAT I WAS GOING FOR!
THEN WHAT WERE YOU GOING FOR?!
YOU WERE TOTALLY INTO IT!!
DON'T GO SAYING AWFUL THINGS ABOUT PEOPLE LIKE THAT!
I MUCH PREFER INNOCENT AND PURE-HEARTED COUPLES!!
THIS IS DOWNRIGHT... DOWNRIGHT SHAMEFUL!
UWAAAAAAAH!
WHY ARE YOU CRYING?!
CALM DOWN, KENTO! LISTEN TO ME!
Gyaaah!
BEEP BEEP
38.2°C
38.2 DEGREES.

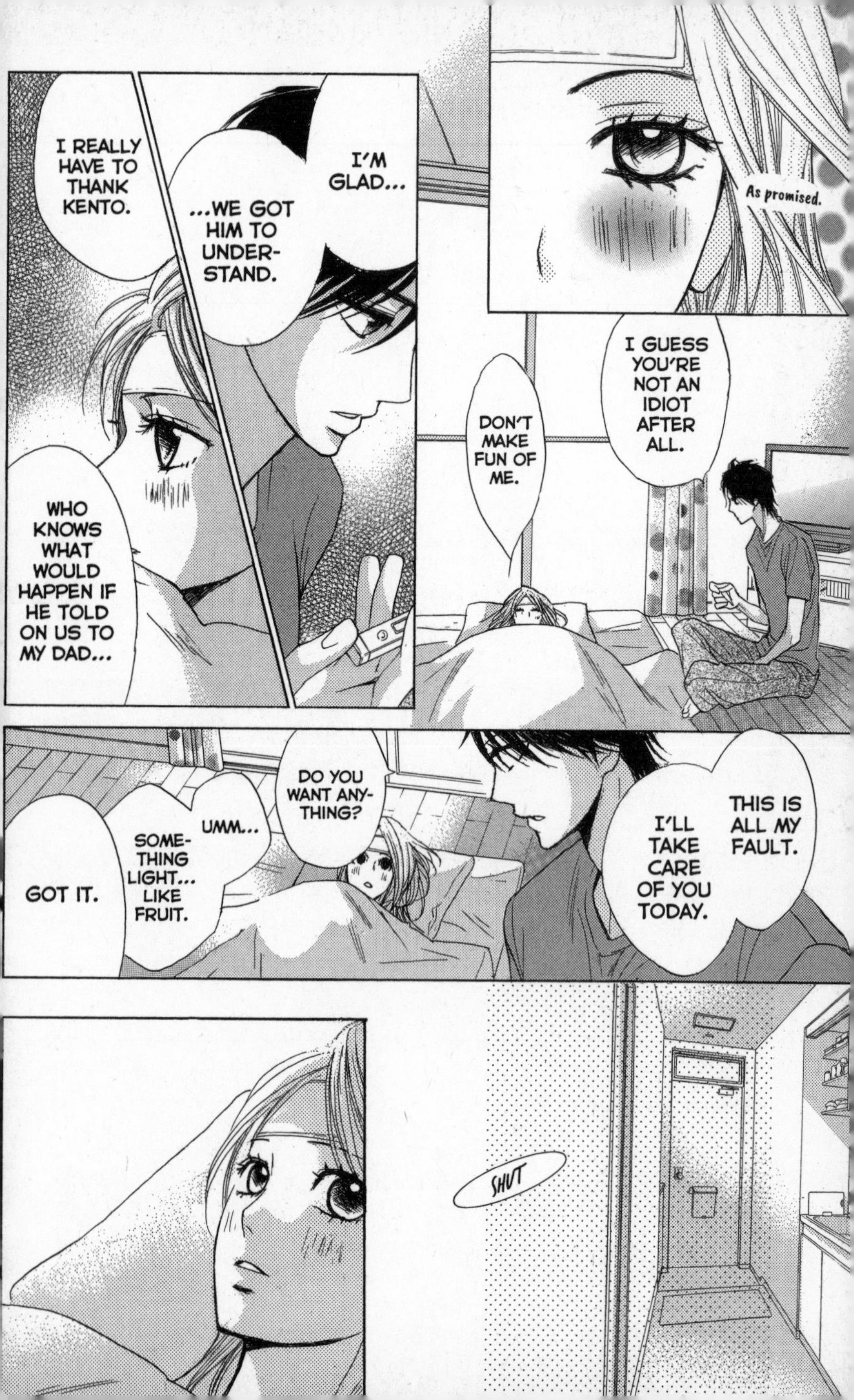
As promised.
I GUESS YOU'RE NOT AN IDIOT AFTER ALL.
DON'T MAKE FUN OF ME.
I'M GLAD...
...WE GOT HIM TO UNDER-STAND.
I REALLY HAVE TO THANK KENTO.
WHO KNOWS WHAT WOULD HAPPEN IF HE TOLD ON US TO MY DAD...
THIS IS ALL MY FAULT.
I'LL TAKE CARE OF YOU TODAY.
DO YOU WANT ANY-THING?
UMM...
SOME-THING LIGHT... LIKE FRUIT.
GOT IT.
SHUT

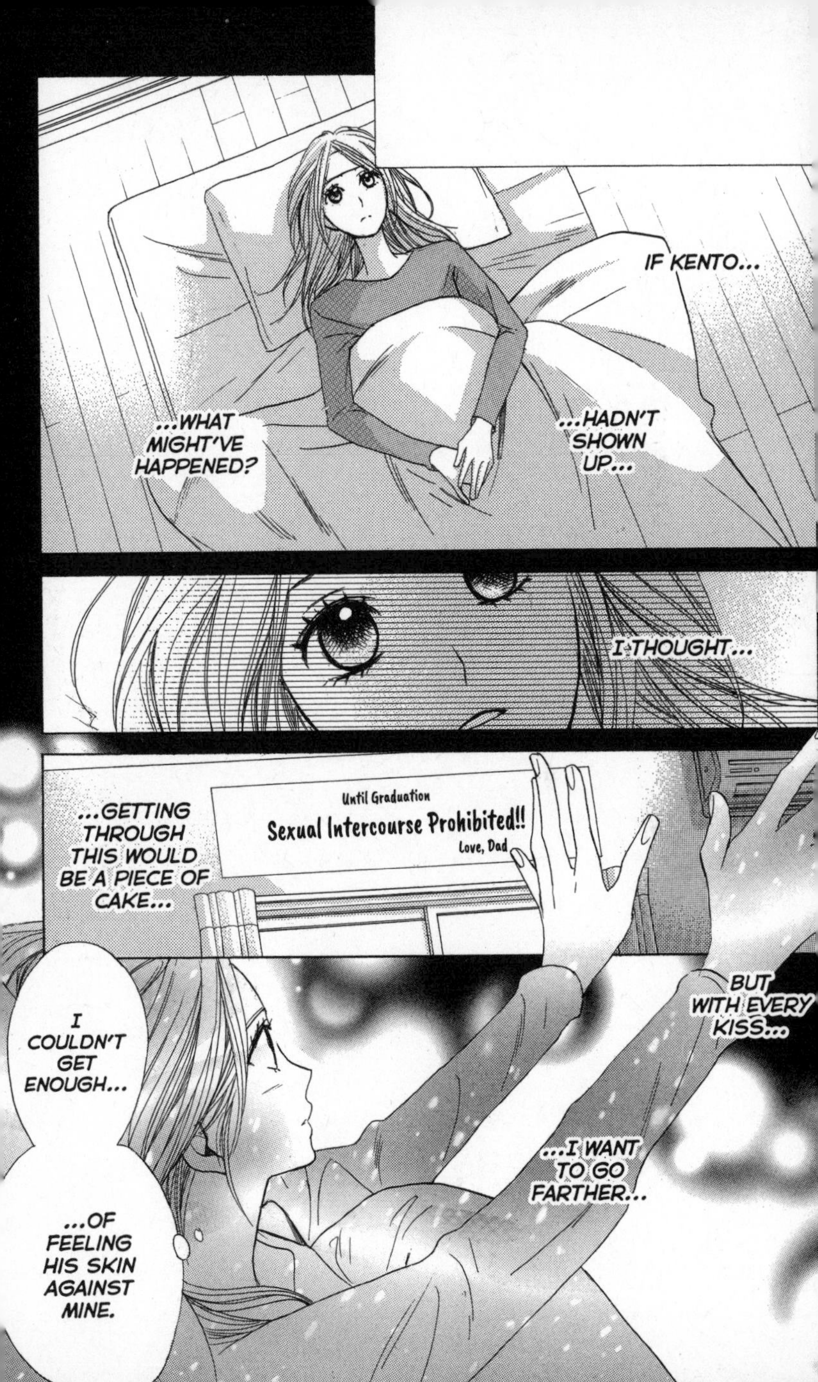
IF KENTO...
...HADN'T SHOWN UP...
...WHAT MIGHT'VE HAPPENED?
I THOUGHT...
Until Graduation
Sexual Intercourse Prohibited!!
Love, Dad
...GETTING THROUGH THIS WOULD BE A PIECE OF CAKE...
BUT WITH EVERY KISS...
...I WANT TO GO FARTHER...
I COULDN'T GET ENOUGH...
...OF FEELING HIS SKIN AGAINST MINE.

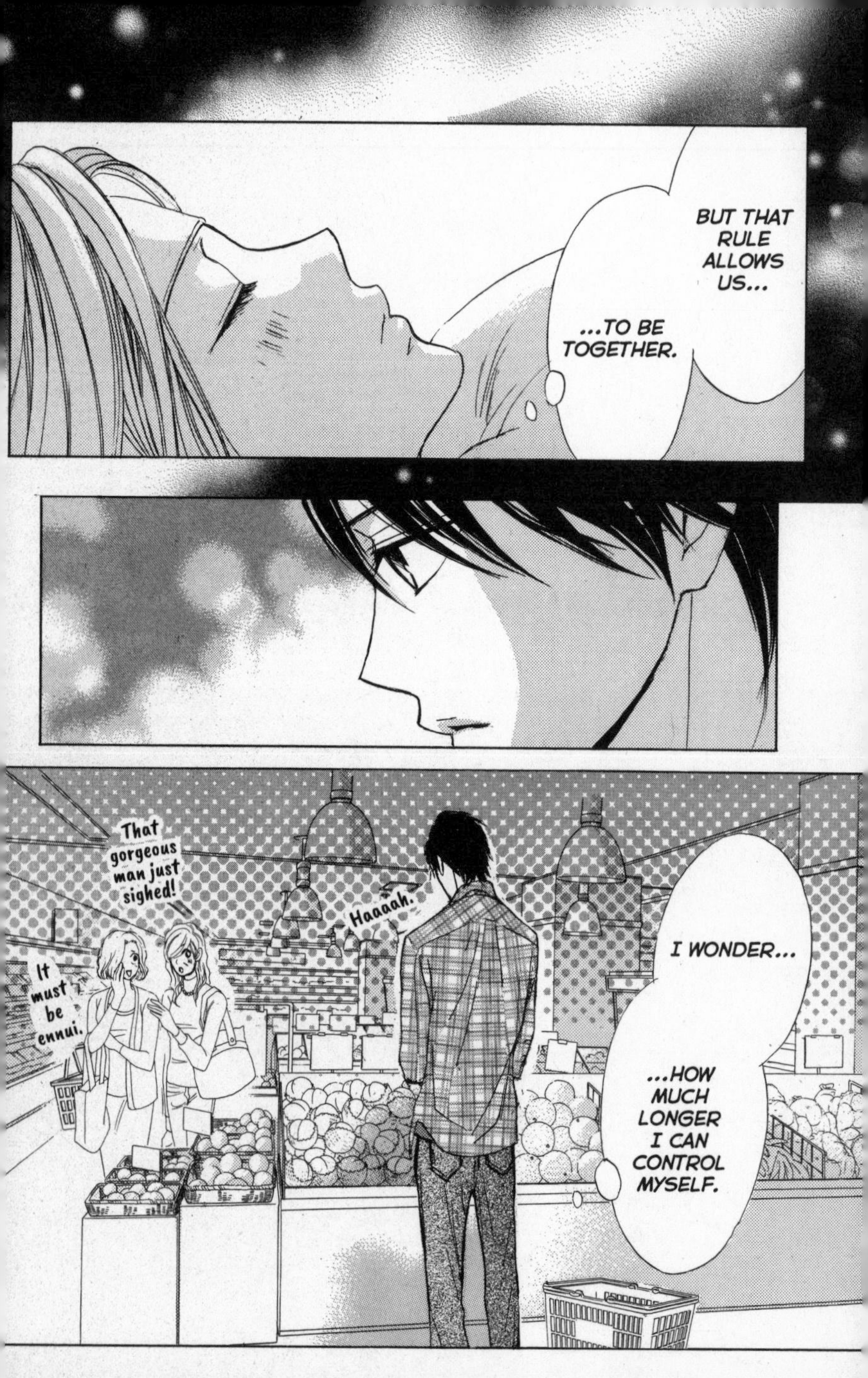
BUT THAT RULE ALLOWS US...
...TO BE TOGETHER.
I WONDER...
...HOW MUCH LONGER I CAN CONTROL MYSELF.
Haaaah.
That gorgeous man just sighed!
It must be ennui.

L♥DK

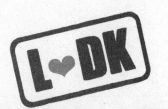

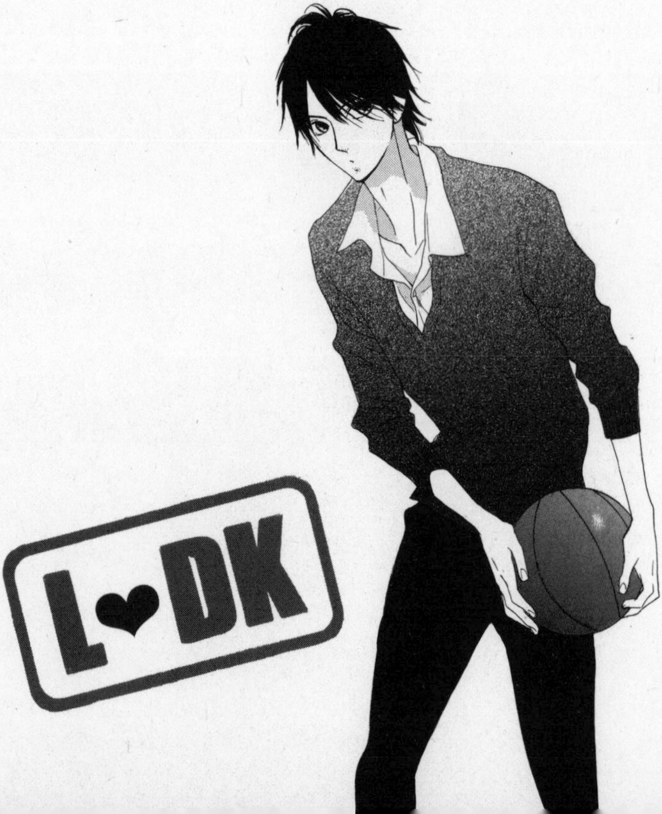
L♥DK

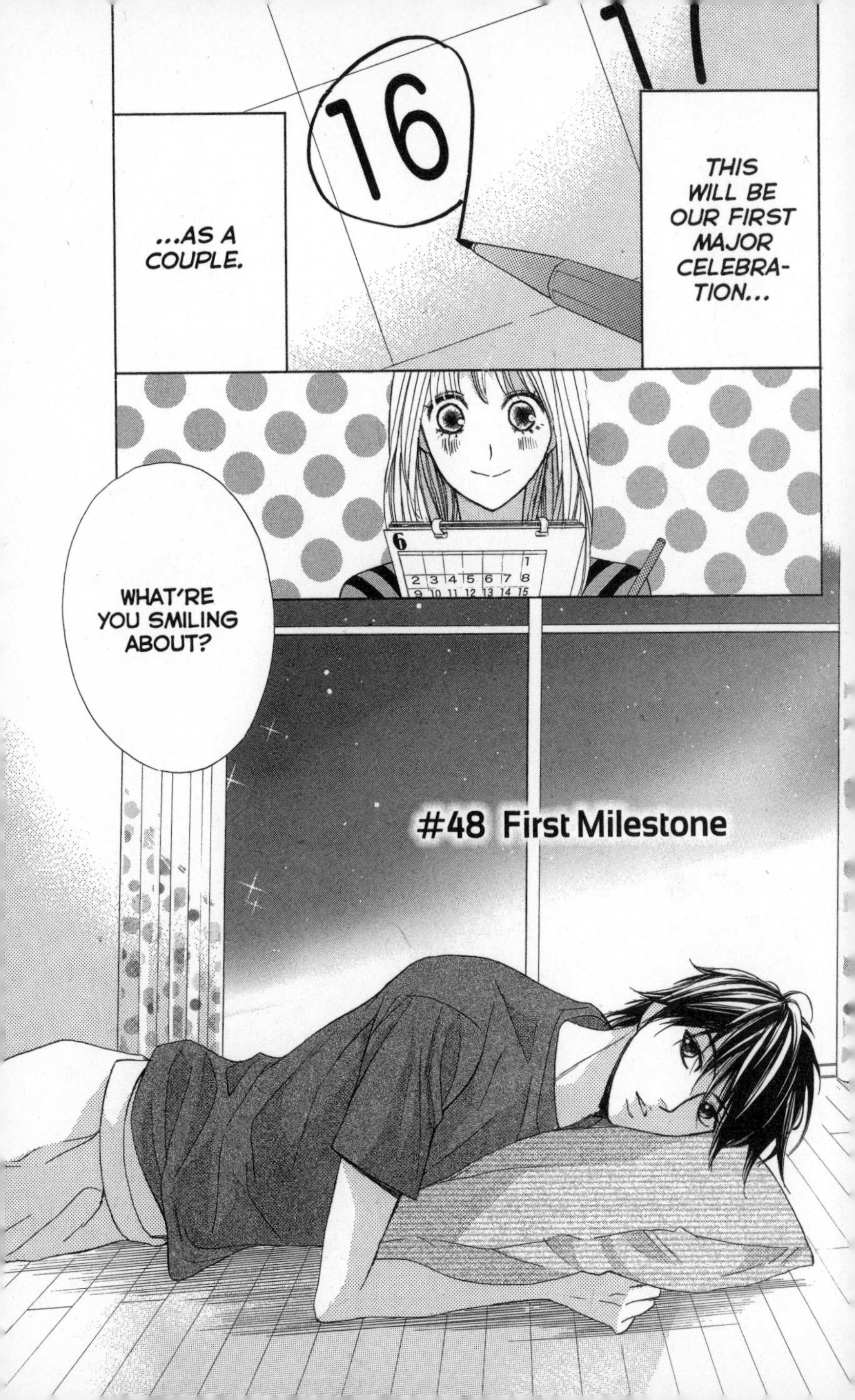
THIS WILL BE OUR FIRST MAJOR CELEBRA-TION...
16
...AS A COUPLE.
WHAT'RE YOU SMILING ABOUT?
#48 First Milestone

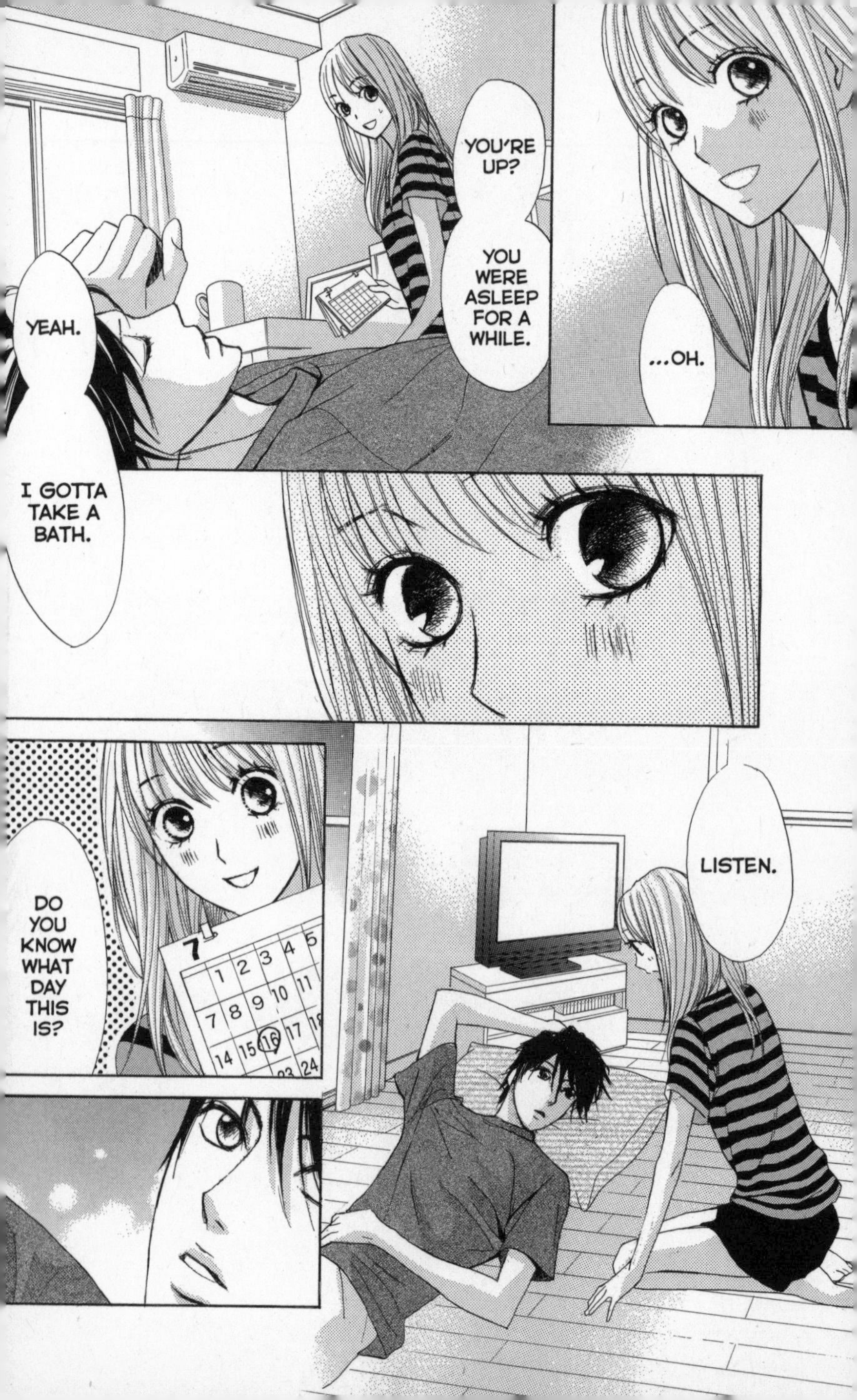
YOU'RE UP?
YOU WERE ASLEEP FOR A WHILE.
YEAH.
I GOTTA TAKE A BATH.
...OH.
LISTEN.
DO YOU KNOW WHAT DAY THIS IS?

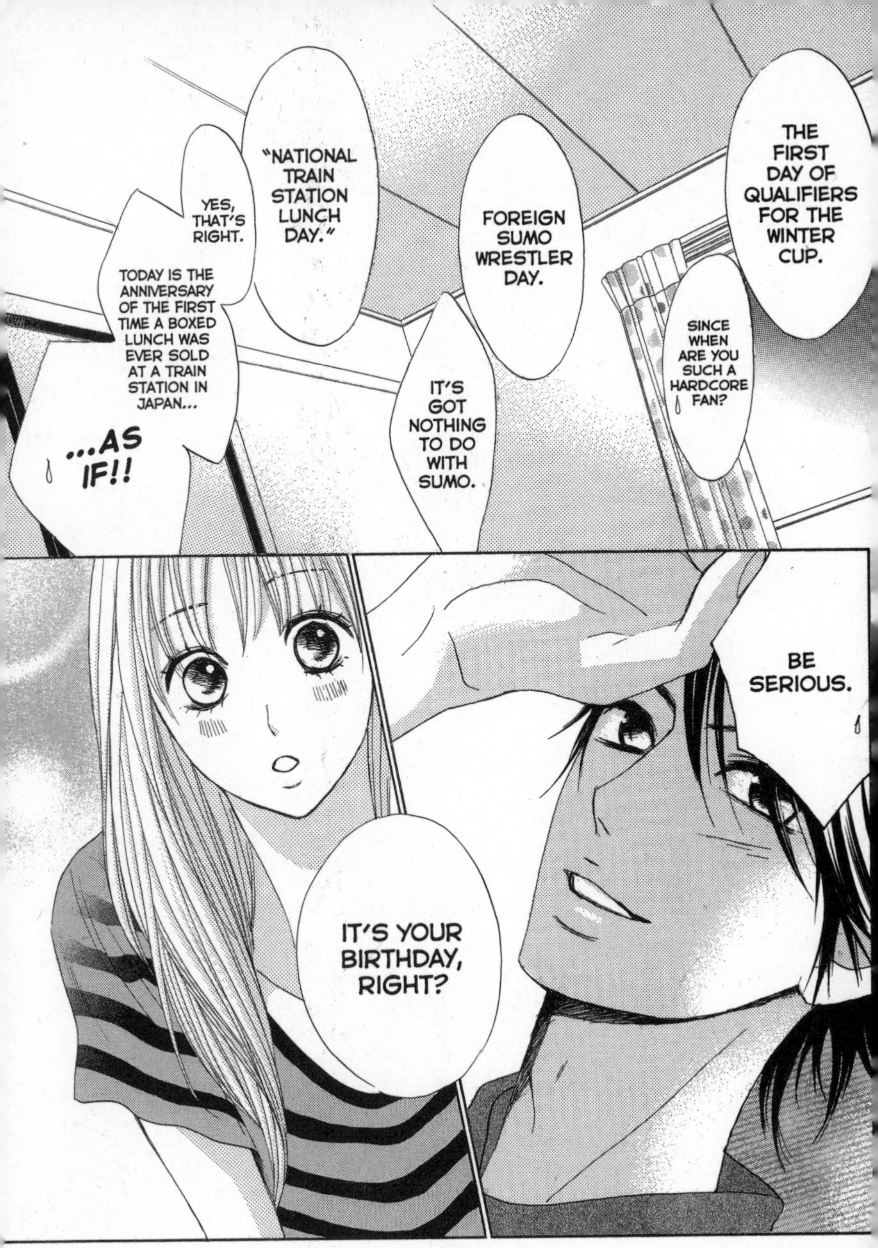
THE FIRST DAY OF QUALIFIERS FOR THE WINTER CUP.
SINCE WHEN ARE YOU SUCH A HARDCORE FAN?
FOREIGN SUMO WRESTLER DAY.
IT'S GOT NOTHING TO DO WITH SUMO.
"NATIONAL TRAIN STATION LUNCH DAY."
YES, THAT'S RIGHT.
TODAY IS THE ANNIVERSARY OF THE FIRST TIME A BOXED LUNCH WAS EVER SOLD AT A TRAIN STATION IN JAPAN...
...AS IF!!
BE SERIOUS.
IT'S YOUR BIRTHDAY, RIGHT?

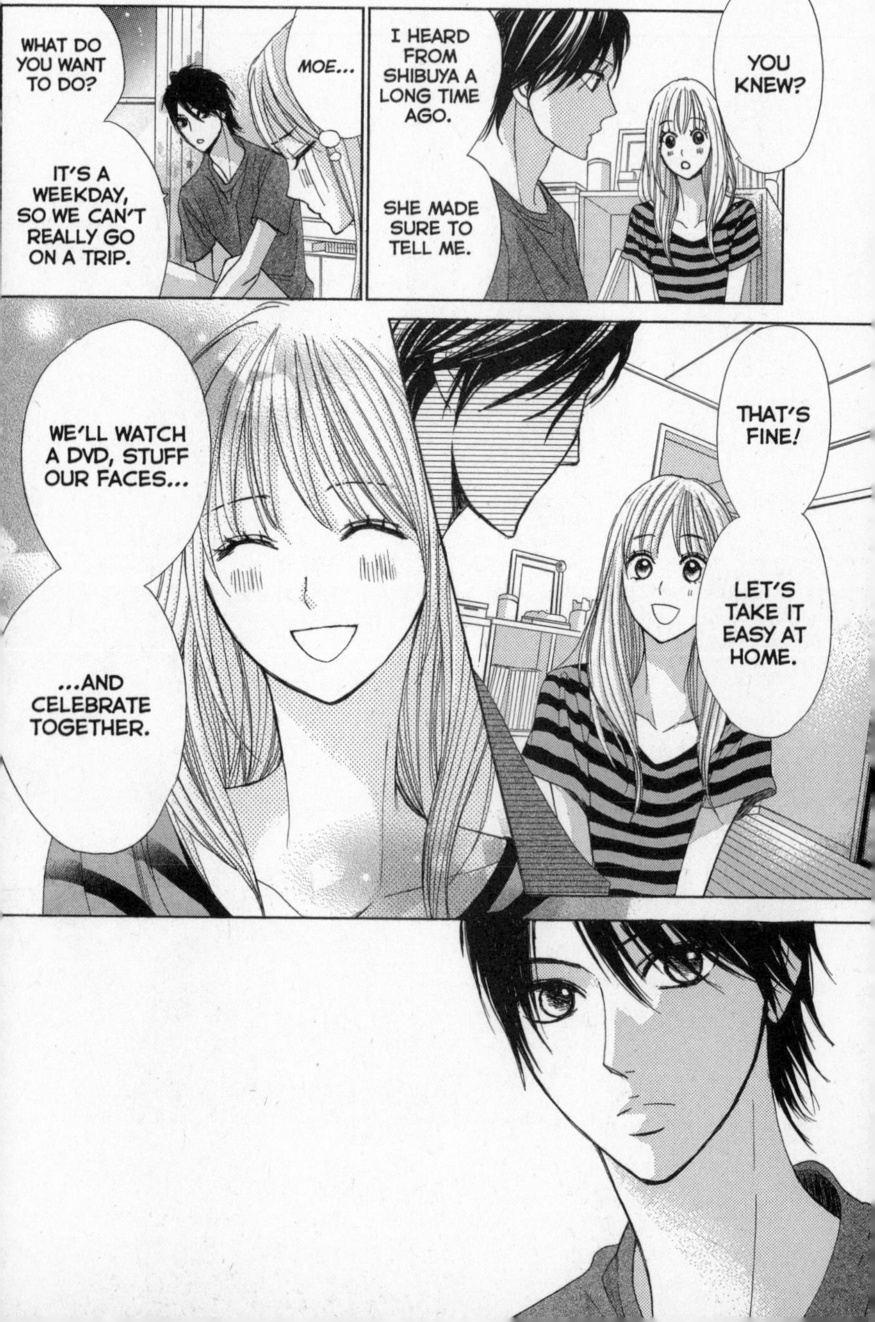
YOU KNEW?
I HEARD FROM SHIBUYA A LONG TIME AGO.
SHE MADE SURE TO TELL ME.
MOE...
WHAT DO YOU WANT TO DO?
IT'S A WEEKDAY, SO WE CAN'T REALLY GO ON A TRIP.
THAT'S FINE!
LET'S TAKE IT EASY AT HOME.
WE'LL WATCH A DVD, STUFF OUR FACES...
...AND CELEBRATE TOGETHER.

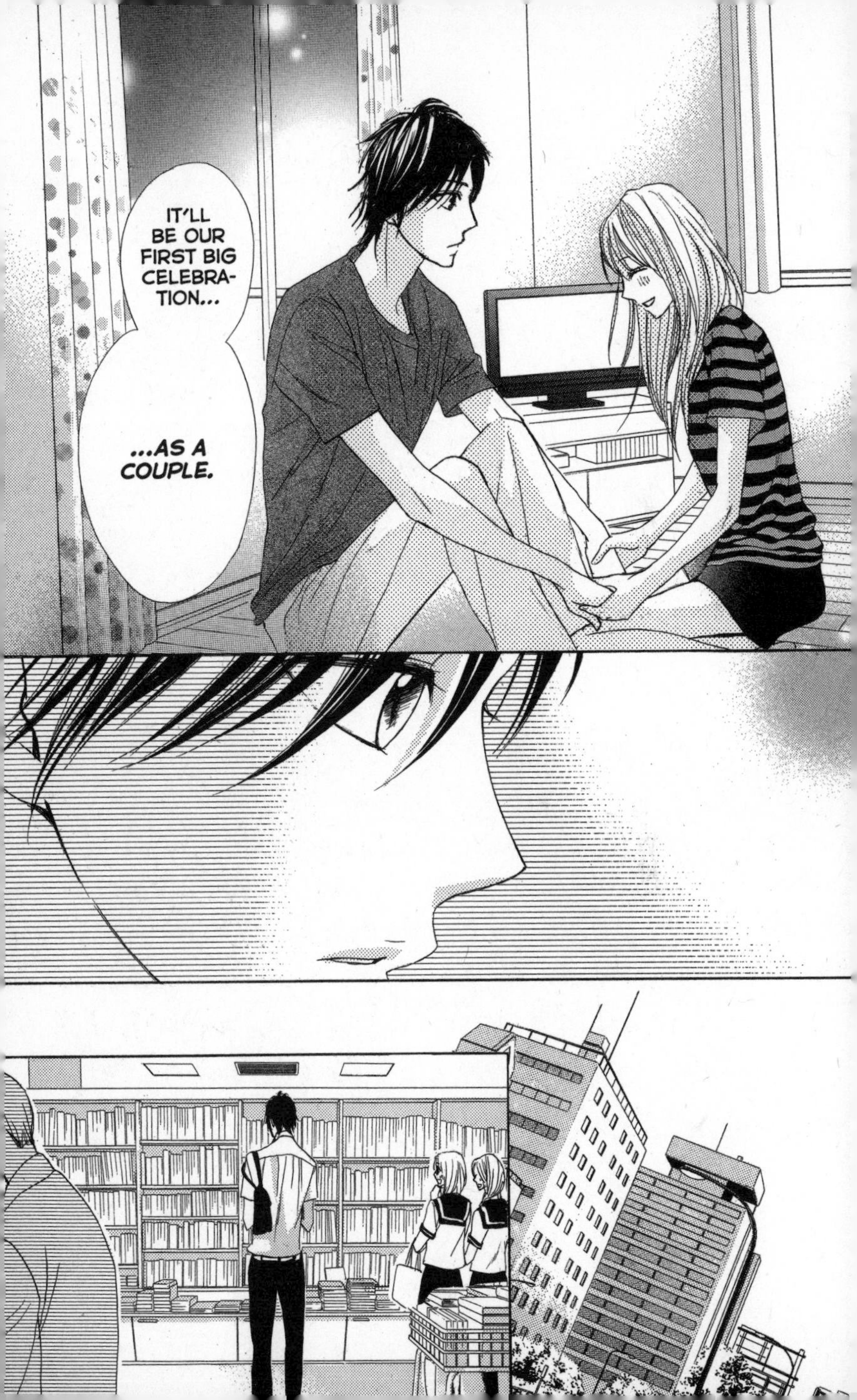
IT'LL BE OUR FIRST BIG CELEBRATION...
...AS A COUPLE.

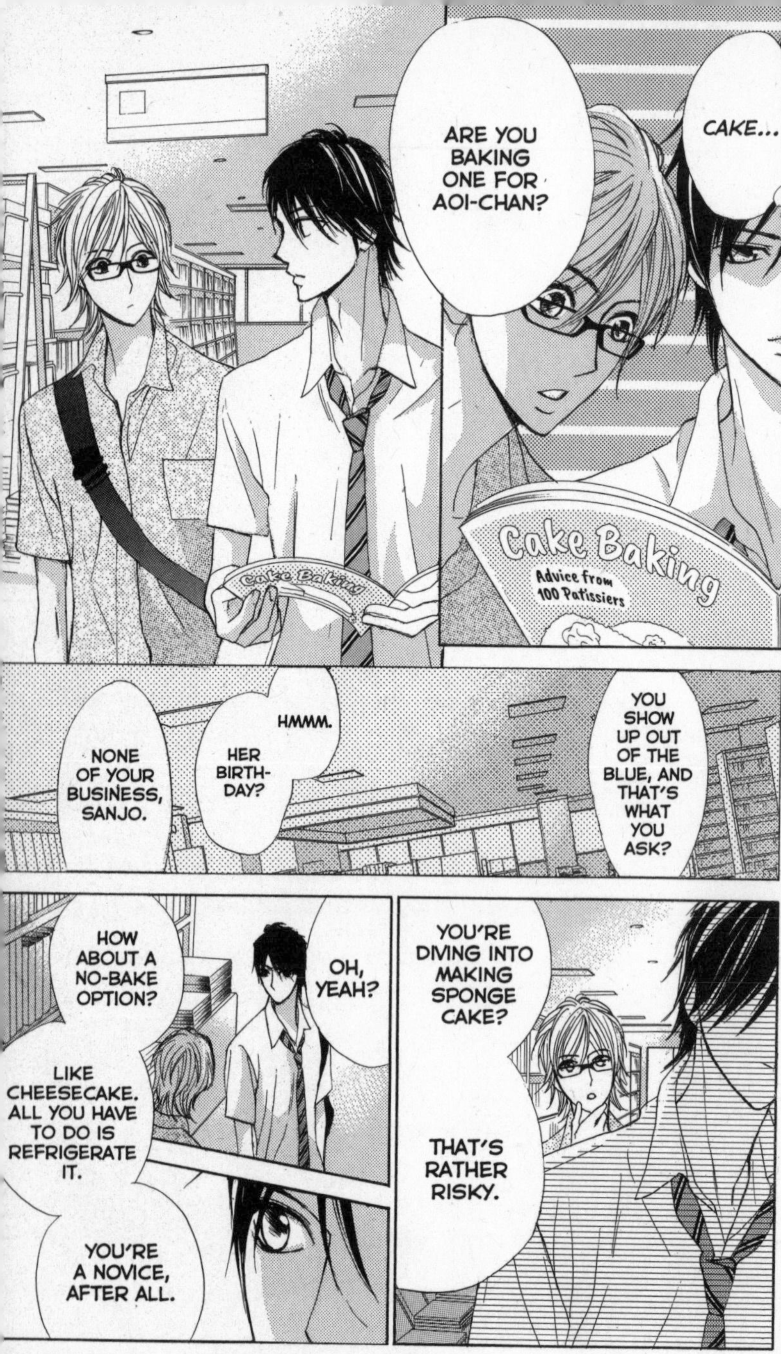
CAKE...
ARE YOU BAKING ONE FOR AOI-CHAN?
Cake Baking
Advice from 100 Patissiers
Cake Baking
YOU SHOW UP OUT OF THE BLUE, AND THAT'S WHAT YOU ASK?
HMMM.
HER BIRTH-DAY?
NONE OF YOUR BUSINESS, SANJO.
YOU'RE DIVING INTO MAKING SPONGE CAKE?
THAT'S RATHER RISKY.
OH, YEAH?
HOW ABOUT A NO-BAKE OPTION?
LIKE CHEESECAKE. ALL YOU HAVE TO DO IS REFRIGERATE IT.
YOU'RE A NOVICE, AFTER ALL.

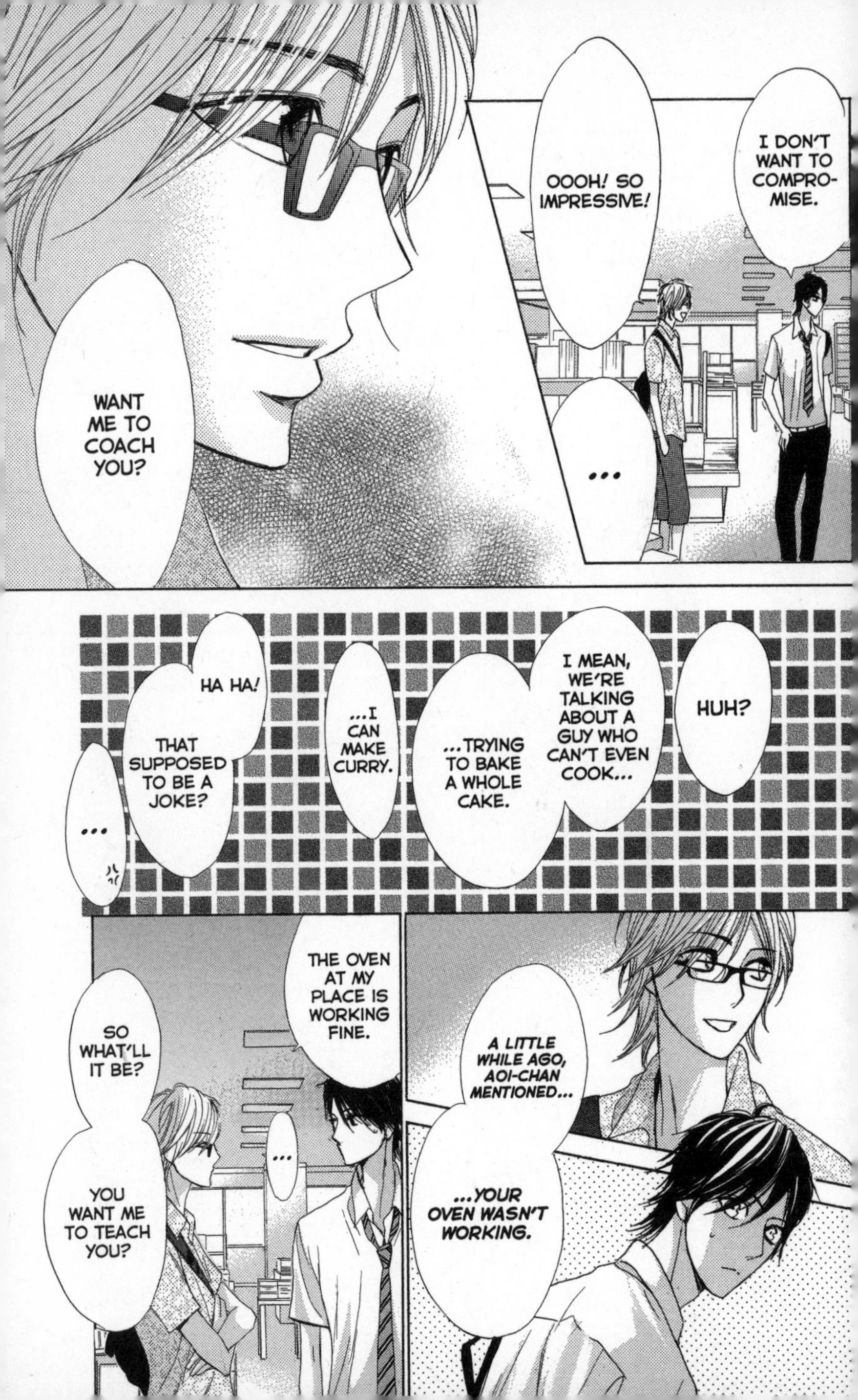
I DON'T WANT TO COMPROMISE.
OOOH! SO IMPRESSIVE!
...
WANT ME TO COACH YOU?
HUH?
I MEAN, WE'RE TALKING ABOUT A GUY WHO CAN'T EVEN COOK...
...TRYING TO BAKE A WHOLE CAKE.
...I CAN MAKE CURRY.
HA HA!
THAT SUPPOSED TO BE A JOKE?
...
A LITTLE WHILE AGO, AOI-CHAN MENTIONED...
...YOUR OVEN WASN'T WORKING.
THE OVEN AT MY PLACE IS WORKING FINE.
SO WHAT'LL IT BE?
...
YOU WANT ME TO TEACH YOU?

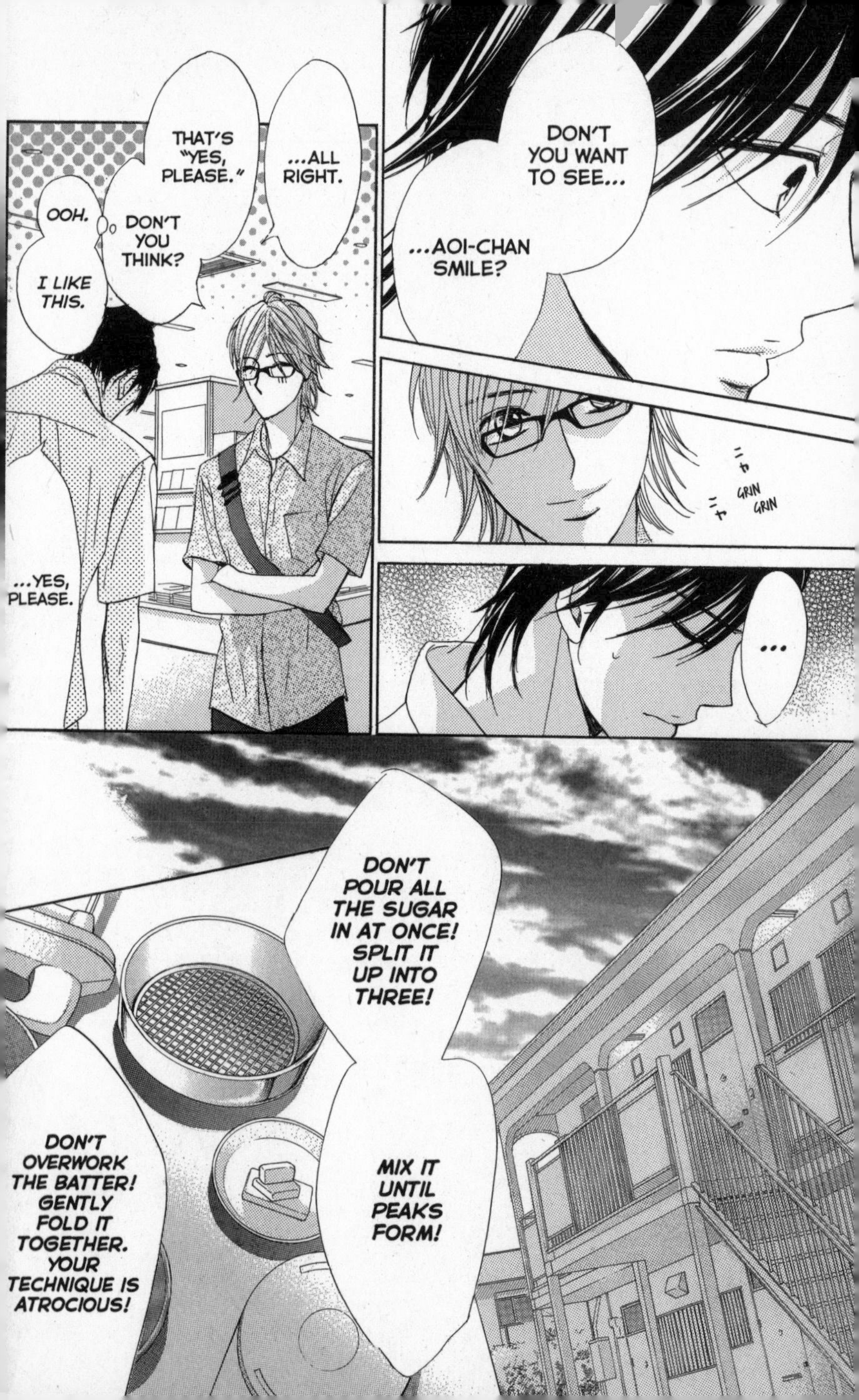
DON'T YOU WANT TO SEE...
...AOI-CHAN SMILE?
ニヤ GRIN
ニヤ GRIN
...
...ALL RIGHT.
THAT'S "YES, PLEASE." DON'T YOU THINK?
OOH. I LIKE THIS.
...YES, PLEASE.
DON'T POUR ALL THE SUGAR IN AT ONCE! SPLIT IT UP INTO THREE!
MIX IT UNTIL PEAKS FORM!
DON'T OVERWORK THE BATTER! GENTLY FOLD IT TOGETHER. YOUR TECHNIQUE IS ATROCIOUS!

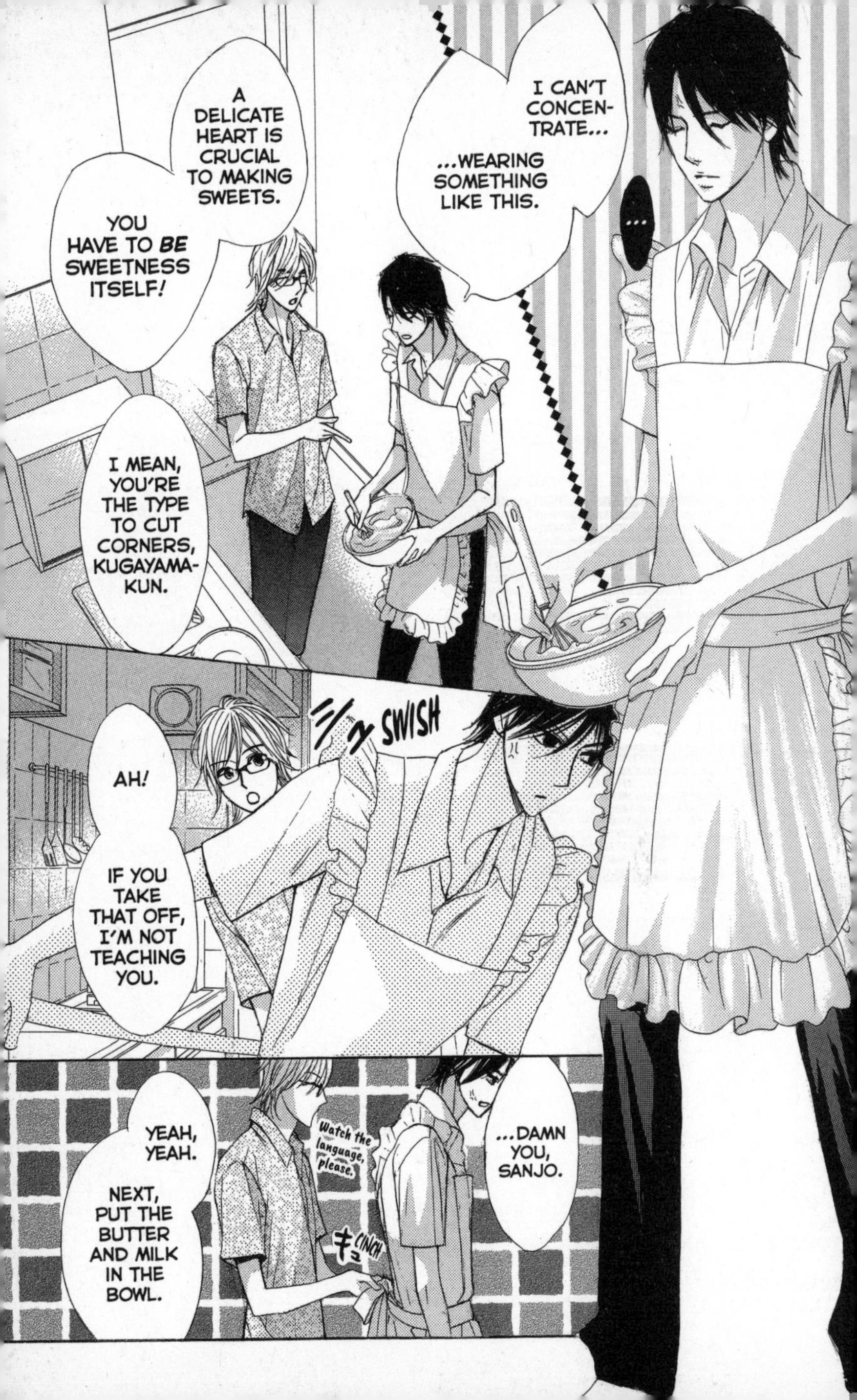
I CAN'T CONCENTRATE...
...WEARING SOMETHING LIKE THIS.
...
A DELICATE HEART IS CRUCIAL TO MAKING SWEETS.
YOU HAVE TO *BE* SWEETNESS ITSELF!
I MEAN, YOU'RE THE TYPE TO CUT CORNERS, KUGAYAMA-KUN.
SWISH
AH!
IF YOU TAKE THAT OFF, I'M NOT TEACHING YOU.
...DAMN YOU, SANJO.
Watch the language, please.
CINCH
YEAH, YEAH.
NEXT, PUT THE BUTTER AND MILK IN THE BOWL.

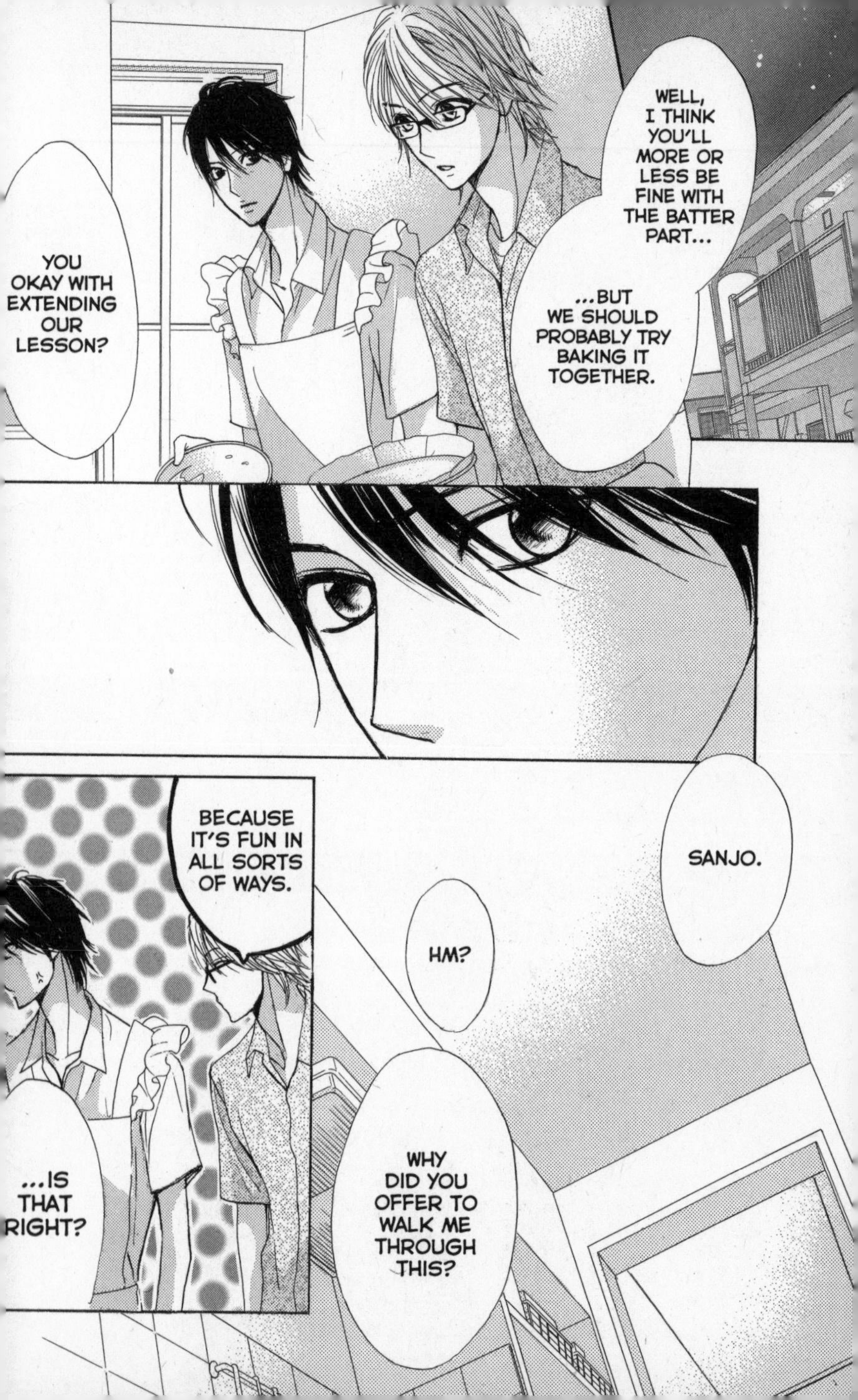
WELL, I THINK YOU'LL MORE OR LESS BE FINE WITH THE BATTER PART...
...BUT WE SHOULD PROBABLY TRY BAKING IT TOGETHER.
YOU OKAY WITH EXTENDING OUR LESSON?
SANJO.
HM?
WHY DID YOU OFFER TO WALK ME THROUGH THIS?
BECAUSE IT'S FUN IN ALL SORTS OF WAYS.
...IS THAT RIGHT?

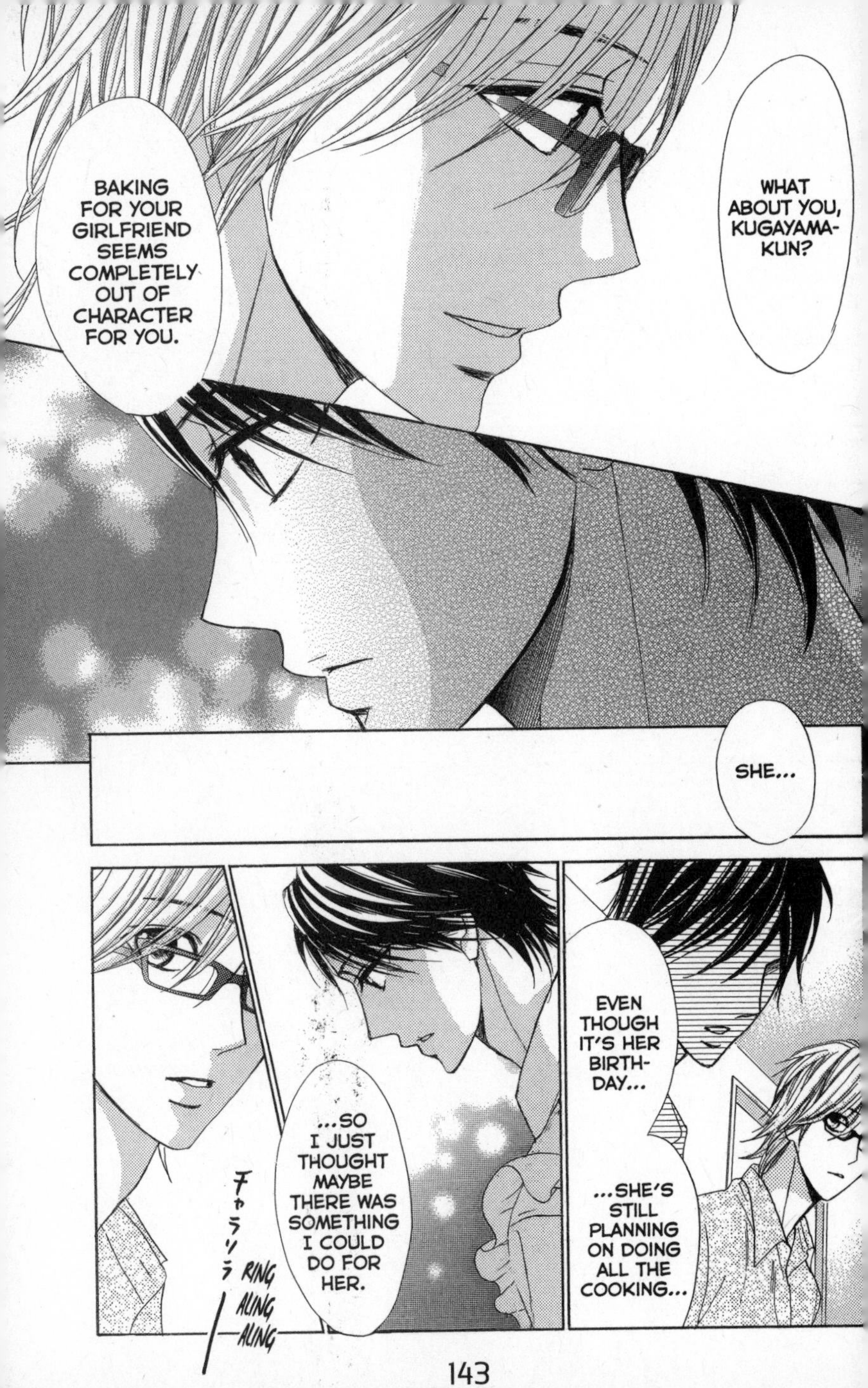

WHAT ABOUT YOU, KUGAYAMA-KUN?
BAKING FOR YOUR GIRLFRIEND SEEMS COMPLETELY OUT OF CHARACTER FOR YOU.
SHE...
EVEN THOUGH IT'S HER BIRTHDAY...
...SHE'S STILL PLANNING ON DOING ALL THE COOKING...
...SO I JUST THOUGHT MAYBE THERE WAS SOMETHING I COULD DO FOR HER.
チャラリラ
RING ALING ALING

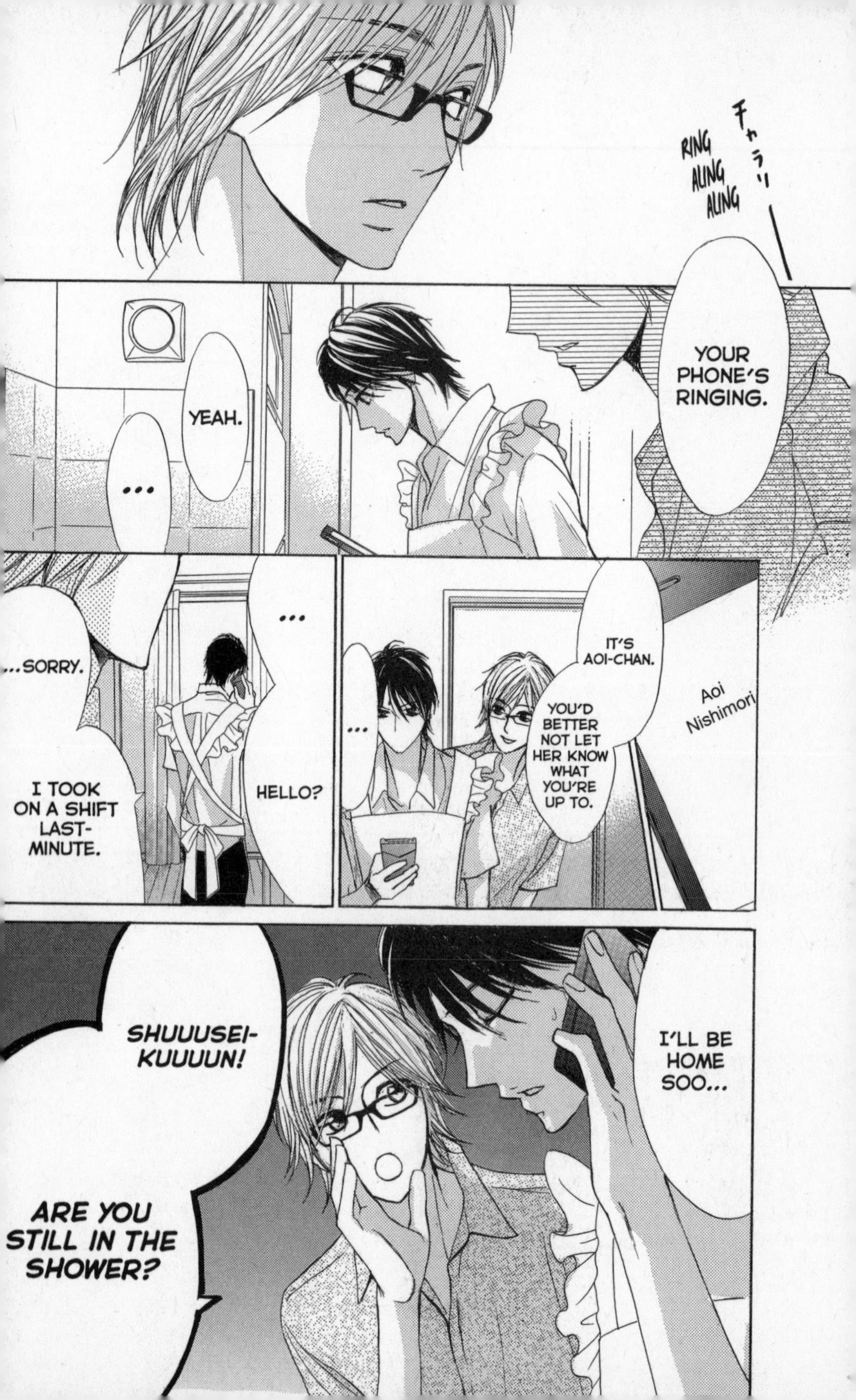

RING ALING ALING
チャラリ
YOUR PHONE'S RINGING.
YEAH.
...
IT'S AOI-CHAN.
Aoi Nishimori
YOU'D BETTER NOT LET HER KNOW WHAT YOU'RE UP TO.
...
...
HELLO?
...SORRY.
I TOOK ON A SHIFT LAST-MINUTE.
I'LL BE HOME SOO...
SHUUUSEI-KUUUUN!
ARE YOU STILL IN THE SHOWER?

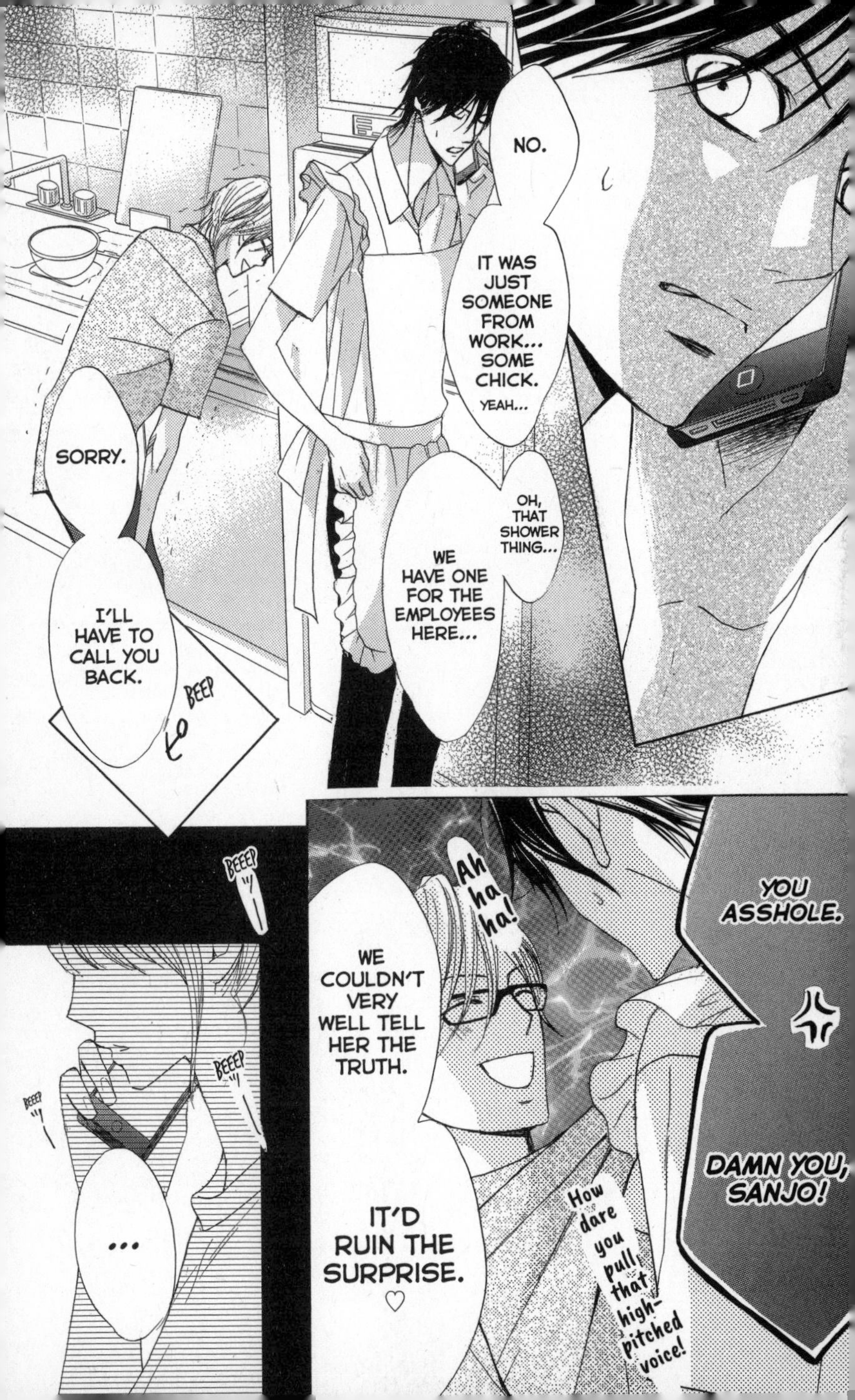
NO.
IT WAS JUST SOMEONE FROM WORK... SOME CHICK.
YEAH...
OH, THAT SHOWER THING...
WE HAVE ONE FOR THE EMPLOYEES HERE...
SORRY.
I'LL HAVE TO CALL YOU BACK.
BEEP
YOU ASSHOLE.
DAMN YOU, SANJO!
How dare you pull that high-pitched voice!
Ah ha ha!
WE COULDN'T VERY WELL TELL HER THE TRUTH.
IT'D RUIN THE SURPRISE. ♡
BEEEP
BEEEP
BEEEP
...

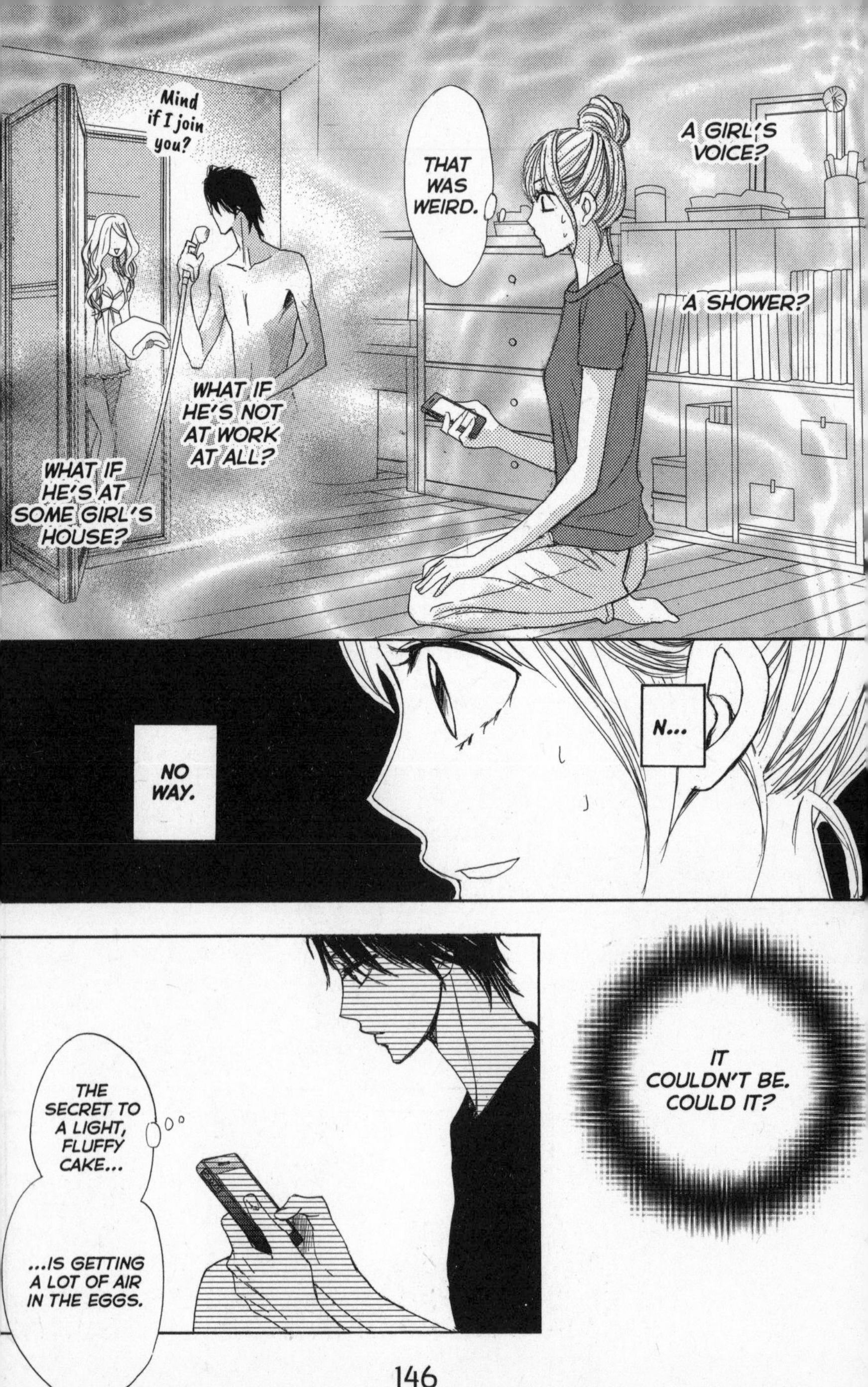
A GIRL'S VOICE?
THAT WAS WEIRD.
A SHOWER?
Mind if I join you?
WHAT IF HE'S NOT AT WORK AT ALL?
WHAT IF HE'S AT SOME GIRL'S HOUSE?
N...
NO WAY.
IT COULDN'T BE. COULD IT?
THE SECRET TO A LIGHT, FLUFFY CAKE...
...IS GETTING A LOT OF AIR IN THE EGGS.

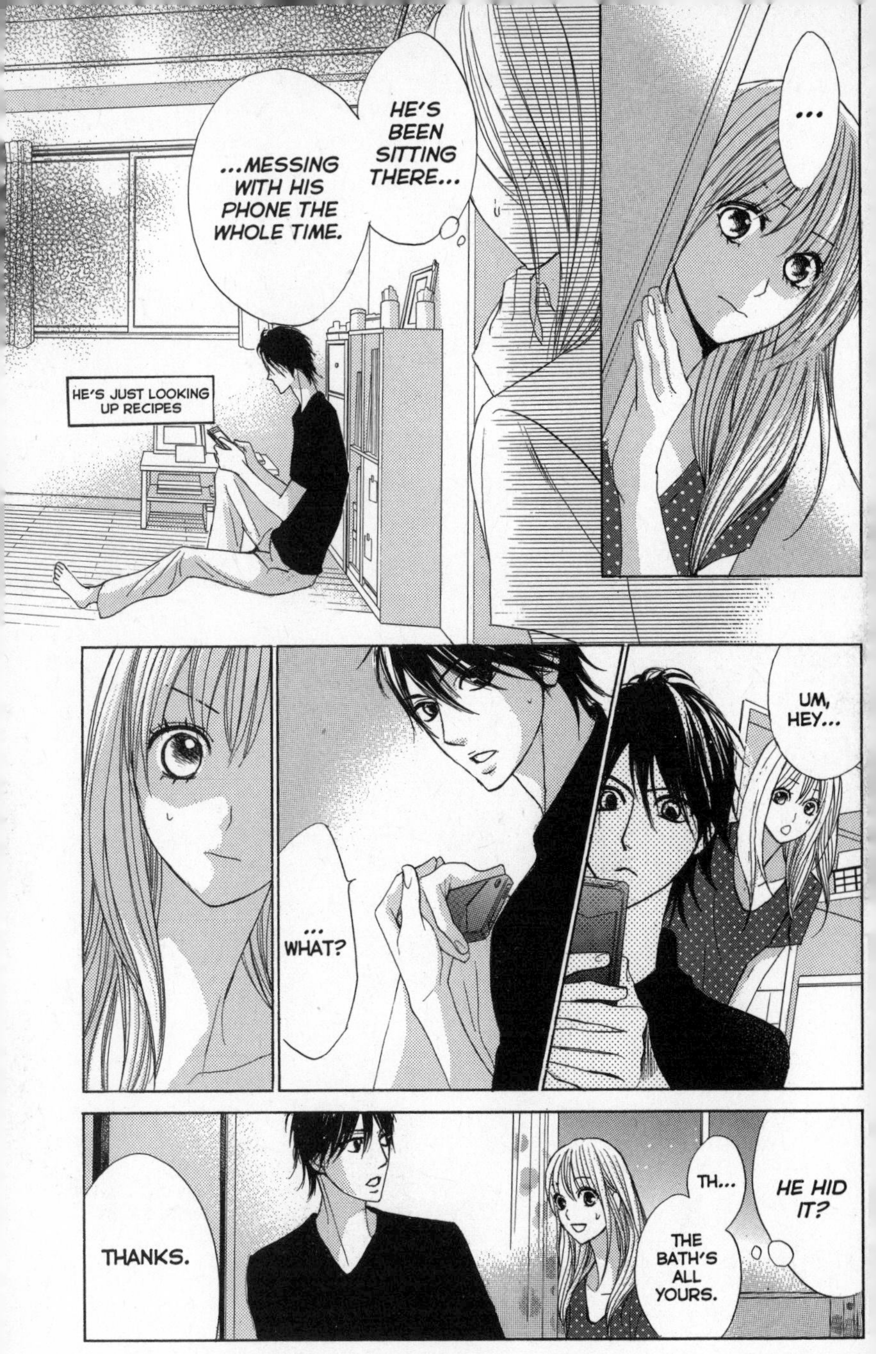
...
HE'S BEEN SITTING THERE...
...MESSING WITH HIS PHONE THE WHOLE TIME.
HE'S JUST LOOKING UP RECIPES
UM, HEY...
... WHAT?
HE HID IT?
TH...
THE BATH'S ALL YOURS.
THANKS.

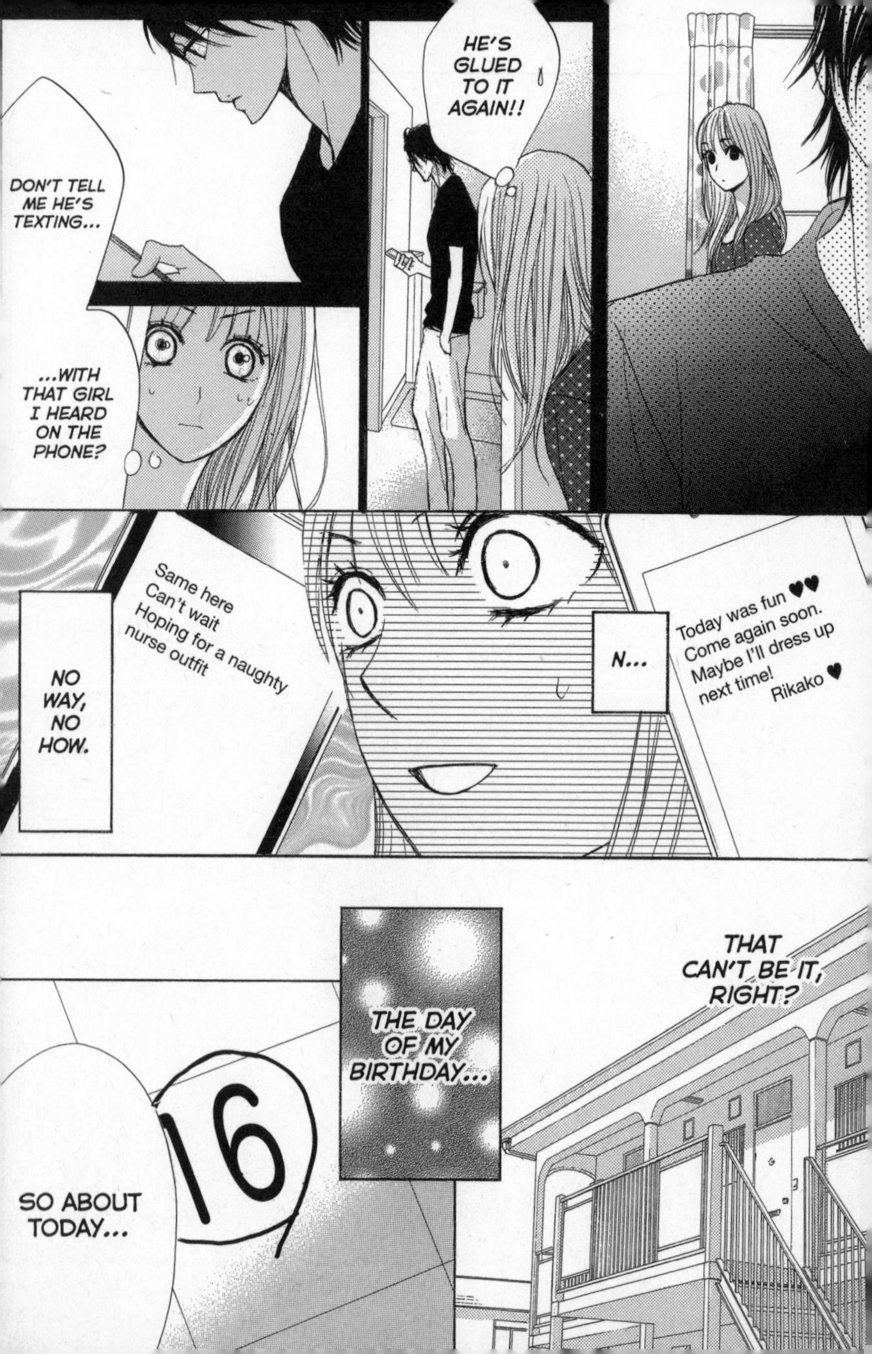
HE'S GLUED TO IT AGAIN!!
DON'T TELL ME HE'S TEXTING...
...WITH THAT GIRL I HEARD ON THE PHONE?
Today was fun ♥♥ Come again soon. Maybe I'll dress up next time! Rikako ♥
N...
Same here Can't wait Hoping for a naughty nurse outfit
NO WAY, NO HOW.
THAT CAN'T BE IT, RIGHT?
THE DAY OF MY BIRTHDAY...
16
SO ABOUT TODAY...

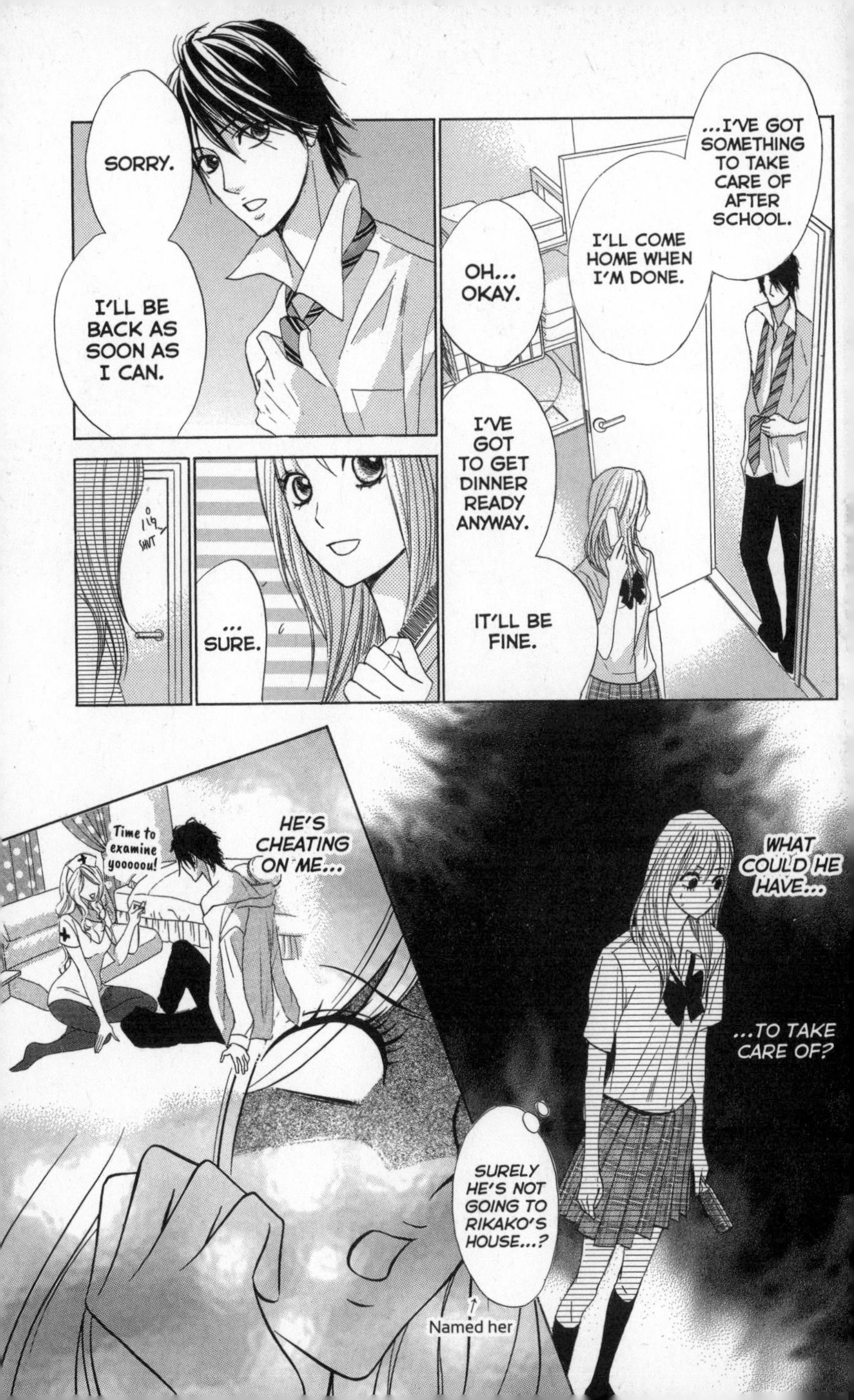
...I'VE GOT SOMETHING TO TAKE CARE OF AFTER SCHOOL.
I'LL COME HOME WHEN I'M DONE.
OH... OKAY.
I'VE GOT TO GET DINNER READY ANYWAY.
IT'LL BE FINE.
SORRY.
I'LL BE BACK AS SOON AS I CAN.
... SURE.
SHUT
WHAT COULD HE HAVE...
...TO TAKE CARE OF?
SURELY HE'S NOT GOING TO RIKAKO'S HOUSE...?
Named her
HE'S CHEATING ON ME...
Time to examine yoooou!

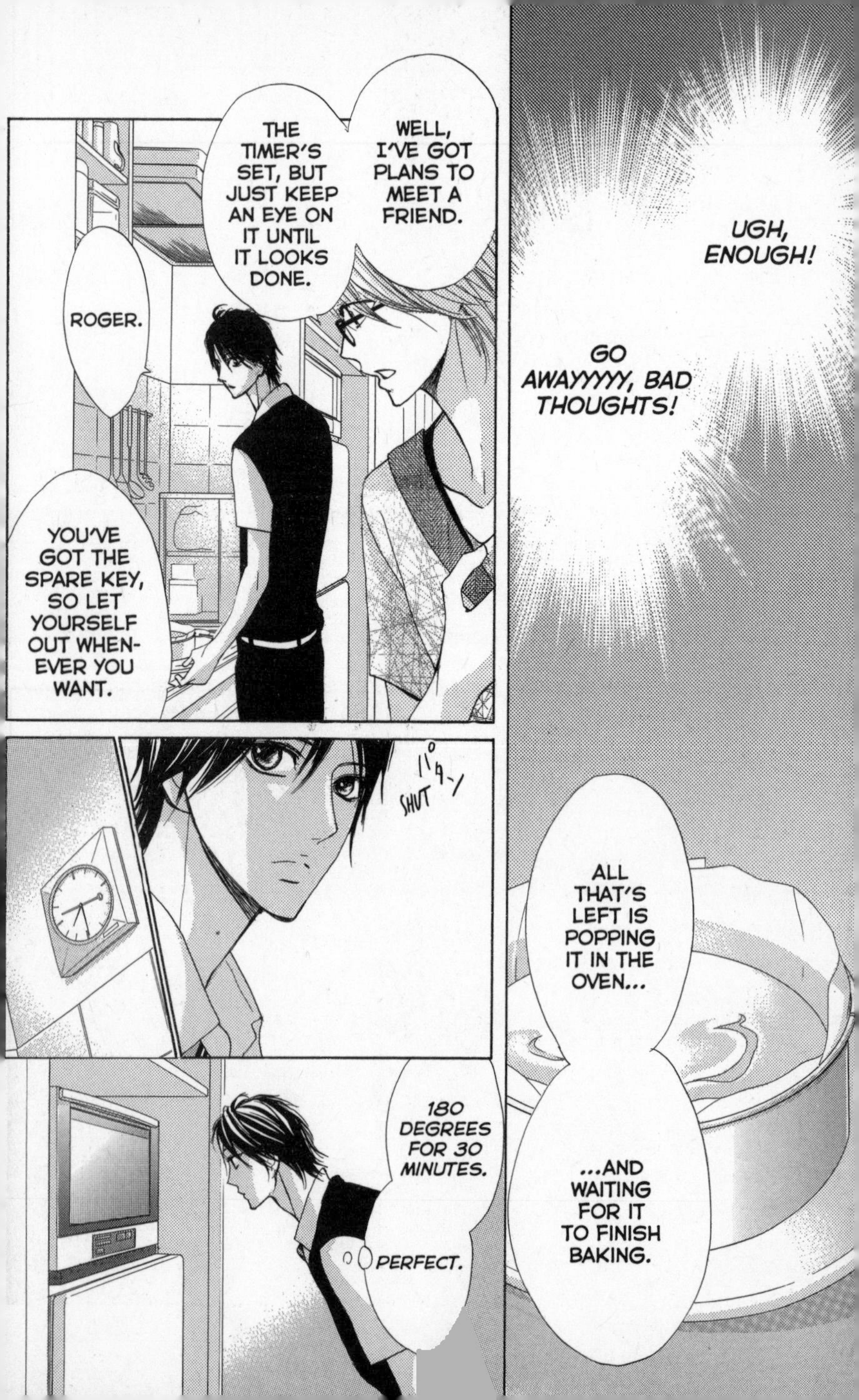
UGH, ENOUGH!
GO AWAYYYYY, BAD THOUGHTS!
ALL THAT'S LEFT IS POPPING IT IN THE OVEN...
...AND WAITING FOR IT TO FINISH BAKING.
WELL, I'VE GOT PLANS TO MEET A FRIEND.
THE TIMER'S SET, BUT JUST KEEP AN EYE ON IT UNTIL IT LOOKS DONE.
ROGER.
YOU'VE GOT THE SPARE KEY, SO LET YOURSELF OUT WHENEVER YOU WANT.
SHUT
180 DEGREES FOR 30 MINUTES.
PERFECT.

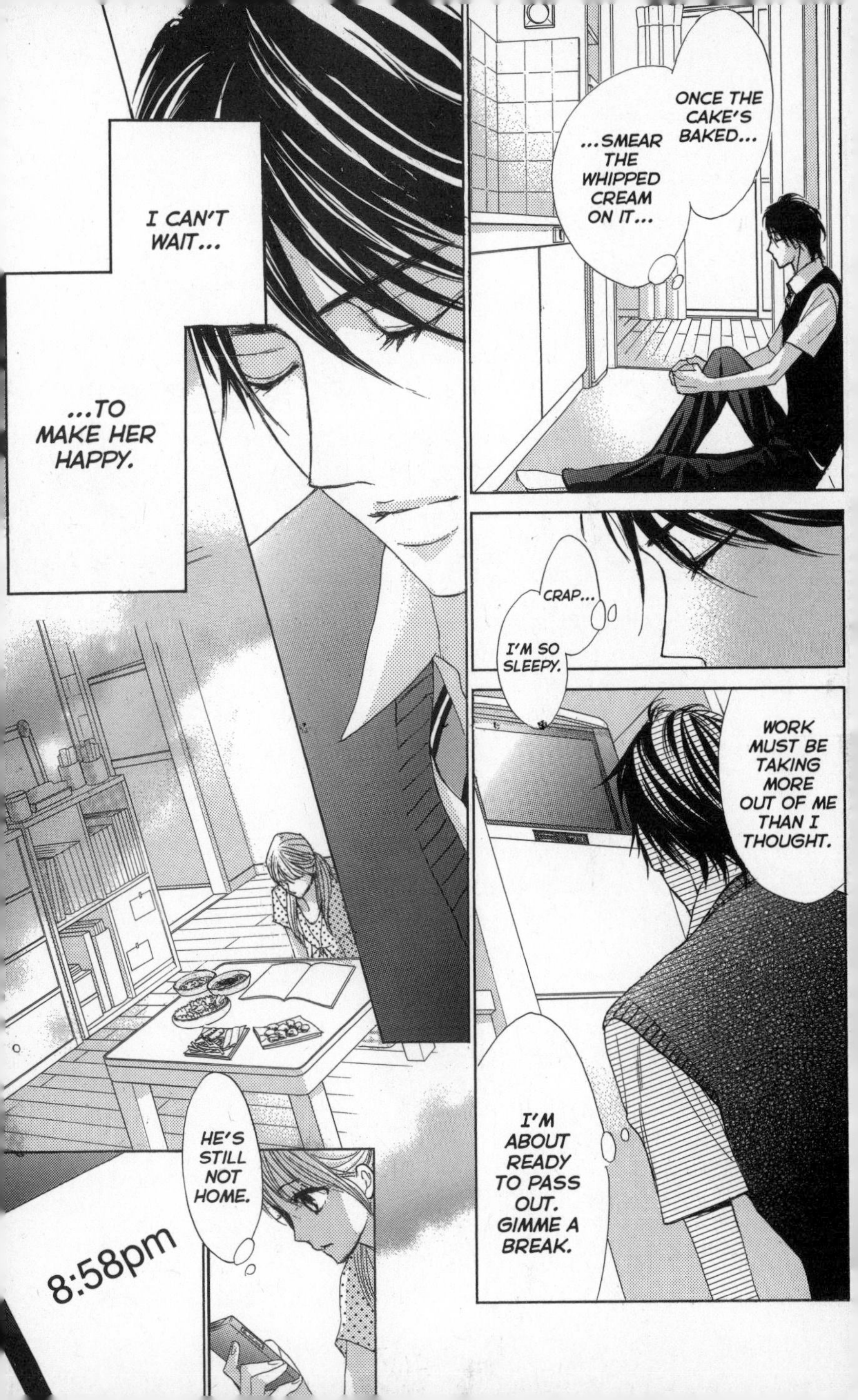
ONCE THE CAKE'S BAKED...
...SMEAR THE WHIPPED CREAM ON IT...
CRAP...
I'M SO SLEEPY.
WORK MUST BE TAKING MORE OUT OF ME THAN I THOUGHT.
I'M ABOUT READY TO PASS OUT. GIMME A BREAK.
I CAN'T WAIT...
...TO MAKE HER HAPPY.
HE'S STILL NOT HOME.
8:58pm

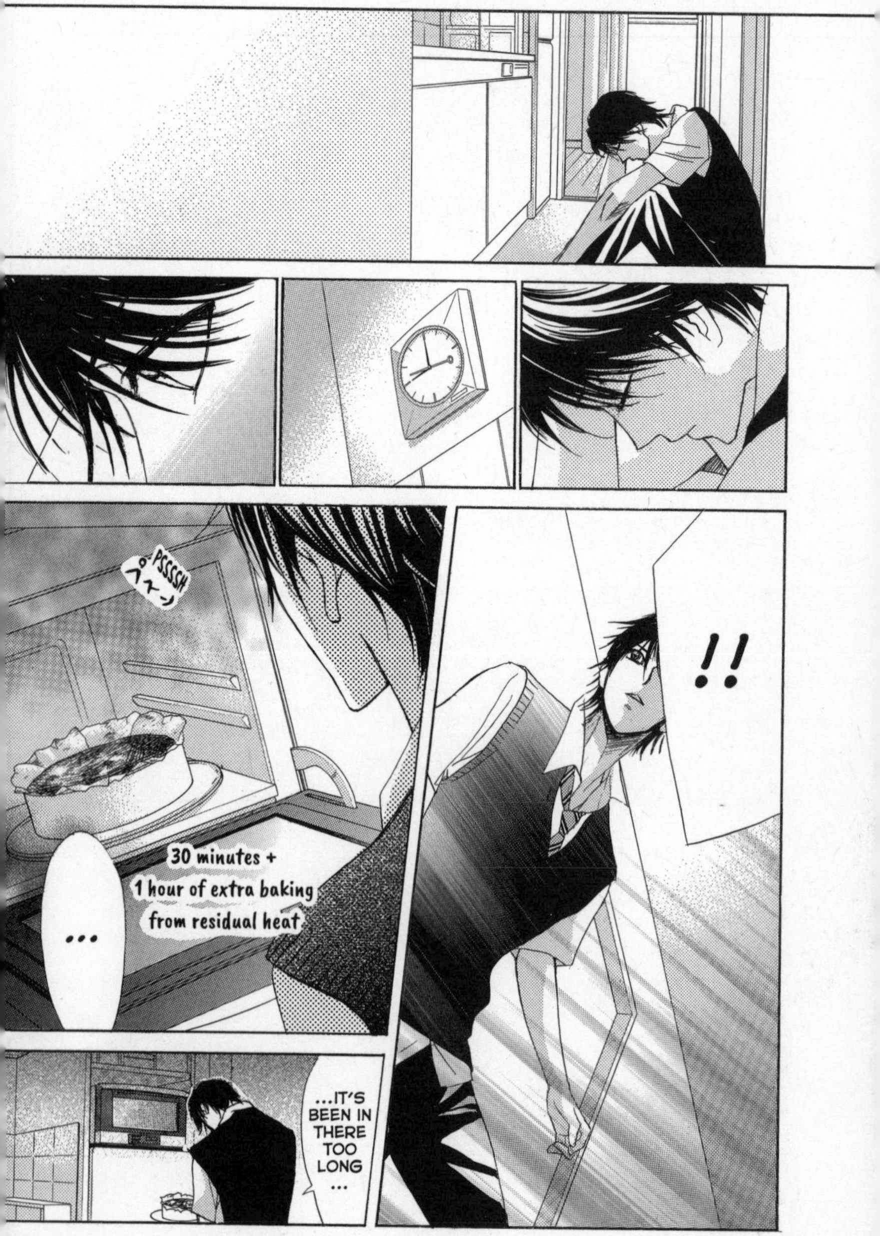
!!
PSSSSH
ペスーン
30 minutes + 1 hour of extra baking from residual heat
...
...IT'S BEEN IN THERE TOO LONG ...

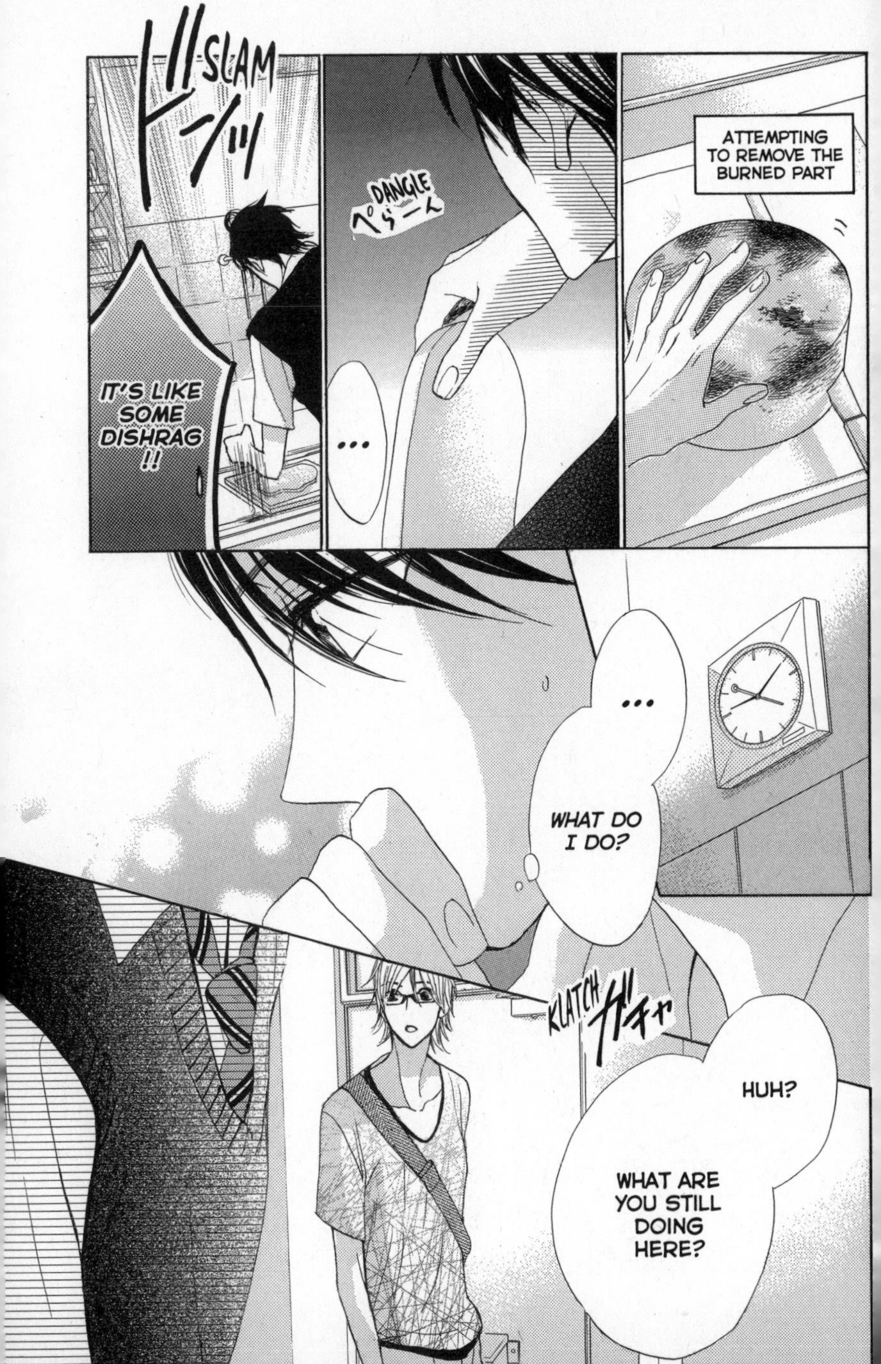
ATTEMPTING TO REMOVE THE BURNED PART
DANGLE ぺらーん
...
SLAM ドーンッ
IT'S LIKE SOME DISHRAG !!
...
WHAT DO I DO?
KLATCH ガチャ
HUH?
WHAT ARE YOU STILL DOING HERE?

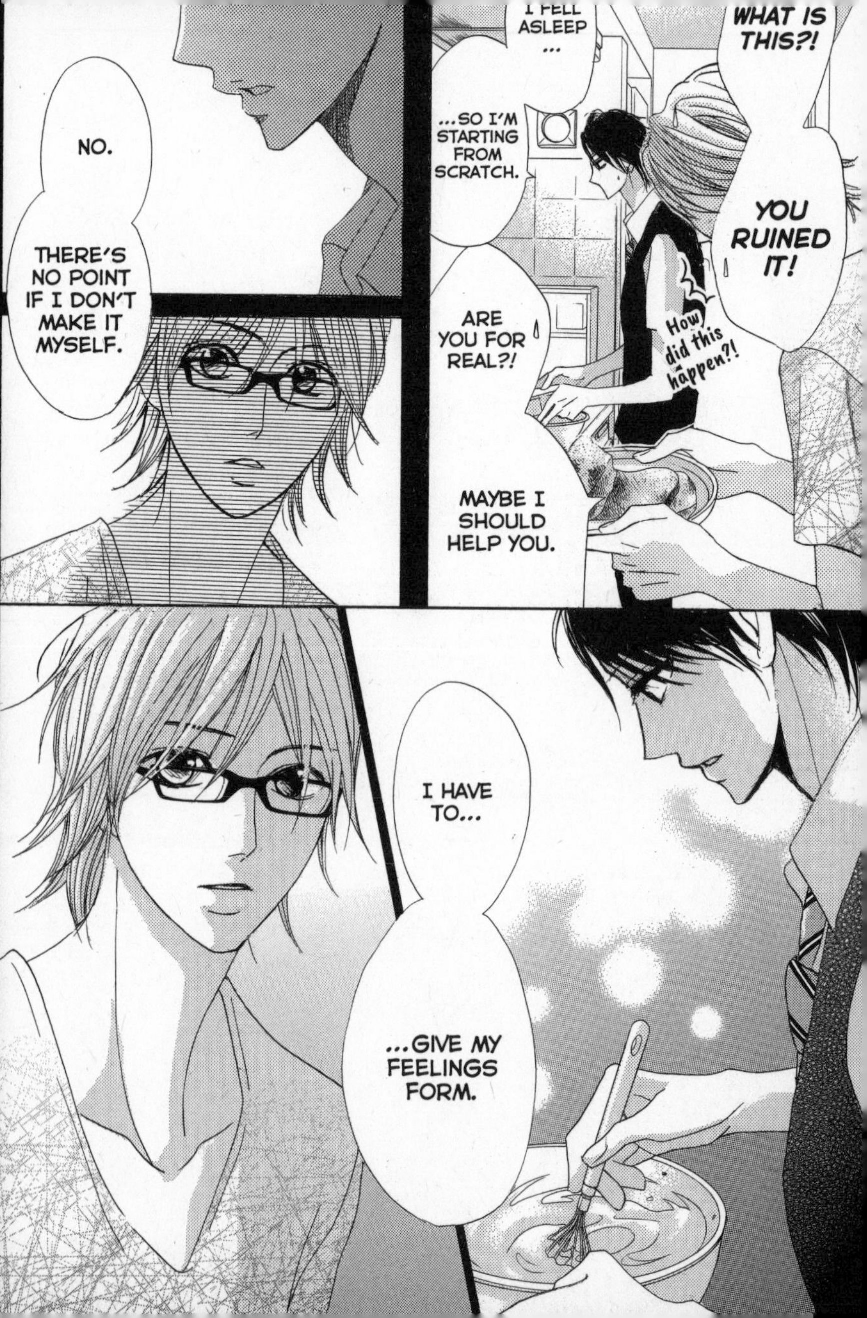
WHAT IS THIS?!
YOU RUINED IT!
How did this happen?!
I FELL ASLEEP ...
...SO I'M STARTING FROM SCRATCH.
ARE YOU FOR REAL?!
MAYBE I SHOULD HELP YOU.
NO.
THERE'S NO POINT IF I DON'T MAKE IT MYSELF.
I HAVE TO...
...GIVE MY FEELINGS FORM.

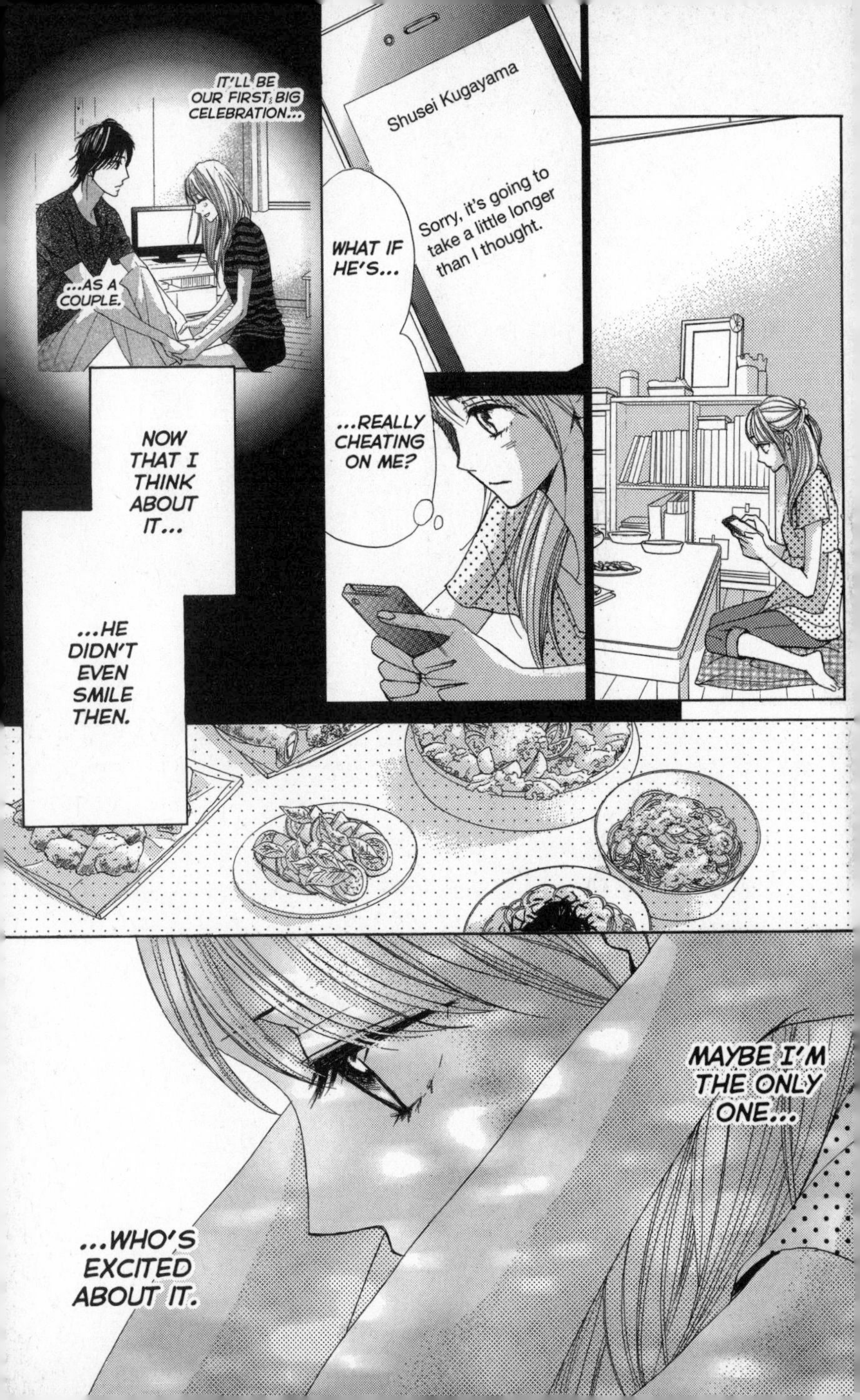
Shusei Kugayama
Sorry, it's going to take a little longer than I thought.
WHAT IF HE'S...
...REALLY CHEATING ON ME?
IT'LL BE OUR FIRST BIG CELEBRATION...
...AS A COUPLE.
NOW THAT I THINK ABOUT IT...
...HE DIDN'T EVEN SMILE THEN.
MAYBE I'M THE ONLY ONE...
...WHO'S EXCITED ABOUT IT.

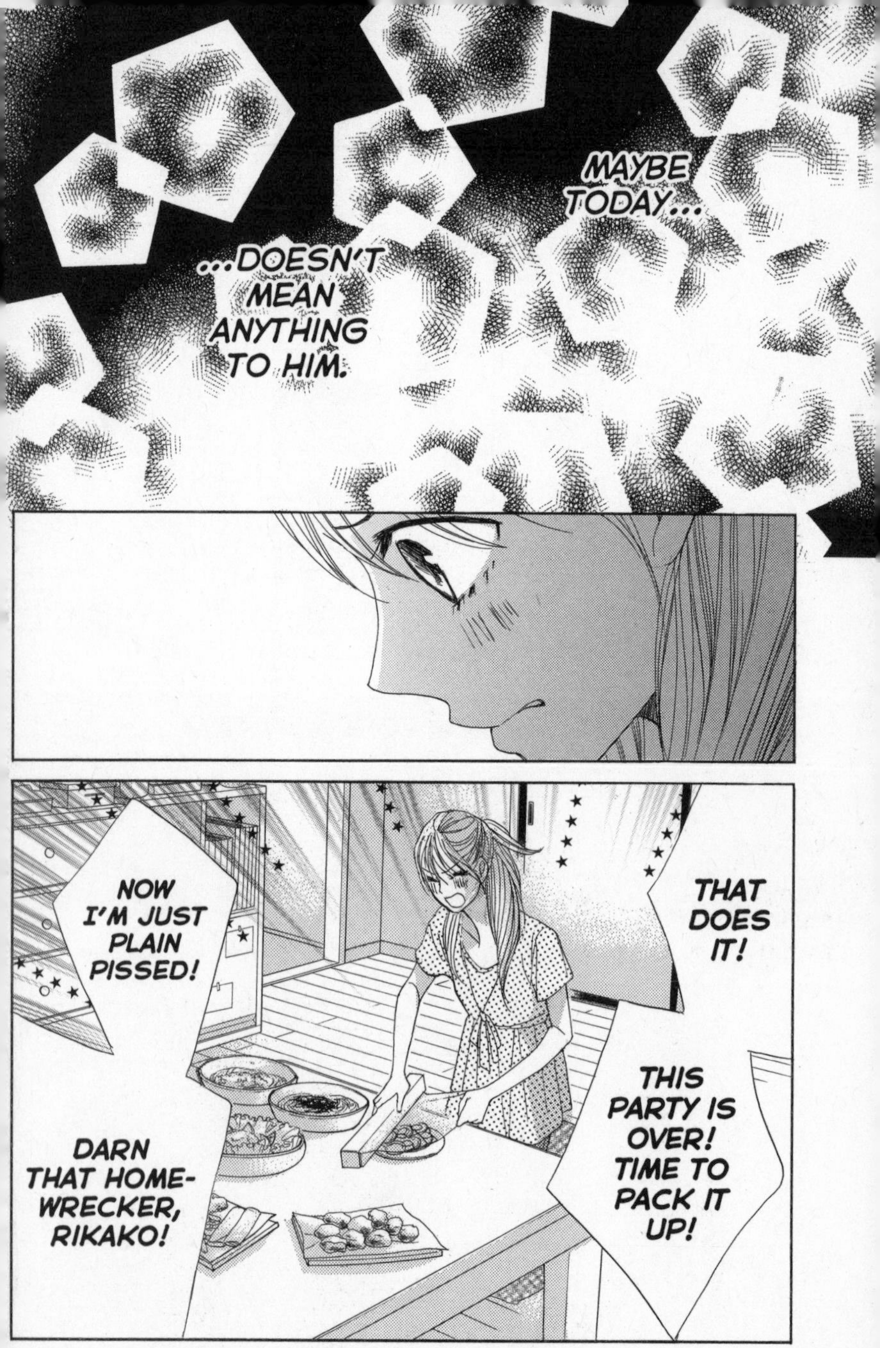
MAYBE TODAY...
...DOESN'T MEAN ANYTHING TO HIM.
THAT DOES IT!
THIS PARTY IS OVER! TIME TO PACK IT UP!
NOW I'M JUST PLAIN PISSED!
DARN THAT HOME-WRECKER, RIKAKO!

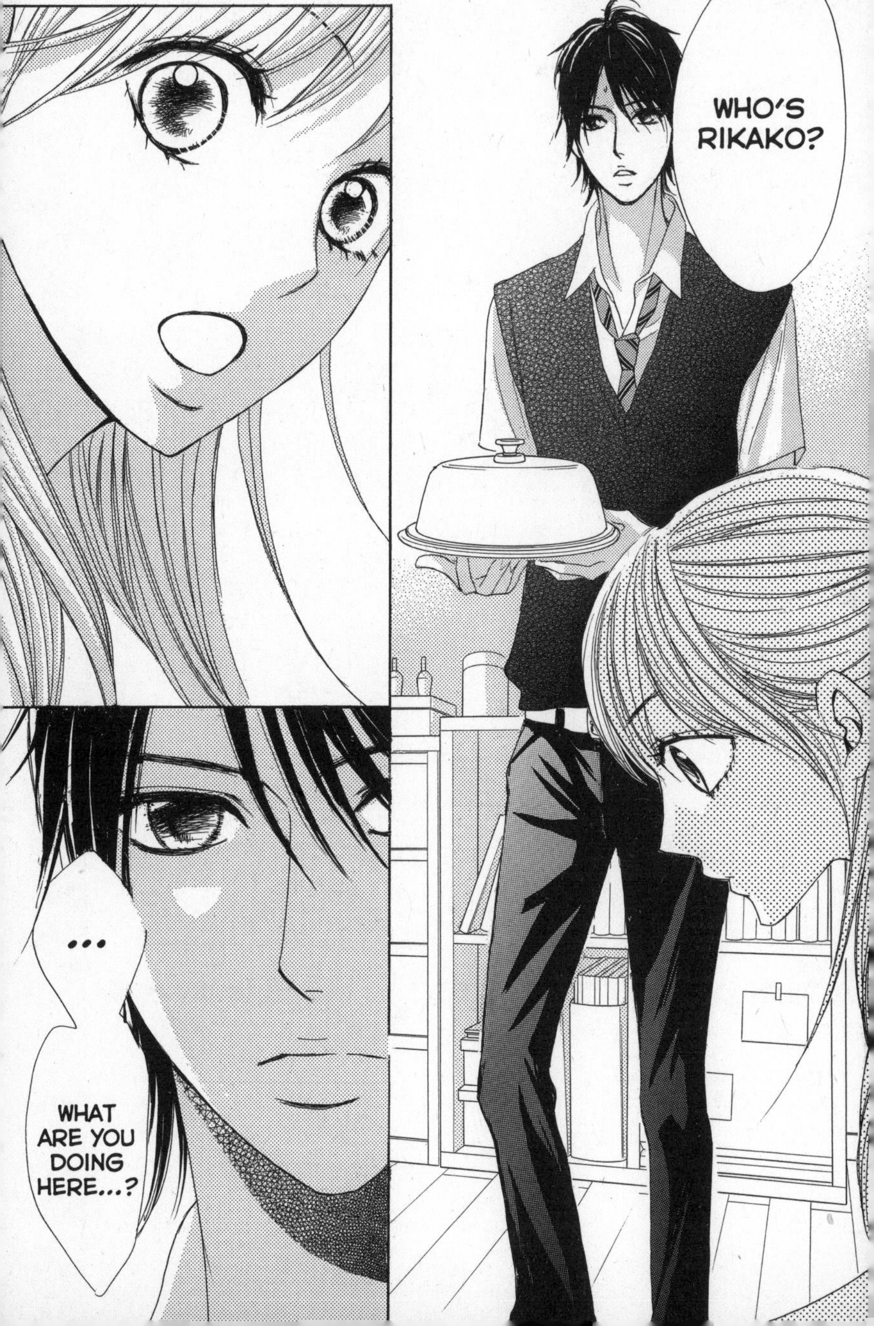
WHO'S RIKAKO?
...
WHAT ARE YOU DOING HERE...?

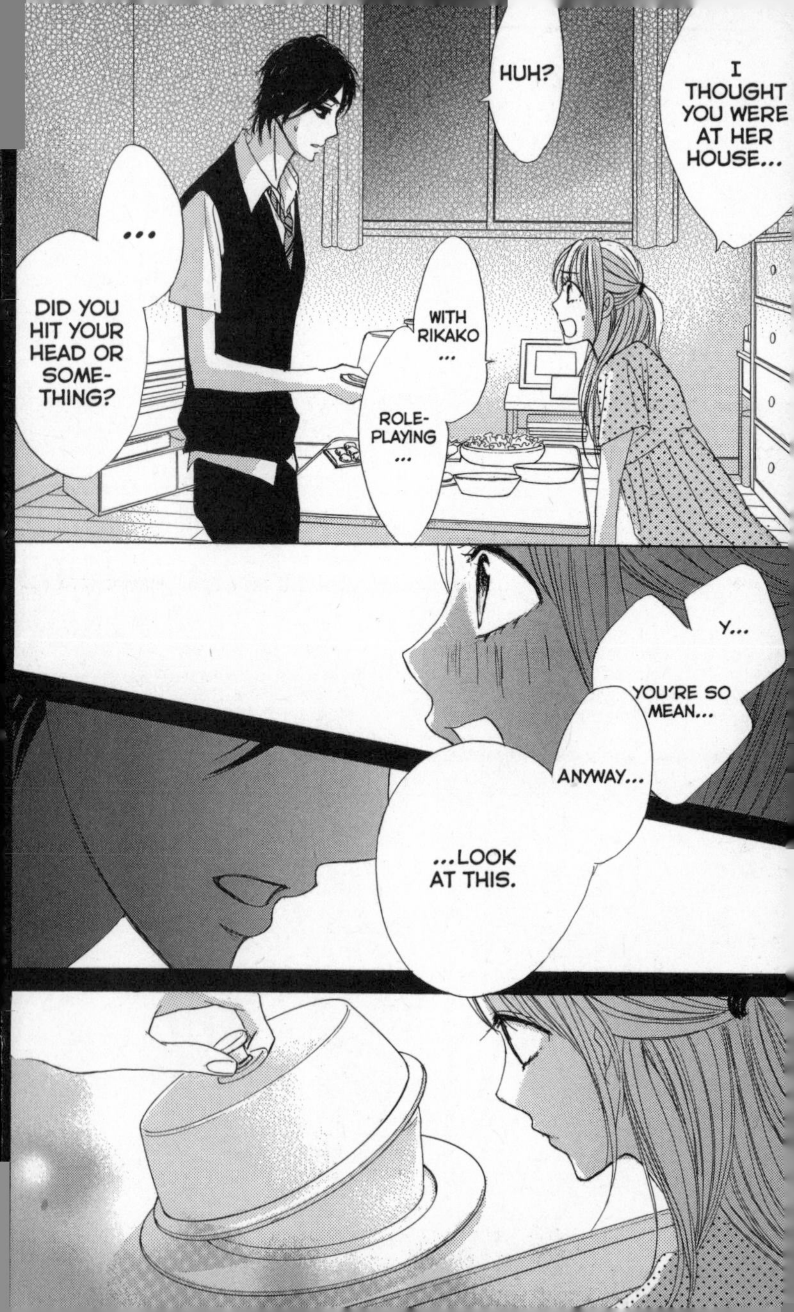

I THOUGHT YOU WERE AT HER HOUSE...
HUH?
WITH RIKAKO...
ROLE-PLAYING...
...
DID YOU HIT YOUR HEAD OR SOME-THING?
Y...
YOU'RE SO MEAN...
ANYWAY...
...LOOK AT THIS.

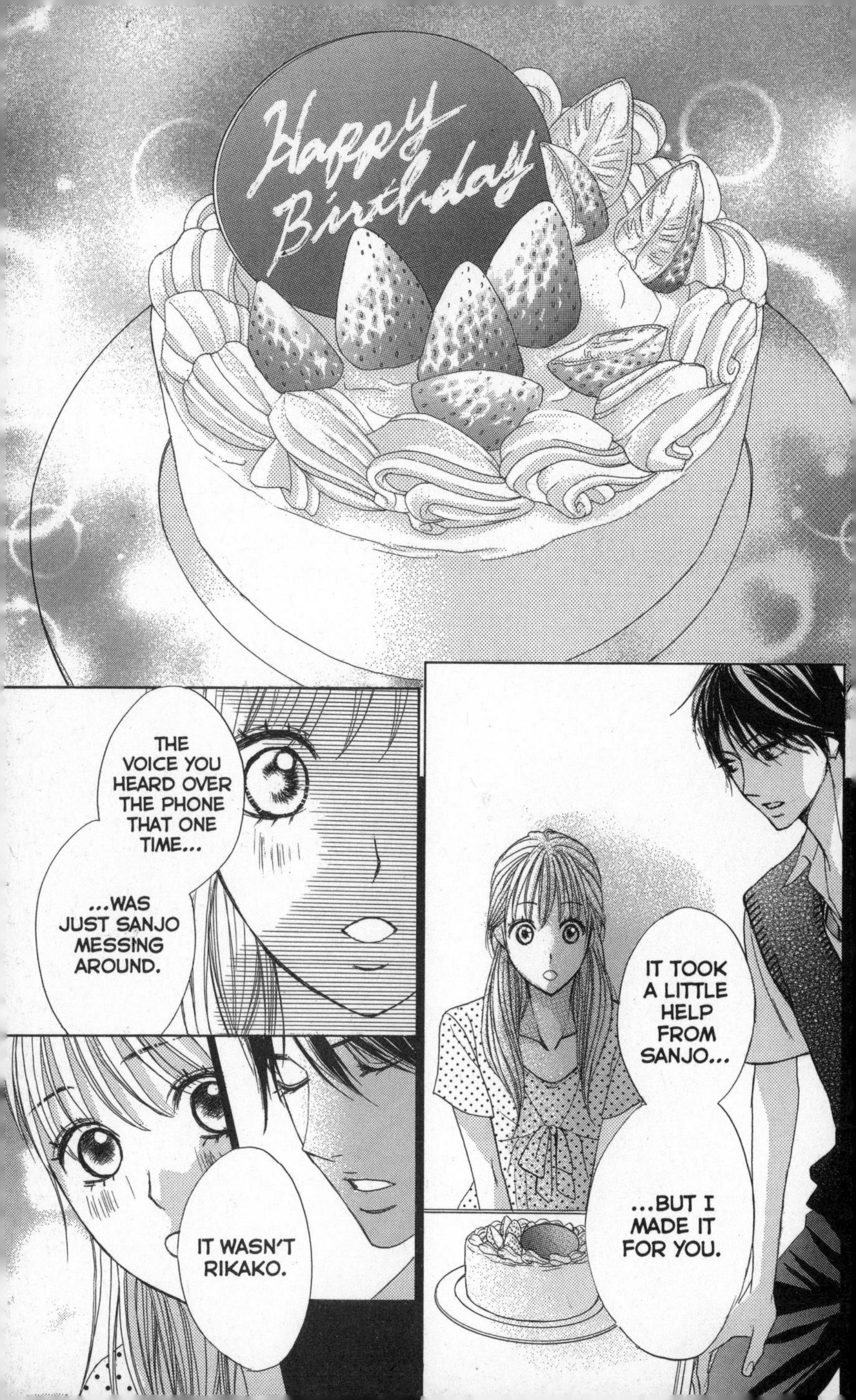
Happy Birthday
IT TOOK A LITTLE HELP FROM SANJO...
...BUT I MADE IT FOR YOU.
THE VOICE YOU HEARD OVER THE PHONE THAT ONE TIME...
...WAS JUST SANJO MESSING AROUND.
IT WASN'T RIKAKO.

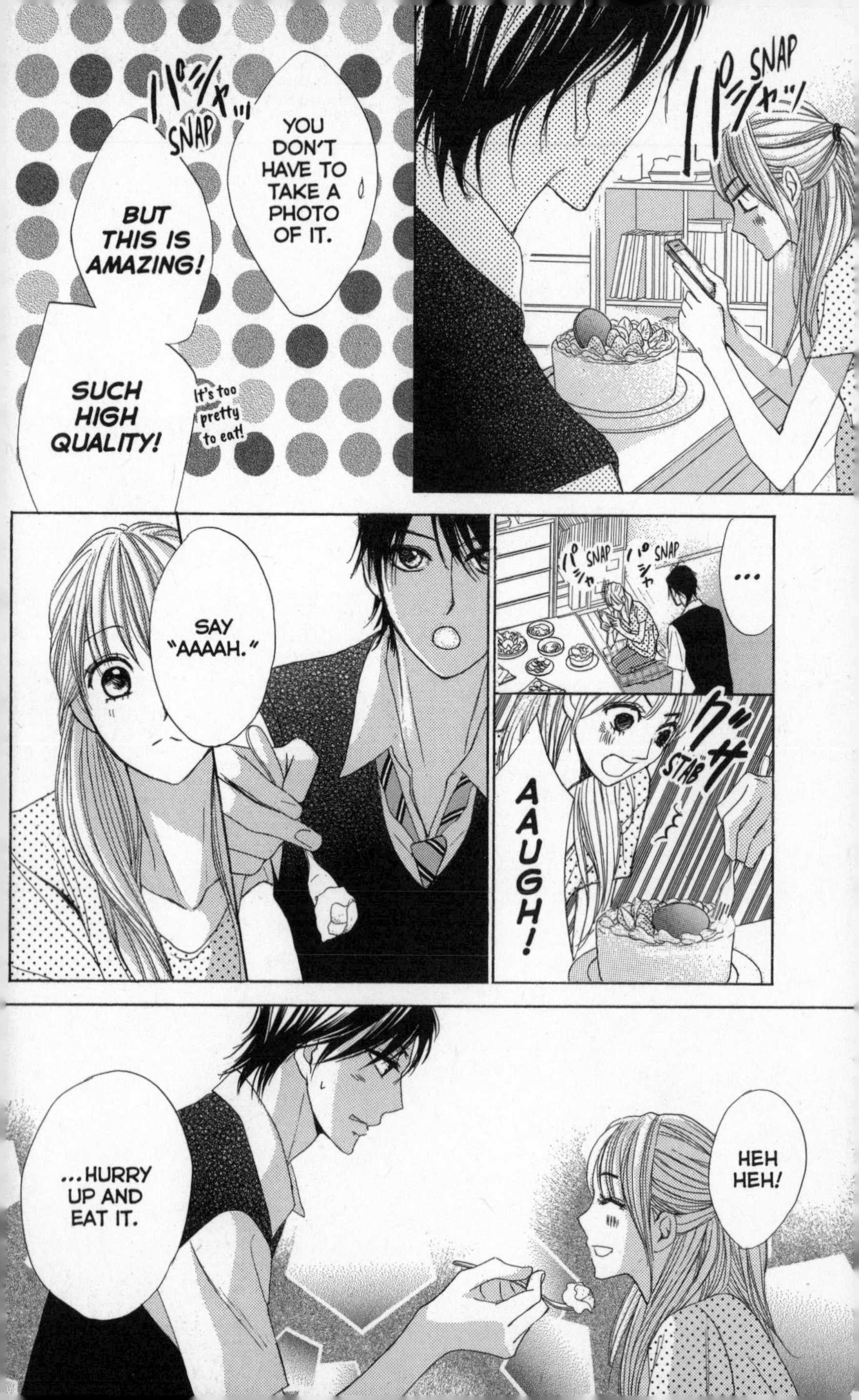
SNAP
YOU DON'T HAVE TO TAKE A PHOTO OF IT.
SNAP
BUT THIS IS AMAZING!
SUCH HIGH QUALITY!
It's too pretty to eat!
SNAP
SNAP
...
STAB
AAUGH!
SAY "AAAAH."
HEH HEH!
...HURRY UP AND EAT IT.

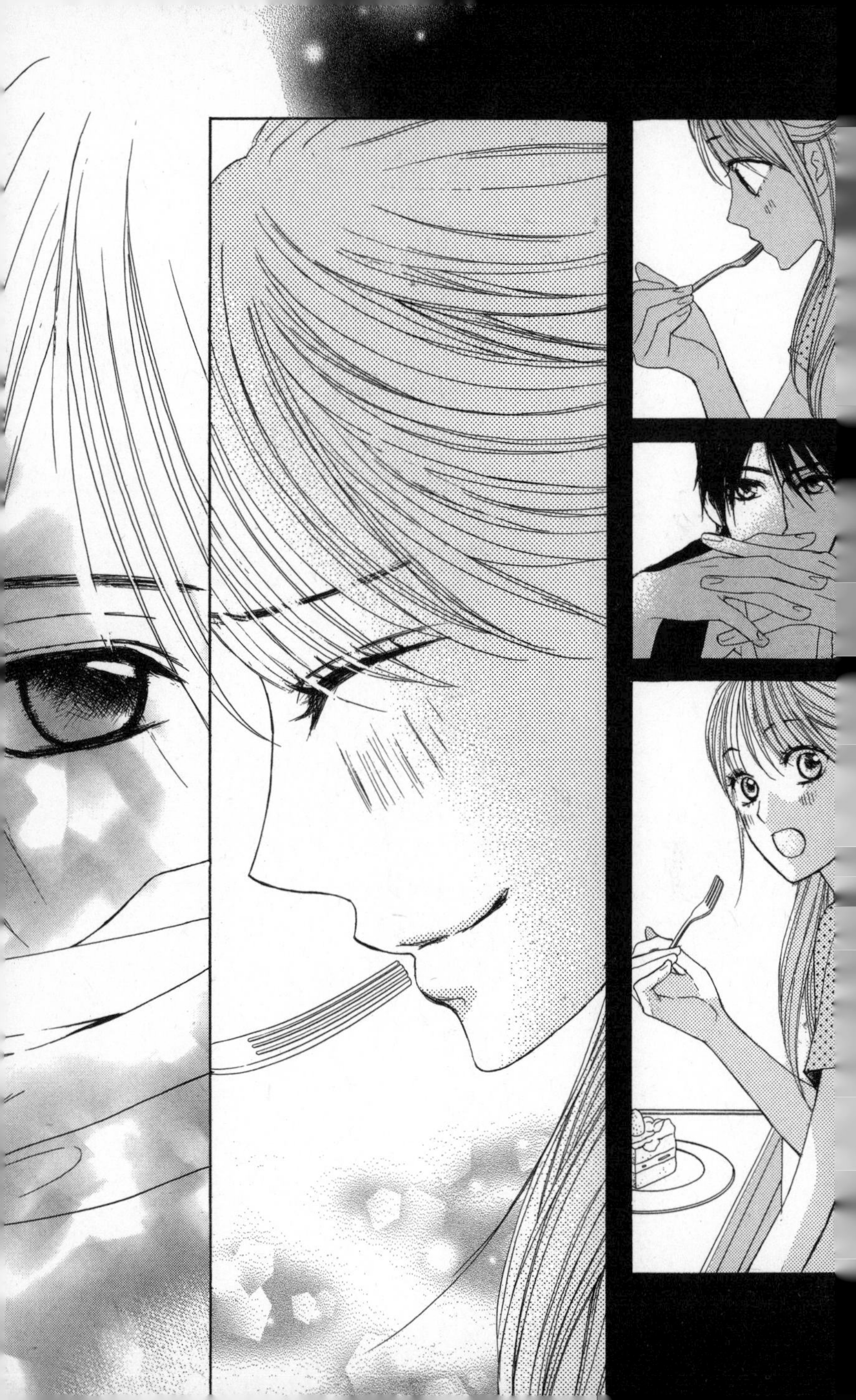

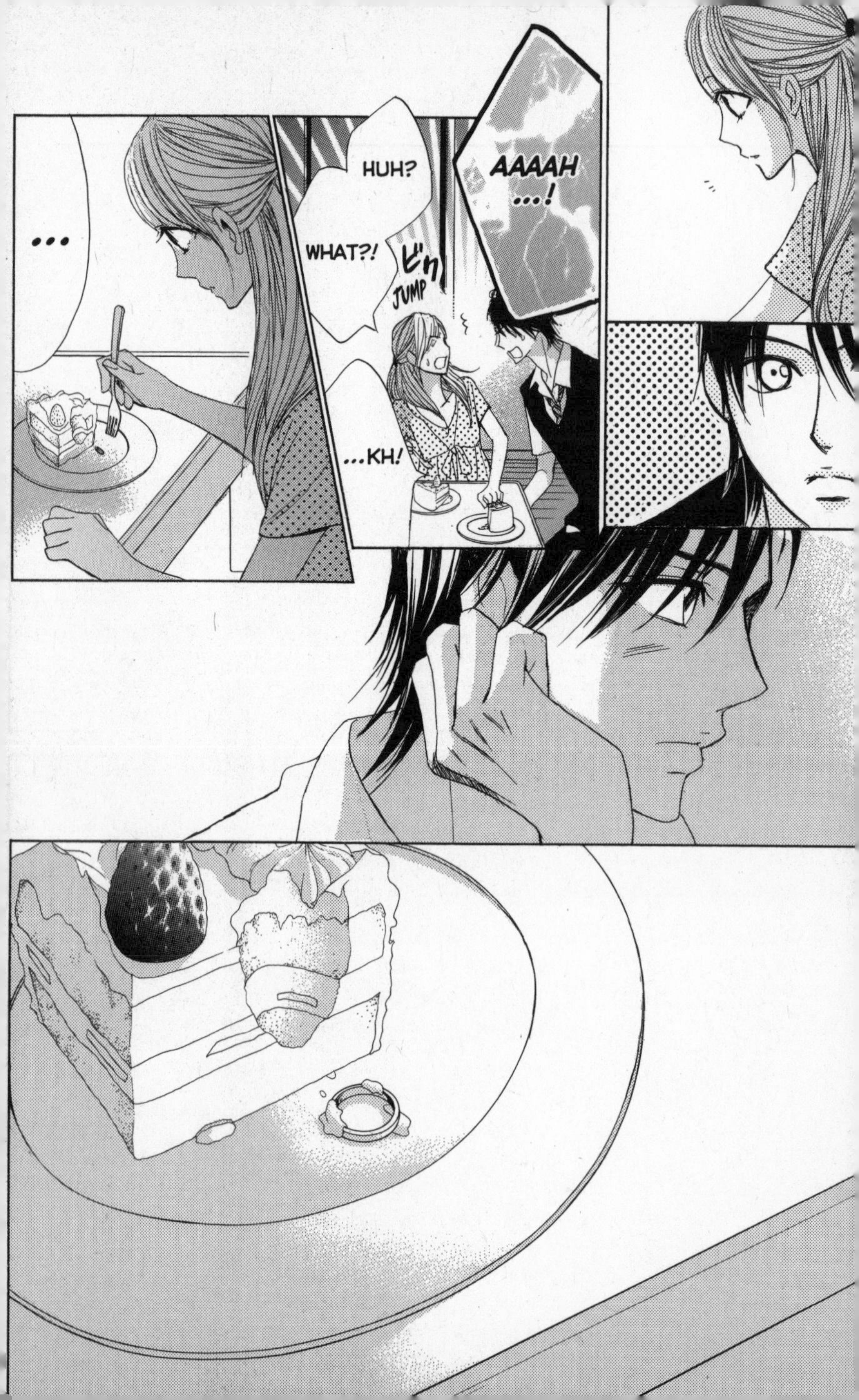
AAAAH ...!
HUH?
WHAT?!
JUMP
...KH!
...

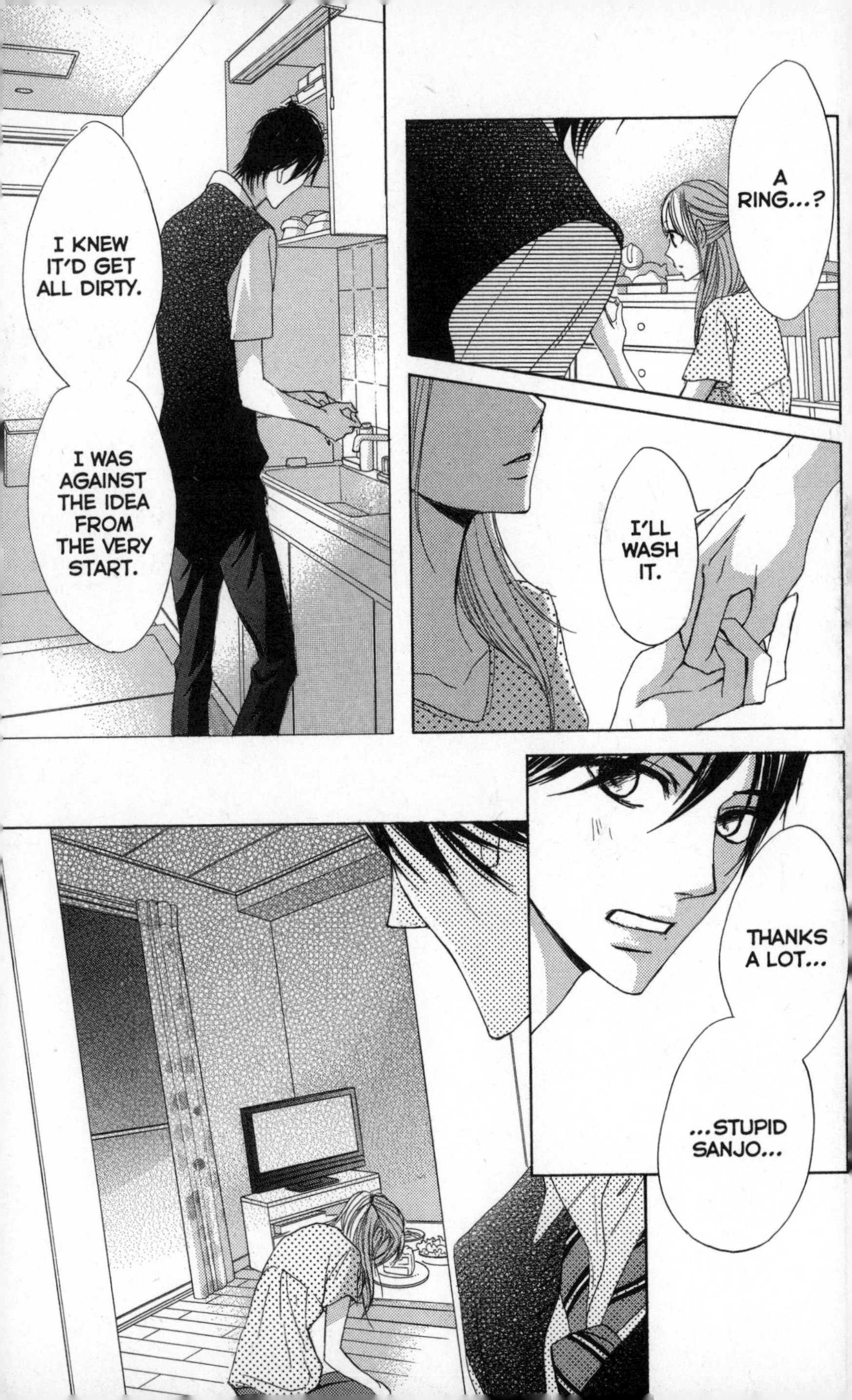
A RING...?
I'LL WASH IT.
I KNEW IT'D GET ALL DIRTY.
I WAS AGAINST THE IDEA FROM THE VERY START.
THANKS A LOT...
...STUPID SANJO...

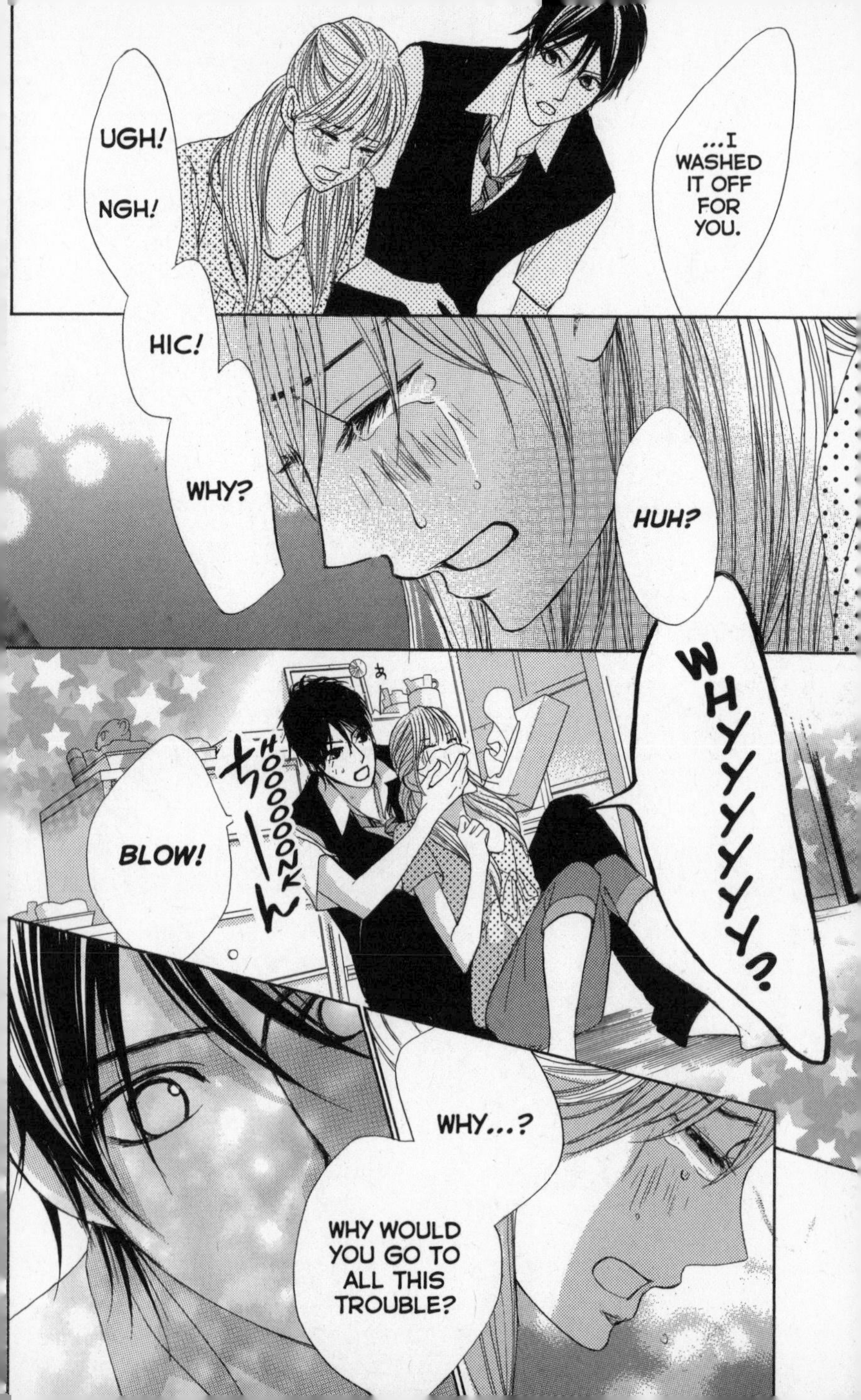
...I WASHED IT OFF FOR YOU.
UGH!
NGH!
HUH?
HIC!
WHY?
WHYYYYYYY?
HOOOOOONK
BLOW!
WHY...?
WHY WOULD YOU GO TO ALL THIS TROUBLE?

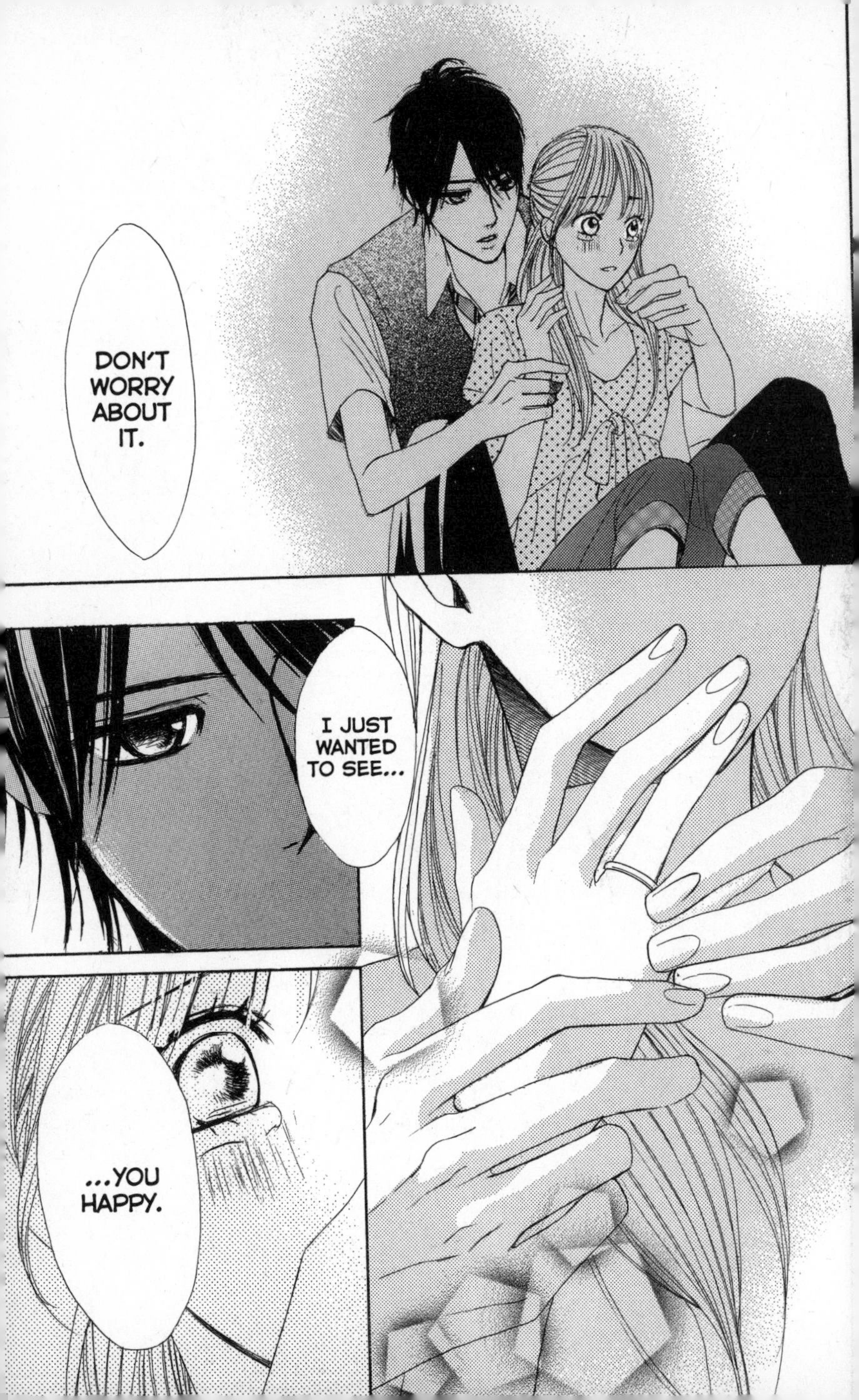
DON'T WORRY ABOUT IT.
I JUST WANTED TO SEE...
...YOU HAPPY.

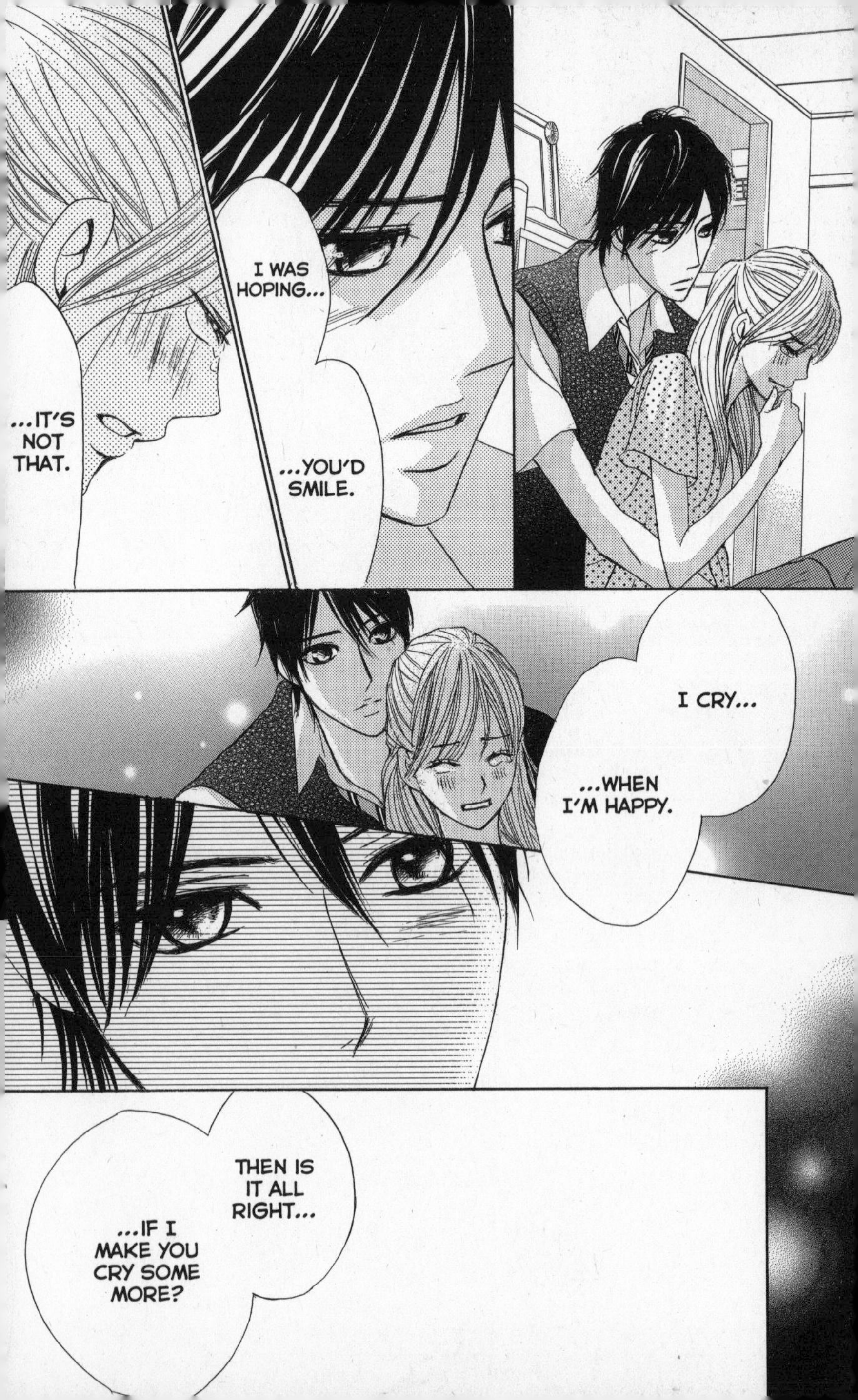
I WAS HOPING...
...YOU'D SMILE.
...IT'S NOT THAT.
I CRY...
...WHEN I'M HAPPY.
THEN IS IT ALL RIGHT...
...IF I MAKE YOU CRY SOME MORE?

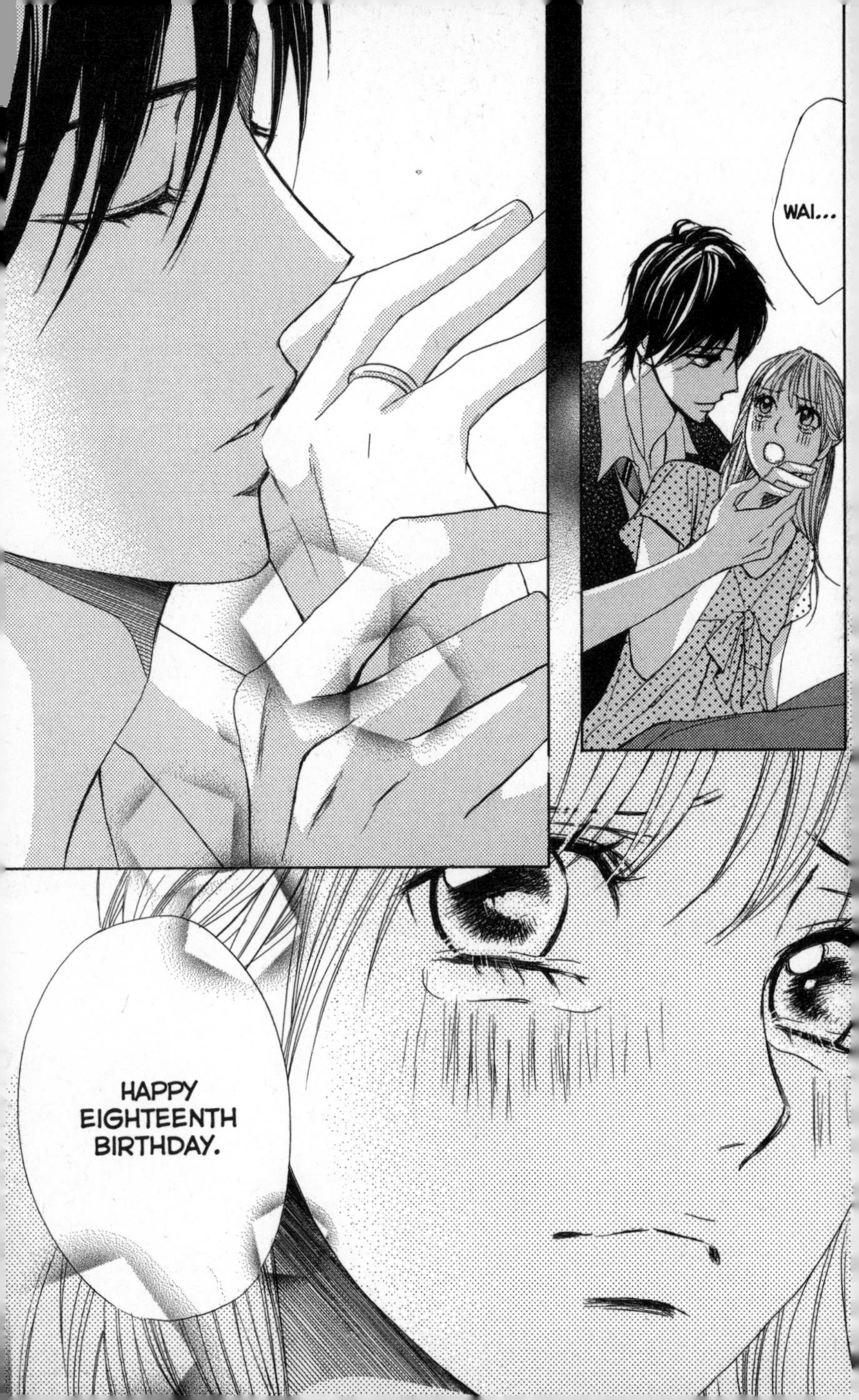
WAI...
HAPPY EIGHTEENTH BIRTHDAY.

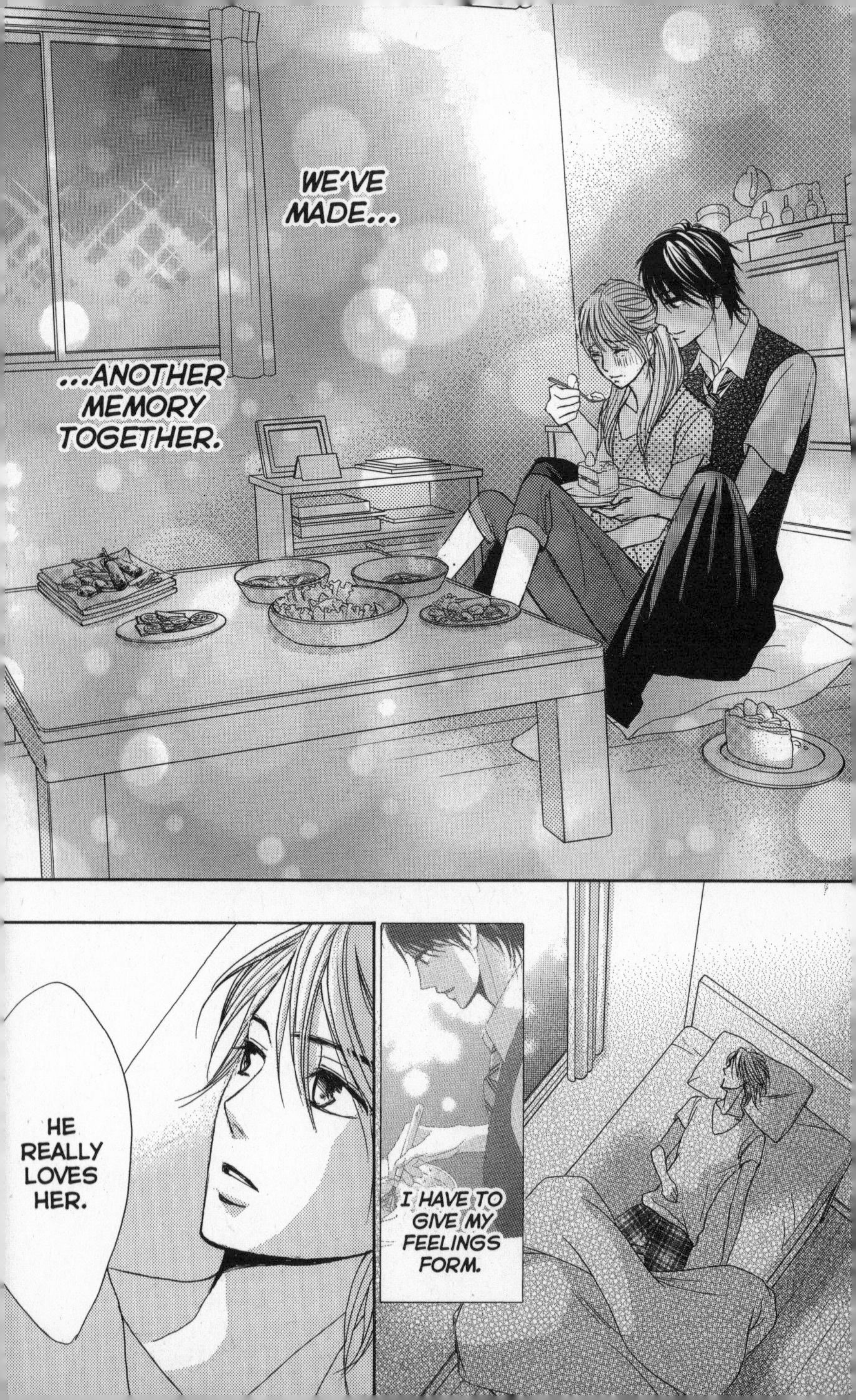
WE'VE MADE...
...ANOTHER MEMORY TOGETHER.
I HAVE TO GIVE MY FEELINGS FORM.
HE REALLY LOVES HER.

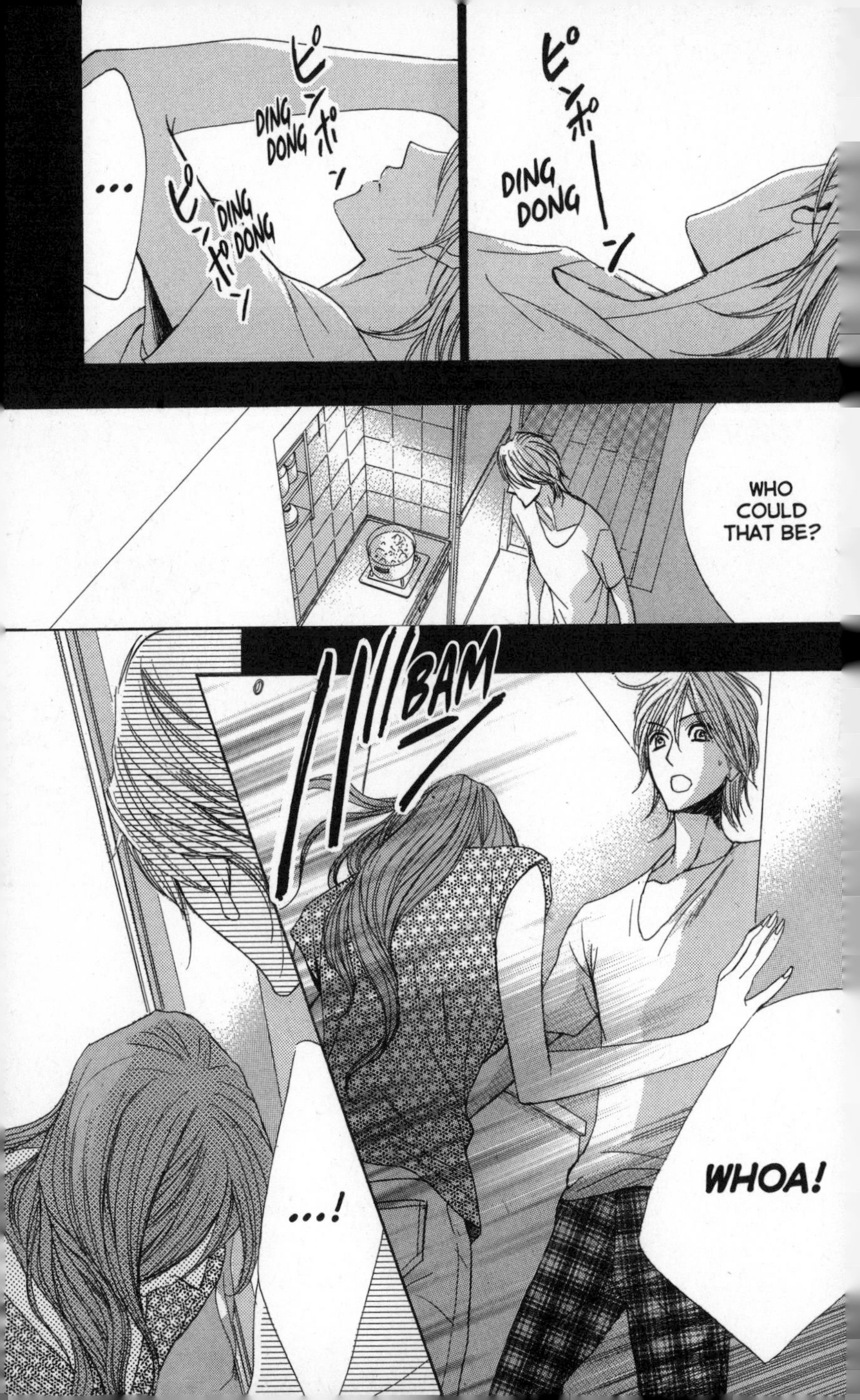
ピンポーン
DING DONG
ピンポーン
DING DONG
ピンポーン
DING DONG
...
WHO COULD THAT BE?
BAM
WHOA!
...!

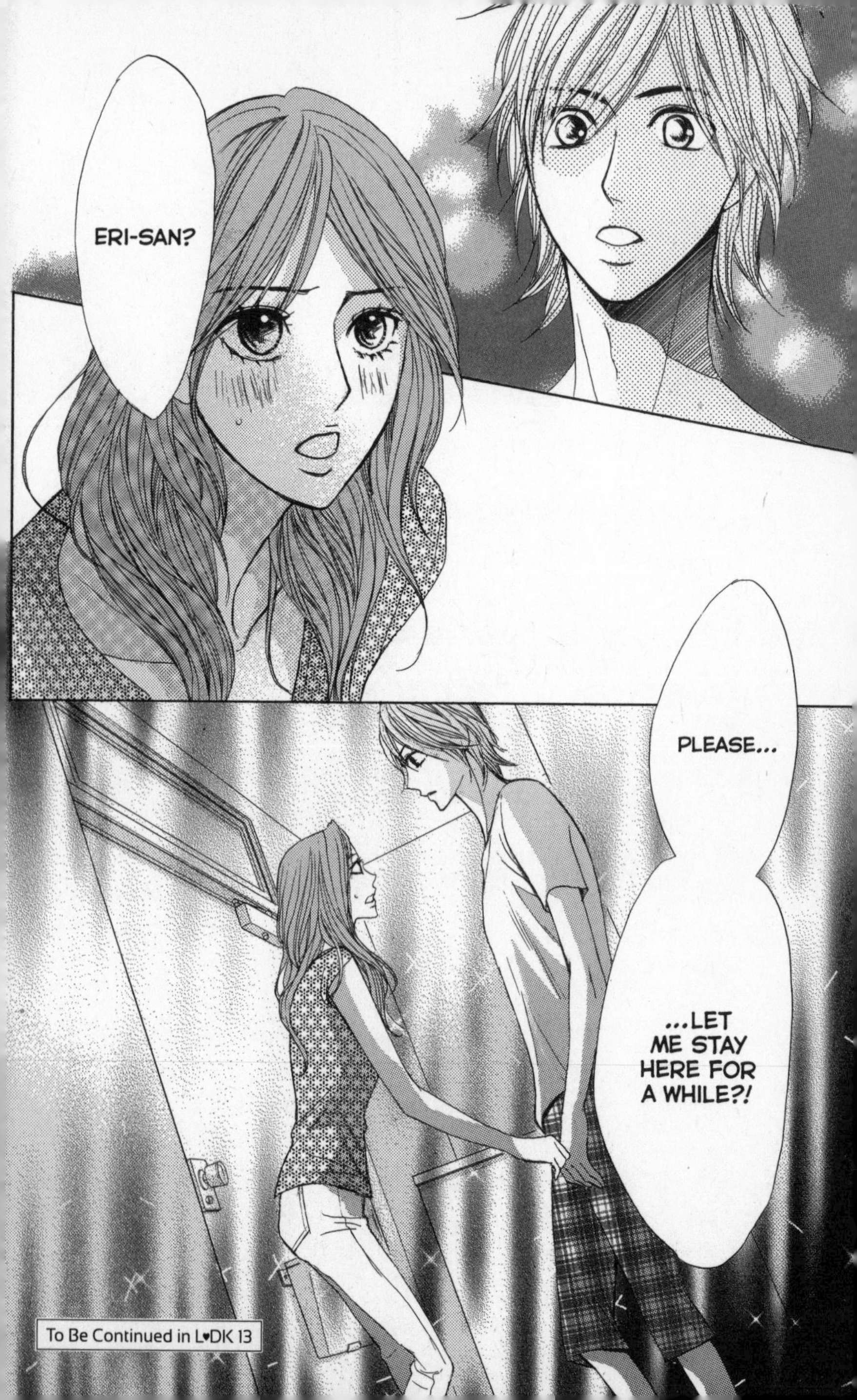
ERI-SAN?
PLEASE...
...LET ME STAY HERE FOR A WHILE?!
To Be Continued in L♥DK 13

L♥DK

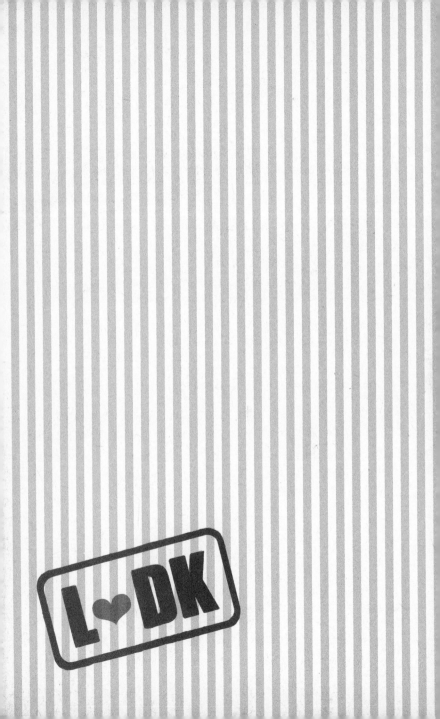

AFTERWORD

Hello, everyone! This is Ayu Watanabe. Thank you very much for picking up volume 12 of L♡DK. W-w-w-would you believe L♡DK is going to be adapted into a film?!!! Whoaaa! I feel sorry and embarrassed and thrilled and honored. I'm sorry. Thank you. Looking back on it all, volume 1 came out in June 2009, and it's been a quick four years since the serialization began. Time really has flown... Kids who were in sixth grade back then are now first-years in high school!! It's just wild to think about. Memories...

When I started the serialization, I had a lot of trouble deciding on all the character backgrounds and the settings, but overcomplicating things just makes my mind wander (lol), so I figured I'd instead go with a simple premise. And that's how this work was born. Taking a standard setup and molding into something entertaining was quite a challenge, and I still work hard at it. I give it my all! And I hold the lesson of being shameless close to my heart (who taught me that lesson anyway?) and focus on keeping things steamy, though I sometimes feel like I went a little overboard on that in the first half of the series. Even now, I still feel a little embarrassed at having the outrageous situation of a guy and a girl getting into a tub together (lol) in only the second chapter.

Eeeee!

Look at you again!

You've really done it this time!!

← Typical reaction to Shusei's actions (lol)

They say manga is just another form of entertainment, and it really is. So it makes me incredibly happy when my readers enjoy it and tell me they found it funny or interesting. Of course, I enjoy it as I'm making it too! Time is precious, and I'm going to keep working hard to keep you invested in the story.
So, until the next volume, take care~!

L♥DK

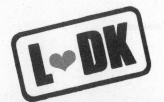

LDK volume 12 is a work of fiction. Names, characters, places, and incidents are the products of the author's imagination or are used fictitiously. Any resemblance to actual events, locales, or persons, living or dead, is entirely coincidental.

A Kodansha Comics Trade Paperback Original.

LDK volume 12 copyright © 2013 Ayu Watanabe
English translation copyright © 2018 Ayu Watanabe

All rights reserved.

Published in the United States by Kodansha Comics, an imprint of Kodansha USA Publishing, LLC, New York.

Publication rights for this English edition arranged through Kodansha Ltd., Tokyo.

First published in Japan in 2013 by Kodansha Ltd., Tokyo, as *L♡DK*, volume 12.

ISBN 978-1-63236-165-3

Printed in the United States of America.

www.kodanshacomics.com

9 8 7 6 5 4 3 2 1

Translation:
Lettering: S
Editing: Tan
Kodansha C

special thanks

K. Hamano
N. Imai
Y. Negishi
Mosuko

my family
my friends

M. Morita
Y. Ikumi
A. Yamamoto

AND YOU

Ayu Watanabe
Apr.2013

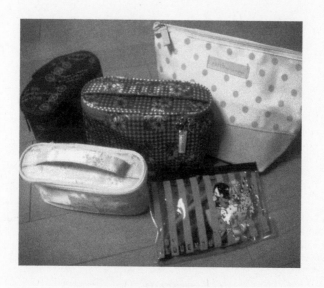

Everyday Essentials, Item 12
Magazine Freebies

This is just a selection of my magazine freebies. I get so giddy when a magazine offers them. I get especially excited when they're pouch-type items. I'll stuff them with all sorts of odds and ends to the point where I don't know what I've put into which ones... (Ha...)